Legal Form and the End of Law

Following the 100th anniversary of Pashukanis' *General Theory of Law and Marxism* (1924), this volume aims to breathe new life into the main category of Pashukanian legacy, the concept of legal form.

This book offers new, deeper and more general, ways in which the concept of legal form can be used to push forward Marxist—post-Marxist or hauntingly Marxist—legal theory. Accordingly, this book does not pledge allegiance to reconstructing and reconsidering the official interpretative legacy of the legal form. Instead, it mobilises the revolutionary conceptual potentialities that this term contains. When investigated thoroughly, and in many dimensions, the legal form becomes a privileged vantage point not only into the greatest law-related riddles of Marxism (such as the relation between economy and the state or withering away of statal apparatuses), but the whole of modernity as the epoch determined by—if not overlapping with—capitalism. This book aims to think *with* the legal form rather than explain this concept. In so doing, it offers a panoply of theoretical perspectives that address legal subjectivity, abstraction, autonomy of the law and, last but not least, withering away of the law.

This contemporary interrogation of the relevance of the concept of legal form will be of considerable interest to scholars and students of legal and political theory.

Cosmin Cercel is Professor of Legal History at Ghent University, Belgium.

Gian-Giacomo Fusco is Lecturer in Law at Kent Law School, University of Kent, UK.

Przemysław Tacik is Assistant Professor at the Institute of European Studies at the Jagiellonian University of Kraków, Poland.

Part of the Nomos Studies in Law, Culture and Power Series

Legal Form
Pashukanis and the Marxist Critique of Law
Edited by Cosmin Cercel, Gian-Giacomo Fusco and Przemysław Tacik

Legal Form and the End of Law
Pashukanis's Legacy
Edited by Cosmin Cercel, Gian-Giacomo Fusco and Przemysław Tacik

A GlassHouse book

For more information about this series, please visit: https://www.routledge.com/

Legal Form and the End of Law

Pashukanis's Legacy

Edited by
Cosmin Cercel, Gian-Giacomo Fusco and Przemysław Tacik

Routledge
Taylor & Francis Group
a GlassHouse Book

First published 2025
by Routledge
4 Park Square, Milton Park, Abingdon, Oxon OX14 4RN

and by Routledge
605 Third Avenue, New York, NY 10158

Routledge is an imprint of the Taylor & Francis Group, an informa business

A GlassHouse book

British Library Cataloguing-in-Publication Data
A catalogue record for this book is available from the British Library

Library of Congress Cataloging-in-Publication Data
Names: Pashukanis, Evgeniĭ Bronislavovich, 1891–1937. | Cercel, Cosmin, 1982– editor. | Fusco, Gian-Giacomo, 1985– editor. | Tacik, Przemyslaw, 1985– editor.
Title: Legal form and the end of law : Pashukanis's legacy / edited by Cosmin Cercel, Gian-Giacomo Fusco, and Przemyslaw Tacik.
Description: Abingdon, Oxon [UK] ; New York, NY : Routledge, 2025. | Series: Nomos studies in law, culture and power | Includes bibliographical references and index.
Identifiers: LCCN 2024027968 (print) | LCCN 2024027969 (ebook) | ISBN 9781032724492 (hardback) | ISBN 9781032724720 (paperback) | ISBN 9781032724713 (ebook)
Subjects: LCSH: Law and socialism. | Law—Philosophy. | Forms (Law)
Classification: LCC K357 .P369 2025 (print) | LCC K357 (ebook) | DDC 340/.1—dc23/eng/20240620
LC record available at https://lccn.loc.gov/2024027968
LC ebook record available at https://lccn.loc.gov/2024027969

ISBN: 978-1-032-72449-2 (hbk)
ISBN: 978-1-032-72472-0 (pbk)
ISBN: 978-1-032-72471-3 (ebk)

DOI: 10.4324/9781032724713

Typeset in Sabon
by Apex CoVantage, LLC

Contents

Contributors

Cosmin Cercel is Professor of Legal History at Ghent University. His research focuses on genealogies of law and politics with specific reference to twentieth-century continental legal history. He is the author of *Towards a Jurisprudence of State-Communism: Law and the Failure of Revolution* (2018) and has co-edited *States of Exception: Law, History, Theory* (2020). His recent publications include: 'Mapping the State of Siege: Law, Crisis and the Antinomies of Liberal Legality' (2022) 12(2) *Romanian Journal of Comparative Law* 193; 'Law, Politics, and the Military: Towards a Theory of Authoritarian Adjudication' (2021) 22 *German Law Journal* 192. He is the recipient of a Consolidator Grant from the European Research Council (ERC) to research the history of emergency legislation during the last century in Europe with a view to offering a legal historical explanation of how the experience of emergency has shaped constitutional and political cultures across Europe in the past century.

Eduardo A. Chia is a doctoral researcher at the Institut für Kriminalwissenschaften und Rechtsphilosophie, Goethe-Universität Frankfurt/Main, Germany. He has a bachelor's degree in law (Universidad Andrés Bello, Chile), post-graduate studies in philosophy (Universidad de Chile, Chile) and a master's degree in legal theory (Goethe-Universität Frankfurt/Main). His research interests include: philosophy of law and jurisprudence, critical legal theory, history of legal thought, comparative law, globalisation and law.

Peter Čuroš is Assistant Professor at the Polish Academy of Sciences in Warsaw. In previous years he worked as a postdoctoral fellow at the Department of Private Law at the University of Oslo. From 2016–2019 he was an assistant professor at the Pavol Jozef Šafárik University in Košice. He spent the academic year 2015–2016 at the Washington and Lee University School of Law, with the research area of professional responsibility and constitutional law. He has published chiefly on judicial reforms, legal ideology, the judiciary in CEE, and judicial ethics. His current focus is an analysis of the judicial ideology using Lacanian psychoanalysis concepts.

Gian-Giacomo Fusco is a lecturer in law at Kent Law School (University of Kent—Canterbury). He has obtained his doctoral degree in law at the University of Kent. His research interests include jurisprudence, critical theory, history of ideas and urban studies. His more recent monograph *Form of Life. Agamben and the Destitution of Rules* (2022), engaged with and developed further Agamben's concept of destituent potential as a critique of the law.

Tormod Otter Johansen is a researcher at the Law Department, University of Gothenburg, Sweden. He works in public law (constitutional law and administrative law) and legal theory. For the moment he is pursuing two main projects with different research groups: one concerning Swedish, European and international legal regulation of crisis management and defence; and one interdisciplinary project on the notion of the 'End of law' in Christian and secular thinking. One of his latest publications was 'Minor law: Notes towards a revolutionary jurisprudence' in *States of exception: law, history, theory*, edited by Cosmin Cercel, Gian-Giacomo Fusco and Simon Lavis., 73–9, 2020.

Hedvig Lärka is a doctoral student of international law and tax law at Gothenburg University in Sweden. She studies the contemporary emergence of global, top-up minimum taxation from a Marxian lens.

Hugo Lundberg is a doctoral candidate in international law at Gothenburg University where his doctoral research is focused on how the regulation of unilateral coercive measures under international law assumes legal form. His interest in Pashukanis comes from convening a reading group on the General Theory of Law and Marxism for the Swedish Centre for Marxist Social Studies (CMS) in 2020. Beyond international law, Hugo's research interests broadly encompass Marxist and critical approaches, especially value-form theory and critical animal studies. He teaches legal theory and treaty law, among other things.

Dimitrios Kivotidis is a lecturer at Goldsmiths, University of London. Prior to this, he held positions at Birkbeck, University of London and Durham University. Dimitrios's research interests lie in the areas of public law, human rights, law and political economy, critical legal theory (in particular Marxist critiques of law), law and social change, comparative law and European Union law. Dimitrios has published on the impact of crisis legislation on fundamental rights, on the relationship between rights and social change, as well as on the relationship between constitutional law and political economy. He is also a member of the editorial collective of the Legal Form, a forum for Marxist analysis and critique.

Christos Marneros is a lecturer in law at the Department of Law and Criminology, Royal Holloway, University of London, United Kingdom and a visiting docent in legal philosophy at Riga Graduate School of Law, Latvia. His research interests are on the intersections between anarchist and anarchic theory and practice, political theory, legal theory, politico-philosophical critiques of human rights and continental philosophy. Christos is the author of *Human Rights After Deleuze: Towards an An-anarchic Jurisprudence*, published in 2022.

Przemysław Tacik is Assistant Professor at the Institute of European Studies of the Jagiellonian University of Kraków, Poland, and Director of the Nomos: Centre for International Research on Law, Culture and Power. A philosopher, lawyer and sociologist by education, he holds doctorates in philosophy (2014) and international law (2016). He has been a visiting scholar at many universities (i.e. Columbia University, Cardozo Law School, SUNY at Buffalo, Université Paris-1, Université d'Orléans, Université Aix-en-Provence, Heidelberg Universität, Max-Planck-Institut für ausländisches öffentliches Recht und Völkerrecht, Salzburg Universität and Lisbon University). In his academic work he combines both philosophical and legal perspectives; attempting to approach them from an interdisciplinary angle. His current research is focused on critical legal theory and contemporary philosophy. He has authored five books as well as over 50 articles and two translations of a poetry volume (from French to Polish). His most recent monographs are *A New Philosophy of Modernity and Sovereignty: Towards Radical Historicization* (2021) and *Deconstructing the Right to Self-Determination in International Law: Sovereignty, Exception, Biopolitics* (2023).

Dennis Wassouf is a doctoral candidate at the Masaryk University, Brno in the field of legal theory and legal history. In his research, he focuses on the intersection of Lacanian political theory, ideology critique and law. Using methods of psychoanalytical and deconstructive critique, he aims at refurbishing the methods of legal critique and thinking about political relevance of critical legal studies movement.

Rosie Woodhouse is a doctoral candidate in Law Studies at the University of Warwick. Her dissertation investigates relations of power and property in recent configurations of neoliberalism and the state, specifically on how these interface with different modes of the 'speculative'. She has obtained an LLM in Law and Political Economy (Birkbeck College, University of London) and a bachelor's degree in art theory and philosophy (Central Saint Martins). She has contributed to and worked as an editor for numerous critical and artistic DIY publications, radio programmes and online platforms, and has presented her research at several international conferences and workshops.

Introduction

The legal form as a conceptual event

Cosmin Cercel, Gian-Giacomo Fusco and Przemysław Tacik

Legal form as a conceptual event

Zhou Enlai famously quipped that almost 200 years is not enough to assess the consequences of the French Revolution. But the 100th anniversary of Pashukanis' *General Theory of Law and Marxism* (1924)[1] is a time long enough to appreciate what kind of theoretical reshuffling this book has produced. And it is also an even better occasion to re-include later discoveries in the original conceptual push, looking for a new, deeper and more general way in which Pashukanis' central concept, the legal form [*правовая форма*], can be used to develop Marxist—post-Marxist or hauntingly Marxist—legal theory.

Accordingly, this book does not pledge allegiance to reconstructing and reconsidering the official interpretative legacy of the legal form, which is a task of the parallel publication.[2] Instead, it aims to mobilise revolutionary conceptual potentialities that this term contains. When investigated thoroughly, and in many dimensions, the legal form becomes a privileged vantage point not only into the greatest law-related riddles of Marxism (the relation between economy and the state, mechanisms of capitalist abstraction, dialectics between capitalism and knowledge about it, irreducibility of the political,

1 Евгений Брониславович Пашуканис, *Общая теория права и марксизм in Избранные произведения по общей теории права и государства* (Наука 1980) 32–181. English translation: Evgeny Pashukanis, *The General Theory of Law & Marxism* (Barbara Einhorn tr, Transaction Publishers 2002). This English translation is based mainly on the German edition from 1929, which significantly—and in many points of the text—differs from the later Russian versions. In particular, the German (and, consequently, English) edition seems more conceptually developed and puts more stress on the notion of legal form, developing it into the central theoretical knot of Pashukanis' more general critique of the law. The detailed trajectory of Pashukanis' thought will not be of main focus in this book, as it attempts to critically rethink the concept of the legal form rather than engage in reconstructive or philological work. On a general context of Pashukanis' theory and main polemics about it see: Michael Head, *Evgeny Pashukanis. A Critical Reappraisal* (Routledge 2016).

2 Cosmin Cercel, Gian-Giacomo Fusco, and Przemysław Tacik (eds), *Legal Form: Pashukanis and the Marxist Critique of Law* (Routledge 2024).

DOI: 10.4324/9781032724713-1

withering away of statal apparatuses) but the whole modernity as the epoch determined by—if not overlapping with—capitalism. Pashukanis often underlined that the abstract form of the law, which assures equivalence necessary for commodity exchange, appears properly under capitalism, although—in a Hegelian-Marxian legacy—it can give insight into previous forms of the law.[3]

Naturally, to release these new interpretative potentialities the concept of the legal form needs to be dissected from the closed horizon of its immediate context. As such, the legal form will be here taken more in its *haunting presence*: as a concept that survives Pashukanis' own theory, its reinterpretations and the Marxism of that era. For authors of this volume, the legal form will be a spectre that returns in various fields of legal theory and philosophy. Precisely as a spectral category in its original meaning, it becomes a foothold for asking novel questions about the most fundamental assumptions of modern legality, its links to the creation of modern subjectivity and the possibilities of its overcoming. Loyalty will be therefore pledged here to the legal form as a still ongoing conceptual event. The legal form has not yet shown the fullness of its potential; it is not an ossified concept, but a process of intellectual development.

Just as the Portuguese language was famously dubbed by Olavo Bilac 'última flor do Lácio', 'the last flower of Latium', so is the concept of the legal form a late blossom of the Marxist tradition that emerged on a territory distant from its main field of operation. Although it appeared in dialogical tension with the Soviet theory of its time, which was much more hostile to the law, it provided a new foothold for Marxist legal scholarship. Although Pashukanis himself was an adherent of the 'withering away of the law' thesis, in whose underpinning the legal form was crucial,[4] his concept

3

> [O]nly in bourgeois capitalist society, where the proletarian figures as a subject disposing of his labour power as a commodity, is the economic relation of exploitation mediated legally, in the form of a contract. This is linked precisely with the fact that in bourgeois society. in contrast to societies based on slavery or serfdom, the legal form attains universal significance, legal ideology becomes the ideology par excellence [*по преимуществу*], and defending the class interest of the exploiters appears with ever increasing success as the defence of the abstract principle of legal subjectivity [*защита абстрактных начал правосубъективности*].
>
> Pashukanis (n 1) 45

4

> The withering away of certain categories of bourgeois law [*Отмирание категорий буржуазного права*] (the categories as such, not this or that precept) in no way implies their replacement by new categories of proletarian law, just as the withering away of the categories of value, capital. Profit and so forth in the transition to fully-developed socialism will not mean the emergence of new proletarian categories of value, capital and so on. The withering away of the categories of bourgeois law will, under these conditions, mean the withering away of law altogether, that is to say the disappearance of the juridical factor [*исчезновение юридического момента*] from social relations.
>
> Pashukanis (n 1) 61. See also Hugh Collins, *Marxism and Law* (OUP 1982) 108–11

offered a new momentum for Marxist analyses. In this function, the legal form opens a new conceptual continent, which—as we will see throughout this volume—allows of meaningful and profound contact between Marxism and various legacies of explaining the law, including messianic, theological and anarchic antinomian traditions. The legal form contains a potential that does not merely *apply* Marxist traditions to the law, but rather returns to the original conceptual moment, in which Marx combined German philosophy, socialist legacy and the British school of economy in a dialectical manner. The scale of Pashukanis discovery was still unclear to him and rightly so—in the context of his work it did not yet mobilise its full potential. If the *General Theory of Law and Marxism* provides an underdetermined, and sometimes vague description of what the legal form really is, it is because real, potent concepts can hardly ever be grasped in their entirety at the beginning. They are rather first established as blurred and all-too-general conceptualisations that only further theoretical work—ramified in various directions—reveals as strong and subtle. Some development of the concept of the legal form was of course achieved in critiques of Pashukanis—for example, the ones addressing his focus on distribution[5] and negligence of labour relations.[6] But apart from these critiques, the concept itself is still open to theoretical honing.

For this reason, the legal form is one of few theoretical inselbergs from the early Soviet period that still offer a re-conceptualising potential instead of a soothing ideological pan-explanation. Already the Soviet polemics around Pashukanis show that the legal form is a fighting notion directed against two poles. First, against imaginary explanations of 'the law in general' (Stuchka)[7] that normalised and perpetualised the law as a social phenomenon. Such a tradition continues the errors of pre-WWI positivist Marxists that ossify dialectics into allegedly solid socio-ontological categories. Second, against the tendency represented by the ideological school (Razumovsky) that reduced the law to the role of cementing the inversion of economic relationships in people's perception.[8] The legal form—against Stuchka's concept of 'form' in law[9]—does not reproduce juridical idealism but perceives *the production of*

5 Nancy E Anderson and David F Greenberg, 'From Substance to Form: The Legal Theories of Pashukanis and Edelman' (1983) 7 *Social Text* 69, 71–72.

6 Colin Sumner, 'Pashukanis and the "Jurisprudence of Terror"' (1981) 11(1) *Insurgent Sociologist* 99, 104–5.

7 Peteris Stučka, 'The Marxist Concept of Law' in *Selected Writings on Soviet Law and Marxism* (M. E. Sharpe 1988) 22–37; Head (n 1) 147–48.

8 Head (n 1) 139–40.

9 Stuchka claimed that '[f]or the bourgeois jurist, law in the objective sense is a form, i.e. a totality of norms. On the contrary, for the Marxist it is the system of relations as *the content* of law.' Peteris Stučka, 'Notes on the Class Theory of Law' in *Selected Writings on Soviet Law and Marxism* (M. E. Sharpe 1988) 38–55. Such a split between form and content mystifyingly separates ontology from epistemology, while Pashukanis was much more aware of the concurrence of the work of the legal form in reality and its recognition.

form as an active work of capitalism. Therefore the concept of the legal form grasps the inner link between modern law and capitalism in a theoretically productive way, penetrating to the core of the basic Marxist dilemma of relations between economy and the legal.[10] This concept is akin to ones that came from the heart of Marx's conceptual forge and inherits their grandiosity, allowing to portray modern, abstract law as part and parcel of the same processes that build up capitalist economy and the nation-state based on popular sovereignty.

In a nutshell, 'legal form' is a concept rather Marxian than Marxist: its ramifications are so diverse that it leaves the safe ground of the great classic Marxist playbook and offers an insight into crucial problems of modern law, subjectivity, revolutions and the end of modernity itself. It opens a path into the philosophical foundations of Marxist dialectics, demonstrating how it remains a counterpoint to capitalist processes of abstraction and universalisation. As such, 'legal form' is a negation of what could be an application of orthodox Marxism to legal theory. If, as Göran Therborn had it, Marxism constitutes Her Majesty's opposition to modernity,[11] then the legal form should appear as a vital locus of criticism of modern society as such. When interpreted audaciously, it allows of piercing the caked officiality of Marxist theory towards fresh sources of thought. Accordingly, this book will attempt to use the concept of the legal form in a fruitful and original way, throwing light not only on the law but also on key questions of Marxism as well.

First of all, we will construct the generalised concept of the legal form drawing from the broadly conceived Marxist legacy but aiming to grasp the dialectics between modern law's specificity and the explanatory power of Marxism as a modern tradition of thinking. Then we will use it to address pivotal issues where Marxist legacy puts modern legality in a piercing light, making visible its boundaries and presuppositions. In order to provide a solid theoretical framework for the legal form, we need to perform a Benjaminian 'tiger jump'[12] and re-inscribe the concept of the legal form, as developed in Evgeny Pashukanis' work, back into the origins of Marx's critique of the law. The generalised concept of the legal form should thus be able to recuperate the conceptual thrust of Marx's analysis of capitalism and modern society. In particular, Pashukanis' limitation to civil law needs to be overcome in order to grasp the legal form *as such*. To this end, Pashukanis' crucial discovery of the affinity between the legal form and Marx's commodity form—based on the capitalist power of abstraction—requires further conceptual work.

10 See Georg Lukács, *The Ontology of Social Being, vol 3: Labour* (David Fembach tr, Merlin Press 1980) 90.

11 Göran Therborn, *From Marxism to Post-Marxism?* (Verso 2014) 66.

12 Walter Benjamin, 'On the Concept of History' in H Zohn (tr), *Illuminations. Essays and Reflections* (Schocken Books 1969) 261.

Back to Marx, or generalising the concept of the legal form

To turn Pashukanis' legacy more universal, we should not treat it as just a particular concept within the Marxist tradition, but rather as a cornerstone of recognition of how modern law—underpinning capitalist society—is structured and how it functions. Contrary to Pashukanis' original focus on commodity exchange (for long criticised under the label of 'economism'[13]), we should rather take the legal form for an embodiment of how the law changes in modernity in counterpoint to the emergence of capitalism. Thus construed, the legal form turns into a matrix of processes that define modern law: abstraction, universalisation, codification, creation of legal subjectivity and its anchoring in the developing of human rights. It is on the basis of these qualities that the legal form corresponds to capitalist society. If so, the link between commodity exchange and legal relationship—which Pashukanis brings forward in his analysis—is perhaps a privileged vantage point of grasping capitalist law, but in no way an exhaustive description of this relation.

The concept of the legal form in this general understanding can—and should—be applied retroactively to Marx himself. Paradoxically, Pashukanis offers a particular key to a more general reconsideration of the Marxist legacy. Marx's critique can be understood as a response to *the emergence of the modern legal form*, associated with the nation-state, abstract creation of subjects, biopolitics and the vision of rational completeness of the legal system. In intellectual history, this modern legal form is represented by Kant and Hegel whom Marx directly addresses as porte-paroles of the all-encompassing and pan-codifying tendency of modern legality, based in fact on forced abstract equalisation. Much as the very concept of 'the form' could be thus linked to ancient Greek philosophy or used to analyse Roman or Canon law, for example, the core of Marxism-informed critique must tackle what is specific to the legal form in modernity: universalising equal exchange and turning human beings into formally equal subjects of it (esp. in the context of exchange of labour).[14]

Consequently, if the concept of the legal form is to be applied anachronically, it can only be done in a way that Pashukanis suggested

13 Daniel McLoughlin and Talina Hürzeler, 'Marx on the Factory Acts: Law, Exploitation and Class Struggle' in Paul O'Connell and Umut Özsu (eds), *Research Handbook on Law and Marxism* (Elgar 2021) 29–30; Head (n 1) 135–45.

14 See Chris J Arthur, 'Towards a Materialist Theory of Law' (1977) 7 Critique 31, 36–37; Isaac D Balbus, 'Commodity Form and Legal Form: An Essay on the "Relative Autonomy" of the Law' (1977) 11 *Law and Soc* 215, 219–22; Vinícius Casalino, 'Karl Marx's Dialectics and the Marxist Criticism of Law' (2018) 9(4) *Direito e praxis* 2268, 2282; Richard Kinsey, 'Marxism and the Law: Preliminary Analyses' (1978) 5 *Brit JL and Soc'y* 202, 215–20.

himself, mirroring Marx's famous argumentation from the introduction to *Grundrisse*:

> Bourgeois society is the most developed and the most complex historic organisation of production. The categories which express its relations, the comprehension of its structure, thereby also allow insights into the structure and the relations of production of all the vanished social formations out of whose ruins and elements it built itself up, whose partly still unconquered remnants are carried along within it, whose mere nuances have developed explicit significance within it, etc. Human anatomy contains a key to the anatomy of the ape. The intimations of higher development among the subordinate animal species, however, can be understood only after the higher development is already known. The bourgeois economy thus supplies the key to the ancient, etc.[15]

Marx inherits here the Hegelian logic of the specimen. Just as pointed out by Žižek[16] (and earlier by Lukács), it is characteristic of modern dialectics that each relation between a given genus and its exemplars is based on a structural overlap between genus and *one* of its exemplars. Thus, capitalism is a key primarily to itself, but at least within its horizon, it seems to solve the riddle of previous epochs. Properly Marxian should therefore take general, transhistorical terms with a grain of salt, given that they are usually part of bourgeois ideology.[17] Similarly, the concept of class struggle may be extrapolated beyond to address historical social relations in their entirety, but only capitalist class struggle is the proper representative of this concept as a *genus*.

The same problem reappears in Pashukanis. While the modern legal form is obviously not the only type of the legal form, within the capitalist universe it is its proper embodiment that remains a key to the 'anatomy' of the legal form as such. The potentially trans-historical generality of the legal form emerges as a corollary to its particular, modern character. Consequently, the modern legal form requires a special place in Marxist critique.

As a result, the structure, origins, and propensities of the legal form in pre-modern epochs require profound reconsideration. Whether and in which aspects the legal form is historically continuous is a question in itself. There seems to exist an elusive dimension of *longue durée* within the law which can be addressed through the concept of the legal form and does not seem limited to modernity. In a nutshell, 'legal form' can connote a dissociation between the socio-economic meaning of a legal provision and its legal content. This

15 Karl Marx, *Grundrisse* (Martin Nicolaus tr, Random House 1973) 105.

16 Slavoj Žižek, *Sex and the Failed Absolute* (Bloomsbury 2020) 212.

17 Still, Marx himself was not entirely free from constructing pan-historical diagnoses. See Mark Neocleous, 'International Law as Primitive Accumulation; Or, the Secret of Systematic Colonization' (2012) 23 *Eur J Intl L* 941, 958–59.

aspect of the law, almost inevitable in the long run, seems to be applicable also to pre-modern legality—Roman law in particular. Problems that may be addressed by the concept of the 'legal form' seem to be rooted in the very status of normativity as displaying an inertia vis-à-vis the reality it is meant to regulate. Addressing the nexus between the *formal continuity* of the law—including the resistance of obsolete legal concepts and devices against the pressure of socio-political reality—and its effective functions is a crucial question. To use Ernst Bloch's term, the law is afflicted by 'the simultaneity of the non-simultaneous' (*Gleichzeitigkeit des Ungleichzeitigen*[18]): outdated and contemporaneous elements coexist within the law on a daily basis. The natural inertia and conservativeness of interpretation suggest that the legal form has its own kind of temporality.

Crucially, however, this trans-epochal understanding of the legal form is secondary at best, as it steers away from the heart of the Marxist approach to legality. As Pashukanis underlined clearly, the concept of the legal form addresses capitalist legality, as it involves commodity exchange based on forced equalisation.[19] For this reason, the application of the legal form to pre-modern legality is naturally possible—and potentially fruitful—but it eclipses the core of the Marxist legacy in explaining capitalist legality.

There is one additional important reason why the concept of legal form should be applied in its intrinsic link to capitalist (modern) society. The legal form cannot be dissociated from the key element of legacy to which it belongs: the idea of the law's disappearance (or, in the Marxist parlance, 'withering away') as a result of overcoming capitalism.[20] As a result, the legal form is interwoven into the thick web of core Marxist problems concerning historicity and the possibility of putting an end to capitalism. Marxism has therefore a special, historically reflexive position in the history of antinomianism and demands focus on addressing the modern legal form.

With these recognitions in mind, we can work toward building a generalised concept of the legal form, which overcomes Pashukanis' limitations in order to retroactively grasp Marxist thinking on legality. In the first approach, the legal form can be conceived of *as the transposition of an arbitrary political will onto the self-sufficient normative level, which produces a surplus of discriminatory symbolic power that exceeds the power directly contained in the command of the lawgiver*. The surplus violence inherent in the law itself lies precisely in the act of normative generalisation, regardless of the content of a norm. The core of Marx's critique is directed at the fact that abstraction on which the transposition of the will into a norm is based is equivalent to alienation. Within the legal form, abstraction and alienation are indifferentiable. Legal form is responsible for the construction of a

18 Ernst Bloch, *Werkausgabe, Band 4. Erbschaft dieser Zeit* (Suhrkamp 1985) 98–116.
19 Pashukanis (n 1) 63–64.
20 See Zia Akhtar, 'Law, Marxism and the State' (2015) 28 *Int J Semiot Law* 661, 672.

normative world parallel to the 'real' one, which deforms it in the process of alienation-through-abstraction and produces inherent injustice. The legal form as a concept, points to this excess of domination and violence present in legal abstraction which—beyond any concrete provisions that may be unjust in themselves—obfuscates power and disarms resistance.

Even more importantly, modern legal form tends towards universalisation of the normative. In the modern state, the law is not an oracle to which we come to solve a dispute or a problem that exists independently of it. It rather aims to build a complete normative system that will not complete social reality and human life but will become *an exhaustive legal basis for them.*[21] The universal subjection to the law is a corollary of Foucault's 'Great Confinement',[22] which leaves the non-legal remainder as a direct object of coercion. The law (and human rights in particular) plays a crucial role in what Enzo Traverso identifies as the crux of modern political evolution: 'the installation of the people as a biopolitical object moulded and built by the new power'.[23] As a result of this 'panjuridification', in modernity we do not come to the law, we are already in the thrall of the law. This is reflected in the language of rights, especially human rights: we live because we have *the right* to live. The assumption of the law's completeness makes the normative world not only formally independent from the 'real' one but gives the former incontestable power over the latter. In other words, it underpins legal fetishism that, in turn, is a prop for commodity fetishism.

Kant—Hegel: Legal form at the heart of modern abstraction

These initial definitions allow us to look back at the debates within the triangle Kant—Hegel—Marx to reconstruct the critique of the legal form in more detail.

For Kant (esp. in *The Critique of Practical Reason* and *The Metaphysics of Morals*), the law—together with ethics—constitutes a self-sufficient normative world, the only one in which human beings are free from constraints of

21 This tendency is visible in numerous processes taking place in modern law: decline of natural law, uptake of private law by structures of public law, great codifications and the emergence of human rights as linked with constitutional law. See Murray Raff and Anna Taitslin, 'Private Law in the Shadow of Public Law: A Legacy of 20th Century Marxism and the Soviet Legal Model' in Thomas Bustamante and Oche Onazi (eds), *Human Rights, Language and Law* (Franz Steiner Verlag 2012) 157–59, 162–73.

22 Michel Foucault, *History of Madness* (Jonathan Murphy and Jean Khalfa trs, Routledge 2006) 44–77. See also Roy Porter, 'Foucault's Great Confinement' (1990) *Hist Human Sci* 3(1): 13.

23 Enzo Traverso, *Revolution. An Intellectual History* (Verso 2021) 101.

nature and causality.[24] This normative world is self-referential and independent from the 'real' world reigned by physical laws. It may, of course, trigger human actions in the natural world, but in themselves its existence and validity remain unaffected by 'reality'.[25] As a result, however, human beings are split into two: *homo phaenomenon*, the one subjected to the reign of nature, and *homo noumenon*, the one who finds her freedom of self-constitution in the law.[26] Thus normativity introduces a rift at the heart of human existence, anticipating Marx's critique of the split *homme/citoyen*,[27] and shedding light on the distinction between the people and the nation Kant's promise of freedom precisely in the legal form is a double-edged device: human beings can enjoy freedom only for the price of subjugating themselves to the alienating harness of the law. Wherever there is legal form, the 'representation of reality' on the normative plane takes precedence over what is represented.

But the link between the legal form and Kant's thinking goes even further than his ethics. The schema of legal form which first abstracts from reality in order to later return under the form of judgment—a relation between the general and the particular—is a recurrent motif in the whole œuvre by Kant. In *The Critique of Pure Reason*, it is responsible for relating concepts and phenomena in transcendental logic.[28] In other words, the legal form corresponds here to epistemological structures. *The Critique of Judgment* investigates cognition through the idea of judgment, which combines the rule with its application. In particular, through the concept of the sublime Kant addresses situations in which the rule bursts through the overwhelming excess of reality to which it is meant to apply.[29]

In this way, Kant brings to the end the claim of the modern legal form to *treat each particularity as a singular case of general norms and concepts*, although he recognises—in the notion of the sublime[30]—that this link may be occasionally ripped apart. In this sense, the sublime is a peculiar counterpart to the legal form's inherent violence. On the one hand, it could seem that the moment when the rule cannot absorb the 'case' due to the latter's incommensurability represents a revolutionary momentum. But on the other

24 Immanuel Kant, *The Critique of Practical Reason* (Werner S Pluhar tr, Hackett 2002) 4.
25 ibid 4–8, 60–61.
26 Immanuel Kant, *The Metaphysics of Morals* (Mary Gregor tr, CUP 1991) 214–15.
27 Karl Marx, 'On the Jewish Question' in Karl Marx and Friedrich Engels (eds), *Collected Works*, vol 1 (Progress Publishers 1975) 154.
28 Immanuel Kant, *Critique of Pure Reason* (Paul Guyer and Allen W Wood trs, CUP 1999) 204–44.
29 Immanuel Kant, *The Critique of Judgment* (JH Bernard tr, Macmillan 1914) 109–20.
30 On the Kantian notion of the sublime see also: See Jean-François Lyotard, *Lessons on the Analytic of the Sublime* (E Rottenberg tr, Stanford UP 1994) 77–146; Jean-Luc Nancy, *Une pensée finie* (Galilée 1990) 169–93.

hand, Kant's sublime connotes a *jouissance*-like pleasure of inadequacy and domination.[31] If so, the sublime would rather represent an imaginary triumph of the legal form over what would try to burst it.

Kant's philosophical revolution has, as Peter Sloterdijk noticed, a Magellanian dimension:[32] it seeks to delimit totality. In this sense, Kant perspicaciously grasps the actual work of modern legal form toward universalisation. His schemata demonstrate how the legal form is at work not only within the strictly understood legal field but penetrates deeply into the *episteme* of the epoch. What can be thus seen is that the inherent injustice of the legal form lies in the violence on particularity exerted by already absorbing it into a system of relations between the general and the particular. Interpretative problems belong only to the normative level, whereas reality is always-already dissected into 'facts' seen through legal categories. The decision on how to classify 'a case' and how to apply a legal term or a legislative norm (the power of adjudication) is a specifically legal form of power, regardless of the power that a norm aims to accomplish (the power of legislation). Common modern prohibition of *non liquet* transforms a linguistic practice into exercise of power through language epitomised by a decision or a judgment, backed up by state power. In this sense, the prohibition of *non liquet* corresponds to the sublime in Kant's account: however reality would wriggle out of the harness of a rule, the latter always has the upper hand, being located in a comfortable, unassailable position.

Finally, rethinking Kant allows of discovering another specific trait of the (modern) legal form. The transformation of political will into positive legal norms is a form of exercising power *in advance*. Contrary to, for example, a particular local decision of the monarch, the power congealed in the legal form encompasses an entire *class* of cases whose boundaries are difficult to predict at the onset. Whoever confronts a particular legal decision, confronts already the entire normative system with its internal logic and independence from reality. In this respect, the legal form expropriates particularity by putting it in the losing position of unsubstantiated negation of universality.

The development of the modern legal form is particularly visible in Hegel's *Philosophy of Right*.[33] According to Hegel, the legitimacy of the law can lie only in its universal form.[34] Meanwhile, 'form in its most concrete significance

31 Kant (n 29) 119–20.

32 Peter Sloterdijk, *Im Weltinnenraum des Kapitals. Für eine philosophische Theorie der Globalisierung* (Suhrkamp 2005) 143.

33 GWF Hegel, *Philosophy of Right* (RW Dyde tr, Batoche Books 2001).

34 For Hegel, the law appears as the highest form of normativity, a condensation of an ethical and political progress that culminates in legal provisions—because they are universal and (thus) rational. As he writes, 'Right and ethical principle, the actual world of right and ethical life, are apprehended in thought, and by thought are given definite, general, and rational form, and this reasoned right finds expression in law.' ibid 15.

is reason, as an intellectual apprehension which conceives its object'.[35] Naturally, this concept of the form is rooted deeply in Hegel's own thought, but precisely in this respect, it grasps the novelty of modernity. For him, the form of the law is the highest development of the will; only the will that conceives of itself in the most abstract form gains full freedom.[36] The will—in this case understood politically—can reach its peak when it does not relate to some accidental situations or objects, but addresses them normatively in advance, as cases of abstract rules. Just as in *The Phenomenology of Spirit*[37] consciousness rises from a simple here and now to the most abstract intellectual constructs of spirit, so does the law achieve its apex when it captures the law entirely with an exhaustive system of rules.

What Hegel's thought reveals here is not only the inherent link between legal form and capitalist modern abstraction but also the role of sovereignty. Through the legal form, the law reaches universality of application, which excludes and pacifies any territory not subjected to universal rules, while building up a normative reproduction of the whole social reality. At the same time, it grasps, *in advance*, the whole of reality. What the form brings to the law is the self-certainty of being in command of the object, not even factually, but through aspiringly universal reason. It is nothing less but a binding between law and sovereignty understood as always having the upper hand. The law based on the sovereign will should always win, because it grasps and predicts everything in advance, turning the whole reality into a set of cases corresponding to general rules. Such a turn is a Copernican revolution in Kant's sense:[38] the law does not *intervene into* reality but rather reproduces it, poses the normative copy as primary and requires factuality to conform to it. The legal form should be understood precisely as the act of making the law a universal rational system based on sovereign reason.

In Hegel's account, the law must be thus based on the translation of a political will into the universal language of normativity and thereby eliminate any kind of 'caprices', that is, arbitrariness or contingency.[39] Apologetic in his approach to the sovereign nation-state, Hegel praises this act of converting a political decision into a universal norm as the highest act of freedom possible on Earth.[40] The state power culminating in abstract law *knows what it wants* in the most abstract way: 'the state knows what it wills, and knows it as something thought'.[41] What in Kant was the real freedom of a human being—legislating for herself—is in truth, only the freedom of the law-giving

35 ibid.
36 ibid 30–35.
37 GWF Hegel, *Phenomenology of Spirit* (AV Miller tr, OUP 1977).
38 Kant (n 28) 110.
39 Hegel (n 33) 39–40.
40 ibid 195.
41 ibid 214.

sovereign. Only the sovereign is actually free because in its position the particular will conflate with the universal form: the sovereign creates not acts or decisions, but entire normative worlds.

In this way, the legal form corresponds to the self-certainty of the law. Stemming from sovereignty, it is equivalent to the certainty that whatever is decided within the normative world will shape reality without the possibility of the latter affecting the former. The legal form constitutes a double move: it makes the law universal and, at the same time, makes everything else particular in relation to the already established universality. This self-sufficiency and independence of the legal form is for Hegel absolute conceptual perfection. For Marx, however, it is the cornerstone of his critique.

Marx: Generalising the critique of the law

Approaching Marx 100 years after Pashukanis requires that we move further from the well-ruminated history of his explicit critique of the law. The concept of the legal form is broader and more potent. Accordingly, we should rather ask: how can the legal form be generalised to address the nature of capitalism?

Marx' explicit critique of the law—and what is the crux of the legal form—can be found mainly in his early writings, although some important insights return in his late work.[42] In *Debates on the Law on the Theft of Wood* Marx addresses precisely the emergence of modern legal form as inherent in positive, universal legal acts.[43] The universality that Hegel praised becomes for Marx the highest injustice.[44] Amassing wood, hitherto a customary practice of the poor, is identified as an actual instance of a general legal term—'theft'.[45] The abstraction at work in the law is a brutal force, which abstracts from the context, historical customs and, most importantly, economic divisions. Marx points out that, subjugation of a particular situation through a universalist

42 It is commonly claimed that 'Marx never offered fully developed critiques of law or the state, let alone theories of jurisprudence or legal history.' Rob Hunter, 'Critical Legal Studies and Marx's Critique: A Reappraisal' (2021) 31(2) *Yale JL & H* 389, 389. This platitude corresponds to the idea of treating the legal form as a conceptual event rather than an ossified theory, which in Marxism is particularly problematic.

43 Karl Marx, 'Debates on the Law on the Theft of Wood' in Karl Marx and Friedrich Engels (eds), *Collected Works*, vol 1 (Progress Publishers 1975) 224–63.

44 As Daniel Bensaïd wrote, 'À travers une législation comme celle sur le vol du bois, les autorités publiques se mettent au service de l'intérêt privé au lieu d'incarner face à lui l'intérêt général'. Daniel Bensaïd, 'Marx et le vol de bois: du droit coutumier des pauvres au bien commun de l'humanité' in *Les dépossédés. Karl Marx, les voleurs de bois et le droit des pauvres* (La Fabrique Éditions 2007) 8. But by doing so, the state does not warp the Hegelian ideal, as Bensaïd suggests, but rather demonstrates how this ideal was inherently warped from the start.

45 Marx (n 43) 225–27.

law is an actual act of violence.[46] The trouble is, this class violence—rooted in crude interests of the bourgeois—is obfuscated with a seemingly logical, almost technical legal argumentation.[47]

Accordingly, we could say that the imminent injustice of the legal form consists in converting effective politico-economic decisions into terminological and logical disputes. In this critique of legal formalism, the very act of *translation* is already an act of violence and *adikia*. As soon as the legal form is established, a decision on whether to punish a certain group of citizens for the actions they have traditionally been performing is veiled in its political character and begins to be perceived just as the allegedly neutral legal decision on how to classify a given case. In this respect, the legal form is masked class violence. *'Classification'* is a perfectly dialectical term to grasp this ambiguous process: by classifying 'cases' into legal categories, the legal form produces, preserves and subjugates the dispossessed class.

With the benefit of deconstructive critique, the legal form may be understood as a radical example of a self-sufficient linguistic world that maintains a relation with social reality through its absorption into legal categories. Seen in the light of the concept of the legal form, the law seeks answers to social dilemmas in its own text; each reference to seemingly extra-legal categories (social justice, customs, mercy) may be performed only through a legal foothold. In this sense, for the legal form *il n'y a pas d'hors-texte*:[48] it muddles the representability of the world on which it is based in order to produce the illusion of the world already shaped by a text and decodable in it.

Marx demonstrates thus that positive law is inherently alienating. It abstracts from age-old customs and popular sentiments on what is a crime and what is not.[49] This new law diverges from people's understanding of justice.[50] The legal form constitutes the normative world, which is inaccessible to the poor, as they have no intellectual capital to understand it and no economic capital to hire a lawyer. As a result, the law always has the upper hand: ignorance of the law is the position to which the dominated class is pushed in order to be ruled.

46 ibid 227–29.

47

> The Assembly, it is true, repudiates the difference between gathering fallen wood, infringement of forest regulations, and theft of wood. It repudiates the difference between these actions, refusing to regard it as determining the character of the action, when it is a question of the *interests of the infringers of forest regulations*, but it recognises this difference when it is a question of the *interests of the forest owners*.
>
> ibid 229

48 Jacques Derrida, *Of Grammatology* (Gayatri Chakravorty Spivak tr, John Hopkins Press 1997) 158.

49 Marx (n 43) 230–36.

50 ibid 235–36.

Marx's critique targets the feature that for Hegel epitomised rational freedom of the law. In producing an abstract class of cases, the legal form violently destroys a thick web of particularities on which the life of the poor depended. Marx gives a telling example: the modern state liquidates monasteries as strongholds of ignorance and exploitation. But it abstracts from the fact that monasteries used to provide charity to the poor. This however, becomes *a negligible particularity which is not seen through the lens of the universal legal form*. By liquidating monasteries, the modern state carries out a general rational principle, but annihilates the labyrinth of contingent elements of social life that allowed the dispossessed to survive.

Contrary to Kant and Hegel, Marx discovers that there can be no 'true' universality that perhaps Rousseau was the last to dream of in his *Social Contract*. Each universality is tainted with particular interest. Therefore, the universality of the modern law—its praised rationality, coherence, predictability, etc.—is, *in fact*, tainted by the private interest of those who established it.[51] As such, it is the most radical exertion of class violence: on the ground of the legal form the possessing and the dispossessed do not meet as equal opponents but as the 'normal' and the 'pathological'. In the purportedly universal tissue of the modern law, the dispossessed have just a spectral presence. The law is not 'theirs' but it aspires to represent everyone. In this double bind the exclusion of the dispossessed is perfect: they are formally granted rights and effectively rendered invisible.

As suggested by Marx, there can be no true equality or justice within the legal form. The process of abstraction, universalisation and normativisation by which it is produced always deforms the world against *some*. There can be no totality without the remainder which both founds it and is excluded by it—in the case of the law, this remainder is a class of human beings. Yet the self-sufficiency of the normative makes the impression that the remainder does not exist. It can be revealed only by critique or *irony* as a particularly Marxian method of revealing particular biases hidden behind the mask of universality. The legal form cannot be criticised directly: in itself, it creates a self-sufficient world that engulfs the critique and, therefore, may only be disclosed through ironic distance. *Rien n'est plus terrible que la logique dans l'absurdité*, says Marx after Benjamin Constant; for him, the legal form is a deformed presentation of a class interest in the form of a logical, coherent and universal system.

51

> The state abolishes . . . the distinctions established by *birth*, *social rank*, *education*, *occupation*. . . But the state, none the less, allows *private property*, *education*, *occupation*, to, act . . . as private property, education, occupation, and to manifest their particular nature. [F]ar from abolishing these effective differences, it only exists so far as they are presupposed; it is conscious of being a political state and it manifests its universality only in opposition to these elements.
>
> Karl Marx, *On the Jewish Question in The Marx-Engels Reader* (Robert Tucker ed, Norton & Company 1978) 33

The inherent inequality of the legal form postulates the imperative of its disappearance, which will coincide with communism. *The Critique of the Gotha Programme*[52] resumes arguments developed in Marx's early thought to criticise the legal form. Although the text itself aims at lambasting the SPD's focus on distribution in the economy instead of production, the core of the argument is in fact of a legal nature. The inherent injustice of the abstract law is that it always selects *some* criteria to grant an entitlement or a resource, and thus contradicts itself:

> it is, therefore, a right of inequality, in its content, like every right. Right by its nature can exist only as the application of an equal standard; but unequal individuals (and they would not be different individuals if they were not unequal) are measurable by an equal standard only insofar as they are made subject to an equal criterion, are taken from a certain side only . . .[53]

When individuals are perceived through the lens of these criteria, they seem to be formally equal. Nonetheless, the law abstracts from the real inequality between them that has been made irrelevant in the process of selection and relegated to the artificially constructed domain of the 'facts'. For example, the norm which demands equal effort from workers abstracts from all circumstances that differentiate the workers: their abilities, health, familial status, living conditions, etc.[54] *Factually unequal law presenting itself as formally equal is a propensity of both capitalist society and its transitional form on the way to communism.*[55]

The communist society, however, is believed by Marx to be founded on the famous principle 'From each according to his ability, to each according to his needs'.[56] This 'principle' is fundamentally antinomian, hence its paradox. *It breaks the legal form by using it to enshrine a relation manifestly unequal in the formal sense, and, consequently, uses a legal expression to crush legal abstraction.* This is, according to Marx, *real* equality: it abstains from comparing through abstract terms and thus achieves a material change in reality. Such a change is more profoundly ontological than its concrete Marxist incarnations, like Lenin's comparisons of 'equal measure' and concrete differences between people ('people are not alike: one is strong, another is weak; one is married, another is not; one has more children,

52 Karl Marx, 'The Critique of the Gotha Programme' in Karl Marx and Friedrich Engels (eds), *Collected Works*, vol 24 (Lawrence & Wishart 2010) 75–99.
53 ibid 86–87.
54 ibid 87–88.
55 See also Lenin's comments on this piece in: Vladimir I Lenin, *State and Revolution* (Haymarket Books 2014) 130–33.
56 Marx (n 52) 87.

another has fewer, and so on'[57]). Marx postulates the crumble of the general ontologico-epistemological machine of abstract comparison, incarnated in the legal form and assuring exchange of value.[58] Where it ceases to work, people's contribution to the economy is, in a sense, an *acte gratuit*, an inner need. The end of the legal form is like the event horizon around a black hole: its inner elements cease to work together, while legal abstraction is supposed to be replaced by the richness of factual reality.

What *The Critique of the Gotha Programme* brings into the field is a crucial identification that later on Pashukanis will approach in his own terms: *whenever socio-economic reality is to be constructed according to some abstract principles, they will be inherently unjust due to their very construction*. The legal form is precisely at the heart of commodity exchange. To assume equal exchange means to abstract from particular circumstances, which entails factual inequality. The legal form is more than the law understood as legal provisions: it is a form of abstract universalisation that capitalism imposes. Therefore, Marx postulates to abrogate the unjust abstraction inherent in the legal form, as it produces pre-selected factuality to match legal norms and perpetuates violence vis-à-vis the discarded elements. Breaking the legal form is not just a task of the juridical; it is, first and foremost, an economic challenge. For this reason, there is no overcoming of capitalism without overcoming of the legal form—not only understood as the classic 'withering away of the law', but most importantly crushing the machine of ruthless abstraction.

Another aspect of Marx's critique of the legal form arises from the conceptual map sketched in the pamphlet *On the Jewish Question*.[59] Here Marx offers a critique of the split that the modern legal form produces at the heart of human beings. This form is based on political emancipation: the modern state translates human beings (*hommes*) into legal fictions named citizens (*citoyens*) and, since this moment, relates to them only as to legal fiction.[60] Human life becomes itself colonised with the legal form: we are no longer human beings, but our legal avatars that participate in social life. To use an Althusserian term, we are always-already interpellated by the legal form.[61] The state positions itself in the role of intermediary between us and our freedom. It allows us to lead our lives only as rights established or recognised by statal apparatuses and records. In this respect, the culture of human rights with its creeping juridicisation of all areas of life is a complex process of creation of subjectivity through the legal form. Yet in doing so, the state abstracts

57 Lenin (n 55) 131.
58 See Oskar Negt, 'Thesen zur marxistischen Rechtstheorie' 6(1) (1973) *KJ* 1, 6.
59 Marx (n 27) 146–74.
60 See ibid 154.
61 Louis Althusser, *Sur la reproduction* (PUF 1995) 311.

from *actual* exercise of rights, real conditions of human beings: it settles for providing a universal grid of rights for its avatars (*citoyens*) and, once again, abstracts from everything else. This void left by the state becomes the realm of capitalism, *bellum omnium contra omnes*.[62] By our inclusion in the normative world through the legal form of citizenship, we are absorbed into the law only partially. What remains—precisely in its 'invisibility' for the state and universality—is the area of brutal exploitation. In this sense, *legal form is the production of visibility and invisibility—a permanent political redefinition of what is socially visible and what is not*. This recognition allows of including the concept of the state of exception within the Marxism-informed understanding of the legal form. With the Benjaminian intuition,[63] it may be claimed that the legal form is *a permanent form of the state of exception* which is veiled behind the mask of objective universality.

This argument brings us to a Marx-based redefinition of the concept of the legal form: *the legal form is a tool of political violence in the class struggle that consists in defining the threshold between social visibility and invisibility*. It governs social life by 'representing' it on the normative plane, but it does so through deforming it in the process of abstraction through alienation. It imposes a seemingly universal linguistic grid upon social reality, but, in fact, universality is created through the expulsion of the dominated class.

Finally, these observations correspond with Marx's analysis from the first volume of *Capital*,[64] which constitutes the closest link to Pashukanis' own theory. What we can observe here is the capitalist work of abstraction which necessarily creates a *form* opposed to matter. This is how exchange value functions in relation to use value: as a soul opposed to a thing's 'body'.[65] In *Capital* Marx identifies the relation of equivalence that the existence of exchange value presupposes between commodities, which makes otherwise qualitatively and fundamentally incommensurable products to be exchanged by entering into a formal relationship between each other—as things that they are not, that is *equal*. This particular formal relationship is also at the centre of the ideological displacement necessary to the emergence of the commodity form, that is commodity fetishism. It conflates and obscures the real social and economic processes of production and presents commodities as having an autonomous and quasi-natural relation to each other without interference. What we are witnessing is a process of congealing and concealing social relations, namely labour, that stay at the basis of the creation of commodities.[66]

62 Marx (n 27) 155.
63 Walter Benjamin, 'Theses on the Philosophy of History' in Harry Zohn (tr), *Illuminations* (Schocken Books 2007) 257.
64 Karl Marx, *Capital. A Critique of Political Economy*, vol 1 (Ben Fowkes tr, Penguin 1976).
65 ibid 126–27.
66 ibid 163–77.

Pashukanis posits the conceptual centre of his work on the equivalence of the legal form and commodity form.[67] In doing so, he models the law after commodity exchange, holding them separate and giving conceptual preference to commodity form. But having in mind the role of abstract, universal form in Kant, Hegel and Marx, should we not rather venture a claim that instead of approaching the legal form to commodity form, we should identify *an underlying form-generating force of abstraction, which—through its ability of normative redoubling and comparing—is intrinsically legal*? It would no longer be modelled after commodity form but would rather focus on *the inherent normative element at work in the capitalist process of abstraction*. In this perspective Pashukanis would appear to have made a step in the right direction, but one instead of two. The legal form works deeper, stronger and more ubiquitously than the typical Marxist antilegal sentiment would like to recognise. If we adapt it in this way, then the concept of the legal form could become a proper locus of reflecting on the equalising, universalising and abstracting work of the capital.

Thinking with the legal form

In conclusion, the analysis of Marx's critique of the law—backed with Kantian-Hegelian context of his work—reveals that the legal form is a very complex conceptual locus, rather than a singular notion. Most importantly, it has two main incarnations: properly legal and general.

The proper legal version connotes a specific modus of legality that emerges in order to uphold, disclose, conceal and congeal the reality of social and economic relations of domination and exploitation and operates as a condition of possibility for law. It provides the necessary conceptual grid, coupled with state apparatuses and modes of coercion, to maintain fundamental features of the capitalist mode of production: exchange, transfer, contract, ownership, guardianship and legal subjectivity. Such an understanding brings into question first the historical inscription of the legal form in the capitalist mode of production, and second, the specific relationship between law and the economic basis—including the endless (and not particularly elucidating) discussion of the law's relation to structure or superstructure.[68]

67 '[T]he existence of the legal form is contingent upon the integration of the different products of labour according to the principle of equivalent exchange. In so doing, he exposes the deep interconnection between the legal form and the commodity form.' Pashukanis (n 1) 63. On the senses of this correspondence see Matthew Dimick, 'Pashukanis' Commodity-Form Theory of Law' in Paul O'Connell and Umut Özsu (eds), *Research Handbook on Law and Marxism* (Elgar 2021) 116–17.

68 Collins (n 4) 22–24, 77–91; Richard Kinsey, 'Marxism and the Law: Preliminary Analyses' (1978) 5 *Brit JL and Soc'y* 202, 206; Karl Klare, 'Law-Making as Praxis' (1979) 40 *Telos* 123, 126–27; Susan Dianne Brophy, 'An Uneven and Combined Development Theory

The more general concept of the legal form does not restrict it to the law *proprio sensu*. Therefore, it would not have to find it subservient to commodity exchange—and, thus, avoid clumsy philosophical bindings between law and economy. A general concept of the legal form could be a lens through which various aspects of capitalist modernity—in its abstracting, equalising, motion-focused machinery—can be viewed. In this perspective, overcoming the legal form would be linked not only to, as Pashukanis posited, overcoming capitalism, but overcoming the whole modern way of functioning that it brings with itself. Attacking the legal form is equivalent to an attack on the whole work of capitalist totality, maintained by bonds of essentially juridical character, that Marxism strives to achieve.[69]

Accordingly, what this volume aims to achieve is thinking *with* the legal form rather than focusing on explaining Pashukanis. The legal form will be here a key to unleashing the potential of Marx's thought rather than a safe, compartmentalised notion of the Marxist antique shop. This way of thinking will, hopefully, do justice to the legal form as a conceptual event.

Presentation of the volume

This volume aims to use the concept of the legal form creatively in order to address some features of legality with a renewed Marxist gaze. The chapters pledge loyalty to speculative analysis, focusing on particular aspects of the modern law.

The first chapter, Przemysław Tacik's *Subjectification through normativity: legal form as a modern device*, addresses the legal form as a tool of producing the modern subject. By discussing Marx, Kant and Rousseau, amongst others, Tacik focuses on the role of normativity in creating the subject as a link in capitalist exchange and a condition of the possibility of modern political communities.

In the second chapter, entitled *The politics of abstraction: property, subjectivity, legal form*, Rosie Woodhouse addresses the key Pashukanisian problem of abstraction, as a dimension in which the law and capitalist exchange overlap. Based on a re-reading of Marx's early writings, this contribution aims to detect splits within the edifice of the capitalist subject and find paths of emancipation.

of Law: Initiation' (2017) 28 *L and Crit* 167, 179–82; GA Cohen, 'Base and Superstructure: A Reply to Hugh Collins' (1989) 9 *OJLS* 95, 95–99. Cf. Michael Mandel, 'Marxism and the Rule of Law' (1986) 35 *UNB LJ* 7, 10; Michael Mandel, 'Marxism and the Rule of Law' (1986) 35 *UNB LR* 7, 10; Alan Stone, 'The Place of Law in the Marxian Structure-Superstructure Archetype' (1985) 19(1) *L and Soc Rev* 39, 48–56.

69 See Moshe Postone, *Time, Labour, and Social Domination. A Reinterpretation of Marx's Critical Theory* (CUP 1993) 79.

The third chapter, Peter Čuroš' *A journey to the center of the legal form—Kelsen's Ought as the missing piece to the master signifier of the legal form* uses psychoanalytical theoretical apparatus in order to re-address the problem of what is responsible for the specificity of normativity. Čuroš provides a meticulous re-reading of Kelsen in order to demonstrate how the legal form is produced, with the creation of artificial Symbolic universality covering up the exceptional core.

Psychoanalytic inspirations continue in the next chapter, *Pashukanis avec Lacan: towards the fantasy of legal form* by Dennis Wassouf. It uses the Lacanian concept of fantasy (as re-read through Žižek) in order to decipher the functioning of the legal form. Fantasy, understood as 'an unconscious narrative creating an ideological structure of our own relation to reality' provides thus a new foothold for understanding the inner split of the law, the production of the legal subject and the textual life of the law.

The fifth chapter, *On the 'relative' autonomy of the modern form of law: from Marx and Engels to Althusser* by Eduardo A. Chia undertakes an erudite journey through the age-old discussion of the relationship between the law and economy. Chia reconstructs meticulously the emergence of the paradigm of 'relative autonomy', as well as its limits and internal rifts. In this portrayal, legal autonomy is not only a pre-condition of its internal agency but also of any emancipation through juridical devices.

In the sixth chapter, *Struggle to see the law: legal form beyond the object totality*, Hedvig Lärka attempts to re-examine the concepts of abstraction and equality that normativity entails. In a move to find a new paradigm of interpretation, she argues 'for a Marxist critique of law that presents the specificity of law not as general equality, but *as equality before the value-form*'. In a creative and inventive philosophical language, Lärka identifies the subject-creating violence of the legal norm, looking for the ways to emancipate humanity.

The seventh chapter, Hugo Lundberg's *From critique of abstraction to speculative legal form* continues the discussion of the concept of abstraction in Pashukanis. Lundberg mobilises dialectical critique, anchored in readings of Gillian Rose and G.W.F. Hegel, in order to argue that thinking with the legal form should be speculative rather than acknowledge the argument of excessive abstraction. With reference to Hegel, the chapter inscribes the legacy of the legal form into a dialectical sublation. Lundberg postulates 'shifting standpoint from relative ethical life, that is, legal form, to absolute ethical life, which for Pashukanis would be communism'.

The eighth chapter, Christos Marneros' *Legal form and the anarchist critique of the law*, opens the concluding part of the book that re-addresses the respectable tradition of 'withering away of the law'. Marneros confronts the conceptuality of the legal form with anarchist critique, pointing out to lacunae in Pashukanis' theorisation of how the law would disappear. Mobilising anarchist critique of social normativity, he demonstrates that the withering away of the law cannot be a process that ensues from economic transformations but requires active confrontation with legality.

In the ninth chapter, entitled *Law beyond the legal form*, Tormod Johansen offers a nuanced and precise account of distinctions within normativity, demonstrating that Pashukanis' concept of the withering away of the law is not tantamount to the disappearance of normativity as such. As Johansen claims, '*after the end of the legal form we will find law*', pointing out to the way in which the legal form and its conceptuality consumed our understanding of what the law can be. Rekindling the messianic spirit of Marxism, he thus attempts to dissociate the legal form from what it has been dominating.

Finally, the tenth chapter, Dimitrios Kivotidis' *The withering away of the legal form: revisiting past debates for future movements*, revisits the withering-away-of-the-law thesis in order to seek new avenues for finding normativity beyond legality. As he proposes, the structurally capitalist law can be replaced with new forms of social consciousness based on the notion of the 'ethical community' (*Sittlichkeit*) and the principle of the 'free and full development of the individual'.

This book, together with a second volume published simultaneously by Routledge (*Legal Form: Pashukanis and the Marxist Critique of Law*), was prepared under the aegis of two research centres—Nomos: Centre for International Research on Law, Culture and Power at the Jagiellonian University in Kraków and Centre for Critical Thought at the University of Kent. The chapters were developed in long discussions culminating in two workshops, at the University of Kent in June 2022 and at the Jagiellonian University in Kraków in April 2023. The research and publication have been supported by a grant from the Faculty of International and Political Studies under the Strategic Programme Excellence Initiative at Jagiellonian University.

Chapter 1

Subjectification through normativity

Legal form as a modern device

Przemysław Tacik

Introduction

If there is something to add to the panoply of literature on the Marxist concept of the law, it probably arises from the belatedness of our historical position. Creative experiments with state socialism are over; the hopes that the 'age of extremes'[1] had nurtured are gone. Capitalism, though ridden with blatant contradictions more than ever, keeps reincarnating through permanent instability,[2] organising now the map of hegemonies around the line of conflict between liberal and authoritarian capitalist forms. With the distance in time that we now have towards the golden age of Marxism and Marxism-Leninism we can notice how many of their constructing elements had been recycled from more foundational thinking about the modern era. Thus, especially in its dialectical layer Marxism is still the privileged *scientia* of modernity. Recognising its inherent link with modernity, like newcomers coming to a party, we would appear to Marx and great Marxist thinkers as spectres. We know too much—cynically—and see more of the whole picture of modernity, which reveals how Marxism branches out into other intellectual currents that reflect the specificity of the modern age.[3] So it is in our belatedness, in the distance towards Marxism which it gives that we can come back to the problem of legal form. Marx cannot be read without the background of the first philosophy that had grasped the onset of modernity—especially Kant and Hegel—and the accumulated thought of our late epoch. Ours is the night in which the owl of Minerva can fly out.

1 Eric Hobsbawm, *The Age of Extremes. A History of the World, 1914–1991* (Vintage Books 1996).

2 Slavoj Žižek, *Sex and the Failed Absolute* (Bloomsbury 2020) 157–58.

3 This recognition by Žižek led him making a significant step back and perceiving Marx within the universe carved out by Hegel. See Slavoj Žižek, *Less than Nothing: Hegel and the Shadow of Dialectical Materialism* (Verso 2012) 193–64.

DOI: 10.4324/9781032724713-2

When addressing the law Marxism plays on a foreign scene, to invoke Derrida's concept.[4] This is its own choice: in opposition to Hegel, Marxism deliberately maintains an active difference between thought and reality. Thought needs to be commanded by something which is outside of it, by the element coded as 'matter' in the term 'materialism' and identified with economic production. In the Marxist *episteme* most phenomena of the social world, including the law, are kept in suspension and referred to the dimension which is supposed to determine or explain them. This automatically entails well-known problems that since long have troubled Marxist legal theory: to which extent is the law autonomous? What is the nature of the law's determination by the economy? What role does the law play in the maintenance of capitalist relations? The ultimate consequence of the gesture of epistemic suspension is the unfortunate distinction between base and superstructure, whose proneness to ossification and positivisation has muddled the Marxist tradition with cumbersome scholasticism.[5]

Such a materialist structure of Marxism makes it an awkward player in the domain of jurisprudence. It knows not only too much about the law as such but knows it in advance. Yet for the very same reason it can hardly engage in jurisprudential disputes, as it does not recognise legal problems otherwise than in order to *see through* them. On its own ground and in the mode of critique, Marxism wins with jurisprudence hands down. But a theoretician who just smashes the law with the Marxist hammer is left with useless debris. Things get even more tricky when Marxism attempts to scrutinise in greater detail the binding between law and economy or actively engage in the construction of a legal system.

The concept of the legal form—at least since Pashukanis[6] the key element of the Marxist tradition in analysing the law—reflects *the structural reference*

4 Jacques Derrida, 'Freud and the Scene of Writing' in Alan Bass (tr), *Writing and Difference* (Routledge 2001) 246–91.

5 Hugh Collins, *Marxism and Law* (OUP 1982) 22–24, 77–91; Richard Kinsey, 'Marxism and the Law: Preliminary Analyses' (1978) 5 *Brit JL and Soc'y* 202, 206; Karl Klare, 'Law-Making as Praxis' (1979) 40 *Telos* 123, 126–27; Susan Dianne Brophy, 'An Uneven and Combined Development Theory of Law: Initiation' (2017) 28 *L and Crit* 167, 179–82; GA Cohen, 'Base and Superstructure: A Reply to Hugh Collins' (1989) 9 *OJLS* 95, 95–99. Cf. Michael Mandel, 'Marxism and the Rule of Law' (1986) 35 *UNB LJ* 7, 10; Michael Mandel, 'Marxism and the Rule of Law' (1986) 35 *UNB LR* 7, 10; Alan Stone, 'The Place of Law in the Marxian Structure-Superstructure Archetype' (1985) 19(1) *L & Soc Rev* 39, 48–56.

6 Pashukanis' understanding of the legal form is in itself quite complex. Apart from preserving the reference to the economy (as 'matter'), it also connotes formalisation seen as abstraction and sublimation of the economic conflict to the position of superstructure):

> the economic relation in its actual workings is the source of the legal relation, which comes into being only at the moment of dispute. It is dispute, conflict of interest, which creates the legal form, the legal superstructure. In the lawsuit, in court proceedings, the economically active subjects first appear in their capacity as parties, that is, as participants in the

to the outside on which materialism is built. The law is to be seen through the lens of form, which does not exist without its matter: the actual economic relations that it names, registers, classifies, upholds and enforces.[7] The legal form allows for treating the law as partly transparent vis-à-vis its economic structure and, therefore, debunks legal fetishism.[8] Nonetheless, in order to avoid the vulgarisation of Marxism,[9] it needs to be a concept that is used with self-awareness of how much its reference to the outside is used. In this sense it functions like an adjustable lens: depending on how autonomously we treat the form, it gives us the focus either on its own construction or on its economic background of the law. What is crucial, capitalism shapes not only the economy that we see through the lens of the legal form: it produces, reproduces and organises this form itself.

Therefore, two crucial methodological postulates for the legal form, as formulated from a belated position, would be the following: first, it should not be treated as a master key for jurisprudence which solves every riddle through a pre-determined victory. Whenever legal form operates as a concept, we should carefully register what it does to the law and drive its piercing blade with due caution and self-awareness. In mathematics the derivative relates the pace of change of the function value to the change of the argument; accordingly, we should relate the transformation of the law's conceptuality under the influence of the legal form—to our use of it.

Second, the legal form needs to be read with a properly Marxist understanding of its modern nature. *Legal form is not the form of the law as such*: it is a structure proper to modernity in the age of capitalism.[10] That means in

> legal superstructure. Even in its most primitive form, the court is legal superstructure par excellence. The legal differentiates itself from the economic and appears as an autonomous element through legal proceedings.
>
> Evgeny Pashukanis, *The General Theory of Law and Marxism* (David Milovanovic tr, Transaction Publishers 2003) 93

Matthew Dimick attempted to map the vague Pashukanis' definitionary elements of the legal form in: Matthew Dimick, 'Pashukanis' Commodity-Form Theory of Law' in Paul O'Connell and Umut Özsu (eds), *Research Handbook on Law and Marxism* (Elgar 2021) 115–17. On Pashukanis in general see: Michael Head, *Evgeny Pashukanis. A Critical Reappraisal* (Routledge 2016). Nonetheless, it needs to be remembered that according to certain scholars Pashukanis' theory is not a Marxist theory of law as such, but a theory of NEP. See Robert Sharlet, 'Pashukanis and the Rise of Soviet Marxist Jurisprudence, 1924–1930' (1974) 1:2 *Soviet Union* 103, 121.

7 See also Peter Binns, 'Law and Marxism' (1980) 4 *Soc and Class* 100, 102.

8 Collins (n 5) 9–13; Isaac D Balbus, 'Commodity Form and Legal Form: An Essay on the "Relative Autonomy" of the Law' (1977) 11 *J Law and Soc* 215, 226.

9 See Csaba Varga, *Contemporary Legal Philosophising* (Budapest: Szent István Társulat 2013) 82; Andrew Vincent, 'Marx and Law' (1993) 20:4 *J L and Soc* 371, 380; Stone (n 5) 40.

10 Pashukanis (n 6) 41–42, 58; Chris J Arthur, 'Towards a Materialist Theory of Law' (1977) 7 *Critique* 31, 32–34, 42; Balbus (n 8) 217; Brophy (n 5) 185.

the first place—proper to the time in which abstraction operates as a mode of circulation of capital, labour force is exploited through surplus value[11] and workers are theorised as individual free subjects. Yet from our historical position, we must also add: the legal form needs to be seen through the lens of the socialist experiments with legality and their subsequent sliding into re-positivisation.[12] In this sense, it is structurally linked to a greater realm than just capitalism—namely modernity. Extrapolation of the concept of the legal form onto pre-modern epochs, although theoretically possible, follows the deceiving logic of *genus* and its example detectable in Hegel's and Marx's *œuvres*.[13] Even if we assume that legal form traverses the entire history of the law, the modern legal form remains its privileged 'example' that reveals how generalisation and abstraction have been applied to its own particularity (not mentioning the fact that generalisation and abstraction *onto* 'the entire history' are possible only through the historicisation inextricably related to modernity[14]). Modernity is both a foundation of a *genus* and its sole proper example; legal form gains its proper dialectical impetus only when seen in close correlation to this epoch. Outside of it, however, it collapses in its function of referring outside of the law and turns into a notion of *Verstand*, not *Vernunft*, which thus pertains to the law solely.

With these postulates in mind, let us now dig beneath the legal form, delving into the murky foundational region where it roots out into structuralities of modernity. Let us treat legal form not as a tranquil part of reality, but as a real abstraction that can be revealed only through methodological abstraction. Legal form appears within the structure of modern law under the hammer of a Marxist investigation: what we need to achieve is precisely the synchronicity between *the movement of discovery and the movement of appearance*. For the starting point of this study, we will take a modern legal symptom well-thrashed by Marxist critique: human rights. Nonetheless, we will attempt to steer off at a tangent of trite observations. What we will ask is how modernity requires the subject to constitute itself through—and in—a binding between will and the law.

The plan for this chapter is an incremental procession toward the roots of legal form. We will begin with some general theory, then pass to the relation between individuality and legal form, only to prepare for the proper descent into the abyss where subjectivity and the law melt into one another.

11 On the link between exploitation of surplus value and the law see: Antonio Negri, 'Rereading Pashukanis: Discussion Notes' (2017) 5 *Stasis* 8, 21.

12 On the evolution of post-revolutionary Soviet law towards ossification and positivisation see: Cosmin Cercel, *Towards a Jurisprudence of State Communism. Law and the Failure of Revolution* (Routledge 2018); Head (n 6) 117–66.

13 Žižek (n 3) 39.

14 See Przemysław Tacik, *A New Philosophy of Modernity and Sovereignty. Towards Radical Historicisation* (Bloomsbury 2021) 69–80.

Legal form, capitalism and modernity

Legal form remains the core concept of Marxist critique of the law. Sparingly used by Marx and Engels (not necessarily under its future name),[15] it gained prominence with Pashukanis for its two dialectically bound aspects. Legal form is peculiar insofar as it refers to the outside of the law (to the economic sense of social relations under capitalism) and, at the same time, allows of reaching into the law's innermost specificity.[16] Legal form is both a form in relation to matter (economy) and a legal garb that economy needs to don in order to turn into a web of social relations underpinned by the state. In other words, through the legal form, we can grasp what is *most properly legal*—and do it precisely through the relation of the law to its socio-economic sense. In Lacanese, legal form is *extime*, both intimate and exterior to the law—it is, as Lacan wrote, 'cet interdit au centre, qui constitue, en somme, ce qui nous est le plus prochain, tout en nous étant extérieur'.[17] From this perspective, legal form only depletes its potential when it is used in order to prove the lack of autonomy of the law. What the legal form demonstrates is that *the law constitutes itself around the legal reworking of the socio-economic sense of relations.*[18] Its autonomy and dependence are not binarily opposable: autonomy is precisely in the way of retaining and moulding the absolute central axis of dependence through the legal form.[19]

15 Michael Head, 'The Passionate Legal Debates of the Early Years of the Russian Revolution' (2001) 14 *Can JL Jurisprud* 3, 8–10.

16 Pashukanis posits as his first discovery the affinity between commodity form and the legal form, from which he later on derives his further claims.

> [T]he existence of the legal form is contingent upon the integration of the different products of labour according to the principle of equivalent exchange. In so doing, he exposes the deep interconnection between the legal form and the commodity form
>
> Pashukanis (n 6) 63

17 Jacques Lacan, *Le Séminaire. Livre XVI—De l'Autre à l'autre* (Seuil 2006) 224.

18 This reworking has naturally an autopoietic dimension, through which the economic reference may appear in a disturbed way. See Niklas Luhmann, 'Legal Argumentation: An Analysis of Its Form' (1995) 58 *MLR* 285, 285–94.

19 Hugh Collins defines autonomy of the law in the following way:

> first, that there is in reality less direct manipulation of political power by the dominant class in modern society than there was in earlier social formations, and second, that the appearance of autonomy conceals deep structural constraints upon the powers of the State apparatus which ensure that it faithfully pursues the interests of the ruling class.
>
> Collins (n 5) 49

See also Rob Hunter, 'Critical Legal Studies and Marx's Critique: A Reappraisal' (2021) 31 *Yale JL & H* 389, 406–7; Sonja Buckel, 'The Juridical Condensation of the Relations of Forces: Nicos Poulantzas and Law' in Alexander Gallas and others (eds), *Reading Poulantzas* (Merlin Press 2011) 163–64. On the map of strategies that define relations between law and economy in Marxism see: Daniel McLoughlin and Talina Hürzeler, 'Marx on the

In this sense, legal form inherits—via Marxism—the legacy of distinction between two kinds of reasoning, *Verstand* and *Vernunft*, developed in German idealism. Despite differences between Kant and Hegel, *Verstand* was for them the work of intellect operating in a determined field with an unreflected set of presuppositions.[20] Hegel noticed that the greatest power of *Verstand* is a forceful dissection of its field of study, which becomes neatly compartmentalised into stable, separate categories.[21] *Vernunft*, on the contrary, is the power which leaves the boundaries of *Verstand* in order to take into account its presuppositions.[22] *Vernunft* dissolves separated categories, relates them to the foundations of the framework in which they were created and thus dialectically puts them in motion. For Kant, *Vernunft* is generally a prohibitive force that keeps *Verstand* in its legitimate boundaries;[23] for Hegel, *Vernunft* is the power of reflection that mediates between particular forms of knowledge.

Legal form partakes in the understanding of science, *Wissenschaft*, as elaborated in German idealism (especially Fichte[24]). *Wissenschaft* is the science of proper reason, *Vernunft*.[25] It reflects and reinscribes the act of reflection into the matter. Accordingly, when Marx claimed to make a scientific discovery of the nature of capitalism,[26] it rested precisely on the reflective ability of recognising the dialectical nature of capitalist relations. In other words, the concept of legal form allows for putting the law precisely in its *distanced dependence on socio-economic reality*. This does not mean, of course, that *Verstand* proper to law is illegitimate. It is nothing less than jurisprudence: a form of knowledge intrinsic to the law, forcefully dissociating its relation from socio-economic reality and *thus* assuring the operativity of the law. Meanwhile, *Vernunft* offers recognition of the law's relation to the core of the capitalist constitution of reality. The problematic status of this knowledge is that it eventually bifurcates into two options: either it calls for a radical act of abolishing the law altogether with capitalist social relations

Factory Acts: Law, Exploitation and Class Struggle' in Paul O'Connell and Umut Özsu (eds), *Research Handbook on Law and Marxism* (Elgar 2021) 28–30.

20 Georg WF Hegel, *The Phenomenology of Spirit* (AV Miller tr, OUP 1977) 79–88.

21 ibid 95.

22 Nonetheless, Hegel underlines that *Vernunft* and *Verstand* constitute two interlocked movements that cannot be isolated. See Georg WF Hegel, *Science of Logic* (G di Giovanni tr, CUP 2010) 460–63.

23 Immanuel Kant, *Critique of Pure Reason* (Paul Guyer and Allen W Wood trs, CUP 1998) 384–408.

24 Johann Gottlieb Fichte, *The Science of Knowledge* (AE Kroeger tr, Trübner & Co. 1889) 21–22.

25 On *Vernunft* in Marx see Raffaele de Giorgi, 'Zur Kritik der sogenannten Marxistischen Rechtstheorie' (1976) 9 *Kritische Justiz* 270, 274; Allegra de Laurentiis, 'Hegel's Legacy in Marx's Conception of Right' (2001) 17 *Southwest Philos* R 25, 32–33.

26 Karl Marx, *Capital. A Critique of Political Economy*, vol I (Ben Fawkes tr, Penguin Books 1976) 166–69, 433.

or leads to an impasse, in which the realisation of how the law participates in exploitation turns into cynicism when it lacks the capability of changing social reality. Marxism exhibits many affinities with psychoanalysis but this one is, perhaps, the most telling one: both offer disillusioned knowledge of the reality that one cannot change otherwise than through some structurally minor reconfiguration[27]—and open the path to disabused passivity.

Whatever knowledge it offers, the legal form is something more than just the normativisation of social relations. Some Marxist accounts focus on how 'legalisation' of power yields legitimation and objectification of the latter, but the law is much more than just a mask for power.[28] Even Foucault recognised a rather subservient role of the law in relation to power, noticing how legal norms homogenise power relations and frame them as prohibitive speech acts ('thou shalt not . . .').[29] Meanwhile, the real question for Marxism is not how the law *masks* power and class domination—this is in many respects established[30]—but rather *why the law offers a dominating matrix for framing basic elements of the capitalist reality.* This riddle is perhaps most conspicuous when transferred to human rights: why does modernity reach for legal language in order to define individuals and render them active? Naturally, a lot may be said—and has been said—about the ideological function of human rights, focused on guaranteeing capitalist individualist formal equality. Pashukanis, himself, assumed the necessity of legal equality for capitalism:[31] *legal form is, at its deepest, the formula of equivalisation demanded by commodity exchange.* Yet the real question is: why modernity offers just a binary device for the construction of subjects—either legal, in which individualism is constituted and shielded by human rights, or biopolitical, which discards the legal sheath around human beings and addresses them as lumps living matter? In a nutshell, why does an individual in modernity need to be constituted with a legal device—through a legal form proper to human rights—or be

27 See Jacques Lacan, *Le Séminaire, vol XXIII—Sinthome* (Seuil 2005) 33–37, 60, 73, 132–33.

28 Karl Klare, 'Law-Making as Praxis' (1979) 40 *Telos* 123, 127; Nancy E Anderson and David F Greenberg, 'From Substance to Form: The Legal Theories of Pashukanis and Edelman' (1983) 7 *Social Text* 69, 70–72.

29 Michel Foucault, *Power/Knowledge. Selected Interviews and Other Writings 1972–1977* (Power Books 1977) 139–40.

30 See for example Pashukanis (n 6) 139–40; Peter Schöttler, 'Friedrich Engels and Karl Kautsky as Critics of "Legal Socialism"' (1986) 14 *IJSL* 1, 13–18; Donald R Kelley, 'The Metaphysics of Law: An Essay on the Very Young Marx' (1978) 83 *AHR* 350, 354; Kinsey (n 5) 219–24; Klare (n 28) 132–33.

31 Anderson and Greenberg (n 28) 70–71; Stephen J Powell, 'The Legal Nihilism of Pashukanis' (1967–1968) 20 *U Fla L Rev* 18, 29; Alan Norrie, 'Pashukanis and the Commodity Form Theory: A Reply to Warrington' (1981) 10 *IJSL* 419, 423. On the role of violence in upholding this aspect of the legal form see: China Miéville, 'The Commodity-Form Theory of International Law: An Introduction' in Susan Marks (ed), *International Law on the Left: Re-Examining Marxist Legacies* (CUP 2008) 109–16.

treated as a bare life governed biopolitically? These questions go far beyond Pashukanis' own theory of the subject as an actor in equalised exchange.[32] Consequently, an expanded theory of legal form should reveal its structural binding with the basic socio-political organisation of modernity.

An expanded theory of legal form should therefore explain why modernity prefers a normative structure of constituting subjects and social relations. The usual set of common Marxist explanations (law solidifies and universalises domination, creates artificial equality, masks power of the state and of the capital[33]) assume a certain level of instrumentalisation of the law by the capitalist system. Nonetheless, in modernity, the turn to normativity is not a search for a better instrument of domination, but rather a result of some primordial binding between the constitution of subjectivity and the normative substratum. As we will see in subchapter 4, Kant's philosophy represents in theory what the French Revolution established in practice: a normative creation of the world. It is just as if the law were the limit of the sequence of social relations towards which they evolve. The modern turn to normativity seems to establish a binary mechanism that splits subjectivity into its normative version—properly registered, recognised and benefitting from rights—and lawless bare life[34] which, in relation to the law, takes the position of the matter. In this sense, legal form is a proper biopolitical mechanism. With this recognition that binds Agamben's legacy with Marxism, we can begin to unite two great traditions so far usually held separately: the Marxist thinking about capitalist social relations based on exploitation and the political tradition that takes sovereignty as its principal object of study.

But how can we bind sovereignty, law and capitalism? The starting point is the recognition that *modern law does not assume that it describes actual human beings—having their rights, interests and obligations—but rather pretends to create them as subjects*. In this lies the revolution sealed by the emergence of human rights: for the first time the law penetrates to the core of human existence, aspiring to describe it exhaustively in legal language. This operation of the law is based on the modern idea of sovereignty formally present in the people but practically exercised by the state. The law becomes the mediating instance between the people as the formal locus of sovereignty and members of the population as subjected to sovereign power.[35]

32 Pashukanis (n 6) 109–33.

33 Christopher MJ Boyd, 'Can a Marxist Believe in Human Rights?' (2009) 37 *Critique* 579, 594; Alan Hunt, 'Law, State and Class Struggle' (1976) 20 *Marxism Today* 178, 178–82; Edgar Bodenheimer, 'Impasse of Soviet Legal Philosophy' (1952) 38 *Cornell LR* 51, 66.

34 Giorgio Agamben, *Homo Sacer. Sovereign Power and Bare Life* (Daniel Heller-Roazen tr, Stanford UP 1998) 71–111.

35 Agamben notices:

> Declarations of rights must therefore be viewed as the place in which the passage from divinely authorized royal sovereignty to national sovereignty is accomplished. This

This also means that legal form should not be assumed to be just normativity; naturally, normativity as such has accompanied humanity for millennia, whereas legal form has not. Neither does this concept mean that the law regulates social interactions that can be meaningfully understood only outside of the legal scene. Such recognition is also quite obvious for almost everybody except for intransigent adherents of law-centrism. Legal form is a concept that allows why modernity obsessively links two categories—will and normativity[36]—in order to give them a foundational role in defining social reality. Modern normativity does not simply accompany or regulate socio-political life: it is ideologically posited as its cornerstone. In other words, *modernity conceives of the law as the construction material of the body politic and individuals that belong to it.* Thus, the emergence of human rights is not just an invention of capitalism that allows it to produce false market equality and conceal exploitation. Human rights remain the symptom of the entire epoch, its singular trace, the privileged site in which will is established as bound with normativity and essentialised into a symbolic *haecceitas* of human beings.

Capitalist exchange and the work of normativity on modern individuals are correlative through one important feature: abstraction.[37] The edifice of Marx's critique of capitalism is built upon the recognition of how abstraction let loose underpins social relations and sets them in motion. At this point we can retake Pashukanis' strategy of investigating structural overlaps between capitalist exchange and the law—not through civil law, however, as Pashukanis postulated,[38] but by enquiring into the necessity of expressing the circulation of capital in legal terms as such. One strategy would be to assume that the law organises social conditions for the reproduction of capital. Yet such a link between the law and capital is too epithelial; we must dig deeper. Normativity brings with itself the fundamental relation between a norm and 'its' case, or, in more abstract terms, between the general and the particular. Expressing social relations through the language of the law automatically thrusts them into the forced interplay between the reproducible rule and

> passage assures the *exceptio* of life in the new state order that will succeed the collapse of the *ancien régime*. The fact that in this process the "subject" is, as has been noted, transformed into a "citizen" means that birth which is to say, bare natural life as such-here for the first time becomes (thanks to a transformation whose biopolitical consequences we are only beginning to discern today) the immediate bearer of sovereignty.

ibid 128

36 Balbus (n 8) 220.

37 See Slavoj Žižek, *Surplus Enjoyment. A Guide For The Non-Perplexed* (London and New York: Bloomsbury 2022) 33; Balbus (n 8) 220; Kinsey (n 5) 210; Oskar Negt, 'Thesen zur marxistischen Rechtstheorie' (1973) 6 *Krit Just* 1, 6.

38 Pashukanis (n 6) 41–42.

particularity produced through the concretisation of abstraction. In other words, elevating normativity to the rank of the foundation of social reality necessarily abolishes real singularity (what Hegel would call the individual[39]) and replaces it with particularity understood as concrete abstraction.[40] Everything that cannot be subsumed under the guillotine of normative abstraction *becomes socially invisible*. The law absorbs singularity and transforms it into particularity: a concretisation of general rules. As a result, human beings are turned into subjects; goods into objects defined by civil law; and social relations into execution of rights.

In this sense, the law in a capitalist society is turned into a strict correlative of money. In the *Economic and Philosophic Manuscripts of 1844* Marx notices that money can be seen as a general leveller (Marx uses a more emphatic term: 'pimp') which provides a common measure for normally incomparable goods and services.[41] The law does the same by providing a language that operates through permanent conversions of the general into the particular and vice versa. Thus, real singularity is fundamentally obfuscated by particularity, which never functions outside of the universalist framework of legality. In capitalist societies, the law is a medium of juxtaposability—of subjects, objects and their relations.

In relation to subjects, the law also plays an additional role. The archetypal modern state is based on the idea of the sovereignty of the people—essentially, as Foucault demonstrated, a particular welding between the inherited category of sovereignty and democratic imagery.[42] Yet the modern state is a paradox in itself: the people are both the sovereign—the imagined supreme commander of the state—and the object of political power. In such a political ideology the state is a vanishing mediator, a set of apparatuses that allow the people to 'govern itself' through temporally designated representatives. Claude Lefort demonstrated how modern political ideology preserves the concept of the void in the political centre of the state:[43] the throne of democracy is essentially empty and seemingly only provisionally occupiable by transient individuals. Nonetheless, this void requires a mediation between the two roles of human beings: subjects of power and objects of command. In fact, both roles can be found already within the concept of the subject—at the same time a *subiectum* (foundation, base) and *subiectus* (a subordinate).[44]

39 Georg WF Hegel, *The Science of Logic* (George di Giovanni tr, CUP 2010) 511–12.
40 Cf. Balbus (n 8) 222.
41 Karl Marx, *Economic and Philosophic Manuscripts of 1844 and the Communist Manifesto* (Martin Milligan tr, Prometheus Books 1988) 136.
42 Michel Foucault, *"Society Must Be Defended". Lectures at the Collège de France 1975–1976* (David Macey tr, Picador 2003) 25–26.
43 Claude Lefort, *Democracy and Political Theory* (David Macey tr, Polity Press 1988) 29–31.
44 Christos Marneros, *Human Rights After Deleuze* (Hart 2023) 20.

The law is precisely the language which binds the two roles.[45] It creates the modern subject as a bundle of obligations and entitlements organised around the central category: will.[46]

Modern subjectivity is constructed from a binding between the law and the will. It produces an individual that can both buy and be bought—exercising its will either to command or to bow to commands. In this sense, the law assures precisely the same redoubling that Marx identifies in the *Capital* as the axis of capitalist exploitation: labour force is the only good that when used produces value.[47] For this reason, buying someone's labour force is a structural fraud, no matter how well she is remunerated: the compensation for buying labour force is incommensurate to the value that it produces when consumed.[48] The subjective will, as created by the law, is precisely the mandrel that binds entitlements and obligations, *subiectum* and *subiectus*, human being capable of work and human being as a chain in the link between capital spent on labour force and a product.

In this way we can bind Marxist tradition with the legacy of political philosophy focused on state and sovereignty. Modern law forms a fold, binding activity and passivity into one unit joint by the subjective will. This legal structure operates both in politics and the capitalist market. *To assure subordination precisely through the creation of individuality as its locus* remains the secret of legal form.

Modern individual as a legal creation

Joining the Marxist tradition with the legacy of conceptualising sovereignty may appear as difficult as finding the unified field theory that in physics is meant to combine general relativity with quantum physics. Yet if it is possible, the cards must already be in our hands; what we need to do is reshuffle them and find the concealed order. The first move may be to notice that

45 Pashukanis himself notices the paradox of the term 'law':

> Law is simultaneously the form of external authoritarian regulation and the form of subjective private autonomy. In the one case, the fundamental, substantive characteristic is that of unconditional obligation [*безусловной обязательности*], of absolute external coercion [*внешней принудительности*], while, in the other, it is the characteristic of freedom, guaranteed and recognised within certain limits.
>
> Pashukanis (n 6) 97

46 Will plays a central role in Hegel's understanding of law, as it remains a condition of property as well the bridge between property and contract. See Georg WF Hegel, *The Philosophy of Right* (SW Dyde tr, Batoche Books 2001) 75–83. On Marx's understanding and critique of the will see Arthur (n 10) 36–37; de Laurentiis (n 25) 25–33; Kinsey (n 5) 215–17.

47 Marx (n 26) 324–26.

48 ibid 716–17. See also Karl Marx, *Grundrisse: Foundations of the Critique of Political Economy* (Martin Nicolaus tr, Vintage Books 1973) 676.

human rights as an anthropologico-legal device appear in correlation with popular sovereignty and the development of capitalism.

Naturally, there seem to be ready-made common Marxist explanations of their position. The first one—rooted in observations that Marx himself left in his text *On the Jewish Question*[49]—would be that capitalism requires as its prerequisite creation of abstract egoist individuals, dissociated from the actual complexity of human existence, which can be later treated as nominally equal parties in actually exploitative legal relations.[50] Another explanation focuses on human rights as a legal shield of the bourgeoisie against the intrusiveness of the state: only a being who can exercise human rights, especially the right to property, can act as a proper capitalist.[51] Finally, a long tradition of Marxist thinking identifies the ideological role of human rights[52]—even if they seem to apply to all human beings equally, they indeed protect the bourgeoisie and are at best useless for the working class.[53] Anatol France's famous quip about the prohibition of sleeping under Parisian bridges, which applies 'equally' both to the rich and to the poor,[54] encapsulates the angle of this critique. All these approaches grasp some role of human rights within capitalist societies but do not treat them as a key symptom that we need to discern.

The previous section ended with the first postulate of such a developed theory: capitalist exploitation taking place through the circulation of capital and state power mediated by the sovereignty of the people are somehow related.[55] In both cases, we encounter a tripartite structure. Circulation of capital assumes—according to Marx' famous analysis[56]—that an initial portion of capital (C) enters into the process of exploitation of labour force only to return to capital (C'), but this time enriched through surplus value extracted from the worker. Meanwhile, in modern politics the political power of the state can be imposed and exercised only through the fiction of a political

49 Karl Marx, 'On the Jewish Question' in Rodney Livingstone and Gregor Benton (trs), *Early Writings* (Penguin Books 1992) 229–32. See also Stathis Kouvélakis, 'The Marxian Critique of Citizenship: For a Rereading of On the Jewish Question' (2005) 104 *South Atl Q* 707, 712–15; Luis Kutner, 'The Human Rights of Karl Marx' (1979) 55 *North Dacota LR* 39, 57; Justine Lacroix and Jean-Yves Pranchère, 'Was Karl Marx Truly Against Human Rights? Individual Emancipation and Human Rights Theory' (2012) 62(3) *Rev Fr Sci Pol* 433, 447–53.

50 Brophy (n 5) 187–88; Vinícius Casalino, 'Karl Marx's Dialetics and the Marxist Criticism of Law' (2018) 9 *Rev Direito e Práx* 2268, 2282.

51 See Steven Lukes, 'Can a Marxist Believe in Human Rights?' (1981) 1 *PRAXIS Int* 334, 342.

52 Boyd (n 33) 592–93.

53 Hunt (n 33) 187.

54 Richard L Abel, 'Capitalism and the Rule of Law: Precondition or Contradiction?' (1990) 15 *LSI* 655, 695.

55 For a brief overview of Marxist disputes on the nature of the state see: Clyde W Barrow, 'The Marx Problem in Marxian State Theory' (2000) 64 *Sci Soc* 87, 89–111.

56 Marx (n 26) 247–339.

citizen, both *subiectum* and *subiectus*, who obeys the statal order because fictionally takes it for her own. Rousseau's famous passage from *The Social Contract* gives the best example of this legitimising strategy when accounting for the equal pact of all members of a society:

> Find a form of association which will defend and protect, with the whole of its joint strength, the person and property of each associate, and under which each of them, uniting himself to all, will obey himself alone, and remain as free as before.
>
> This is the fundamental problem to which the social contract gives the answer. . .[E]ach in giving himself to all gives himself to none, and since there are no associates over whom he does not acquire the same rights as he cedes, he gains the equivalent of all that he loses, and greater strength for the conservation of what he possesses.[57]

Kant advocates a similar argument:

> The legislative authority can belong only to the united will of the people. For since all Rights is to proceed from it, it *cannot* do anything wrong by its law. Now, when someone makes arrangements about *another*, it is always possible for him to do the other wrong; but he can never do wrong in what he decides upon with regard to himself (for *volenti non fit iniuria)*. Therefore only the concurring and united will of all, insofar as each decides the same thing for all and all for each, and so only the general united will of the people, can be legislative.[58]

Moreover, he describes freedom understood as receiving—through law—an order to whose giving we authorised political power through social contract as the proper form of freedom as such:

> And one cannot say: A state, man in a state has sacrificed a *part* of his innate outer freedom for the sake of an end, but rather, he has relinquished entirely his wild, lawless freedom in order to find his freedom as such undiminished, in a dependence upon laws, that is, in a rightful condition, since this dependence arises from his own lawgiving will.[59]

What both Rousseau and Kant grasp is a mechanism of replacing the pre-modern bipolar relation between the sovereign and the subject with the

57 Jean-Jacques Rousseau, *The Social Contract in Discourse on Political Economy and The Social Contract* (Christopher Betts tr, OUP 1999) 55–56.

58 Immanuel Kant, *The Metaphysics of Morals* (Mary Gregor tr, CUP 1991) 125.

59 ibid 127.

modern reduplication of the subject which plays both the role of the virtual sovereign and the subordinate. In this tripartite structure the subject 'fuels' the state with political power by transferring to it its freedom and, subsequently, is commanded by the reinforced power of the state. This structure corresponds to the structure of economic exploitation (capital—labour—capital) described above.

Therefore, economic exploitation and sovereignty of the people are two structurally akin methods of *producing power*, economic or political,[60] through legal devices that enmesh individuals into alienated forms of subjectification.[61] In both versions of this structure, we have an initial quantum of accumulated power (capital, statal order)[62] which can subsist in time only through a process of replication. Such replication is a permanent test of whether power will be able *this time* to have an effect (will the worker toil for one more day in exchange for her remuneration? will the citizen obey one more order of state authorities?). If it does have an effect, power gains an added value. Power invested traverses both labour force and the subject-citizen in order to re-emerge as power *spent and regained*. Capital needs to reconstitute itself through a permanent process of exploitation; political power reconfirms its existence through citizens' obeyance.

Seen from this perspective, power in its two incarnations—economic and political—displays this peculiar fold that Marx recognised in labour force. *Power is a particular resource insofar as an act of 'spending' it (imposing a task, using, commanding, ordering) does not exhaust it, but, contrariwise, reinforces it.* Power needs to be spent in order to replicate itself. Power, which is preserved, unused, or taken out of exchange, withers away.

The law and money are two languages that sustain this permanent work of replication of power. They both equalise the exchange through which both economic and political power reconstitute themselves by investing it in an individual and collecting the gain. In particular, the law is a symbolic framework of constituting subjects—'juridical persons'[63]—in their necessarily twofold construction: as *subiectum* (an independent subject governing itself and entering voluntarily into legal obligations) and as *subiectus* (a subject subordinated to a labour contract or obeying state orders). The law upholds both

60 On the relation between economy and politics as two intertwined forms of power see: Jonathan Nitzan and Shimshon Bichler, *Capital as Power. A Study of Order and Creorder* (Routledge 2009) 25–64; Cohen (n 5) 96–99.

61 For a complex analysis of relations between subjectification, rights and the political see Jacques Rancière, 'Who is the Subject of the Rights of Man?' (2004) 103 *South Atl Q* 297, 303–6.

62 On the primitive accumulation that leads to this point and then, *in permanence*, upholds it, see: Mark Neocleous, 'International Law as Primitive Accumulation; Or, the Secret of Systematic Colonization' (2012) 23 *Eur J Intl L* 941, 949–54, 960–62.

63 Kinsey (n 5) 204.

the two positions, the difference between them and their point of overlap, just as it maintains 'the separation of labourers from the conditions of labour independent of capital'.[64] In other words, *the law is precisely the medium in which individual freedom and subjection to alienated relations enter their zone of indifferentiation.* The law builds the modern subject as based on the common core—will—which binds freedom and subjection. In this sense Colin Sumner was right in claiming that the heart of capitalist legal form is not commodity exchange as such, but labour exchange[65]—that is, the reduction of human beings to exchangeable abstract constructs. *Subiectus* and *subiectum* are the primordial commodity constructs to be established, interlocked, and sucked into exchange. Consequently, the legal tissue is a medium of flow between freedom and subjection which first creates them as separate positions only to later bind them through subjectivity.

Althusser noticed how interpellation through ideology produces a double subject—the subject as a free individual welded with the subject as a subordinate:

> [S]ubject in fact means: 1) a free subjectivity, a centre of initiatives, author of and responsible for its actions; 2) a subjected being, who submits to a higher authority, and is therefore stripped of all freedom except that of freely accepting his submission. This last note gives us the meaning of this ambiguity, which is merely a reflection of the effect which produces it: the individual *is interpellated as a (free) subject in order that he shall submit freely to the commandments of the Subject*, i.e. in order that he shall (freely) accept his subjection, i.e. in order that he shall make the gestures and actions of his subjection 'all by himself'. *There are no subjects except by and for their subjection.*[66]

Bourgeoisie operates with legal ideology, claims Althusser.[67] Nonetheless, the law itself plays here a crucial role. In Althusser's perspective ideology creates the subject as already given. The subject recognises *itself* in the discourse pre-emptively provided through ideology:

> [o]ne interpellates only a subject which is presumed to already exist—and one gives them their IDs in order to prove to them that they really are *this* subject which has been interpellated.[68]

64 Neocleous (n 62) 960.

65 Colin Sumner, 'Pashukanis and the "Jurisprudence of Terror"' (1981) 11(1) *Insurgent Sociologist* 99, 105–6.

66 Louis Althusser, *On the Reproduction of Capitalist Ideology and Ideological State Apparatuses* (GM Goshgarian tr, Verso 2014) 269.

67 Louis Althusser, *Sur la reproduction* (PUF 1995) 260–64.

68 Louis Althusser, 'Trois notes sur la théorie des discours' in *Écrits sur la psychanalyse. Freud et Lacan* (STOCK/IMEC 1993) 138 [author's translation]. Parenthetically, Rancière offers a

Transposing this remark onto our previous investigations, we can notice that modern law produces a split subject in which active and passive capacity is joined through the will. In other words, the subject is constituted as already capable of willing. In a peculiar legal fiction, which resembles Schelling's doctrine of a primordial choice that pre-exists and pre-constitutes human being rendering it free,[69] *modern law assumes that the subject has already chosen its own constitution, that it wants itself as a subject*. Interestingly, the law must refer here to the will as a category which belongs to the political rather than the legal. The well-known paradox which Giorgio Agamben recognised in *Homo sacer*[70]—that in the exception the law withdraws from its application, as if in a peculiar *tsimtsum*—applies therefore to the subject's will. This will arise in correspondence with the map of withdrawals through which the law constitutes the subject. Consequently, the legal subject is 'born' as wanting already what the law predetermined it to want through its withdrawal, and thus wanting itself, produces as its own axis the concentrated will.

Here we finally reach the question of what status human rights occupy within modern law. Their main function is to constitute the modern legal subject as a twofold entity, composed of: 1) the will and 2) particular rights that channel and predetermine what can be wanted. Through listing entitlements, they circumscribe the subject's will as always corresponding to a claim. Yet they go much further than the rights of civil law, for example. Human rights elevate normativity to the formative platform of human being 'as such': they naturalise the legal subject *as* a human being.[71] This proper biopolitical operation binds the modern legal subject to its *human substratum*. To use Agamben's term, human rights found the anthropological machine[72] in which a human being is invented as an already given legal subject that wants and claims what it wants.[73] In this sense, the audacity of the concept of human rights is unparalleled: *modernity begins by the law's claim not even to describe or control, but to constitute a human being*. Normativity—and the political sphere within the subject created by its

more complex picture, in which subjectification is a permanent oscillation within the field of fight between human rights and their sombre ineffectivity. As he writes,

> There is no man of the Rights of Man, but there is no need for such a man. The strength of those rights lies in the back-and-forth movement between the first inscription of the right and the dissensual stage on which it is put to test.
>
> Rancière (n 61) 305

69 See Slavoj Žižek, *The Indivisible Remainder. On Schelling and Related Matters* (Verso 2007) 13–22; *The Parallax View* (MIT Press 2009) 118.

70 Giorgio Agamben, *Homo sacer* (Daniel Heller-Roazen tr, Stanford UP 1998) 17–18.

71 See Rancière (n 61) 300.

72 Giorgio Agamben, *The Open. Man and Animal* (Kevin Attell tr, Stanford UP 2004) 33–38.

73 See Gian-Giacomo Fusco, 'Notes on the Person and the Anthropological Machine of Law' in Thanos Zartaloudis (ed), *Law and Philosophical Theory. Critical Intersections* (Rowman 2018) 81–83.

withdrawal—becomes the operational centre of transposing a living human being into a modern subject.

Consequently, human rights as a legal device seal the self-recognition of human beings as *already constituted* legal subjects.[74] To be such a subject means: to be born as free to want and already accept itself as a subject. In this role subjects, as we remarked before, are constructed within a fold between activity and passivity. They are axes in which economic and political power are spent and re-enforced. In this sense, *human rights offer a matrix of the most primordial binding between freedom and subjection*, a pre-emptive trade-off that makes the subject ready to enter the position of being economically and politically exploited upon its fictional will. Human rights are an irrefutable blackmail: how could we not want to have them, if they *are* the embodiment of the human?[75] But when we have them, we accept the flow of economic and political power through our position of the legal subject.

It is now clear that in modernity human rights are pre-economic and pre-political in the sense that as an anthropologico-constitutional device, they offer a condition of possibility for economic and political power. They elevate the binding between the law and the will to the core of human subjectivity. In doing so, human rights replace civil law—hitherto perceived as rooted in natural law pertaining to individuals, but not defining them—with a normative concept not only defining human beings but also anchored in the power of the state.[76]

But a crucial question needs to be asked: if modern law converts pre-political freedom into political subjection, or work into labour force performed under a contract, what is the pre-legal and pre-political status that we tradeoff for human rights? As we will see, the answer is to be found, unsurprisingly, in Kant. *We give up humanity as part of the broader animal condition; in return, we gain human rights*. This is why the modern legal subject is based on the fundamental condition: the ability to understand a legal commandment and act upon it. Whoever cannot understand the law or make it determine her actions, is excluded outside of the scope of humanity.

According to the well-known argumentation, Kant opposes the domain of nature, which is subject to empirical necessity, that is, causal links and the domain of freedom. Freedom escapes the realm of physical determination thanks to reason, whose autonomy, in turn, consists in the self-imposition of

74 As Bernard Edelman noticed, 'la personne humaine est juridiquement constituée en sujet de droit, en " toujours-déjà-sujet ", indépendamment de sa volonté même'. Bernard Edelman, *Le droit saisi par la photographie* (Flammarion 2001) 22.

75 See Anat Biletzki, *Philosophy of Human Rights. A Systematic Introduction* (Routledge 2020) 4. Cf. Lukes (n 51) 344.

76 Murray Raff and Anna Taitslin, 'Private Law in the Shadow of Public Law: A Legacy of 20th Century Marxism and the Soviet Legal Model' in Thomas Bustamante and Oche Onazi (eds), *Human Rights, Language and Law* (Franz Steiner Verlag 2012) 157–88, 157.

law.[77] Consequently, whatever creature cannot formulate a legal principle, must be wholly determined by causality and its actions are nothing more than actions of nature itself.[78] Between law and nature there is an unbridgeable gap, which cannot be grasped intellectually—through means of pure reason—but *might be observed in practice, in the act of self-determination by legislative reason.*[79]

Before we investigate this theory in its application to the normative construction of the modern subject, suffice it here to notice that producing a legal subject through human beings assumes *normative possibility of self-awareness*. Animals are classified into those which possess it in advance and those who will lack it categorically. The possibility of governing oneself as a cornerstone of the human condition abstracts from its actual incarnations: a human being may be incapacitated or unconscious, but this does not deprive her of human rights (although it may preclude criminal responsibility). At the onset of modernity non-human animals are explicitly precluded from entering legal subjectivity,[80] which can be

77 According to Kant, the act of self-imposition of law accounts for its own legitimacy; its very possibility proves its freedom:

> For if as pure reason it is actually practical, then it proves its reality and that of its concepts through the deed, and all subtle reasoning against the possibility of its being practical is futile. With this pure practical power of reason, transcendental *freedom* is now also established—taken, moreover, in that absolute signification in which speculative reason needed this freedom, when using the concept of causality, in order to rescue itself from the antinomy into which it unavoidably falls when it wants to think the *unconditioned* in the series of causal linkage. Speculative reason was able to put this concept forth only problematically, as not impossible to think, without securing the concept's objective reality.
>
> Immanuel Kant, *The Critique of Practical Reason* (Werner S Pluhar tr, Hackett 2002) 4

78 ibid 4–8.

79

> [P]ure reason can be practical, i.e., that it can on its own, independently of everything empirical, determine the will; specifically, it establishes this through a fact wherein pure reason does indeed prove itself in us practically, viz., the autonomy in the principle of morality by which pure reason determines the will to the deed. At the same time the Analytic shows that this fact is inseparably linked with the consciousness of the freedom of the will—indeed, that it and this consciousness are one and the same. Through this consciousness of its freedom the will of a rational being that, as belonging to the world of sense, cognizes itself as necessarily subject to the laws of causality like other efficient causes, is yet in the practical [sphere] at the same time conscious—on another side, viz., as a being in itself—of its existence [as] determinable in an intelligible order of things.
>
> ibid 60–61

80 This process bears numerous affinities with the emergence and development of modern concept of sovereignty. The link between both has been extensively theorised by Jacques Derrida in *The Beast and the Sovereign*. As Derrida claims, even though both the sovereign and the 'beast' occupied opposite positions, they did not belong to the domain of law—the former guaranteeing the functioning of law, but not being bound by it, the latter being an outlaw. Jacques Derrida, *Séminaire. La bête et le souverain, vol I (2001–2002)* (Galilée 2008) 38.

observed by the rapid extinction of previously quite widespread animal trials.[81]

In conclusion, human rights constitute the primordially legal anthropological machine that produces human beings as legal subjects, composed of legal entitlements and will arising in the zone of withdrawal of the law, but in counterpart to rights granted by the law. Their emergence definitively excludes non-human animals from legal subjectivity, precisely in order to assert the very quality of humanness as built on a binding between activity and passivity in legal relations.

As Kant notices in his *Metaphysics of Morals*, this binding is apparently a contradiction:

> If the I *that imposes obligation* is taken in the same sense as the I *that is put under obligation*, a duty to oneself is a self-contradictory concept. For the concept of duty contains the concept of being passively constrained (I am *bound)*. But if the duty is a duty to myself, I think of myself as *binding* and so as actively constraining (I, the same subject, am imposing obligation). And the proposition that asserts a duty to myself (I *ought* to bind myself) would involve being bound to bind myself (a passive obligation that was still, in the same sense of the relation, also an active obligation), and hence a contradiction.[82]

—but only until we notice that the human subject, normative in nature, is essentially split:

> When man is conscious of a duty to himself, he views himself, as subject of duty, under two attributes: first as a *sensible being,* that is, as man (a member of one of the animal species), and second as an *intelligible being* (not merely as a being that has reason, since reason in its theoretical capacity could well be an attribute of a living corporeal being). The senses cannot attain this latter aspect of man; it can be recognized only in morally practical relations, where the incomprehensible property of *freedom* is revealed by the influence of reason on the inner lawgiving will. Now,

81 On this topic see Przemysław Tacik, 'Repetition in Law and Exclusion of Non-Human Animals from Norm-Application' in Maria Gołębiewska (ed), *Cultural Normativity: between Philosophical Apriority and Social Practices* (Peter Lang 2017) 137–51. Animal trials have been discussed in the following classical works: Karl von Amira, *Thierstrafen und Thierprocesse* (Innsbruck 1891); Carlo d'Addosio's *Bestie delinquenti* (Napoli 1892); Edward P Evans, *The Criminal Prosecution and Capital Punishment of Animals* (William Heinemann 1906). See also Jen Girgen, 'The Historical and Contemporary Prosecution and Punishment of Animals' (2003) 9 *Animal L R* 97; Günter Teubner, 'Rights of Non-Humans? Electronic Agents and Animals as New Actors in Politics and Law' (2006) 33(4) *J L and Soc* 497.

82 Kant (n 58) 214.

> man as a *natural being* that has reason (*homo phaenomenon)* can be determined by his reason, as a *cause,* to actions in the sensible world, and so far the concept of obligation does not come into consideration. But the same man thought in terms of his *personality,* that is, as a being endowed with *inner freedom (homo noumenon),* is regarded as a being that can be put under obligation and, indeed, under obligation to himself (to the humanity in his own person). So man (taken in these two different senses) can acknowledge a duty to himself without falling into contradiction (because the concept of man is not thought in one and the same sense).[83]

Consequently, human beings enter modernity as split into two parts: rational and animal. This would not differ much from pre-modern theorisations under the auspices of the Aristotelian ζῷον λόγον ἔχων, if it had not been for the fact that the rational part is understood as structurally based on normativity. In other words, beyond normativity in modernity, there is no proper humanness, just animality. To make the situation even more complex, *modern human beings, constituted as legal subjects, are split between their normative, ruling part and animal incarnation subjected to legal commands.* The legal subject is a binding between activity and passivity precisely because it tames, manages, trains and commands its animal part. In this sense, modern human beings are *their own* animals vis-à-vis the law. Human rights contain thus *in nuce* the structure of paradoxical binding incorporated in two crucial redoublings: 1) the people as sovereign and the subordinate to the statal power, and 2) work as a buyable exchange value and source of added value that contributes to the capital.

Kant adds that '[t]he subject that is bound, as well as the subject that binds is always *man only*'.[84] Consequently, modern law can produce a legal subject only from human beings, whose animality is to be tamed by normativity to achieve 'proper' humanness. Animality is thus put before the law: either rejected altogether or allowed to pass in order to produce a substratum for human beings, under the control of normativity. It is in this latter position that it gains the role of bare life in Agambenian parlance.

The last path we need to traverse concerns the pivotal question: why is normativity supposed to create humanness and how does it do it?

Point zero of the legal form: freedom-through-law

In his perspicacious study, *Droit saisi par la photographie* Bernard Edelman noticed that the law invents as the basis for its relations the illusion of free will, through which rights and obligations are created, imposed and

83 ibid 215.
84 ibid.

accepted.[85] The legal subject is naturally linked to private property; legal ideology is based on the postulate that 'l'homme est naturellement un sujet de droit, *i.e.* un propriétaire en puissance, puisqu'il est de son essence de s'approprier la nature'.[86] But apart from all material property that the subject may possess, there is even a more powerful incarnation of this ability to appropriate. In modern law, the human being *is the owner of herself*.[87] The legal subject is its own capital, of which she disposes 'freely', thus being both a subject and object.[88] Edelman notices—in the spirit of Marx's analyses of commodity fetishism—that '[l]a chose est devenue la personne, et la structure du sujet, celle de la chose'.[89]

In other words, the legal form should be properly understood as a binding between subjectivity and objectivity within the same being, a self-taming of animality—rendered bare life through its forceful reconstitution within the area deserted by the law—by the normative core and will as its supplement. Human rights serve as a specimen of how normativity with its shadow of voluntariness can be used in order to define humanity. Modern human beings can be defined as a unit that self-manages its formerly animal substratum.

Interestingly, this link was grasped by first modern philosophers already before Marx. The key breakthrough should be identified with Kant; his distinction between *homo phenomenon* and *homo noumenon* anticipates the more political Marx's critique of the split subject.[90] It is based on a very peculiar assumption—namely that human beings are necessarily twofold because seen from the outside, as part of broadly understood nature, they are subject to laws of nature.[91] Not only through their bodies and senses humans are objects; 'in inner intuition even *the thinking subject is merely an appearance to himself*'.[92] Nonetheless, the special feature of rational beings, represented as a genus only by human beings, consists in reason—*Vernunft*, the same that we encountered earlier while investigating the status of the concept of legal form. *Vernunft* is limited by senses when it comes to cognition (as pure reason), but in its practical dimension, it allows us to direct our actions voluntarily and thus experience freedom.[93]

Yet the biggest paradox ensues later. In Kant's theory, real freedom is not free will (*Willkür*), because this one takes empirical ('pathological' in Kant's

85 Edelman (n 74) 15, 80–81, 123.
86 ibid 19.
87 ibid 40–41. See also Dominique Manaï, 'Les juristes marxistes occidentaux face au phénomène juridique' (1979) 3 *Déviance et société* 279, 286–87.
88 Edelman (n 74) 77.
89 ibid 96.
90 Marx (n 49) 233–41.
91 Kant (n 77) 8–9.
92 ibid 9.
93 ibid 23–25.

parlance[94]) impulses for reasons of actions. In other words, if I crave anything and then act to get it, I am not free, because I am still acting on the influence of the empirical world. *Freedom is to be found only in the normative form*, when the subject formulates for herself a 'maxim' of behaviour, which needs to pass the test of universality through the categorical imperative.[95] In a crucial passage of *The Critique of Practical Reason* Kant claims:

> If a rational being is to think of his maxims as practical universal laws, then he can think of them only as principles that contain the determining basis of the will not by their matter but merely by their form.
>
> The matter of a practical principle is the object of the will. This object either is the determining basis of the will, or it is not. If it [were to] be the will's determining basis, then the rule of the will would be subject to an empirical condition (viz., to the determining presentation's relation to the feeling of pleasure and displeasure), and consequently would not be a practical law. Now if from a law all the matter, i.e., every object of the will, is separated (as a determining basis), nothing remains of the law but the mere *form* of a universal legislation. Therefore, a rational being either cannot think of *his* subjectively practical principles, that is, maxims, at the same time as universal laws at all, or he must assume that the principles' mere form by itself alone, whereby they *are fitting for universal legislation,* makes them practical laws.[96]

It is therefore precisely the legal form that gives freedom to the Kantian subject. Freedom is not to be found just in normativity—a certain legal obligation may correspond to an empirical object and thus 'taint' the will with a pathological motive. Moreover, no norm can be claimed to be valid universally on the basis of its material content. What gives freedom in Kant's understanding is the moment of *determining the will through a norm that becomes referred to the possibility of its universalisation*. The content of the norm is irrelevant to this calculus: just as in the equation 'x' divided by 'x' gives always '1' (for $x \neq 0$), what matters is the correspondence between the norm and its universalisation, not the concrete 'value' of the norm. It is not—as human rights ideologies would like to claim—primordial freedom protected by law, but freedom constituted by and present only within *legal form*.

This theory is more than just Kant's individual propensity to blend philosophy with legal concepts. Precisely at the very same historical moment, during the French Revolution, human beings are posited and defined through human rights. Both events synchronically recognise the binding between

94 ibid 29–30.
95 ibid 29–33.
96 ibid 40.

humanness, law and freedom: the very quality of being a human is from now on constituted through legal form which renders human beings both disposable for the capitalist market and active in pursuit of their own obligations. What Kant theorises in *The Critique of the Practical Reason* serves as a counterpart to the sudden rise of human rights to prominence: *to be 'free' means to situate oneself in a universal normative framework*—through the legal form—and fundamentally crush one's interests, likes and dislikes, not to mention suffering, under the yoke of the law. It is just as if one could not be 'free' locally, irrationally, a-legally. Kant's theory of practical reason is a direct record of how human beings were forcefully subjectivised at the onset of modernity, with the law playing not only the role of the medium of exploitation and subjection but the core tissue from which subjects were crafted.

The Kantian vision of freedom-through-law is a take from a different perspective on the same phenomenon which Marx analysed as a concrete abstraction. As we noticed earlier, capitalism works in only insofar as it turns real incomparable singularity into particularity, a local investment of the general concept. What Kant grasps even better than Marx is how concrete abstraction is, in fact, legal form, insofar as it partakes in the creation of the modern subject as a condition for exchange.[97] Human rights, so often denounced by Marxism just as bourgeois hypocrisy (and sometimes defended on Marxist grounds)[98] are in this sense deeply entrenched in how modernity produces subjects. Marx himself had an ambivalent position vis-à-vis rights.[99] He did not reject them in total, especially insofar as political rights (such as freedom of speech) were concerned; he criticised rather the link between rights and the creation of an abstract, individualist and egoist subject.[100] Yet the question that Marxism should answer is whether the modern entanglement between rights, creation of subjectivity and capitalist exploitation can be broken without finding a new formula for humanity.

The bipolar creation of modern human beings as composed of the normative fold and bare life means that the abolition of the capitalist mechanism without undermining the modern framework produces *just* bare life.[101] Perhaps then attempts at overcoming capitalism founder on the inability at overcome modernity and the anthropological machine that it involves. The

97 See Lon L Fuller, 'Pashukanis and Vyshinsky: A Study in the Development of Marxian Legal Theory' (1949) 47 *Mich LR* 1157, 1162.

98 Brad R Roth, 'Retrieving Marx for the Human Rights Project' (2004) 17 *LJIL* 31, 37–54, 62–66.

99 Lacroix and Pranchère (n 49) 51–64.

100 Amy Bartholomew, 'Should a Marxist Believe in Marx on Rights?' (1990) 26 *Socialist Register* 244, 246–52; Boyd (n 33) 580–82.

101 This claim corresponds to Agamben's argument on the camp as a truth of modernity. See Giorgio Agamben, *Remnants of Auschwitz: The Witness and the Archive* (Daniel Heller-Roazen tr, Zone Books 2012).

survival of the law or its utility for non-capitalism is a secondary matter as long as this machine will be defused.[102] If normativity—including human rights—is subtracted from the construct of the modern human being, but this machine is not abolished, it begins to produce bare life. The defective machine which in Kafka's *Penal Colony*[103] writes the final judgment on the body of its previous operator resembles, ominously, the anthropological machine deprived of its normative component. Modern human subjects deprived of normativity do not return to any pre-modern entity: it rather resembles flesh let loose, a pure object of power, exploitation, or torture, awaiting passively another forceful act of taking in possession.

Conclusions

What would then mean to get rid of legal form? Even more than getting rid of capitalism, just as if this were an easy task. To abolish legal form would also mean to emancipate bare life not only from the yoke of normativity but from itself. In other words, we experience life as a substratum of the normative core through which we are constituted into subjects. In itself, this life is no longer animal, but neither it is human. As a generator of resources, economic and political, it is thrown by legal form into the status of *a link in the chain of exchange*.[104]

Legal form corresponds thus to the position of sovereignty, as a matrix of (self)-domination over life, through which its role as the object and subject of obligations and rights is made possible. Therefore, legal form is a counterpart not necessarily of commodity form, as Pashukanis suggested,[105] but rather of money as the universal lubricating oil to the wheels of exchange. Just as money, it organises the proper framework of capitalist concrete abstraction: it is the law that allows for recalculating the general into the particular and back.[106] Money allows for comparing and exchanging *accumulated time of life*: it condenses the time spent on production and is necessary in order to sustain life through expenditure on means of survival. Where money forms the temporal tissue of life, the legal form assures its *structural organisability* into economic and political relations.

102 Hence projects for the law regulating proper socialism—see Alan Hunt, 'A Socialist Interest in Law' (1992) 192 *NLR* 105, 112–14; Brian Leiter, 'Marx, Law, Ideology, Legal Positivism' (2015) 111 *Va LR* 1179, 1182.

103 Franz Kafka, 'In the Penal Colony' in *The Complete Stories* (Schocken Books 1971) 140–67.

104 See de Laurentiis (n 25) 31–33; Kinsey (n 5) 213, 223–25.

105 Pashukanis (n 6) 38–42, 85–86, 168–69. See also Casalino (n 50) 2285–87. On the critique of Pashukanis' focus on commodity form and civil law see: Mike Macnair, 'Law and State as Holes in Marxist Theory' (2006) 34 *Crit* 211, 228–29.

106 See also Arthur (n 10) 37–38.

As soon as legal form appears in modernity, it throws us into a dual device of the subject being composed from normativity and bare life. Normativity is the tissue of power—economic *and* political—that flows from its accumulated resources, through subjects, and then back to accumulation. For this reason, legal form is a cunning machine of blackmail: either we choose subjectification through law, and thus receive a mandate to self-govern our bodily machines of production, or we renounce them, thereby being reduced to abject bodiness over which power is exercised through pure violence. Subject-related presuppositions of modern law—such as the individual capacity of understanding, the requirement of making the law public so that everyone can learn it—create a subjectivity as a link in the chain of exchange that upholds the capitalist machinery.[107] Beyond the construct of the self-governing subject modernity offers the abyss of ruthless direct exploitation and domination.

As Byung-Chul Han argues, today the rift between freedom and subjection is diminishing: as free entrepreneurs of the self we become our own masters, in the service of the capital.[108] This model is of course territorially located. Those who are less lucky to be created entrepreneurial subjects are dominated directly, through coercion and violence. These two poles of the continuum connote the options offered by capitalist modernity: the true communist thought should be able to find a different way.

If so, then it should be the main task of the Marxist tradition—the tradition that operates with the concept of legal form—to think outside the scope of subjectification via normativity. To do it without falling back into absolutisation of bare life *as bare resource* seems a daunting challenge. It seems parallel to—if not identical with—the actual realisation of the 'withering away of the law' as the irremovable core of Marxism.[109] What needs to be done is ripping apart the law from subjectification: finding a law without a subject and life beyond the subject that does not need to defend itself through human rights.

107 Balbus (n 8) 219.

108

> Today, everyone is an *auto-exploiting labourer in his or her own enterprise*. People are now master and slave in one. Even class struggle has transformed into an *inner struggle against oneself*. . . .[T]he illusion prevails that every person—as a project free to fashion him or herself at will—is capable of *unlimited self-production*.
>
> Byung-Chul Han, *Psychopolitics. Neoliberalism and New Technologies of Power* (E Butler tr, Verso 2017) 5–6

109 Christine Sypnowich, 'The "Withering Away" of Law' (1987) 33(4) *Stud Sov Thought* 305, 327–28; Head (n 6) 19; Robert Sharlet, 'Pashukanis and the Withering Away of Law in the USSR' in Sheila Fitzpatrick (ed), *Cultural Revolution in Russia, 1928–1931* (Indiana UP 1978) 169–88.

Chapter 2

The politics of abstraction

Property, subjectivity, legal form

Rosie Woodhouse

Introduction

As arguably the most significant contribution to a Marxist theory of the legal form, Evgeny Pashukanis places the processes of abstraction that produce private property—and the juridical notion of subjectivity that it legislates—at the heart of his general theory. Drawing on the theoretical tools that Karl Marx developed in *Capital*, for Pashukanis the modern legal form and its subject hinge on the abstractions that underpin commodification in the capitalist mode of production. In this rubric, the legal form appears with the emergence of capitalism at the point where pre-existing ways of organising, using, and conceptualising land are overwritten by private property, abstracting from these relations to render land a commodity that can be 'freely disposed of in the market'.[1] The 'free disposal' of landed property at the market implies a legal subject who can acquire, possess, and exchange commodities as they please. As Marx writes in *Capital*, '[c]ommodities cannot themselves go to market and perform exchanges in their own right', and so require a juridical relation of individual possessors who recognise one another as the private owners of commodities.[2] Without which, the whole process would descend into the continual appropriation of the property of others rather than their *exchange*, predicated on the freedom and equality of individuals guaranteed by the modern legal form.

Likewise, given that under capitalism workers are 'free' to alienate their labour-power in return for a wage, the wage relation necessitates a self-possessive conception of personhood where labour itself becomes a commodity, determined by the logic of modern private property and enclosed by the legal subject as distinct from the serf or slave, who must forcibly submit their labour to production processes. This chapter will question Pashukanis's

1 Evgeny B Pashukanis, *The General Theory of Law and Marxism* (first published 1924, Barbara Einhorn tr, Transaction Publishers 2002) 110.

2 Karl Marx, *Capital: A Critique of Political Economy*, vol 1 (first published 1857, Ben Fowkes tr, Penguin Books 1976) 125.

DOI: 10.4324/9781032724713-3

treatment of relations of ownership and separating out of historical relations of slavery which, as many have scrutinised, risks collapsing capitalist property relations into individual private property as property's *only* legal form.[3] Yet a more sensitive and politically useful Marxist theory of the legal form as such should, as Pashukanis does, begin with the dynamics of ownership and abstraction that tie the legal form so intimately with the socialisation and reproduction of capital.

This chapter will provide a rereading of Marx's early writings on Hegel, law, and the state that similarly focus on property relations to adumbrate a specific, politically grounded critique of abstraction that can reconceptualise the legal form beyond the groundwork already laid by Pashukanis. A Marxism that focuses on the explanatory potential of commodity-based abstractions can risk positing all relations otherwise to those that are directly value-productive, such as race and gender and the non-economic forms of sociality that materialise them, as either subsumed by capital or irrelevant for critique.[4] Relatedly, to follow Pashukanis in the suggestion that the legal form can be made synonymous with private law insofar as it expresses the commodity form, and so public law becomes at best an ideological extension of private capitalist exchange, would leave how the legal form and capitalist society works as a heterogenous whole intact. This is crucial because, as some have argued, the expansion and reassertion of the modern legal form under neoliberal accumulation regimes has had the effect of sedimenting private relations of exchange as an unquestionable fact of social organisation.[5] The legal form in this determination has provided a vehicle for a social and political reality which increasingly disavows meaningful recognition of each other and ourselves: as in the privatisation and depoliticisation of the social sphere.[6] Yet this insight also implies that what is at stake in theorising the form the law takes on critical Marxian terms requires not shoring up or re-totalising those relations that appear obscenely predominant.

In this vein, this chapter will put forward a critique of abstraction that gauges antagonism within its own determining processes. Expounding the

3 Paul Hirst, *On Law and Ideology* (Macmillan 1979) ch 5.

4 For a discussion on differing critical theories of (real) abstraction and how these move beyond the critique of political economy to the critique of the reproduction of capitalist society at large, see Chris O'Kane, 'The Critique of Real Abstraction: From the Critical Theory of Society to the Critique of Political Economy and Back Again' in Antonio Oliva, Ángel Oliva, and Iván Novara (eds), *Marx and Contemporary Critical Theory* (Springer International Publishing 2020).

5 See Honor Brabazon (ed), *Neoliberal Legality: Understanding the Role of Law in the Neoliberal Project* (Routledge 2017).

6 See for example, Robert Knox, 'Law, Neoliberalism, and the Constitution of Political Subjectivity: The Case of Organised Labour' or Honor Brabazon, 'Dissent in a Juridified Political Sphere' in Brabazon (n 5).

social relations of property will not draw a final equivalence between private law and the legal form but open out its contradictory content onto its modern historical origins. From here, where the public or political sphere is corrupted by private property and economic interests, so too is civil law deeply braided with political contentiousness despite at first glance its depoliticising effects.

After exploring the legal form's separations and inversions to get to its own internal countertendencies rather than coherence by depoliticised private economic relations, this chapter will then bring this proposal to bear on some political exigencies of the present. Specifically, concerning the historical emergence and continuing problematics of juridical self-possessed subjectivity as the legal form's claim and conceit. Drawing on contemporary readings of Marx's formulation of abstract labour and the historical mediation of questions of subjective freedom by legacies of enslavement, the fantasy of self-possession will be considered as undermining its own conditions of possibility. Dispossessing the 'proper' subject of ownership on historical terms will be argued to not only yield a critique of juridical abstractions that reproduce the subjective and objective dimensions of capitalist society, but necessary to attend to the colonial dynamics of property inscribed in the legal form, pointing toward a politics that stresses the un-foreclosed social terrain of these contradictions.

Property and the legal form: Hegel to Marx

The prevalent Marxist focus on civil law is unsurprising given that Marx tasked himself with critiquing the historical character of modern bourgeois civil society and civil law concepts. Criticising the 'mystifying' character of his predecessor GWF Hegel's logical method, Marx argued that Hegel's 'uncritical positivism' resolves the conditions of bourgeois civil society through the state as the ideal unification of legalism, moral action, and freedom.[7] For Marx, a materialist critique that would turn Hegel's idealist philosophy back on its feet would demonstrate instead how law is founded upon social reality, as to posit that society is founded upon law would be to perpetuate legal fiction. Leading him to write in the Preface to *A Contribution to the Critique of Political Economy*: 'legal relations as well as forms of state are to be grasped neither from themselves nor from the so-called general development of the human mind, but rather have their roots in the material conditions of life'.[8] The historiography of Marx's writings is significant here. Whilst initially studying law in Bonn and then Berlin, the German legal system's strict separation of public law and private law (where public law is referred to as *Staatsrecht*, or state law) was internalised by Marx as the 'falsity' of using

7 Karl Marx, *Early Writings* (Rodney Livingstone and Gregor Benton trs, Penguin 1992) 385.
8 ibid 425.

civil rules to justify social institutions which in actuality undermined ideas of the common good.[9] Marx's profound disillusionment with the principles of conventional jurisprudence spurred his later move to critically expounding the actual effects of possession and property on the material basis for life's reproduction; in other words, the anatomy of the capitalist mode of production.

This is not to say that Marx disregarded the intellectual questions thrown up by his engagement with jurisprudence in favour of 'unmasking' economic relations, of which law is a simple expression. Rather, the criticism of his juridico-political philosophical heritage would, he believed, turn his work 'not toward itself, but toward problems which can be solved only by one means—practice'.[10] Crucially, as Lucio Colletti contends in his 1975 Introduction to Marx's *Early Writings*, Marx derived his understanding of the alienating effects of abstraction not from the critique of bourgeois economics but from Hegel's philosophical writings on law and the state. It was not only that this had chronological priority but that the stakes of Marx's conceptual struggles underlying his later work found prescience through an engagement with the structure of Hegel's logic, which Marx viewed as reflecting the very real conditions of a 'self-destructive' modern society.[11] The significance of reattending to this lineage goes beyond philosophical historiography, or debates over the correct way to 'read' Marx via Hegel. It is to recognise that the critical study of law has always been closely associated with Marx's most influential—and occasionally most radical—arguments. Early dissatisfaction with the developmental disjunct of jurisprudential ideals from social and political reality, Donald R. Kelley tells us, yielded 'the first Marxian prefiguring of historical materialism', where the back-and-forth temporality of contemporaneous legal and political struggles indicated for Marx the complex heterogeneity of what structures reality and experience.[12]

In his introduction, Coletti sets out the stakes of Marx's relation to and divergence from Hegel around the question of alienation's nature. For Hegel, as modern bourgeois society was structured by private property, he saw the potential reappearance of the social atomism associated with the 'cold' experience of Roman society. In particular, the Roman formulation of legal personhood which he historio-logically traces as persisting in the abstract subjective rights granted by the French Revolution.[13] Unlike in the

9 Donald R Kelley, 'The Metaphysics of Law: An Essay on the Very Young Marx' (1978) 83 The American Historical Review 350, 354.
10 ibid 251.
11 Lucio Colletti, 'Introduction' in Marx (n 7) 10.
12 Kelley (n 9) 355.
13 See GWF Hegel, *The Philosophy of History* (J Sibree tr, Dover Publications 1956).

ideal Greek *polis*, Roman society for Hegel fatally drove apart particular interests, needs, and desires from the legalistic public arena of the state, whose 'harsh and unethical' legal system foreclosed the possibility of genuine social integration and the attainment of harmonious ethical life.[14] The separation of abstract personality (which endows formal equality as *persona*) from the concrete content of actually existing individuals encourages both social fragmentation and a certain political nihilism. That is, abstract Roman legal *persona* hollows out individuals' public or communal existence due to the way it renders each interior life opaque to the other.[15] Rather than allowing people to exist in harmony with the state, juridical personality impoverishes social experience and so subordinates human beings to a despotic state, which binds its atomised citizens to their individual stations through legal constraints and hard coercive dichotomies between rulers and the ruled.[16]

Of this movement, Hegel writes: 'the [Roman] development consists in the purification of inwardness to abstract personality, which gives itself reality in the existence of private property; the mutually repellent social units can then be held together only by despotic power'.[17] The role of private property here is twofold: Hegel recognises the alienating effects of property ownership in creating 'mutually repellent social units'; yet private property was likewise centred as the basis for the subject's 'inward Freedom' in Rome. Hegel hence sought to retain the Roman right to private property as the right of individuals to exclude others from a certain thing (*res*), which was in both instances 'sacred', yet such 'inward Freedom' needed to be emancipated 'from the sphere of the Limited and the External'.[18] 'External' as the aforementioned abstract subjectivity fundamentally mismatched internal freedom with objective freedom; 'Limited' as not all subjects were free in Rome.[19] The Roman legal form for Hegel hence presupposed 'Freedom of Spirit' within itself as the unity of the owning subject, whose self-proprietorship indicates 'wealth

14 GWF Hegel, *Elements of the Philosophy of Right* (HB Nisbet tr, CUP 1991) §180R.
15 Hegel (n 13) 306.
16 ibid.
17 ibid 300.
18 ibid 307.
19 Whilst Hegel criticised the Roman legal categorisation of slaves, women, and children as *res* for the purposes of the slave trade, reproducing a patriarchal social order, and inheritance transmittance respectively, Hegel's philosophy was apologist for these realities. For instance, his highly abstract treatment of slavery rendered the actual practice of slavery a legitimate and 'necessary' evolutionary step in the historical and ethical development of freedom. See Brenna Bhandar, 'Disassembling Legal Form' in Costas Douzinas, Matthew Stone, and Illan rua Wall (eds), *New Critical Legal Thinking: Law and the Political* (Birkbeck Law Press 2012).

of spirit', with an external, universal Spirit of a social context in which the individual can feel 'at home'.[20]

Hegel writes:

> [w]hile [the Romans] have thus bestowed on us a valuable gift, in point of *form*, we can use and enjoy it without becoming victims to that sterile Understanding—without regarding it as the *ne plus ultra* of Wisdom and Reason. They were its victims, living beneath its sway; but they thereby secured for others Freedom of Spirit.[21]

The possibility of 'using and enjoying' the legal form requires mediating the particular and universal toward the unity of subjective freedom (possessed rights) with objective freedom (social context); a mediation which occurs through rediscovering Abstract Right via private property as an '*existential* justification of right as such'.[22] In Hegel, property is co-constitutive with the subject as property in the thing represents the materialisation of the subject's activity or will. As the thing 'has no such end in itself and derives its destiny and soul from his will', man has an 'absolute right of appropriation . . . over all "things"'.[23] Overcoming the schisms of property then hinged on returning the thing-in-itself to the postulate of the subject's individual activity. In other words, if there is no thing-in-itself but only the self-conscious realisation of the owner's will, no human being can be categorised as *res* and all can express their will through creating property in something. From here, the individual can perceive himself and hence others as free persons, calling forth ethical institutions to mediate a sociality based on mutual recognition. Freedom in Hegel's ordering is thus understood as the unification of the particular and universal so that the free will of the subject is a perceivable individualisation of the general will, of which the state is the highest and most concrete (as in, mediated) actuality.[24] More specifically, property acquisition by positively self-actualised subjects becomes expressions of the Idea, eliding the separation of the public and private through the form of the state which conjoins

20 'Wealth of spirit' indicates that Hegel endows much praise upon the subjective capacities of freedom that property entails, as it correlates the owning of objects with self-proprietorship through which human beings come into reason and self-knowledge. He writes: 'the rationale of property is to be found not in the satisfaction of needs but in the supersession of the pure subjectivity of personality. In his property a person exists for the first time as reason'. Hegel (n 14) § 41A. See also § 187R.

21 Hegel (n 13) 307.

22 Daniel Loick, '"Expression of Contempt": Hegel's Critique of Legal Freedom' (2015) 26 *Law and Critique* 189, 195. Emphasis added.

23 Hegel (n 14) § 44.

24 ibid §260A.

subjective freedom with objective freedom. As Jacob Blumenfeld explains, in Hegel property becomes an end in itself, as

> [t]o see property only as a means to an end is to reduce it to an economic standpoint of particular needs and wants; to see property as an end is to treat it normatively from the standpoint of universal freedom and right.[25]

'Private' property relations, which for Hegel disclose the potentiality of subjective desires to self-destroy through 'a spectacle of extravagance and want as well as of the physical and ethical degeneration common to them both', thus would not come into conflict with public matters or ethical life.[26] Rather, they are figured as an expression of the latter from which they derive rational and existential legitimacy.

To return to Coletti, Marx regards Hegel as a philosopher of the modern state precisely *because* his abjuration of French bourgeois society via Roman antiquity yields a 'vision of the contradictory and self-destructive character of modern society [that] is so lively'.[27] Simultaneously, Hegel's philosophical aspiration for the state then becomes the means for Marx to critique the existing conditions of modern society and law in *On the Jewish Question*. Hegel argued that the surviving infrastructures of the Prussian feudal order could integrate private property's associated freedoms into a more ethical whole analogous to the antique *polis*.[28] These feudal institutions represented an elementary way to 'effect a basic reconciliation of private interests among themselves' because they structurally conjoined economic distinctions with political ones.[29] For instance, serfs and lords were economic and political positions simultaneously held within estates, unlike modern representative forms of state which splinter economic life from political existence. For Marx, however, rather than providing a historical explication of Prussia's institutions they become in Hegel metaphysical instantiations of the Idea; Hegel's 'uncritical idealism', he writes, acknowledges reality only in abstract thought.[30]

25 Jacob Blumenfeld, 'Property and Freedom in Kant, Hegel, and Marx' in Victoria Fareld and Hannes Kuch (eds), *From Marx to Hegel and Back: Capitalism, Critique, and Utopia* (Bloomsbury Collections 2020) 80.

26 Hegel (n 14) §185.

27 ibid 30.

28 Daniel Loick highlights how in projecting back and forth between Ancient Rome and bourgeois France Hegel aims to criticise the modern form of the latter, which then 'leaves the task of rejuvenating Greece, i.e. the creation of true ethical life, to the Prussian state'. Loick (n 22) 193.

29 Coletti (n 11) 31.

30 Marx (n 7) 385.

Yet does Hegel's philosophy invert reality to find a solution to the destructive egoism of bourgeois individualism, or disclose something specific about the actual conditions of modern society itself? Coletti suggests that Marx's axiomatic relationship to Hegel's philosophical logic—which Marx saw as standing on its head—was pursued in his early writings to the point where Marx began to identify that Hegel's inverted thinking did not originate from *within* his philosophy as such.[31] Hegel's thinking rather expressed the inverted nature of modern reality itself. Marx's charge of Hegel's upside-down-ism lies within the question of abstraction, which he similarly traces to the modern rupture between the political state and the particularities of civil society. In other words, a juridico-political form of abstraction—formulated on the 'public' side of the state—is rooted in historically specific social relations. Hegel depicted the state in an abstract way not because that was the reality he sought to impress upon it but because the modern form of the political state was, in reality, abstract. As Marx writes, '[t]he abstraction of the *political state* is a modern product', and so 'Hegel should not be blamed for describing the essence of the modern state as it is, but for identifying what is with the *essence of the State*'.[32] The criticism Marx levels at Hegel then is that he substantiates this inversion, so that the modern political state becomes a totalising, self-sufficient universal that exists in its own right—that is, it is real because the empirical or finite simply expresses it.

Early Marx: property and abstraction

With this in mind, I want to return to Marx's earlier political writings on law which can tell us something specific about a Marxian critique of abstraction, and its importance for the theory and operation of the legal form and the critique of the capitalist mode of production alike. The character of modern abstractions was initially formulated not as an *effect* of capitalist exchange relations to be read back onto the legal form, but as a political problem arising out of the inverted structure of the modern society. Within this, the legal form's content becomes antagonistic rather than subsumptive, insofar as the legal form includes and separates itself from the presuppositions of the old society which persist as countertendencies in its seemingly unitary form. For example, the problem of private property is that, in an inversion of the Roman principles on which it is based, it is mistaken with political power insofar as it is separated from general public wealth: 'the political constitution at its highest point is the constitution of private property'.[33] In an 1842

31 Coletti (n 11) 33.
32 Marx (n 7) 90, 100.
33 ibid 165.

article in the German newspaper *Rheinische Zeitung* on the 'Debates on the Law on Thefts of Wood', Marx—albeit in an ultimately liberal, idealistic way—argued against the criminalisation of peasants gathering fallen wood, a customary right based on need that existed under feudalism. In Marx's view, as the wood had already fallen from the trees there had been no violation of property, and to classify the gathering of wood as theft would twist the law to the *'interests of the forest owners'* subsequently collecting the fines incurred through criminalisation.[34] Marx writes:

> the [legislative mind] forgot, however, that even from the standpoint of civil law a twofold private right was present here: a private right of the owner and a private right of the non-owner; and this apart from the fact that no legislation abolishes the privileges of property under constitutional law, but merely divests them of their strange character and gives them a civil character.[35]

The *theft* of fallen wood then amounted to a 'customary right of the aristocracy' which, insofar as customary rights persisted under civil law, should be the recourse of 'this lowest, propertyless and elemental mass' because the aristocratic privileges of property persisted.[36] Marx argues that 'customary rights of the aristocracy conflict by their *content* with the form of universal law' because they contradictorily raise what already exists *de facto* to the universal level of right.[37] Seemingly rejecting the German jurisprudential justification of property rights based on the fact of possession, the problem of possession here prefigures Marx's later stance to property. By not conflating fact with right in a kind of 'chaotic conception of the whole', to use his language in the *Grundrisse*, Marx turned attention to the abstract determinations which society ascribes to possession.[38] Which is to say, how social relations are organised through differential relations of ownership and how, by keeping open the relational gap between *de jure* and *de facto* as the juridical structure of right and the social context which through which that right is actualised, these processes of abstraction can reveal the political problems that constitute the heart of private property.

The 'Law on the Theft of Wood' has been taken as an early adumbration of a determining economic material base which is expressed by a

34 Karl Marx, 'Debates on the Law on Thefts of Wood' in *Marx and Engels: Collected Works*, vol 1 (Lawrence and Wishart 1975) 228.

35 ibid 223.

36 ibid 230.

37 ibid.

38 Karl Marx, *Grundrisse: Foundations of the Critique of Political Economy* (first published 1953, Martin Nicolaus tr, Penguin Books 1973) 33.

juridico-political institutional superstructure.[39] However, a more open reading suggests that Marx identifies the kernel of something that troubles the '[legal] form of the universal interest'.[40] What appears as a self-sufficient universal is really an uneasy unity of discrete, contradictory, and inconsistent elements; in Marx, there would never be a true or complete universalism. In Marx's principle understanding of modern Germany and Europe, civil law's development proceeded 'on the basis of the Roman Codex'—including the common law tradition in England to the extent that Roman legal principles were integrated to develop movable property with arising capitalism.[41] Within the Roman model, a person can seize a thing (*res*) and exclude anyone else from physically acting upon that thing, which develops in German civil law into the custom *Besitz*.[42] Yet *Besitz* does not automatically constitute a legal relation of property (*Eigentum*), nor will it necessarily become so.[43] This inheritance from Roman law means that the process of transmuting the former into the latter requires, then, the acquisition of socially derived relations which meaningfully constitute 'property' as such. So, the independence of factual possession or occupation from property's legal form remained despite being newly endowed with a 'civil character'. The basis of Marx's argument that the customary right to gather wood should amount to legal property is founded on an assessment that the institutional development of legal protection in the dominant interest of the forest owners is the product of historically specific juridic determinations rather than natural phenomena.[44] The critical discrepancy or 'radical non-relation between the [legal] institution and the world of the natural', as Yan Thomas phrases it, is not what is significant for our purposes here, however.[45] Rather, that this allows Marx to make

39 For a contemporary debate on the utility and distractions of the base/superstructure metaphor, see Nate Holdren and Rob Hunter, 'No Bases, No Superstructures: Against Legal Economism' (*Legal Form,* 15 January 2020) <https://legalform.blog/2020/01/15/no-bases-no-superstructures-against-legal-economism-nate-holdren-and-rob-hunter/#:~:text=The%20base%2Fsuperstructure%20metaphor%20allows,and%20exchange%20as%20co%2Doriginary> accessed 11 January 2024.

40 Marx (n 7) 127.

41 Kelley (n 9) 365.

42 Jean Axelrad Cahan, 'The Concept of Property in Marx's Theory of History: A Defense of the Autonomy of the Socioeconomic Base' (1994) 58 *Science & Society* 392, 398–99.

43 ibid. Jean Cahan show that Marx learnt the difference between *Besitz* and *Eigentum* from his teacher in Berlin, Carl von Savigny, whose comprehensive historical study of Roman law conceived of the Roman principle of *Besitz* as a separate constituent of Roman culture and legal thought, rather than necessarily a legal relation. Cahan argues, '[i]t cannot be overemphasized that Savigny's concern and project was to demonstrate that "Besitz ist kein Rechtsverhältnis": *Besitz* is not a legal relation, nor was it an historical forerunner of the legal relation *Eigentum*'.

44 Marx (n 34) 218.

45 Yan Thomas, '*Fictio legis*: L'empire de la fiction romaine et ses limites médiévales' (1995) 21 *Droits* 17.

a *political* argument (based on use and need) for the rights of non-owners in the matrix of civil law and private rights. So for Marx, even *within* civil law, there are competing notions of property at play which can be used to emphasise capitalism's necessary social condition of *propertylessness*, both real and personal.

If then the Marxian argument reveals how law and institutions have their roots in 'the material conditions of life', this should not be mistaken as a general claim on the reducibility of all law to dominant economic relations or subsumed by a supernal logic of the *capitalist* as the universal interest. The question of a critical understanding of the movement of abstraction arises here as one that does not inadvertently assume and re-inscribe its totalising effects. This gains importance for a critical Marxian theory of the legal form which, as many of the contributions to this book demonstrate, can be characterised as asserting its own universality over the different particularities texturing material reality. The formal equality of legal form sublates actual inequalities to create a self-sufficient, universal representation of reality which appears independent of and dominant over social and personal experience. Unequal relations between people are likewise overwritten in their recognition by the law as formally equal legal subjects. In turn, the uneven distribution of wealth, violence, and democratic power is legitimated, as the formal equality of rights is transmuted into the only authentic mode of relating to one another, nullifying the class antagonism on which it depends. The eradication of particularities that are tantamount to the 'violence' of abstraction is perhaps a received truism of Marxist social critique.[46] However, for the purpose of a *critical* theorisation of the legal form, it is important to avoid reproducing the appearance of totalising abstractions in theory. To paraphrase Stuart Hall in his seminal text on the 1857 Introduction to the *Grundrisse*, Marx's critique is

> *of a certain distinctive kind*—one which *not only* lays bare the 'real relations' behind their 'phenomenal forms', but does so in a way which *also* reveals as a contradictory and antagonistic necessary content what, on the surface of the system, appears only as a 'phenomenal form', functional to its self-expansion.[47]

Positing capitalism as self-reproducing through an essential core—as, for example, private property dovetailing into commodification—can risk only emphasising *homogeneity* in and through differing facets of personal and social life, including those opposing elements to dominant relations. Whilst

46 See Peter Osborne, 'The Reproach of Abstraction' (2004) 127 *Radical Philosophy* 21.

47 Stuart Hall, 'Marx's Notes on Method: A "Reading" of the "1857 Introduction"' (2003) 17 Cultural Studies 113, 141.

not discounting the problem of depoliticisation and ascendency of private relations within our contemporary predicaments, such a mode of critique can inadvertently characterise sites of power as self-enclosed and autonomously self-replicating rather than politically contestable, as in the Hall quote above. In a kind of reworked anti-formalist critical theory of the legal form, the aim of this chapter is to expose the legal form to where its own fundamental presuppositions break down and bring in the textures that puncture its apparent unitary legitimacy. Reconceptualising the legal form on these terms is significant if we are to avoid, as Marx critically viewed jurisprudence and Hegel, hypostasizing the abstractions which need unpacking to gauge the legal form's effectiveness in reproducing capitalism's relations of production.

Marx's dialectic: "On the Jewish Question"

What are the stakes for re-apprehending the legal form from this perspective of such a mode of abstraction, configured by the separation and inversions of modern society that Marx learnt from Hegel's insight into the reality of the abstract political state? In *On the Jewish Question*, Marx does not simply reverse the determining positions of the state and civil society in a crude or vulgar dialecticism, despite his critique of the political emancipation afforded by individualistic bourgeois rights. Following Hegel, Marx traces the dissolution of the feudal order and the struggle for civic emancipation that pushed civil law into its modern phase.[48] Above all, the juridical development of private property cleaved the political community—the modern representative state—from the life of civil society—where autonomous individuals could privately pursue their material and spiritual interests independently of the community—which had been previously conjoined within the feudal order. Emphasising the splitting of 'Man' and 'Citizen' in the constitutionalised articles of the Declaration of the Rights of Man and of the Citizen, Marx argued that the 'so-called rights of man' are dovetailed by the Declaration *as* the rights of members of civil society.[49] The state, on the other hand, figures its Citizens as members of a political community that possess equal rights. In so doing, it abstracts from the unequal interrelations of Man to achieve a social unity that stands above and against civil society's warring private wills. Civil society thus 'perfects' its materialism insofar as '"Man" now inevitably appears at the *natural* man' contra to the idealised political Citizen.[50]

Because of the rupture between the political and economic, or public and private, human beings come to be related by law 'just as men in estates and

48 Marx (n 7) 232.
49 ibid 233.
50 ibid 234.

guilds were related by privilege'.[51] The dissolution of the feudal community's privileged status' for particular religions and stipulations of rank and property for political participation consecrated individualistic rights 'in one and the same act'.[52] The inversion of modern society thus places the completion of politics as such *within* the realm of civil society. In turn, civil society's political dimensions are jettisoned (i.e., depoliticised) wherever bourgeois Man abnegates his identification as a communal Citizen to pursue the individual significance of his particular activities. 'The political revolution', Marx writes, 'regards civil society, the world of needs, labour, private interests, civil law, as the basis of its existence, as a precondition not requiring further substantiation and therefore its natural basis'.[53] The emancipation granted by bourgeois rights amounted in Marx's terms to an emancipation from religion and feudal restrictions yet into alienating bourgeois property relations which are refigured as 'natural', as in, external to the abstract social bond. The abstract state in a real sense represents Hegel's treatment of property as an end rather than a means, as the general political interest's horizon merges with estranged bourgeois property relations.

On the one hand, politics, in the modern sense, is restricted to the means of participation in civil society and the 'right of self-interest', where liberation is shored up as 'freedom from others'. Yet on the other, Marx identifies the *positive* moment of Jewish political emancipation and formal equality within modern law. Akin to Marx's 'selective' use of forms of property which retains those which work in favour of the legally propertyless, Marx praises the civic freedoms that are abandoned at the point where they come into conflict with the right to participate in political life.[54] Expounding this further, the reduction of political institutions to the interests of egoistic Man is balanced in *On the Jewish Question* by Marx's critique of civil society as an 'egoistic *spirit*', whose seeming naturalism is a mystification given that civil society becomes political emancipation's end-point.[55] The abstract political form of the state is revealed to be rooted in material life, but this process works the other way: the 'materialism' of civil society is perfected insofar

51 ibid 233.
52 ibid.
53 ibid 234.
54 As Marx emphatically writes,

> [w]e impractical people [communists] take up on behalf of the politically and socially propertyless masses what the learned . . . so-called historians [of jurisprudence] have invented as the true philosophers' stone . . . we vindicate on behalf of the poor the right of customary use [*Gewohnheitsrecht*]. . . . We go even further and only maintain that by their nature such rights can belong *only* to the elemental, propertyless masses.
>
> Marx (n 34) 230

55 Marx (n 7) 234. Emphasis added.

as it becomes an *ideal* representation of an emancipated community. 'Egoistic spirit' in this sense exceeds the depoliticised, atomised individualism of civil society as it performs a socially binding, or integrative function in the modern sense of the political. Yet in their very separation, which is both an abstraction from themselves and each other, the state and civil society presuppose one another and continually antagonise their respective independence. Due to bourgeois civil society, the political state cannot achieve its claim of common social unity; yet the promised freedoms of individuals are continually negated by a coercive state attempting to assert such unity over a discordant political community.[56] Egoistic man's self-interestedness is not recapitulated by Marx as human individuality's natural reality but revealed to be a radically contingent order of spirit undercut by the abstract legalism which renders it legible.

What critical purchase does this mode of abstraction yield, that could exceed a delimited modern meaning of politics toward a politics of antagonism? The separations and struggles between the state and civil society, politics and economics, the public Citizen and private Man, are thus *internally related and posed within the legal form*, insofar as Marx recognises that modern law and juridical subjectivity arise from these social conditions. Abstraction here, which is figured as an internal separation, can shift a normative depiction of the legal form from a self-sufficient register to one of self-destructiveness. The layering of liberation and constriction, freedom and unfreedom, can be proposed as an irresolvable condition in the sense that such oppositions are internally rather than externally related. 'Property' is never fixed nor collapsed by Marx into the pure unfreedom of bourgeois market society as property relations can be remade via the social relations that give property its meaning. Through his sensitivity to the Roman treatment of property which forms the basis of his critique of private property's basic nature in Hegel, Marx recognises that human nature is a characteristic of abstract social relations mediated by objects that, insofar as the objects we make change and effect our mutual relationships in turn, take different forms. The claim of the modern legal form is that the juridical structure of right can only be actualised in a social context wherein liberation is constituted as the freedom to pursue one's individual self-interest in the marketplace. Yet the abstract *political* conditions upon which the modern legal form is founded reappear to disturb its apparently interlocking juridical and 'natural' structure, mediating the actualisation of this claim as closer to an impossibility. Within this, the 'depoliticised' realm of civil law can be extrapolated as undermining its own preconditions, yielding an antagonism that delinks the individualistic structure of (property) right from the (capitalist) social order.

56 For more on how this kind of reading of *On The Jewish Question* has been developed, see Gillian Rose, *The Broken Middle: Out of Our Ancient Society* (Blackwell 1992).

In other words, the 'real relations' of private economic exchange underpinning the legal form cannot be wholly universalised to explain either its logic or structure. As Coletti and many others have pointed out, this would have significant implications for Marx's criticism of the method of bourgeois economists who substitute, for example, the specificity of wage-labour for the timeless metabolic category of labour-in-general, as well as his own mature approach to the capitalist mode of production.[57] To again paraphrase Hall, any account of the unity which the mode of production—or, we can add, the legal form—appears to us as must also emphasise the elemental differences of the process so that such unity is not inadvertently re-totalised in critique, transforming those elements into realisations of a determining category which is the mistake of Hegel and bourgeois political economy.[58] If we follow however Marx's discernment of Hegel's relationship to modern social reality beyond perhaps what Marx himself acknowledged, Hegel intimates that the entwinement of subjective freedom, property, and an objectively free social context is not realised by capitalism but delimited by modern society's split and inverted structure. By keeping open as Marx does the interplay between positive moments in the juridico-political development of modern society—with the property structure of right, emancipation/freedom, and mutual recognition—and grounded social conditions which *cannot* fulfil these bases, the social structure can be critiqued in a way that *also* makes a political argument for non-capitalist forms through which to actualise them. This is not to say that the heterogenous modes of abstraction constitutive of the legal form presented here can be relied upon to self-negate in practice but to determine where the legal form's internal countertendencies cannot be synthesised or disintegrated. That is, to exclude the historically specific separations and inversions of modern society posed within the legal form by positing them in their subsumption by a supernal universal would amount to a theory of the legal form that is theoretically self-enclosed and politically unimportant.

Property and labour: juridical subjectivity dispossessed?

Just as modern society is conditioned by the separation between the state and civil society, so too is human experience internally split, i.e., abstracted from itself via juridical subjectivity, between the political Citizen and egoistic private Man. This introduces a profound insecurity into the seemingly unitary legal subject of the legal form predicated by modern property on full self-possession. Property in oneself, or the relationship between property and labour, has pretexted conceptual explorations of freedom within classical

57 Coletti (n 11) 28.
58 Hall (n 47) 127.

political economy, modern jurisprudence and, more partially, Marxism. To return to Pashukanis, property in oneself is presumed in a way that enables him to fuse the legal subject with Marx's economic subjectivity presented in *Capital*. Paul Hirst has argued that in defining the essence of the legal form as private law, Pashukanis limits his understanding of right (which cannot exist without the 'subject') through analogy with possession. This slippage operates on the terrain of alienable, moveable property where, as a possessor of alienable rights, the legal subject can be seen 'as a development of the subject of commodity exchange, who is the possessor of alienable things capable of entering into an exchange of equivalents with another possessor'.[59] By flattening property with possession Pashukanis' legal subject folds the contradictory positionalities of the worker (who owns only labour-power) into the capitalist (who owns the means of production) and so elides their social differentiation. More than this, the figure of the capitalist is imitated without remainder: 'the subject of property right, the subject actually possessing the means of production, and the subject who engages in economic calculation and exchange all coincide in the person of the "capitalist"'.[60] We have already established that in order to understand property as a structuring social practice it cannot be treated independently of non-economic processes of abstraction. So within this, what of the relations of ownership that produce real conditions and experiences of propertylessness? To shore up the legal subject as the self-possessed individual and others as dispossessed of legal forms of recognition and control over the will, not only substantiates modern private property but elides the actual practices of property as it relates to mutable contexts of power for the poor, gendered, and racialised.

To give this point valence is to consider Patricia Williams' evaluation of the complexities in averring property in oneself in the wake of slavery. In *The Alchemy of Race and Rights*, Williams explores the paradoxes that arise in variably claiming bodily, reproductive, and intellectual autonomy, writing that:

> [r]eclaiming that from which one has been disinherited is a good thing. Self-possession in the full sense of that expression is the companion to self-knowledge. Yet claiming for myself a heritage the weft of whose genesis is my own disinheritance is a profoundly troubling paradox.[61]

In acknowledging the conflictual desire to affirm her self-proprietorship, self-determination and autonomy through an inherited juridical and social structure that rendered enslaved people an object of property, Williams

59 Hirst (n 33) 117.
60 ibid 99.
61 Patricia J Williams, *The Alchemy of Race and Rights* (Harvard UP 1992) 217.

confronts the possible aggregation of domination or dispossession with property rights extended to those historically 'un-righted'.[62] Williams here does not simply honour self-possession by contrasting it with the violence experienced through objectification, which may reinscribe (capitalist) self-possession as a legitimate sanctum that must be maintained as such. By holding apart property right from possession, the legitimate reclaiming of self-possession is in this instance experienced as truncated and paradoxical; objectification persists. In this way, Williams writes through conjunction and conflict not to resolve this paradox but 'dispossess the self who seeks dispossession';[63] as in, dispossessing the dominant conception of personhood as a bounded and racially exclusive subject of ownership that risks being preserved through the phenomenal shell of property right.[64]

However, by not rejecting the possible relation between freedom and property in oneself or dismissing this conjunction only as an idealist fantasy (which is likewise present in Marx), Williams works to undermine how that relation *currently* appears in juridical subjectivity and so introduces variation into its meaning and material effects. In this register notions of dispossession and self-proprietorship are social conditions—as in, mediated by histories of enslavement and emancipation—rather than ontologically prior or primary.[65] Because they are underpinned by property's historically contingent forms, both are abstractions that are lived rather than impermeable (gendered, racialised) conditions of human experience. Crucially, colonialism's survival and its current permutations amount to the *impossibility* of actualising freedom of the self within social relations that are currently given. As the artist-activist collective International Imagination of Anti-National Anti-Imperialist Feelings (IIAAF) reminds us, '[n]o one is pure in a colonized world. We all live by our contradictions'.[66] Our present is they add an 'entangled dystopia' in which, for instance, you can struggle to pay rent and

62 ibid 227.

63 Katharine T Bartlett, 'The Alchemy of Race and Rights' (1992) 14 Sydney Law Review 393, 395.

64 The construction of this subject over and against others has, materially and historically speaking, been instrumentalised in colonial and settler colonial situations to enact dispossession and oppression. For example, Brenna Bhandar explores its use as a tool of domination by settlers in Palestine, Canada, and Australia in Brenna Bhandar, *Colonial Lives of Property: Law, Land, and Racial Regimes of Ownership* (Duke UP 2018). Robert Nichols has developed Williams' work on 'Black antiwill' as the logical antithesis of the self-possessed person that produces deadly social conditions for Black and Indigenous people. See Robert Nichols, *Theft is Property!: Dispossession and Critical Theory* (Duke UP 2020) ch 4.

65 For more discussion on the antinomies of 'dispossession' as an ontological category, see Nichols (n 64).

66 International Imagination of Anti-National Anti-Imperialist Feelings, 'The Strike MoMA Reader' (*Verso*, 24 December 2021) <https://www.versobooks.com/en-gb/blogs/news/5235-the-strike-moma-reader> accessed 8 January 2024.

simultaneously displace another, teach at a university yet want to tear the educational system down, or be oppressed in one site of experience and contribute to other people's oppression in another.[67] The task then is to heighten and open out these contradictions and how their overlaying is lived and legitimated to undermine the principles which rigidify their seeming polarisation.

In the previous sections of this chapter, a Marxian critique of abstraction derived from his early writings on law and the state that could be useful for reconceptualising the legal form was proposed as an internal separation. The historical lineages of colonialism within the legal form and how it shapes contradictions of the present can sharpen this proposal. Before developing this point, however, it is important to first qualify this through a rereading of the supposed apex of Marx's articulation of abstraction that Pashukanis draws from *Capital*. A certain version of Marxism which relies on the commodity form can lapse into understanding abstraction as the obliteration of all 'external' particularities through the abstraction and commodification of labour. For Marx, abstract labour is the substance of capitalist value given concrete existence in money, or the value-form.[68] The predominance of capitalist value-making processes within social life oversees that all specific or experiential differences of identity are subsumed into abstracted units of labour, being labour's alienated social form which can be interchanged with capital.[69] Yet stopping at abstraction as homogenisation and labour as the substance of value—and both as the fundamental unit of social interpellation—can misinterpret the real social contradiction between labour and capital and the experience of alienation therein. If we remain in the register of affirming labour as the primary constitutive agent of value-making processes then the possibility of freedom from capitalism is recast positively and immanently to the capitalist system, where all that seemingly remains is wresting control of production processes from capital and re-placing them into the hands of workers.[70] Labour however is not the 'real' subject of the process: because

67 ibid.

68 Marx (n 2) 165.

69 Ellen Meiskins Wood's demonstrates this mode of Marxist critique in arguing that

> [u]nlike previous modes of production, capitalist exploitation is not inextricably linked with extra-economic, juridical or political identities, inequalities or differences. In fact, there is a positive tendency in capitalism to undermine such differences, and even to dilute identities like gender or race, as capital strives to absorb people into the labour market and to reduce them to interchangeable units of labour abstracted from any specific identity.
>
> Ellen Meiskins Wood, 'Capitalism and Human Emancipation' (1988) 167 NLR 3, 5–6

70 Examples of how this mode of critique has practically played out can be seen in struggles over intellectual property, where the critique of intellectual labour's 'commodification' can be accompanied by the moralistic complaint that the value generated through intellectual property should be the purview of labour to which it rightfully belongs. See Bob Jessop,

the fetish-forms of capital are perverted forms of social practice which take place behind our backs, abstract labour is posited as the substance of capitalist value which constitutes labour as a historically specific social form *negatively*. Marx writes: 'objectified labour is, in this process, at the same time posited as the worker's *non-objectivity*, as the objectivity of a subjectivity antithetical to the worker, as *property* of a will alien to him'.[71] As labour has become alienated from the worker and given concrete existence in money as the value-form, it comes to dominate them in turn. Because abstract labour is how all labour is structured, socialised, and concretely existing under capitalism, labour's productivity as the simultaneous not-property of the worker reproduces the capital relation. Capital then emerges as an 'automatic subject' that is continually proved in action, assuming the appearance of self-sufficiency by positing the (inverted) material world of human social practice and claiming the subject's self-possession as its truth content.[72]

Taking this further, it is hence impossible for Marx to conceive of an 'internal, dumb generality' for human subjectivity or collapse labour into a timeless metaboliser of human nature.[73] His focus stays with the historically *negative* relationship between labour and ownership that configures the conditions of human existence, of capital as the property that escapes the worker and becomes an alien will 'antithetical' to her, which must be constantly renewed and sustained. Labour's alienated social form, which under capitalism amounts to a striving to *dispossess* the subject of the wilful alienation of her labour, is already presupposed, which undermines the possibility of the worker's very existence. That is, to sustain the negative capital-labour relation, labour is constantly de-valorised in accordance with capital accumulation. Where Marx writes that 'a surplus population of workers is a necessary product of accumulation or of the development of wealth on a capitalist basis', he is arguing the capitalist mode of production depends on the creation of a disposable and surplus 'industrial reserve army' not necessarily engaged in work, but 'always ready for exploitation by capital in the interests of capital's own changing valorisation requirements'.[74] This condition both *undermines* capital's own basis of wage-labour, as its 'true' human social practice, and is consistent with it. The value created by abstract labour both suppresses socially necessary labour-time and expels labour from production processes, concomitantly increasing the immiseration of the remaining

'Intellectual Property Rights' *Bob Jessop* (9 February 2014) <https://bobjessop.wordpress.com/tag/intellectual-property-right/> accessed 7 March 2022. See also Peter Drahos, *A Philosophy of Intellectual Property* (ANU Press 1996) ch 5.

71 Marx (n 38) 512.

72 Marx (n 2) ch 4.

73 Marx (n 7) 423.

74 Marx (n 2) ch 25.

workforce both within nation-states and in globally interconnected yet asymmetric ways.

Reading this into more contemporary crises of capitalist economies, the Endnotes Collective explain that, because

> wage-labour is inseparable from the accumulation of capital, from the accretion of labour-saving innovations, which, over time, reduce the demand for labour . . . the reduction of socially-necessary labour-time—which makes goods so abundant—can only express itself in a scarcity of jobs, in a multiplication of forms of precarious employment.[75]

The argument here is that even at the very abstract level of the logic of capitalist value, the process bifurcates at different levels of the mode of production in ways that can destabilise its logical and actual reproduction. Abstract labour hence does not simply represent the homogenisation (commodification) of labour but inscribes the real contradictions between the de-valorisation and immiseration of the social body, the unviability of self-reproduction articulated with the *expansion* of abstract wealth. Short-circuiting the gap between labour and ownership, or conceiving labour as an independently self-determining power, stops at egoistic Man's seemingly natural state, which is the mystification that ultimately serves the interests of capital. In so doing, the person with alienable free will is re-conflated with commodified labour, which can only *politically* argue for a legitimate relationship between labour, ownership, control, and value as it appears within capitalist society. In other words, it resolves the split between political Citizen and egoistic Man back into the appearance of self-possessed juridical subjectivity rather than expounding the necessary social condition of propertylessness that this split implies.

Here it is crucial to ask: what makes the disconnect between labour and ownership within the matrix of juridical subjectivity possible? The racialised saturation of who can alienate their labour and who cannot have stratified those not cognisable to a theory of the legal form that operates on a stable, self-possessive conception of juridical subjectivity.[76] This chapter is seeking to go beyond this, however. In historical terms, the utility of slavery to capitalist development and social order has resided not with its externality to modernity but its liminality.[77] Similarly, relations of dispossession of

75 Aaron Benanav and Endnotes, 'The Moving Contradiction: The Systematic Dialectic of Capital as a Dialectic of Class Struggle' (2010) 2 Endnotes 20, 32–33.

76 These are the terms that Bhandar criticises Pashukanis's presumption of the legal subject on, which cannot attend to processes of subjectivation via juridical forms of property in situations of colonialism and settler colonialism where the legal form has been instrumentalised. Bhandar (n 64) 100.

77 See Nichols (n 64) ch 4.

the will are similarly not simply excised from the legal form but occupy an antagonistic, liminal position to it. Commodified labour-power, is one mode of dispossession legitimately enclosed by the legal form that mediates human and interpersonal experience. This point, however, can be rendered problematic if it is taken to simply destabilise the conceptual status of the legal subject. As Robbie Shilliam has contended, there exists a 'comforting tendency' within Marxism to posit the 'essence' of capitalism as the struggle between unfreedom (relations of dispossession, barred from the means of subsistence and production) and freedom (relations of property and formal equality).[78] This tendency becomes problematic when it logically ascribes the possibility of a real and radical freedom as 'immanent within commercial society that ultimately makes up for its acts of dispossession and exploitation'.[79] From the perspective of Shilliam's incisive work on the determining relation of Atlantic slavery for arising English capitalism, the commodification of labour becomes, in fact, a *qualification* of the radical unfreedom of enslaved Africans as 'labouring things'.[80] Due to constrictions of space, Shilliam's work cannot be fully explicated here, but I want to clarify the juridical relationship between property, labour, and freedom (what Shilliam calls the 'hermeneutic of English common law') through his proposal that the regulatory 'thingification' of slaves as objects of property represents the 'ultimate' form of commodified labour.[81] That is, what is objectified is not part of the person but personhood itself. Thingification and commodification are on the other hand not entirely severable historical, legal, and economic categories but related processes insofar as slavery's regulation determined and conditions the development of capitalism's wagers of social order and liberty. During the 18th century integration of commercial society, the thingified status of slaves could not be resolved into the English legal universe because their entirely alienable political and personal status was 'impossible' on free English soil.[82] Simultaneously, as 'objects' seen to be severed from relations of social dependency, enslaved Africans represented the possible shattering of pre-existing hierarchies of dependence, patriarchy, and servitude that had to be maintained by a sociality based on civic freedom *and* private relations of domination, making the full outlawing of thingification in England

78 Robbie Shilliam, 'Forget English Freedom, Remember Atlantic Slavery: Common Law, Commercial Law and the Significance of Slavery for Classical Political Economy' (2012) 17 New Political Econ 591, 605.

79 ibid.

80 ibid 598.

81 ibid 604. More specifically, common law's hermeneutic makes the moral and political argument for individual freedom predicated on the intertwinement of property and labour which, as we know, works to reproduce the capital relation above all.

82 ibid 597–98. Shilliam demonstrates the hard labour that English and Scottish Enlightenment jurisprudence, moral philosophy, and classical political economy performed to excise slavery from English civil liberty.

unworkable. For Shilliam, then, thingification was qualified as commodified labour which gained legitimacy through being fused with the relative political freedoms of property (i.e. personhood pertaining to free will), meaning that the hermeneutic of capitalism's social order cannot be posed as either *radically* free or unfree unlike the Atlantic economy out of which it grew. In other words, labour cannot be salvaged as a fully emancipatory force as it exists as capital's necessary and negative pole.

Yet this chapter has adumbrated a Marxian critique of the legal form which emphasises the irresolvability of this struggle insofar as it is an internal antagonistic relation. From the perspective of how processes of thingification were absorbed (as commodification) and suppressed (with the excision of radical freedom that thingification implies) from the co-development of capitalist social relations, the legal form, and the legal subject, we can give better valence to this proposal's political orientation. As human experience is conditioned via juridical subjectivity by the internal split between freedom and unfreedom, property and propertylessness, then these contradictions as social conditions can be confronted rather than resolved back into the legal form's self-perpetuating stability. By first decoupling the sanctimony of the self-possessed, free individual *from* the capitalist social order (which is the legal form's claim and conceit), then an argument can be made for a non-capitalist world which might realise self-possession and freedom in genuine form. If, as Shilliam suggests, radical freedom escapes the hermeneutics of Marxism, Marxism can critically theorise where this dynamic cannot be resolved within capitalist social relations: hermeneutics stops and practice begins.

Conclusion

Closing their Strike MoMA Reader, which was disseminated as a form of direct action and utilised as an organising instrument, the IIAF outline their political solidarity's strategic choices:

> [w]e can see contradictions as impediments and be consumed by frustration, ambivalence, and despair, or we can acknowledge and heighten them. . . . large or small: each act we take further undermines the principles that sustain this system.[83]

This chapter has attempted to refurbish a critical conceptualisation of the legal form through its constitutive abstractions that are founded upon internally heterogenous social practices, so as to not take its principal claims for granted. The legal fiction that Marx reveals in *On the Jewish Question* is

83 International Imagination of Anti-National Anti-Imperialist Feelings (n 66).

law's generation of the state as the modern locus of politics, which naturalises private law and civil society as depoliticised and to which political possibility is made reduceable. However, this chapter has countered depoliticisation as a primary methodological critique insofar as the internal separations of the legal form's historical basis manifest as the proliferating contradictions in how social life is experienced. It then follows that the task of Marxian critique is to render the legal form normatively foundationless insofar as the decoupling of the legal form—and the capitalist social order it preserves—from the logic of self-possessed individualism is already presupposed. By focusing on such separations and their inverted social enunciations, the aim is to reinvigorate the politics of Marxian legal theory in a way that does not inadvertently become politically hegemonic. Or, in the words of Alberto Toscano, to theorise 'in ways that do not reproduce the bourgeois imperative of super-unification, and thus the historical complicity of philosophers with the state' in its reproductive role within capitalist society as a whole.[84] Further, by turning historical conditions of dispossession back onto the self-enclosed subject of property, then any commitment to a notion of possession that justifies freedom in its thoroughly capitalist sense may be undercut and exceeded by a political argument for a new sociality that can actualise it.

84 Alberto Toscano, 'The Detour of Abstraction' (2015) 43 Diacritics 68, 85.

Chapter 3

A journey to the center of the legal form—Kelsen's *Ought* as the missing piece to the master signifier of the legal form

Peter Čuroš

Introduction

Legal form plays a crucial part in both branches of the dichotomy of the material and ideal. This dichotomy is one of many, for instance, nature v. culture, immanent v. transcendent, factual v. normative, which have in common an existence of more than one level of reality. They all claim that there is a world where humans are passive and dependent on elements other than their own. And then, there is another world where human consciousness is a creator, a sculptor molding the world. While the natural world limits humans due to its physical laws, transcendence, on the other hand, allows creation without any limits. Accepting transcendence opens the door to organizing life by asking the question: How ought one live? The normative orders such as morality, ethics, religion, or law have changed their social influence ranking in the past. However, a law with a characteristic universal form proved to be the most efficient in social organization. Unlike other normative orders, it provided a new reality in which subjects are, at least partially, free from causality, and outcomes of this freedom are backed and sanctioned by material authority. In materialist theories, the legal form spreads through all social relations and is normalized by the authority of law.[1] In this chapter, I plan to introduce a different way of seeing the legal form by looking for its essence, which is at the core of the authority of law. The following chapter will use Hans Kelsen's formalist theory to explain the legal form and location. The aim is to answer the question: Where does the core of the legal form reside? From there, another question arises: How does legal form work?

In this venture, the chapter will look for the essence of the legal form, starting by excluding the legal form from any other normative form using Kelsen's views on naturalistic fallacy. When the legal form is distilled, we move toward the various concepts of legal form in Kelsen's oeuvre, in which

1 Evgeny Pashukanis, *The General Theory of Law and Marxism* (2nd edn, Transaction Publishers 2003) 137.

DOI: 10.4324/9781032724713-4

we will look for the essence that is a necessary part of the legal form. By picking his final concept of OUGHT—the empowerment (*Ermächtigung*), we explain how this essence of the legal form represents a surplus in Master discourse. Finally, we will conclude that the core of the universal legal form is the exception and that the universality and formality of law ultimately depend on the functionality of the categorical imperative for the legal officer to apply the sanction.

The form by the materialists and the formalists

In the works of materialist authors, there is a line of expectations for the development of the legal form. For Marx and Engels, it was a matter of historical determinism that the state and law would disappear, along with the end of the class struggle and bourgeois economic system. For Marx, a gradual process of the state withering away would make the phenomenon later coined as a legal form redundant, as there would be no call for apparently universal means to enforce the ruling class's will.[2] Marx was slowly abandoning the statist vision of Communism, for which Mikhail Bakunin criticized him in the First International. For Marx, the state as it existed could not work for working-class purposes. The state was, by nature, bourgeois. Therefore, the legal form would diminish with 'state (which) must be transcended and replaced by free associations of producers who autonomously without any mediator decide all questions of public importance.'[3] The revolution starts with the crash of capitalist institutions and ends with the emergence of the community without conflicts. The liberated humanity will not need the form of gains of the bourgeois society, such as the state, rights, representative democracy, or negative freedom, as all these are instruments to solve the conflicts stemming from antagonistic interests.

The revolution required overcoming the desire to own an object. For Marx, it is possible to enjoy the thing without owning it. Communism was supposed to be the positive supersession of private property as human self-estrangement. Hence, the true appropriation of the human essence

2 Karl Marx, 'Critique of the Gotha Programme' <https://www.marxists.org/archive/marx/works/1875/gotha/ch01.htm> accessed 31 January 2024. Later in 1872, Marx corrected his predictions when he, in the Preface to *Communist Manifesto*, included the experience from the Paris Commune:

> One thing especially was proved by the Commune, that the working class cannot simply lay hold of the ready-made state machinery, and wield it for its own purposes.
>
> Karl Marx, 'Communist Manifesto (Preface)' (German edn, 1872) <https://www.marxists.org/archive/marx/works/1848/communist-ma, nifesto/preface.htm> accessed 21 January 2024

3 Mihailo Marković, 'Stalinism and Marxism' in Robert C Tucker (ed), *Stalinism: Essays in Historical Interpretation* (W.W. Norton 1977) 313.

through and for a human being.[4] For Marx, the economy in such a form would change drastically. The outcomes were the abolition of alienated labor and the fetishism of commodities, the transcendence of the narrow division of labor, the reduction of working hours, and the liberation of free activity.

Marx saw the alienating effects of the legal system. He argued that the abstractness and universality that legal form claimed led to the alienation of individuals from their labor and the products of their labor. As a part of the superstructure, the legal system has been divorced from the base of material conditions, perpetuating the separation of individuals from their true human essence.[5] When Marx criticized legal form, he observed the early outcomes of the codification process. He was right about the influence of a relatively new element in modern society. Soon, the legal form became an effective tool to secure the organization of large communities.

In continuity with Marx, Evgeny Pashukanis saw legal form as an outcome of the desire to own an object. For Pashukanis, the legal form was intimately tied to the capitalist mode of production. In capitalist societies, the legal system regulates and maintains capitalist relations of production, including private property, contracts, and wage labor. Legal relations, such as property rights and contractual obligations, are essential for the functioning of capitalist economies. The characteristic qualities of the legal form were proprieties that differentiated law from any other phenomenon—universalism, formalism, abstraction, and reification.[6] The legal form was essentially connected to market relations, and the form's existence depended on its existence.[7]

However, thanks to its claimed universality, the law has experienced growing influence in secularized countries since the 18th century. It would not be wrong to call the upcoming period the era of the Great Law. The law became an omnipotent phenomenon. If it explicitly mentions a relation, it creates a legal relationship. However, if it doesn't mention the relation, nonetheless, the relationship may be considered legal since it is allowed by law by not explicitly forbidding it to exist. The legal form has gradually encompassed society. No relationship is unrecognized by law, either as permitted or banned. Marxist critique accused the legal form of hiding a class interest behind a logical, coherent, and universal system. It was directed mainly at this subject-creation by awarding an identity within legal relations opposite to the subject's economic interest.

Although the materialist critique provides an extensive view of the legal form's consequences and development, it does not focus primarily on its

4 Karl Marx, 'The Economic and Philosophical Manuscripts: 3rd Manuscript' <https://www.marxists.org/archive/marx/works/1844/epm/3rd.htm#s2> accessed 21 January 2024.

5 Karl Marx and Friedrich Engels, *The Economic and Philosophic Manuscripts of 1844 and the Communist Manifesto* (Prometheus Books 2009) 69.

6 Pashukanis (n 1) 156.

7 ibid 14.

essence. Therefore, the following subchapter will shift toward formalist theory, leading us to the legal form's core.

The form by the formalists

We will follow Hans Kelsen's path in our quest for the kernel of the legal form. Kelsen's *Pure Theory of Law* builds on separating the law from the non-law based on the form, not the substance. The legal form as the focus of legal science separated it from other disciplines. Hans Kelsen opened with his dichotomy of IS and OUGHT[8] a legal rabbit hole. Because every time one might think she is already at the bottom of the problem, a new dimension of OUGHT appears. Every new connotation of OUGHT opens a question: how is it, and should it be connected to what IS?

The OUGHT realm consists of values mainly deduced from facts from the natural or social world. The response to such deduction varies, from approval that different facts should serve as a source of inference for values through a dissent on which facts should be valid to denying the possibility of inference of OUGHT from IS. The latter approach accuses the former two of committing a naturalistic fallacy. Kelsen's claim against the naturalistic fallacy goes even further. He wanted the legal OUGHT to be pure, pure of IS, and pure of any kind of OUGHT, different from the legal OUGHT.

To determine what legal OUGHT is, we will get through the question of what OUGHT is not. That question will portray the mistakes we often commit while using language. In philosophy, such an error is referred to as a naturalistic fallacy.[9] Although G.E. Moore coined the term, the IS/OUGHT gap by David Hume and later Immanuel Kant echoed long before. These conceptions also influenced Kelsen's view of naturalistic fallacy more than Moore's. David Hume recognized the gap between statements of facts and statements about values.[10] Hume claimed that moral requirements cannot come from rationality, as reason is and ought only to be the servant of the passions and never pretend to any other office than to serve and obey them. Therefore, fact

8 I shall use capital letters to detach the concept of IS and OUGHT from usual usage of verbs is and ought to differentiate the terms of IS and OUGHT from ordinary use of verbs of is and ought to. I will use the English terms of IS and OUGHT, instead of SEIN and SOLLEN.

9 The term naturalistic fallacy comes from G.E. Moore, who originally meant the impossibility of defining the Good due to its open-question nature. Moore criticized attempts to explain the concept of Good and connect it to natural properties. George Edward Moore, *Principia Ethica* (CUP 1993).

10

> In every system of morality, which I have hitherto met with, I have always remarked, that the author proceeds for some time in the ordinary way of reasoning, and establishes the being of a God, or makes observations concerning human affairs; when of a sudden I am surprised to find, that instead of the usual copulations of propositions, is, and is not, I meet with no proposition that is not connected with an ought, or an ought not.
>
> David Hume, *A Treatise of Human Nature* (Courier Corporation 2003)

statements established through reason cannot infer moral statements that arise from desire. Hume's view is visible in Kelsen's dichotomy of the proposition and its meaning.

Kant also influenced Kelsen's views, such as the distinction between natural and normative science and pure and practical reason. However, his view on naturalistic fallacy and the most crucial influence on Kelsen is covered by the distinction of categorical and hypothetical imperative seen in Kelsen's location of OUGHT to empowerment.

There are several spots where Kelsen's view on what a naturalistic fallacy is demonstrated. In his early work, he pointed out the specific relationship between legal and natural science.[11] Later, he criticizes confusion about the ethical content and legal form.[12] In *What is Justice*, he points to the 'derivation of norms from other norms that do not originate in human will.'[13] Moreover, finally, in the *General Theory of Norms*, he puts under criticism various theories that do not detach the IS from the OUGHT, starting with Plato, followed by Aristotle, Thomas Aquinas, Moritz Schlick, Hermann Cohen, and others. Here, Kelsen mentions that the error these authors make is that they either reduce IS to OUGHT (Plato, Aristotle, and Aquinas),[14] aim to get rid of OUGHT (Bentham), refuse the existence of OUGHT (Schlick), or reduce OUGHT to IS (Mauthner) or attempted reduction of OUGHT to IS (Cohen).

The following lines explain how Kelsen concludes on the naturalistic fallacy through his attempts for independence and autonomy of legal science, the specific nature of legal normativity, and the concept of OUGHT, which developed over the oeuvre of Kelsen.

Independence of the legal science and autonomy of the legal form

By emancipation jurisprudence and getting rid of the 'metaphysics' of what the law ought to be, Kelsen has in mind detaching jurisprudence from psychology, biology, ethics, and theology, which got part of it.[15] In other words, Kelsen would like to see jurisprudence built according to 'proper' science while being completely independent of any other science.

He knew that detaching legal science from the physical world might be problematic. As the behavior of law subjects always takes place in the physical world, Kelsen decided to detach the realm of being and norms. We can apply this process to any situation we foresee in law. A person is driving 55km/h within city limits—this is what is happening in the immanent world.

11 Hans Kelsen, *Hauptprobleme Der Staatsrechtslehre Entwickelt Aus Der Lehre Vom Rechtssatze* (JCB Mohr (P Siebeck) 1923) 72.

12 Hans Kelsen, *Allgemeine Staatslehre* (J Springer 1925) 131.

13 Hans Kelsen, *Was Ist Gerechtigkeit? [Was Bedeutet Das Alles?]* (Reclam Verlag 2016) 47.

14 Hans Kelsen, *General Theory of Norms* (OUP 1991) 73.

15 Hans Kelsen, *Pure Theory of Law* (University of California Press 1967) 1.

While in the transcendent world, the person has just committed speeding. This first step created Kelsen a realm, which he called a normative realm. It is a transcendent world of the ideal, where the actions are happening in the physical–natural world and are looking for their legal-normative meanings.[16]

While the first step was methodological, his next step was substantial. Kelsen was stepping toward emancipating jurisprudence—detaching it from morality and other normative orders.[17] The act of will creates both legal and moral norms. Both need to be positive to be an object of science. The main difference between law and morality is the presence of sanctions.[18]

These two surgical cuts detached law as an object of legal science, securing the purity of legal science against a sociological point of view that uses causal sciences to appropriate the law as a part of nature and against the claim of the natural law theory that mixed legal theory with ethics.[19] He also brought back transcendence[20] in the form of refurbished normativity as an ideal level of reality detached from immanence. He showed that the connection between the norm and the sanction is arbitrary. Kelsen's normativity was a new platform for reality. Instead of the world of facts, which is limited by physical and social laws, normativity offers an opportunity to build a new

16

> For if you analyze any body of facts interpreted as 'legal' or somehow tied up with law, such as a parliamentary decision, an administrative act, a judgment, a contract, or a crime, two elements are distinguishable: one, an act or series of acts—a happening occurring at a certain time and in a certain place, perceived by our senses: an external manifestation of human conduct, two, the legal meaning of this act, that is, the meaning conferred upon the legal meaning of this act, that is, the meaning conferred upon the act by the law. For example: People assemble in a large room, make speeches, some raise their hands, others do not—this is the external happening. Its meaning is that a statute is being passed, that law is created.
>
> ibid 2

17 ibid 59.

18

> A difference between law and morals cannot be found in what the two social orders command or prohibit, but only in how they command or prohibit certain behavior. The fundamental difference between law and morals is: that law is a coercive order, that is, a normative order that attempts to bring about a certain behavior by attaching to the opposite behavior a socially organized coercive act, whereas morals is a social order without such sanctions. The sanctions of the moral order are merely the approval of the norm-conforming and the disapproval of the norm-opposing behavior, and no coercive acts are prescribed as sanctions.
>
> ibid 62

19 Bonnie Litschewski Paulson, *Introduction to the Problems of Legal Theory: A Translation of the First Edition of the Reine Rechtslehre or Pure Theory of Law* (Clarendon Press 1992) xx.

20 If one wants to cognize norm, one has to believe there is OUGHT. Jörg Kammerhofer, 'Hans Kelsen as the Epitome of Legal Modernism' (2007) SSRN 4 <https://papers.ssrn.com/sol3/papers.cfm?abstract_id=1566432>

world where designers set limits. Where the world of facts rewards long teeth or bodily power, the normative may prefer intelligence.

This distinction is close to Schopenhauer's distinction of Idea and Will, where paradoxically, the OUGHT resembles the world captured by human consciousness, as this is the world in which the meaning exists. On the other hand, the will exists outside meaning and human consciousness.[21]

Normativity resides in the symbolic world. Although law, social and political institutions, morals, economics, languages, and human behavior, all of these relations are run through rules of language,[22] Kelsen did not fancy the concepts of normativity prevalent at his time. First, normativity was an outcome of social efficacy; second, normativity was based on the authority of a divine being, where validity is dependent on transcendental authority.[23] These types of normativity make the law dependent on its legitimacy—either in compliance with social rules or other normative orders, such as morality. Kelsen was looking for a specific type of normativity, one different from the content-dependent normativity[24]—which, for Kelsen, was ideological.[25] He wanted to purify the legal science. Like a researcher in a laboratory, he was trying to get an outcome of the pure form by over and over cleaning the object until nothing other than the law appeared. This outcome must have been cleaned of anything resembling morality or factuality. Legal normativity was the unique relation essential to legal norms, which only legal science with its methods can discover. Kelsen successfully maintained a normative thesis claiming that law is explicated independently of fact and a separability thesis claiming the separation of law from morality.[26] However, where this concept of normativity resided and how it works varied in different stages of Kelsen's career.

21

> The world is my idea: this is a truth which holds good for everything that lives and knows, though only man can bring it into reflected, abstract consciousness. If he really does this, philosophical discretion has evolved in him. It then becomes clear to him, and certain, that he knows not the Sun and not an Earth, but only an eye that sees the Sun, a hand that feels the Earth, that the world which surrounds him exists only as an idea—that is, only in relation to something else, the one who conceives the idea, which is himself.
>
> Arthur Schopenhauer, *The World as Will and Representation*, vol 1 (Courier Corporation 2012)

22 Gordon P Baker and Peter Michael Stephan Hacker, 'Language, Sense and Nonsense' (1985) 175 *Revue philosophique de la France et de l'étranger* 256.

23 Tradition of the natural law theory.

24 The content-dependent normativity is visible in natural law theories (NLT): 'As Augustine says, that which is not just seems to be no law at all.' NLT is based on the dichotomy but also the dependence of human law on transcendent objective values that are knowable to human reason.

25 Visible in Hans Kelsen, *The Communist Theory of Law* (Library of World Affairs 1955).

26 Stanley L Paulson, 'Continental Normativism and Its British Counterpart: How Different Are They?' (1993) 6 *Ratio Juris* 227, 231.

Problem of ought: various oughts in Kelsen's thought

The independence and autonomy of law are the legal OUGHT's independence and autonomy. However, OUGHT is one of the most elusive concepts in Kelsen's theory.[27] It also evolved dramatically during Kelsen's academic career.[28] Kelsen used OUGHT in various relations, and it could be helpful to elucidate which relations he used it in.

First, from Hume's guillotine, OUGHT is impossible to derive from IS. The IS-OUGHT dichotomy is generally about human cognition's incapacity to derive what 'ought to be.' It is a thesis of skepticism of human cognition. Hume, Kant, Kelsen, and many others say that those who make such claims—from IS to OUGHT—commit a naturalistic fallacy.

Kelsen uses the dichotomy for its usefulness in normativism for critical appraisal of legal positivism, faith in the role of logic in legal decision-making, and for criticism of relativist theories of law, which reduce law to facts and predictions of facts. Furthermore, the dichotomy is a helpful argument against natural law theories that derive norms from man or society's alleged factual nature. Finally, the dichotomy is the foundation of the methods and concepts of the *Pure Theory of Law*.[29]

However, neither IS nor OUGHT have a definition in Kelsen,[30] so their meaning depended on the context in which they were used. Kelsen himself did not reveal much about IS and OUGHT when he first defined the norm as a meaning of the act through which behavior is commanded, permitted, or authorized, and then added that the difference between IS and OUGHT cannot be explained any further.[31]

If IS and OUGHT are different in logic and language, it should be possible to divide two linguistic expressions into IS-class and OUGHT-class. This dichotomy builds on logical dualism[32] that the meaning of the speech act describing something differs from the meaning of an act of will that prescribes something.[33]

However, this distinction does not offer a proper categorization. There is no certainty that descriptive statements are distinguishable from normative statements just by looking at them. That the grammatical form would

27 Carsten Heidemann, 'Facets of 'Ought' in Kelsen's Pure Theory of Law' (2013) 4 *Jurisprudence* 246.

28 His theory of normative cognition can be divided into four different phases, which might be called the constructivist phase, the neo-Kantian phase, the realist phase, and the analytical phase. Ibid 250.

29 Jerzy Wróblewski, 'Kelsen, the Is-Ought Dichotomy and Naturalistic Fallacy' (1981) *Rev Int Philos* 508, 509.

30 ibid 510.

31 Kelsen (n 15) 5–6.

32 ibid 6.

33 Wróblewski (n 29) 513.

tell—this is description such: 'Life is beautiful' and 'Life ought to be beautiful' as prescription. However, it is not. Descriptive statements hide in modal sentences, while normative statements use a form of descriptive verbs. Let us see the difference. Using: 'Life should be more enjoyable' in a situation of despair does not deliver the message of a norm but is more a descriptive statement about the person not enjoying life. On the other hand, saying: 'All life pursues enjoyment' while writing down a document as a statement of the political community tells us more than just a simple descriptive sentence. It is a prescriptive statement. It cannot be a decisive factor in a statement, whether the modal verb is used or not.[34]

Therefore, Kelsen's view on normativity went further, as OUGHT had a logical-semiotic, epistemic, ontological, and practical level in his conception. The epistemological level of IS and OUGHT distinguished between two ways of cognizing reality. While the IS proposition could be recognized, the OUGHT meaning must have been understood. Furthermore, at the ontological level, IS and OUGHT were two types of existence—the existence of a fact and the validity of a norm. It created the dichotomy of the world of facts, where the proposition appeared, and the world of values, where norms—as ideal, transcendent meanings existed.[35] An act of will belonged to IS, while the meaning of the act of the will belonged to the OUGHT.

Various stages of OUGHT

For this chapter, we leave out the distinctions that Kelsen makes in Pure Theory of Law, such as ought in the broad and narrow sense, prescriptive and descriptive ought, and objective and subjective ought.[36] Instead, we focus on what OUGHT is. Is OUGHT/normativity/norm a specific existence of meaning? Or is it a relationship that does not reflect necessity but possibility? Or is OUGHT rooted in a particular appearance of the norm—in its modality? Or is it based on a categorical element of the norm—empowerment?

Firstly, it is OUGHT as a separate realm of meaning. Kelsen used the concept of OUGHT as a specific reality of meaning. This meaning of OUGHT came from the ontological dualism of IS and OUGHT and the differentiation between an act of will and the meaning of this will. This use was typical of Kelsen's early career stage[37] when he posed himself against traditional

34 For instance, saying: 'the age of criminal liability is 15' is a description but is considered normative. Therefore, it is not the verb is or ought/should and the grammatical form of the sentence that makes it descriptive or normative. It is not a grammatical form but a meaning of the speech act that makes the sentence prescriptive or descriptive.

35 Kelsen (n 14) 172.

36 Kelsen (n 15) 7. See more in Ulises Schmill, 'The Dynamic Order of Norms, Empowerment and Related Concepts' (2000) 19 *L and Phil* 283.

37 First phase—mainly in his Habilitationsschrift: Hauptprobleme der Staatsrechtslehre (1911), and Allgemeine Staatslehre (1925) constructivist phase and neo-Kantian phase. See Stanley L

positivism. It was primarily a reaction to Jellinek's *Allgemeine Staatslehre* and his concept of the normative force of factual. Kelsen emphasized how it was impossible to derive law from social facts. Therefore, the naturalistic fallacy resulted from deriving the norm from the fact, criticizing Jellinek's position that a norm was standard to the subjects due to the factual situation. It said that OUGHT could not be derived from IS and vice versa, that law was solely a matter of OUGHT, and the concept of law available to Kelsen must have been derived from its use in legal practice and legal science. OUGHT had an exceptional quality. It spoke a language of a norm. Metaphorically, it was a vision that recognized the norm.

Kelsen's *Stufenbautheorie* supported the legal OUGHT that law consisted of a layered structure, where the lower norms needed authorization from higher norms to be valid. Thanks to the OUGHT principle, these norms were considered normative, and thanks to the unique quality of the Basic Norm, they were even considered to be of the unique normative quality. They were legal if the pedigree led to the legal Basic Norm. In this sense of OUGHT, the meaning of the legal proposition (material sentence in the text) did not recognize legal subjects' actions but the meaning of the actions of legal subjects.

Secondly, it was an OUGHT in the sense of imputation. Law was a matter of OUGHT concerning imputation—a relation between condition and consequence. Imputation was an analogical relation to cause and effect, which required an act of will for this connection to happen. The outcome, a legal norm, was a hypothetical judgement of legal science imputing a sanction to a specific act. The unique connection between the antecedent and consequence in law differed from the connection between cause and effect because it is not caused by necessity but constructed by the will. Moreover, to have a pure legal form, Kelsen distinguished between various kinds of normativity: when the naturalistic fallacy happens when the limits of ethical content and legal form are misunderstood.

It stemmed from a criticism of the public subjective rights when he claims that these do not fall within the realm of law. At this time, Kelsen's notion of legal OUGHT is situated in the imputation between the breach of command and a consequence in the form of a sanction. The law, therefore, cannot guarantee the obligation not to steal. It can only punish the thief if she commits such a crime. 'Legal order can sanction a theft, but it does not guarantee a right not to be robbed.'[38]

In *What is Justice*, Kelsen formulated the naturalistic fallacy as deriving norms from other norms that do not originate in human will.[39] Such a

Paulson, 'Toward a Periodization of the Pure Theory of Law' in Letizia Gianformaggio (ed), *Hans Kelsen's Legal Theory: A Diachronic Point of View* (Giappichelli 1990) 24.

38 Kelsen (n 15) 127.

39 Hans Kelsen, *What is Justice? Law, and Politics in the Mirror of Science* (University of California Press 1957) 7.

formulation is influenced by his definition of natural law where the divine being is the supreme source of value, this divine being guarantees absolute validity, and this law arose outside human will. Moreover, it is based on principles without sanction. According to Kelsen, natural law systems were not positive norms because they were not the sense of actual acts of will. They were fictional norms because they were made by scholars that presupposed acts of will.[40]

Thirdly, he used OUGHT in practical terms, such as how Kant distinguished the hypothetical and categorical imperative. A duty, OUGHT, is to follow the categorical OUGHT that stems from the presupposition of the Basic Norm. According to Kant, OUGHT could not be connected with any content of Good.[41] The only Good can be the universal form of a categorical imperative. Therefore, in Kelsen, it is the same approach—OUGHT could not be connected to any content, only to the form of law. Under Kant's influence, Kelsen's OUGHT seemed more like an a priori category.[42]

The norm should be perceived as a meaning of the proposition—perceived by the senses and recognized by reason as a legal norm. Only then should such a norm be followed, and the motivation for its following should be a duty. The OUGHT, then, must be a synthetic a priori judgement. It comes through the senses. However, the meaning is understood. Normativity is a pure *a priori* category for comprehending the empirical legal material.[43]

As the OUGHT evolved, the naturalistic fallacy also evolved. If the OUGHT were a specific reality of meaning, the fallacy would have been committed if it did not recognize its particular nature. In such a way, it could be even legal textualism—in a way, when a judge did not 'translate' the party's behavior as a meaning—as subjective ought. Still, the opposite, the judge was turning the behavior into a social fact. In the description of this fact, the judge was looking for the same qualities in the written text of the proposition.

Secondly, perceiving OUGHT as the relation of imputation—*if a happens, there ought to follow b*, the naturalistic fallacy, would be any argument that something ought to be because—it is suitable, desirable, profitable, or

40 Kammerhofer (n 20) 5.

41 Immanuel Kant, *Groundwork of the Metaphysics of Morals* (CUP 1997) 13.

42

> There can be no doubt that all our knowledge begins with experience. For how should the faculty of knowledge be called into activity if not by objects which affect our senses and which partly produce representation, and thus to convert the raw material of our sensible impressions into a knowledge of objects which we call experience. With respect to time, therefore, all knowledge begins with experience. But although all our knowledge begins with experience, it does not follow that it arises from experience.
>
> Immanuel Kant, *Critique of Pure Reason* (CUP 1998) 127

43 Hans Kelsen, 'Pure Theory of Law, The-Its Method and Fundamental Concepts' (1934) 50 *LQ Rev* 474, 475.

humane. In other words, any inference of the consequence after some condition different than it 'ought to be, for the sake of duty.'

Thirdly, perceiving OUGHT as a part of a legal norm depends on where the legal OUGHT is located. If the legal OUGHT was situated in the hypothetical norm: 'if a happens, then bought to follow,' it was already a fallacy as the legal OUGHT was not located in this hypothesis but in the empowerment that came if the obligated subject did not follow its obligation, and then the duty of the state official encountered, with empowerment—'If the subject does not fulfill the obligation, then the state official ought to apply a sanction.' This concept of OUGHT, which corresponds to empowerment, will be further referred to as Kelsenian OUGHT.

Legal form fixing the unstable meanings

At this point, we have established where the essence of a legal form resides. The Kelsenian OUGHT resides in the empowerment of the legal officer to apply the sanction. However, we still do not know how the legal form managed to capture social relations in such an overwhelming scope and whether the legal form is something we can get rid of, as Friedrich Engels anticipated.[44] For this further discussion, the approach using Žižekian and Lacanian terms will be helpful. This approach will show that what Kelsen presents as the center of law—the legal OUGHT is simultaneously a radical non-law. At the end of the chapter, it will be shown that when the judge commits the categorical imperative of the legal OUGHT, she is approaching an exception.

Lacanian theory has three registers of experience—Symbolic, Imaginary, and Real. If focusing on the individual, the unconscious subject is initially negative, defined by the lack emerging at the entrance to Symbolic order. At that moment, the Real register was suppressed by entering the realm of the big Other, of language, where words and signs cover the Real and signify everything that does not resist signification: 'The symbol first manifests itself as the killing of the thing, and this death results in the endless perpetuation of the subject's desire.'[45] This lack became structured upon the system of signifiers. The need existing in the Real was transformed into desire, which slides on the signifiers of Symbolic order. The chain of signifiers is working thanks to that lack, which the desire struggles to fill. This chain will always defer the meaning since signifiers are not attached to signified by any necessary

44 The state is not 'abolished', it withers away. Friedrich Engels, *Anti-Dühring* (Boitempo Editorial 2017).

45 Jacques Lacan, *Ecrits: The First Complete Edition in English* (W.W. Norton & Company 2006) 262.

connection. However, the subject's desire is to attain completeness; it is the desire for wholeness—totality.

It is a totality of the dissolution of the subject within the object. It is a totality of meaning, a condition of consciousness that makes the floating signifiers stable, what can happen only if they are anchored to their signifieds. In social practice, individuals are subject to the Symbolic order that stabilizes the meaning of the signifiers and does not offer any space for doubting this meaning. In the totality of meaning, a subject is determined by its position within the structure. The signifier standing for the subject is undetachable from its signified position in the structure. Moreover, this position is not up to the subject to change. However, the nature of signifiers is the opposite. They float. Their connection to signifieds is socially constructed and, therefore, not stable. Thus, the totality of meaning happened to be unachievable.

In Hegel, such totality is visible in the concept of *Sittlichkeit*, where the subject—consciousness—overcame all the previous stages, complied with its objective conditions, and became fully aware of its position within the structure.[46] In other words, everybody is where they are meant to be and doing what they are intended to do. The idea of a totality was a reaction to the Enlightenment way of thinking in modernity, which furthered the concept of an autonomous subject with an agency to act upon objects. The emancipation of the Enlightenment subject needed to weaken the stable meanings, as progress was defined by looking for new ways of thinking.

Simultaneously, alienation became a concept noticed as going hand in hand with this way of thinking—the alienation from stable identities, or in other words, stable meanings. Suppose the subject was suddenly allowed to change its position in the system and connect the signifier 'I' with new signifiers. In that case, the objective conditions that keep her in the position make her feel alienated because she is not in charge of the objective conditions. She cannot influence them to the point she wants.

Alienation can then be overcome in two ways: First, it can be made powerful enough to rule the objective conditions; second, it can become part of the objective conditions determining the subject's position. In other words, overcoming alienation should make the subject feel 'at home.'

The problem of alienation in philosophy has been handled as a gradual separation of subject and object. For Hegel, history begins in the stage of an absolute spirit defined by the totality of subject and object.[47] In the second stage, the subject and object become detached. The material world without consciousness and consciousness with limited access to the material world. That is the moment of alienation. The alienation might be overcome when the consciousness controls its subjectivity within objective conditions. Then,

46 Georg Wilhelm Friedrich Hegel, *Philosophy of Right* (Kitchener 2001) 132.
47 Georg Wilhelm Friedrich Hegel, *The Phenomenology of Spirit* (rev edn, OUP 1977) 58.

the subject and object will become united again. In the *Lectures on the Philosophy of History*, Hegel sees historical development as a continual growth of the human agency, as a march from development in itself to development for itself. A man gains self-knowledge about his liberty through history and broadens his potential.[48]

According to Lacan, the totality of subject and object is impossible to attain, as we can only replace one master signifier for another, not attach it to the signified. The desire will, therefore, never perish. It may only be redirected. Whatever we do, we remain trapped in a virtual world of signifiers.[49] We will always desire unstable signifiers, so we will never be in a stable state of totality. We are immersed in the totality of signifiers, which are not connected to the signifieds by any necessary condition. The split subject does not know anything outside signifiers, although it considers them to be the thing itself. Although the system of signifiers—the Symbolic is always totalitarian in that it covers all of the Symbolic realm, it does not allow the subject to understand outside the signifiers. That means the Symbolic constitutes and governs the subject subordinated to this Symbolic order.

A violent force of immense intensity tried to fix the meaning from evasion, but it was unsuccessful. Despite the gap between signifier and signified, which cannot be crossed, a forced solution of alienation came under 20th-century totalitarian regimes. These regimes proposed frantic attempts to fight 'alienation' from the meaning, break the resistance, and reconcile man with his 'true' sociability. Unlike the theories of Hegel and Marx, which aimed to understand the subject of alienation and what is wrong for him in this world and then shape the world in a way when everyone feels at home and not alienated. Acquiring the state of totality, the idea of the totalitarian state was based on making the subject think he is not alienated by violence. That would require making the subject think entirely like the authority wanted him to.[50]

A totalitarian state attempted to use the legal form to solve the fragility of the stable meanings by the forced connection of those stable meanings. The meaning behind signifiers had to be stable; therefore, disobedience or

48 Andrzej Flis, 'From Marx to Real Socialism' in Martin Krygier (ed), *Marxism and Communism: Posthumous Reflections on Politics, Society, and Law* (Rodopi 1994) 21.

49 Marc De Kesel, 'Act without Denial: Slavoj Žižek on Totalitarianism, Revolution and Political Act' (2004) 56 *Studies in East European Thought* 299, 302.

50 Several points characterize the regime that attempts to unitize subject and object by force: '1) a totalitarian ideology, 2) single party committed to this ideology and usually led by one man: 'the dictator', 3) fully developed secret police and three kinds of monopoly: mass communication, operational weapons, and centrally planned economy.' Carl J Friedrich, 'The Evolving Theory and Practice of Totalitarian Regimes' in Carl J Friedrich, Michael Curtis, and Benjamin R Barber (eds), *Totalitarianism in Perspective: Three Views* (Praeger Publishers 1969) 126.

doubt about the stable meanings of key signifiers was punished severely.[51] Of course, such an effort took immense resources for violence. It meant the authority would have to control the language and its use. In a narrow sense, the state could become totalitarian only if it successfully attempted to grasp the Symbolic order. This means that the state's authority can control the meaning behind all signs within the social reality. The objective conditions controlled by the state would entirely comply with the subject's consciousness. There would be no conflict in such a state since the objective conditions would fully constitute the subject's position. To do so, the state would have to acquire the whole Symbolic and diminish any other influence from outside the state itself. The subject would be wholly subordinated to the system of signifiers governed by the state, fully determining his place. Through the legal form, the state would have to be in charge of the language and how the subjects unconsciously use that language. Suppose we consider totality a political system where all social ties have been entirely replaced by the state-imposed organization and all groups and individuals act only according to the state's goals.[52] It would require the utter destruction of civil society. The state and legal form would be the only way of social life, where all activity—political, economic, and cultural is allowed only when it follows the state's goals. Simply put, every individual would be the state's property.

Ideological fantasy

For a society to function, some meanings must be stable. The big Other must provide quilting points in the language, which anchor the meaning that all the cooperating members understand. Thanks to these quilting points, signifying chains on which a language works can provide an identity for the subject, who then projects her position in the social structure. The subject fills the Imaginary register by acquiring identities corresponding to this position. This fantasy is shared among the members and serves as an ideological fantasy.

The Kelsenian OUGHT is the last piece in the ideological fantasy, representing how individuals or societies construct beliefs or narratives to maintain their ideological frameworks.[53] Fantasy helps to structure the narrative so that an individual can make sense of his experiences and desires. These fantasies can be deeply ingrained and shape one's perception of reality.

51 Therefore, the new ways of an interpretation of the Marxist authors were discouraged from happening.

52 Leszek Kołakowski, 'Marxist Roots of Stalinism' in Robert C Tucker (ed), *Stalinism: Essays in Historical Interpretation* (W.W. Norton & Company 1977) 285.

53 Slavoj Žižek, *The Sublime Object of Ideology* (Verso Books 2019) 96.

Fantasy is an imaginary image. It serves to overcome the gap rooted in the instability of the connection between a signifier and a signified.

The subject's perception of the legal form is based on ideological fantasy. The outcome of the fantasy is what it OUGHT to be, which is shared within the community. The fantasy provides imaginary support for the otherwise nonsensical order of the authority and allows an individual to rationalize the fulfillment of this order.

In other words, the rule of law as a metaphor[54] aspires as an ideological fantasy to explain that the law is not the will of an individual or a group that imposes the rules upon the community members. On the contrary, it is an elaborated cloud of rules that either predict all the possible relations in the community or make it possible to find a solution for all the issues that were not initially anticipated, with the help of those rules. The officer who applies the rule and decides upon a situation, may it be a judge, is only a well-educated expert who maintains the application of impersonal rules.

Furthermore, we can observe a symptom in the metaphor.[55] The symptom manifests unresolved tensions or conflicts repressed or concealed within the discourse. In the case of an individual subject, the symptom is a message from the unconscious, a form of communication that reveals hidden desires, anxieties, or traumas. To understand the symptom is to understand the subject's relation to the Symbolic. On the community level, we can observe the symptoms of ideological contradictions, cultural practices, or political unrest.[56] However, the symptom is not just a random anomaly but a meaningful expression of underlying tensions and contradictions within the social order. Understanding the symptoms can also reveal why the solutions do not work. The symptom reveals the gaps, inconsistencies, and repressed antagonisms that characterize the functioning of ideology and power relations in society.[57]

It is a symptom that stems from the controversies within the Symbolic register.[58] The symptom reveals itself through a series of signifiers, which form a metaphor. We may observe such a metaphor in various utterances. For instance, look at the Latin definition of law—*Ius est ars boni et aequi*. This metaphor should not be explained. It works only when used as a metaphor

54 A metaphor refers to a process of substitution or displacement in which one signifier is substituted for another. This substitution creates a symbolic relationship between signifiers, producing meaning through resemblance or analogy. It operates by substituting one element for another within the symbolic order. This substitution is not arbitrary but is guided by unconscious processes and social structures.

55 A symptom is the awareness of the lack of the object of desire expressed in a displaced ss—in the metaphor.

56 Žižek (n 53) 156.

57 ibid 147.

58 Symbolic is defined by otherness—by the big Other, the unconscious.

in a position of a quilting point, which holds the whole metaphor together. The subject knows how the law OUGHT to be—good and equal; at the same time, it stays foggy about what it stands for in practice, where the law is neither applied as art nor can it fulfill good and equal at the same moment. The loose connection between particular signifiers in the definition becomes quickly apparent. The metaphor reveals its symptom that the definition of the law, which is repeated to the students of law, and which decorates aulas at the law schools, is non-sensical. The connection of signifiers is not only loose but missing.

The metaphor of the rule of law works on a similar principle. It developed by replacing the original signifier, which was the rule of the sovereign. The unconscious process is defined by the desire for the stable meaning of the signifiers—the totality of the world created by stable meanings leads towards a desire for the form that could guarantee that reality has a stable condition. However, the original signifier of the sovereign's rule is still present, haunting from the forgotten memory of the signifying chain.[59]

Similarly, in the metaphor of Kelsenian OUGHT, a symptom haunts from the background that should have been forgotten. The symptom is a distrust that the judge will not decide by the legal OUGHT but based on his personal interest or preference. Therefore, it is essential to have the ideological fantasy present, which makes it undoubtful that the Rule of Law works, that the exception is repressed, and that the judge is not a corrupt weakling but an honorable authority.

This center of the legal form, as Kelsen defined it—the categorical imperative of a legal officer to apply the sanction when conditions of the disposition are fulfilled, cannot avoid the metaphorical expression. Therefore, the most profound of all symptoms of the legal form is its essence—the Kelsenian OUGHT. We may see it in Kelsenian OUGHT when the legal officer applies the norm. At this moment, we may realize who this person is and what is his entitlement to sanction me. Slavoj Žižek touches on it in the analysis of the fetishistic disavowal:

> I know very well that things are the way I see them, that the person in front of me is a corrupt weakling, but I nonetheless treat him respectfully since he wears the insignia of a judge so that when he speaks, it is the law itself which speaks through him. So in a way I really do believe his words, not my eyes. This is where the cynic who believes only hard facts falls short: when a judge speaks, there is in a way more truth in his words (words of

59 See the concept of hauntology in Jacques Derrida, *Specters of Marx: The State of the Debt, the Work of Mourning and the New International* (Routledge 2012).

an institution of law) than in the direct reality of the person of the judge, if one limits oneself to what one sees, one simply misses the point.[60]

Accepting the metaphor is crucial for the sustainability of the legal form. As Kelsen explains in the imputation principle, there is no necessary connection. This connection should only be created by will. This Kelsenian OUGHT is the metaphor that reveals the symptoms of the community. The unbearable truth that cannot be said loudly is that the whole ideological system of the legitimacy of power is a theatre because, at the decisive moment, it is no system of rules that automatically sanctions but an officer who connects the sanction to the action. Ultimately, without the ideological fantasy, it is only up to the officer if and how she decides to do so.

The legal form then reveals its darkest secret, which depends entirely on the ideological fantasy.[61] The ideology must fix the metaphor problem, which resides in the revelation that the meaning and the signifier are not connected. The task is to convince the subject not to ask the simple question: How come one individual is entitled to punish another? This is the question that the judge herself should never ask. If she does, it might be the beginning of the doom of her job.

Categorical imperative in master's discourse

The master discourse is crucial for legal form because it refers to a particular configuration of language and power that plays a central role in forming subjectivity and social structures. The master discourse represents a Symbolic order and framework within which individuals construct their identities and understand their place in society. A hierarchical relationship between the master signifier and other elements characterizes the whole discourse.[62]

The master signifier (S1)[63] is the center of the master discourse. It is a foundational and often arbitrary symbol that holds power and authority within a given social or cultural context. This signifier organizes and regulates meaning within the discourse, providing a sense of coherence and stability. The master discourse assigns subjects specific positions or roles within the social order. The master suppresses or marginalizes alternative forms of knowledge

60 Slavoj Žižek, *Less than Nothing: Hegel and the Shadow of Dialectical Materialism* (Verso Books 2012) 334.

61 Žižek (n 53) 27.

62 Jacques Lacan, *Le Séminaire. Livre XVII, 1969–70* (Seuil 1991) 27.

63 The master initially appears to have power and authority over the slave. However, the master's sense of selfhood depends on the recognition of the slave, who is seen as an object to be controlled. As a result, the master's self-consciousness remains incomplete and dependent on the slave's recognition. See Hegel (n 47).

or ways of speaking that challenge its authority. It establishes certain truths or norms as dominant while relegating others to the margins. This process of subjugation helps maintain the power dynamics inherent in the discourse. Subjects within the master discourse are compelled to identify with and internalize its norms and values, shaping their desires and aspirations accordingly.

The Kelsenian categorical imperative for the legal officer to apply the norm is structured like that. The master signifier is in the center of the discourse. It is detached from the subject, and the subject cannot decide for or against the master signifier. However, the master signifier is meaningless, as it only pretends its relation to the signified. Master serves as a quilting point,[64] which stabilizes the meaning. However, this stabilization is only imaginary, and in the metaphor, which serves as a revelation of the master signifier, the subject may detect that while it seems to be the strongest connection spot to the signified, it is just like any other signifier—fluid. Through the *point de capiton*, meanings or interpretations become temporarily 'quilted' together, giving the illusion of stability and certainty.

To understand it, the master signifier has to be connected to a chain of signifiers. This signifying chain is dependent on the subject, as it is the subject that can speak and bring the master signifier to life. The master signifier, on the other hand, is connected to the product—the surplus (a). Kelsen's categorical imperative structure puts the judge in the position of the subject, who has to act as the legal OUGHT prescribes in the signifying chain. The judge (subject $) needs to create the knowledge S2 to justify S1 (master signifier). What the master needs from the subject is the surplus. The surplus belongs to the master, not to the subject. The surplus is the Kelsenian OUGHT, the categorical imperative.

The categorical imperative is a guiding principle for moral decision-making and the ideological fantasy par excellence in every rational and humanist social system. A surplus is an excess or extra amount beyond what is needed or expected in the economy. In the master discourse, it is redundant over the master's needs. As the subject complies with the principles of universality, respect for humanity, and autonomy, she contributes to the legitimacy of the master, who longs for this surplus.

As presented above, Kelsenian OUGHT is the center of the legal form. It is the 'object a' as the surplus is, in this case, absolute allegiance to the master. However, this allegiance depends on the function of the ideological fantasy supported by knowledge—by the signifying chain (S2), the whole Symbolic order. This Symbolic order—the big Other—must fool the subject into thinking that acting by duty is the only option. For the effectivity of the legal form, the Kelsenian OUGHT is the crucial knot.

64 The *point de capiton* acts as a stabilizing or anchoring point within this linguistic flux. It functions as a nodal point or 'knot' within the symbolic structure, temporarily fixing the sliding signifiers and providing a sense of closure or coherence to meaning.

The rule of law in a metaphor reveals the symptom: that it depends only on the functioning ideological fantasy in the judge's unconscious. Carl Schmitt was a living example of this symptom: that it is not the rule of law but the sovereign who has the last word. The rule of law is an imaginary ideological construct; however, it benefits the community's well-being.

Why does the subject follow the master? The reason is neither utilitarian nor metaphysical, but for the simple reason—that the master requires it. Although the subject creates the surplus, it belongs to the master, which means that Kelsenian OUGHT belongs to the master, not to the subject. When the master is in the position, there is no way that the subject could decide about the surplus. If she does, the master will sanction her. Therefore, the categorical imperative is not questionable. Unlike the hypothetical imperative, it does not allow discussion of any element other than the duty itself. It does not matter whether the master possesses any content requirements. It only matters that it is in the master position or that the law is binding because it is the law and 'the law rules.' The effectiveness of the legal form in governing all human relations depends on the allegiance to the Master—on the fundamental fantasy that the Master exists as a Master.

Ideology as crucial part

For the effectivity of the master signifier, the working ideology is crucial. Ideology resides in the Symbolic register. However, it presents itself fully in the Imaginary while driven by the signifying chains stemming from the Symbolic. Just like Symbolic is the system of representations,[65] ideology reflects this Symbolic in the Imaginary, in the subject's fantasy about herself. Ideology fills the empty spots, where the subject guesses the answer to the question: 'What do you want from me, big Other?' It is a blind guess to that unanswered and unanswerable question: *Che vuoi?* The subject guesses and constantly asks: Is that what you want? It is the unknown known—'we do not know, that we already know' as the ego presents itself in a particular way, based on the signification stemming from the unconscious subject of the Symbolic, that is, the discourse of the Other. They are the disavowed beliefs and suppositions we are unaware of adhering to ourselves, but which determine our acts and feelings.[66] The split subject does not know she performs the determined pattern, even though she might be aware of its existence.[67]

65 Louis Althusser, *On the Reproduction of Capitalism: Ideology and Ideological State Apparatuses* (Verso Trade 2014) 231.
66 Slavoj Žižek, *How to Read Lacan* (Granta 2006) 52.
67 For example, in thinking about own behavior and asking, why 'I' behave in the same way as the others.

Subjects do not perceive this influence as artificial or secondary but natural, authentic, or apparent.[68] Because subjects believe these ideas to be self-evident, they act upon them and reproduce the status quo. Ideology is a consistent, integrated pattern of thoughts and beliefs explaining a human being's attitude towards life and her existence in society, advocating a conduct and action pattern responsive to a commensuration with thoughts and beliefs.[69] The symptom is a revelation of the systemic contradiction. The metaphor then gives us several contradictory meanings. If the ideology is weak, many interpretations of the metaphor are possible. However, if the ideology functions well, one particular meaning comes to mind and usually is not disputed.

In order to maintain the illusion of the same meaning behind the master signifier, the master must be set in a certain spot of the signification chain, which is secured by the usage of the tropes—metonymy and metaphor. These give the subject an odd feeling of insecurity in the meaning. Lacan, for instance, celebrates metaphor as it represents a place for the liberation of the subject.[70]

For the efficacy of the social existence of the subject, this *point de capiton*—the metaphor must be knotted to a particular meaning.[71] 'The result of the metaphor is to tie a specific meaning to particular words without regard to an absolute referent.'[72] The quilting point is where the signifier seems to be attached to the meaning,[73] although this connection is just imaginary. It is a task for ideological fantasy to establish quilting points.

The chain of signification is a metonymic line of signifiers the subject misrecognizes as standing for particular signifieds or material objects. Every once in a while, there is a metaphor within the metonymic chain. This metaphor manifests the object cause of desire, as desire shows itself as incomplete. The metaphor is a unique spot because it connects two spots in the discourse. The discourse of the master reveals how the master signifier is connected with the surplus (a).

The rule-of-law master signifier connects itself with a surplus. The surplus is the master's need for obedience. While craving this obedience, the metaphor reveals the symptom. This symptom is revealed in a particular moment, which is also why Lacan calls it a moment for celebration. For instance, in

68 Louis Althusser, *Lenin and Philosophy and the Other Esseys* (NLB 1971) 172.

69 Karl Loewenstein, 'Political Systems, Ideologies, and Institutions: The Problem of Their Circulation' (1953) 6 *Western Political Quarterly* 689.

70 Lacan (n 45) 423.

71 Jacques Lacan, Jacques-Alain Ed Miller and Russell Trans Grigg, *The Seminar of Jacques Lacan, Book 3: The Psychoses 1955–1956* (W.W. Norton & Company 1993) 268.

72 Bruce Fink, *A Clinical Introduction to Lacanian Psychoanalysis: Theory and Technique* (Harvard UP 1999).

73 Žižek (n 53) 112.

Hans Holbein's painting of *The Ambassadors*, the skull reveals itself only at a certain angle. Similarly, Lincoln in Dalivision reveals itself only from a certain distance. The subject recognizes the symptom only under a certain angle of vision while looking at the painting, or in a specific connotation of the signifiers when reading a text. The cause of the symptom is quite simple: it is a desire for totality and wholeness, stable meanings, correct answers, and foreseeable outcomes—as in Hegel's totality—of dissolving the subject and an object into one.

Kelsen's idea of OUGHT is in this weak spot, revealing the master's desire for legitimacy resulting from obedience. However, in the knowledge (S2), the master suppresses the surplus (a) behind the knowledge—that the master's position is the only necessary reason for the validity and following obedience. The master (S1), however, needs the surplus (a) to convince the subject (S) to create the knowledge (S2). The OUGHT, as a duty of the legal officer, to apply the rule would not be possible without the officer's conviction that the categorical imperative is binding.

Kelsen unwillingly revealed the most confidential information about the OUGHT: that the pure legal OUGHT must function as a categorical imperative. The catch about the categorical imperative is that any utilitarian analysis cannot dispute it. The imperative must be followed from duty. This duty stems from the subject's position in the structure, defined by ideology.

The key function of public officeholders is to occupy the place of what is called 'the subject supposed to know.' A person in the position of the legal subject believes that the judge knows what OUGHT to be, revealed in Latin as *iura novit curia*, which establishes an illusory but fixed connection. The task of ideology is to fool the legal officer into thinking she knows why she is doing what she is doing.

Conclusion

When we bring Kelsen back to our discourse and apply his notion of the legal OUGHT, we find out that the quest of the master signifier is to maintain stability. The master, in this case, is the legal form, which reveals itself through the metaphorical rule of law. The legal OUGHT resides in the empowerment of the officer applying the legal norm on a particular situation to connect otherwise independent signifiers and create meaning. Until this very act of, for instance, a judge reading the judgement, sanctioning the person for some behavior, the norm has no stable meaning. Only then we can think of the stable meaning when the judge connects the signifiers of the disposition and the sanction. All of it is, however, illusory. There is no connection, as there is no meaning behind signifiers. Nevertheless, the subject is not used to sustain in such meaningless limbo. Therefore, the identity must be illusively stable, through the legal form.

This is precisely the problem of Raskolnikov in Dostoyevskyi's *Crime and Punishment*. Even though he is proud of being a nihilist, he cannot sustain the fact that the punishment is not coming for him. To maintain his identity, he needs confirmation that he is a subject. Therefore, he is seeking a legal form to punish him. The OUGHT must happen. Otherwise, his devious act would not make sense. Paradoxically, Raskolnikov needs to confirm the meaning of the fact that he despises any meaning in the world. In other words, even though Raskolnikov claims there is no OUGHT, he is so immersed in the ideological fantasy that he needs this OUGHT to happen.

We all need confirmation of the meaning. And legal form can deliver that because it creates another level of reality where the human will is capable of controlling actions and consequences. I remember a Slovak nationalist politician, Andrej Danko, claiming on television that the parliament can do anything, even to say that the Sun orbits the Earth. There was a massive laugh from the intellectual community about his oblivion of causal and imputable consequences. However, the lawyer in me did not laugh. The politician was right in an illusory way. The legal form can illusorily connect meanings with signifiers. As it is impossible to know things in themselves, the Symbolic, not the Real, creates the truth.

Despite the factual flaw, if a judge would sanction by death a man saying that the Earth orbits the Sun, the judge would be empowered to do so if such legal form stipulated so. The judge would be even correct because the law prescribes what OUGHT should be and illusorily connects signifiers with signifieds. But as was already written, there are no signifieds, and signifiers have no stable positions. It is the incredible power of the legal form that makes reality stable, regardless of whether it is true or false.

Chapter 4

Pashukanis avec Lacan

Towards the fantasy of legal form

Dennis Wassouf

Introduction

Today's legal edifice lost a lot of its past glory of majestic monument that watches over its obedient subjects; the testament of asceticism asking its subjects to restrain their enjoyment in order to live in a functioning society has withered away. But that is in no way to say that we are dealing with the end of law, much less are we facing the end of coercive power. The crucial question lying ahead of us is how the relationship between law and power has changed? Through what forms does law shape our reality in the age of seemingly permissive society where more is allowed than restricted? Or in a much more condensed way: in this situation, how are we to proceed with a more efficient critique of law?

Some might say answering these questions inextricably depends on the concrete object of our critique. It certainly matters whether we are criticizing judicial decision-making, legal institutions or legal education. But my point is, rather, that we can discern the underlying logic of law enabling us to formulate a shrewd and radical critique. I argue that the possible way of accomplishing this task leads through a return to the concept of legal form, however, conceived in a different methodological way which goes beyond its traditional understanding. Trajectory of my thought begins with the legal form itself in which I read methodological and critical potential and go through insights of Lacanian political theory. Let me briefly sketch this starting point present in the works of Karl Marx, Friedrich Engels and Evgeny B. Pashukanis.

Legal form, as theorized by Pashukanis, derives its logic from commodity-form. Commodities transformed from incommensurable things to equal objects relied on the transformation of labor processes producing them. To render commodities exchangeable, they need to be considered equal and representable by an abstract and ultimate commodity, money. This logic can be summarized in three movements: 1) as a movement deriving form

DOI: 10.4324/9781032724713-5

from the content, 2) abstraction and 3) universalization.[1] For the capitalist system of commodity exchange to be fully operative, another level of abstraction is needed, specifically, a level of social agency which can be obtained by creating legal subjectivity as an abstract and universal concept of free individual oriented rationally in the market. At the same time, this concept requires an idea of equality allowing individuals to enter into contracts. Although individual subjects are obviously not equal because of their unique histories, desires, distinct characters, attributes and dreams, their contractual activity is possible only through the abstract notion of equal citizens.[2] Now, we could say that the economical principle of commodification present at the beginning, simultaneously gave rise to the legal principle of formalization, creating one common metric.[3] As Karl Marx succinctly pointed out in his Notes on Adolph Wagner's *Lehrbuch der politischen Ökonomie*:

> [F]or him [Adoph Wagner] the law is first, and then comes commerce; in reality it is the other way round: first there is commerce, and then a legal system develops out of it. In the analysis of the circulation of commodities I have demonstrated that in developed bartering the participants tacitly acknowledge one another as equal persons and owners of the respective goods to be exchanged by them; they already do that while offering their goods to each other and agreeing to trade with each other. This actual relation, which only arises through and in the exchange, is later given legal form in the contract, etc. but this form neither creates its content, the exchange, nor the relationship between the persons inherent in it, but vice versa.[4]

For Marx, as for Pashukanis,[5] legal form is the result of an economic principle expressed in commodity form, in other words, legal relations, as well as

1 Isaac D Balbus, 'Commodity Form and Legal Form: An Essay on the 'Relative Autonomy' of Law' in Roger Cotterrell (ed), *Sociological Perspectives on Law*, vols I and II (Routledge 2001) 218.

2 ibid 219. Also see Morton J Horwitz, 'The Historical Foundations of Modern Contract Law' (1974) 87 *HLR* 917.

3 Evgeny Bronislavovich Pashukanis, *The General Theory of Law* (Transaction Publishers 2003) 82.

4 Karl Marx, 'Notes on Adolph Wagner's Lehrbuch der politischen Ökonomie (Second Edition), Volume I, 1879' (*Marx/Engels Internet Archive: Works of Karl Marx*, 1881) <https://www.marxists.org/archive/marx/works/1881/01/wagner.htm> accessed 7 March 2023.

5 Pashukanis draws practically the same conclusion:

> Only under this condition [existence of commodity and money economy] does the legal subject have its material base in the person of the subject operating egoistically, whom the law does not create. but finds in existence. Without this base, the corresponding legal relation is a priori inconceivable.

See Pashukanis (n 3) 93

their actors, grow out of economic relations. That being said, we can without difficulties anticipate the subsequent approach of Marx and Pashukanis, that is a critique of legal form as a kind of ideology concealing the real state of things. Pashukanis, in his polemics with Mikhail Reisner, defended the Marxist notion of *ideology as a distortion* against the latter's staunch perceptivism. As he wrote in his reading of Reisner:

> [S]tate power as the creature of as many psychologies as there are individuals, state power which manifests as many different models as there are diverse group—and class—based environments, will naturally assume a completely different shape in the consciousness and behaviour of a minister and that of a peasant as yet unfamiliar with the idea of the state.[6]

Pashukanis' position remained fully dedicated to the Marxian definition of ideology as: 'the production of ideas, of conceptions, of consciousness, [which] is at first directly interwoven with the material activity and the material intercourse of men, the language of real life'.[7] So, if commodity and legal form distort the authentic state of things by creating fictitious social relations, the task of *ideologiekritik* is to make the reality visible again. Ideology may be for Marxists a powerful, yet fragile force relying primarily on a primitive operation of inversion, that is, for example, making people think they are created by law whereas the exact opposite is true; law is a creation of human consciousness.[8] Pashukanis contends that there is a hard kernel of reality resisting the distorting ideological force and, in order to fight ideology, one has to turn his sight on material relations expressed in it.[9] Now, it was none other than Friedrich Engels who exposed the gravest shortcoming of such an approach, especially in relation to the law:

> [T]hus to a great extent the course of the 'development of law' only consists: first in the attempt to do away with the contradictions arising from

6 Pashukanis (n 3) 77. Also perceptible in addendum by Karl Korsch, see ibid 195.

7 As way laid down by Marx and Engels in their *Critique of German Ideology*; for them, ideology as much as all epistemic and cognitive capacities are derived from material conditions:

> Conceiving, thinking, the mental intercourse of men, appear at this stage as the direct efflux of their material behaviour. The same applies to mental production as expressed in the language of politics, laws, morality, religion, metaphysics, etc. of a people.
>
> see Karl Marx and Friedrich Engels, *A Critique of The German Ideology, 1932* (xxx original year of writing) (*Marx/Engels Internet Archive*, 2000) <https://www.marxists.org/archive/marx/works/download/Marx_The_German_Ideology.pdf> accessed 7 March 2023

8 Marx illustrates inversive operation by famous example of *camera obscura*, ibid.

9 Pashukanis (n 3) 75. Pashukanis also explicitly states: 'if we wish to expose the roots of some particular ideology, we must search out the material relations which it expresses' ibid 140.

> the direct translation of economic relations into legal principles, and to establish a harmonious system of law, and then in the repeated breaches made in this system by the influence and pressure of further economic development, which involves it in further contradiction. . . . The reflection of economic relations as legal principles is necessarily also a topsy turvy one: it happens without the person who is acting being conscious of it; the jurist imagines he is operating with a priori principles, whereas they are really only economic reflexes; so everything is upside down. And it seems to me obvious that this inversion, which, so long as it remains unrecognised, forms what we call ideological conception, reacts in its turn upon the economic basis and may, within certain limits, modify it.[10]

What Engels is describing here is the mechanism of how law (as an example of ideology) constitutes its legitimized authority over its subjects. The ideology of legal form does not constitute itself through obscenely open violent acts but through the process of its disavowal. So, it is not that law comes to the scene as a violent intrusion, on the contrary, law comes as the herald of an order and consistency, providing a coherent sense of reality because law appears first and foremost as consistent with itself. Class struggle or other social contradictions or discrepancies have seemingly nothing to do with law, all the more so it brings their resolution. Consequently, *ideology forms and modifies our relation to reality and conceals this very formation*. Then it gets nearly impossible to locate any stable notion of reality since all of reality is ideologically constructed while the act of construction is disavowed.

There are two basic ways how to tackle the ideological disavowal of contradictions. First, it is the standard Marxist approach outlined above which can be in a more concrete way demonstrated on the example of a worker as the primal contradiction of capitalism. The worker is not only someone who sells her labour as commodity but she is also a 'disavowed (but necessary) contradiction: someone who is both inside the circuit of commodification (selling labour power) and externally constitutive of it (producing the surplus value that is continuously recycled)'.[11] Disavowal is produced by the legal form creating the illusion that it is the worker who voluntarily sells her labour[12] and by entering the contractual framework regulated by norms

10 Friedrich Engels, 'Letter to Conrad Schmidt. Marx and Engels Correspondence' (*Marx/Engels Internet Archive*, 2000).

11 Glyn Daly, *Speculation, Politics, Ideology, Event* (Northwestern UP 2019) 74.

12 Note the fact how often we can encounter the sentence 'the employer gives you a job' or 'the job is provided by an employer' and so on. It gives us the impression of an employer as being superior and at the same time independent of worker while worker is fully dependent on the employer as a provider of work. Hierarchy is introduced by this barely noticeable rhetoric gesture. *Cf.* Karl Marx, 'What are Wages? How are they Determined. Karl Marx: Wage Labour and Capital' (Online) (*Marx/Engels Internet Archive*, 2000).

of labour law, the worker is considered equal to the employer. Thus, the legal form gives us a perfect illusion of a symmetrical relationship whilst it makes all kinds of shady variants of contractual employment unnoticed (hiring through agencies, zero work hours, etc.).[13]

The second approach focuses primarily on the legal form as a frame through which we perceive reality. As we have seen, this frame has the quality of making some things visible to us while not allowing us to see others, so we have something to do with the duality of exclusion/repression, and strategical questions distinguishing this approach from the traditionally Marxist one goes as follows: *through what operating mechanism of exclusion/repression, does this universal frame itself emerge?*[14] What precisely are we getting here?

Slavoj Žižek in his most famous and inaugural work *The Sublime Object of Ideology* outlined two critical methods: symptomatic reading and phantasmatic critique.[15] The former corresponds to the already mentioned critique seeking to undermine the dominant ideology by pointing out the gap between what is officially promoted (equality, freedom, wealth, possibilities of unbridled creativity, etc.) and what we get instead (increase of poverty, racism, misogyny, etc.). This mode of critique basically relies on the good old Freudian dictum about repression: 'it is not the repression itself which produces substitutive formations and symptoms, but that these latter are indications of a return of the repressed'.[16]

In this light, the symptomatic reading aims at interpreting symptoms indicating some deeper repressed contradiction, and, in the political-critical sphere, the goal is to bring these symptoms to the surface and expose them as consequences of unresolvable contradiction of capitalism, thus opening up a space for formulating political demands and subsequently systemic change. This is also why Žižek, using a Lacanian reading of Marx, famously called Marx as the inventor of the symptom, in a sense that Marx discovered a certain imbalance between 1) *how things appear to us* and *how they really are* (i.e., commodity fetishism where relations between people are transposed on relations between things); and 2) *universal notion* and *particular representation* (i.e., how particular representation of, let's say, equality, undermines its universal form). Žižek adds that:

> [T]his procedure thus implies a certain logic of exception: every ideological Universal—for example freedom, equality—is 'false' in so far as it

13 Ruth Dukes, 'Critical Labour Law: Then and Now' in Emilios Christodoulidis, Ruth Dukes, and Marco Goldoni (eds), *Research Handbook in Critical Legal Theory* (Elgar Publishing 2019) 356.

14 Judith Butler, Ernesto Laclau and Slavoj Žižek, *Contingency, Hegemony, Universality—Contemporary Dialogues on the Left* (Verso 2000) 258.

15 Slavoj Žižek, *Sublime Object of Ideology* (Verso 2008) 26–27.

16 Sigmund Freud, *General Psychological Theory: Papers on Metapsychology* (Atria 2008) 103.

> necessarily includes a specific case which breaks its unity, lays open its falsity. Freedom, for example: a universal notion comprising a number of species (freedom of speech and press, freedom of consciousness, freedom of commerce, political freedom, and so on) but also, by means of a structural necessity, a specific freedom which subverts this universal notion.[17]

To rephrase it, the fetishistic relationship between universal notion and its element responds to *the species subverting its own genus*.[18] It follows that symptomatic critique strives to reveal this irremovable imbalance. But if we get back to Freud's quotation mentioned above and we read it closely, we realize that a symptomatic approach is not enough. In reality: 'it is not the repression itself which produces substitutive formations and symptoms, but that these latter are indications of a return of the repressed and *owe their existence to quite other processes*'.[19]

What Freud had in mind was, simply put, that symptoms indicate a return of repression and are not creations of repression itself, that is to say, repression is only a defense mechanism against that which is repressed, and symptoms are signs of something more primordial starting to claim the floor. What is this something? Question about these processes brings us finally to the latter mode of critique: fantasmatic critique. What does the critique have to aim at in order to subvert the ruling ideology? Žižek's basic premise is that, in today's era of prevailing cynicism, we are more than keen to acknowledge the gap between what ideology promises and what it actually delivers. From this standpoint, it seems like symptomatic critique has to be met with a dull exclamation: "so what?" We can imagine such a situation pretty easily: in November 2021, it was revealed that Bill Gates had given 319 million dollars to major media outlets; BBC, CNN and Daily Telegraph. While being promulgated as perfectly legal and even altruistic gesture of goodwill, what is really at stake is a billionaire's power to set public agenda.[20] In January 2022, Financial Times, one of the donation-backed media houses, published an article about Gates investing 15 billion dollars in clean tech which was viewed as a breakthrough allowing engineers to realize projects on sustainable aviation.[21] Connecting these exemplary news together, we get the picture

17 Žižek (n 15) 16.

18 'Commentary on Žižek's The Sublime Object of Ideology (Chapter 1)' (*The Dangerous Maybe Blog*, 2019) <https://thedangerousmaybe.medium.com> accessed 14 March 2023.

19 Freud (n 16) 103 [emphasis mine].

20 Alan McLeod, 'Documents Show Bill Gates Has Given $319 Million to Media Outlets' *Mint Press News* (November 2021) <https://www.mintpressnews.com/documents-show-bill-gates-has-given-319-million-to-media-outlets/278943/> accessed 14 March 2023.

21 Leslie Hook, 'Bill Gates-Backed Fund Aims to Invest $15bn in Clean Tech' *Financial Times* (10 January 2022) <https://www.ft.com/content/f25fd95d-e2d8-43f8-b786-1552a1f0059e> accessed 14 March 2023.

of cynical ideology which to the shocking revelation replies 'what is wrong about that, it serves a purpose'. Is this not precisely what Žižek means when he says that:

> [T]his cynicism is therefore a kind of perverted 'negation of the negation' of the official ideology: confronted with illegal enrichment, with robbery, the cynical reaction consists in saying that legal enrichment is a lot more effective and, moreover, protected by the law. As Bertolt Brecht puts it in his Threepenny Opera: what is the robbery of a bank compared to the founding of a new bank?[22]

Phantasmatic critique confronts us with the question about the operating mechanism making the creation of symptoms possible and leads to the acceptance that ideology does not function solely on the plane of consciousness, but also on the level of the unconscious, that is, on the level of fantasy. While having a lucid account of ideology's shortcomings and thus not taking it seriously, on the unconscious level we still follow it; that is to say, we nonetheless subscribe to ideological phantasmatic narrative. Žižek inverts the known formula proclaimed by Marx *they do not know what they are doing* into *they know exactly what they are doing and they do it anyway*,[23] or as Octave Mannoni says *je sais bien mais quand même*. . . . It is not only that this inversion marks a certain shift in a function of ideology but—in a much more radical way—sheds a ray of light on what this shift makes possible, that is, on the very formal condition of the shift. Such formal condition is to be searched in the split of the subject and the very structure of the subject's reality; Mannoni here recalls Freud who:

> once had a patient who was told by fortune-teller that his brother-in-law would die of shellfish poisoning that summer. After the summer had passed, the patient said to Freud, in sum, 'I know very well that my brother-in-law hasn't died, but, all the same, that prediction was wonderful.[24]

This sentence left Freud amazed and made him to remember certain duplicity of the ego known at least from the time of St. Paul,[25] whom Freud considered to be a remarkable analytical figure who successfully brought the repressed into light and managed to disconnect himself from primordial guilt

22 Žižek (n 15) 26.
23 Slavoj Žižek, *For They Know Not What They Do: Enjoyment as a Political Factor* (Verso 2008) 245–46.
24 Octave Mannoni, 'I Know Well but All the Same' in Molly Anne Rothenberg, Dennis Anne Foster, and Slavoj Žižek (eds), *Perversion and the Social Relation* (Duke UP 2003) 71.
25 ibid.

echoing from depth.[26] Now, the necessity of fantasy and its critique became quite obvious, but how does it relate to Pashukanis' idea of legal form and critique of ideology? Let's jump straight to the definition of phantasmatic function provided by Žižek:

> [T]he ontological paradox—scandal, even—of the notion of fantasy lies in the fact that it subverts the standard opposition of 'subjective' and 'objective': of course, fantasy is by definition not 'objective' (in the naive sense of 'existing independently of the subject's perceptions'); however, it is not 'subjective' either (in the sense of being reducible to the subject's consciously experienced intuitions). Fantasy, rather, belongs to the 'bizarre category of the objectively subjective'—the way things actually, objectively seem to you even if they don't seem that way to you.[27]

The unconscious fantasy thus bears certain material and objective qualities while at the same time, structures the most intimate subjective notion of reality. Fantasy is straddled between the subject´s interior and objective exterior and its basic function is to assure we practically act consonant with ideology, even though we might consciously distance ourselves from it.

Two things are even more obvious now: 1) if critique of the notion of legal form is based on the assumption of undistorted reality behind the ideological curtain, then it needs new dynamics; fantasy undermines standard opposition of subject-object rendering legal form in its orthodox appearance unconvincing 2) if we cannot look for this dynamic in the realm of symptomatic reading—albeit revised—we need to dive into phantasmatic critique. The outcome is that we need to conceive *legal form as an ideological fantasy*.

Legal form as an ideological fantasy gives us a new methodological tool for uncovering processes underlying today's legal apparatus. To be able to proceed in this way, I will apply the findings of Lacanian political theory to the concept of legal form. In this chapter, I undertake a tour of psychoanalytically informed critique of ideology in order to map the possible connection between legal form as a legal theoretical concept and fantasy as an object of ideology critique. My aim is to show that fantasy is useful in new understanding of Pashukanis' heritage. I claim that to move beyond Marxist theory of law requires a psychoanalytic reading.

The structure of my contribution is as follows. First, I am going to describe the clinical and psychoanalytical concept of fantasy, its formal logic and the

26 Sigmund Freud, *Moses and Monotheism* (Hogarth Press 1939) 139–42. For more detailed history of St. Paul figure in Freud's *oeuvre* see Herman Westerink, 'The Great Man from Tarsus: Freud on the Apostle Paul' (2007) 76(1) *Psychoanal Quart* 217.

27 Slavoj Žižek, *Fragile Absolute: Or, Why is the Christian Legacy Worth Fighting For?* (Verso 2009) 83.

role it plays in the constitution of subjectivity. In the next step, I connect the notion of legal form as an ideological fantasy to Lacan's declaration about law that is split between public law (codes, institutions, symbols) and its obscene remainder of the superego. The fantasy of the legal form will be conceived as a formal structure, and as a frame, which constitutes the mechanism mediating between the level of public law, in a sense of legal textuality, and superego. Superego as an empty formal injunction, 'enjoy!' creates a delicate relation between law and its transgression, and at the same time, forms the base of late capitalist permissive society where it seems that law lost the grip over its subjects, whereas law, on the contrary, got stronger than ever. Permissive society is defined as follows:

> [R]ather than demanding that its members give up their individual enjoyment for the sake of the whole, the society of enjoyment commands their enjoyment—private enjoyment becomes of paramount importance—and the importance of the social order as a whole seems to recede.[28]

An echo of Thatcherite slogan 'there is no society, only individual men and women' gets apparent here and we also get how the connection between superegoic command 'enjoy!' and legal form promoting the idea of a free and rational subject might look like: *superego as the Real of capitalism is a backbone of legal form sustaining fantasmatic frame of today's ideology.* Connecting legal form and enjoyment seems to be indispensable for maintaining the project of radical yet consistent critique being able to account for the unconscious legal mechanisms, without resigning to its textual representations. The primary goal is to create a concept of legal form as a critical tool enabling the critique of ideology at the level of the unconscious fantasy while not downplaying the textual dimension of law. In this way, it is possible to obtain at least a preliminary outline of a newly understood legal form that respects both the Marxist foundations of ideology critique and contemporary psychoanalytically inspired methods.

Just a sweet sweet fantasy

As the most prominent Lacan's interlocutor Jacques Alain Miller emphasized, one is not only a rational animal but first and foremost fantasizing animal (*animal fantasmatisant*).[29] We are not dealing here with a mere aphorism but with a matter of utmost importance bearing grave consequence: it is not that

28 Todd McGowan, *End of Dissatisfation: Society of Enjoyment* (SUNY Press 2004) 3.

29 Jacques Alain Miller, 'Du symptôme au fantasme, et retour' in Kirk Turner (ed), *Lacanian Fantasy: Image, Language and Uncertainty* (Routledge 2023) 205.

rationality is a condition of fantasy but, in an opposite way, fantasy grounds the possibility of sentience and rationality. As Kirk Turner remarks:

> [F]antasy acts as both a 'filter' between perception and consciousness, i.e., as a support for the consistency and completion of the experience of an individual 'self'; and that which, in respect to our engagement with the world, as mediated by language, 'fills out' our experiential and sense-making capabilities.[30]

In Lacanian parlance, juxtaposing reality and fantasy is misleading since the former is not only conditions the latter but in fact, fantasy is seemingly a window to the reality that is structured by the unconscious scenario provided by fantasy.[31] Lacan, in his return to Freud, who understood fantasy mainly as a scene of wish fulfilment,[32] described fantasy as a support of the subject's desire. What does it mean? It will be instructive to introduce the Lacanian formula (*mathème*) of fantasy which takes the form $ ◊ a.

On the left side, we get a symbol for Lacan's notion of barred subject (hence the line cutting 'S' symbol athwart). An individual, in order to become a speaking subject, has to be subjected to the law of the signifier, that is, to the order of language. To become a subject, the individual needs to go through the process of symbolic castration or symbolization. Since language is a referential system based on differences between signs, it cannot allow us an immediate experience of the world around us, the only thing we can do is to refer to it.[33] In this way, we are, in a sense, violently thrown into language, a move by which we are removed from the world of immediate enjoyment (*jouissance*), the sphere of a pre-linguistic existence in which we could not distinguish between our body, the body of our mother and the world around us.

Leaving this world behind, we become subjects of language forever scarred by the loss of an object. This loss creates an irremovable void inside the subject who is conceived as split (or barred, constituted by the gap).[34] The lost object in question is not meant to be some particular kind of an object,

30 ibid 20.

31 ibid 128, Alenka Zupančič, *Ethics of the Real: Kant and Lacan* (Verso 2000) 158.

32 Sigmund Freud, 'The Case of a Wolf Man' in Muriel Gardiner (ed), *The Wolf-Man and Sigmund Freud* (Karnac Books 1989) 183; Sigmund Freud, *Introductory Lectures on Psycho-Analysis* (W.W. Norton 1977) 238. This Freudian understanding of fantasy through the case of Wolf Man is supported by Lacan himself, see Jacques Lacan, *Four Fundamental Concepts of Psychoanalysis: The Seminar of Jacques Lacan, Book XI* (W.W. Norton & Company 1998) 54.

33 Richard Boothby, *Death and Desire: Psychoanalytic Theory in Lacan's Return to Freud* (Routledge 1991) 149–51.

34 Bruce Fink, *Lacanian Subject: Between Language and Jouissance* (Princeton UP 1996) 45–47.

but what Lacan calls *objet petit a* (*object a*), which is considered to be a remainder of symbolization and also *an object-cause of desire*. *Object a* is for Lacan purely formal category standing for the subject's void.

Fantasy comes to help the subject to overcome the sense of emptiness by concealing the void inside her by making the 'absolutely unreachable infinity seem like something that could one day be attained, and that is desirable. The infinity of the trace is given a positive (imaginary) form as the regulative ideal that is the object of desire'.[35] This operation creates an infinite chain of desire and a subject chasing after a mythical object believing that one day the void will be filled; it is an endless process because the object, as a purely formal category, is not able to actually merge with any concrete object (a dream job, a car, romantic love, etc.), but can only indirectly represent it, thus at the same time positivizing the void. And logically, a positivized void is still a void.[36]

The way in which fantasy structures our reality is thus essentially twofold: 1) it sutures the wound within the subject, thereby covering the constitutive void (the subject as such is then defined as the inability to fill this void[37]) and 2) it sets an endless process of desire into motion jumping from one object to another in the belief that one day we will reach wholeness.

$ <> a can be translated as a barred subject of void searching for the elusive X that is able to make $ into S. The symbol of the lozenge shows the total impossibility of this relationship, for whenever the subject succeeds in physically obtaining the object of her desire, *object a* slips through her fingers and desire moves elsewhere. That is why we can say that fantasy *does not tell us what to desire but how to desire*.[38]

Since symbolization is the domain of linguistic order, in Lacanese called the symbolic register or the Symbolic, which could be called a 'realm of normativity', in a sense of grammatical, mathematical, cultural, moral and legal normativity,[39] that is also what entitles Lacan to formulate one of his most famed catchphrases that *desire is always desire of the Other*:

> Freud reveals to us that it is thanks to the Name-of-the-Father that man does not remain bound to the sexual service of his mother, that aggression toward the Father is at the very heart of the Law, and that the Law is at the service of the desire that Law institutes through the prohibition of

35 Michael Lewis, *Derrida and Lacan: Another Writing* (Edinburg UP 2008) 166.
36 Richard Boothby, *Freud as a Philosopher: Metapsychology after Lacan* (Routledge 2001) 245–48.
37 Žižek (n 15) 236.
38 Jason Glynos, 'The Grip of Ideology: A Lacanian Approach to the Theory of Ideology' (2001) 6 *Journal of Political Ideologies* 191.
39 Jacques Alain Miller, 'Other Without the Other' (2013) 10 *Hurly Burly. The International Lacanian Journal of Psychoanalysis* 15–29.

incest. . . . Desire is desire for desire, the Other's desire, as I have said, in other words, subjected to the Law.[40]

What Lacan states here is another way of describing the process of symbolization but this time in a more technical way, with an emphasis more on the mechanism itself than on its effect, that is the subject. In this process, we focus on the difference between desire and drive, which, under any circumstances, cannot be conflated with animalistic instinct.[41] Drive, or libido, is a way for the subject to get satisfaction in other ways than sexually (e.g., eating, working, reading, etc.). Desire is the name given to the impossibility of attaining any satisfaction. The difference between desire and drive is that the drive presupposes a way of getting satisfaction by circling around the object of desire forever and getting satisfaction from this repetitive process. Drive thus does not strive for actually getting the object, it aims at the very process itself which becomes desired. While desire appears to be a cunning force always deferring our pleasure, drive accepts the desired object's elusiveness and embarks on a journey that is its own goal. Another way of sketching the difference is to say that whereas drive is intentional (it aims at a concrete object), desire is something we are caught in and what only produces back the enjoyment (*jouissance*), which is the exact opposite of pleasure, since it has more to do with pain than pleasure, or to be precise, finding pleasure in pain.[42]

Therefore, the process of symbolization in relation to this difference can be described as a way in how bodily instinct gets trapped in the cobweb of the law of the signifier (Name-of-the-Father), which produces desire as its main product and drive as a by-product.[43] The name-of-the-father is the primordial 'no!', a commandment to tame the instinct and to shape it into a law-abiding flux of 'moderate satisfaction'. Drive is a remainder of desire's creation and each has a different relation to the symbolic structure: 'desire is essentially linked to the law, since it always searches for something that is prohibited or unavailable'.[44] The law of the signifier is what plots the trajectories of our desire and that is why desire belongs to the realm of the Symbolic: the Symbolic introduces us to the pleasure principle, which is to be understood here

40 Jacques Lacan, *Écrits* (W.W. Norton & Company 2007) 723.

41 ibid 722.

42 Slavoj Žižek, *The Ticklish Subject: The Absent Centre of Political Ontology* (Verso 2009) 297.

43 According to Žižek, common mistake in interpreting the process of symbolization (also known as graph of desire) is to think that drive is what we have before the symbolization and by introducing law of the signifier, we end up with desire. It is rather that drive is by-product of symbolization, see ibid 296.

44 Renata Salecl, The Satisfaction of Drives' in David G Collins, Joan Copjec and Jacques Alain Miller (eds), *Umbr(a): On the Drive* (A Journal of the Unconscious 1997) 106.

as 'the symbolic law, a safeguard, a homeostasis which tries to prevent the irruption of the *jouissance* that is linked to the satisfaction of drive'.[45] Drive, on the other hand, undermines law and thus belongs to the Real as the realm of what cannot be symbolized and what threatens the reality constructed by means of the Symbolic. Drive is a certain force of transgression going against the grain of legal desire. But as we are about to see, law and transgression are not autonomous opposites, but they bear witness to the Janus-faced nature of the law.

Because it is the symbolical big Other (representing law, culture, morality, etc.) who moulds us as desiring subjects, we tend to perceive big Other as an agency holding keys to the mystery of our desire; big Other, from our perspective, has all the answers on how to finally reach the climactic point of satisfaction. To put it differently, we 'want to be wanted', that is, we want to be desired by the big Other, in order to get the answer.[46] The subject poses an impossible question, by Lacan formulated as *Che vuoi?* (what do you want?), addressed to the big Other. This question is impossible in a sense of, the impossibility of arriving at any answer whatsoever. What does the big Other want from us? To obey the law; to follow our desire? If so, then in what way it wants us to obey; and obey what exactly? By these questions, we are bound to the big Other as well as to the law.

And here it is where we return to the fantasy from which we never really strayed. Let us recall the famous example with Freud's daughter who was once eating a strawberry cake and saw her parents happy about the way she was enjoying it, which led her to desire the cake. Now, the question is, if I consciously want something, where does this desire come from? How do I know I really want what I want?[47] It is the unconscious level of desire described in the formula of fantasy ($ <> a) which stages our conscious desires, our particular position in the symbolic order and our perception. Here, we stumble upon the moment when the question (*Che vuoi?*) coincides with the answer because this question by means of which we are attached to the big Other forms the fantasy which, in turn, gives us the answer: big Other wants us to *desire to be desired* by the big Other.[48]

But in order to build our argument for the fantasy, we need to be precise and look at what is the *object a* as the object-cause of desire. As I already noted, *object a* is a formal category giving positive shape to the subject's void. Because it is this object towards which our desire is directed., it is the

45 ibid.
46 Bruce Fink, *Lacan to the Letter: Reading Écrits Closely* (University of Minnesota Press 2004) 119.
47 Slavoj Žižek, *Parallax View* (MIT Press 2006) 38.
48 Slavoj Žižek, 'Che Vuoi?' in Slavoj Žižek (ed), *Jacques Lacan: Critical Evaluations in Cultural Theory*, vol III (Routledge 2003) 362.

object a which is the central point of the fantasmatic screen, or as Todd Mc Gowan points out:

> *objet a* stains the field of perception because we are desiring subjects, we cannot perceive straight on neutrally, *objet a* is a name for this inability to perceive straight on the? perceptual field . . . *objet a* is a thing that names our inability to perceive without a distortion of desire . . . every perceptual field is organized around desire which makes neutral perspective on that field impossible. *Objet a* not only distorts but also makes the perceptual field accessible. So, what opens up the perceptual field also makes it inaccessible without distortions.[49]

It is clear that if we are to claim that fantasy is what creates the unconscious *mise-en-scène* of our desire and our reality, then it is through the *object a*. This would mean that fantasy is, apart from being a narrative or a screen, an operational mechanism using *object a* as its tool. *Object a* as a part of a phantasmatic scenario plays the role of a distortion in a sense that by positivizing the lack in the subject, *object a* gives us the idea there is no lack in the subject, no constitutive gap whatsoever.[50] From the point of phantasmatic view, the subject is complete, not lacking. In sum, the constitutive gap, which is the Real threatening the Symbolic with its idea of wholeness, is given the Imaginary form of a fantasy—imaginary in the manner of an image we identify with and which provides us with a semblance of structural unity.[51] Here we get Lacan's basic ontological model of three registers *Symbolic–Imaginary–Real*, which forms three entwined knots, in the midst of which *object a* is situated as that which: 1) conceals the Real void by standing in its place;[52] 2) we identify with in the Imaginary; 3) and what grants us the access to the Symbolic reality.[53] As we have seen, symbolic reality stands on the fantasmatic realm which should be understood:

> [A]s a narrative that covers-over or conceals the subject's lack by providing an image of fullness, wholeness, or harmony, on the one hand, while conjuring up threats and obstacles to its realization on the other. When successfully installed, a fantasmatic narrative hooks the subject—via the

49 Todd McGowan, 'Lacan's 'objet a' (Video)' *Lacan in Scotland* (6 March 2023) <https://www.youtube.com/watch?v=jiXdNBcMCvI&t=859s> accessed 15 March 2023.

50 Lewis (n 35) 187.

51 Fink (n 34) 59–60.

52 As Lacan puts it: 'the Real supports the Phantasy. Phantasy protects the real', see Jacques Lacan, *Four Fundamental Concepts of Psychoanalysis* (Routledge 2004) 41.

53 Arka Chattopadhyay, *Beckett, Lacan and the Mathematical Writing of the Real* (Bloomsbury Academic 2019) 138.

enjoyment it procures—to a given practice or order, or a promised future practice or order, thus conferring identity.[54]

To summarize, we can name a few characteristics of fantasy: 1) it conceals the traumatic void of our subjectivity, as well as of the social structure itself; 2) it is an unconscious formation; 3) it sets desire into motion, organizes it by telling us how to desire; 4) and by virtue of this operation it structures our reality. Virtually the same properties can be assigned to the legal form as an ideological fantasy, as I am about to argue.

Fantasy of legal Form

There are many ways of thinking about law as fantasy. The basic fantasmatic function is to conceal the contradiction in the heart of the law, bearing witness to the economical and class nature of legal conflicts.[55] Such fantasy of legal form helps to build an image of law as determinate, predictable, systematic and logically coherent system, where passions, inextricably associated with political agony, cannot be present. The role of such legal fantasy is to banish from its domain anything that might undermine systematicity and predictability, and that is why law, according to Peter Goodrich referring to Pierre Legendre, is:

> [A] far more pervasive and obscure phenomenon than our conventional learning allows. Indeed, Law in this sense is not especially the province of lawyers; lawyers deal with Law quite unwittingly. They are, for Legendre, the practitioners of sophisticated sort of imbecility.[56]

What lawyers basically do is to repress the awkward presence of enjoyment that seems to have no place in law, for the law deals exclusively with serious matters that have nothing to do with neither desire nor enjoyment. Lawyers' taxonomical aspirations on judicial arrangement of things follow the necessary staging of the impression that law is un-desiring.

Another explanation of the phantasmatic legal characteristics has to do with abstraction and co-ordination (meaning the initiation of an order of semblance), constructing an image of non-coercive market exchange, deliberately ignoring the difference in wealth between workers and capitalists. The

54 Jason Glynos and David Howarth, *Logics of Critical Explanation in Social and Political Theory* (Routledge 2007) 130.

55 Rafał Mańko, 'Legal Form, Ideology and the Political' in Adam Sulikowski, Rafał Mańko, and Jakub Łakomy (eds), *Legal Scholarship and the Political: In Search of a New Paradigm* (C.H. Beck 2020) 35.

56 Alan Pottage, 'The Paternity of Law' in Costas Douzinas, Peter Goodrich, and Yifat Hachamovitch (eds), *Politics, Postmodernity and Critical Legal Studies* (Routledge 1994) 149.

law then must 'abstract from this difference in what is owned and treat each party as having the same right to dispose of his property irrespective of what that property is'.[57] The construction of the homogeneous legal subject had to necessarily be conceived ensuring the functionality of the juridical sphere as a site of balancing interests; in other words, new methods and metrics had to be introduced to measure the incommensurable.[58] It is worth noting that in a sarcastic way, Anatole France in his novel Red Lily described where exactly lies the majesty of law's yardstick: 'the law, in its majestic equality, forbids rich and poor alike to sleep under bridges, to beg in the streets, and to steal their bread'.[59]

Both approaches reflect, on the one hand, the Marxist conception of law as an oppressive instrument serving the ruling class, and the Weberian focus on formal legal characteristics such as rationality or legal certainty.[60] Nevertheless, for my purposes, these two outlined accounts on legal fantasy (or on the fantasy of legal form) are *two sides of the same coin*. I claim that fantasy is to be rather located on the level mediating between these two sides. What is described above are representations of this phantasmatic mediation, rather than fantasy itself. The first side represents the law as the domain of textuality and institutional apparatuses, as well as methods of interpretation and legal reasoning; the second side speaks to the underlying unconscious mechanism bringing certain forms of libidinal investment into the first domain. That is to say, complex transactions taking place between the two parts cannot be properly understood without putting them into context of desire and enjoyment. For the time being, the initial thesis is the phantasmatic mechanism of the legal form supporting the abstraction of the equal and free subject is the mechanism of desire and enjoyment: the subject of legal relations, and likewise the subject of capitalism, is the subject of desire. In such configuration, law must be considered in a strictly Lacanian sense, that is, as a symbolic structure (the big Other), which, as we have seen, is marked by constitutive split.

When we say that it is not only the subject but also big Other who is split, it provokes a question between what is split; what two halves emerge from constitutive fracture? Law, which is in Lacanian theory another name

57 Jeffrey Reiman, 'The Marxian Critique of Criminal Justice' in David S Caudill and Jay Steven Gold (eds), *Radical Philosophy of Law: Contemporary Challenges to Mainstream Legal Theory and Practice* (Humanity Press 1995) 127.

58 Dragan Milovanovic, 'Postmodern Law and Subjectivity' in David S Caudill and Jay Steven Gold (eds), *Radical Philosophy of Law: Contemporary Challenges to Mainstream Legal Theory and Practice* (Humanity Press 1995) 38–53, 40.

59 Andrew Sepielli, 'Law's Majestic Equality' (2013) 32(6) *L and Phil* 673.

60 Harold J Berman, *Law and Revolution: The Formation of Western Legal Tradition* (Harvard UP 1983) 542–47.

for the big Other, is split between public law, that include codes, institutions or legal rituals, and the superego as its obscene underside.

In the conventional Freudian treatment of the superego, it is considered to be the internalized moral agency, the State in the mind of the subject, so to speak. But Freud's understanding is far more nuanced; albeit he connected the superego with obedience, he understood it as a site of 'psychical personalities' producing commandments (he mentions 'moral', but also 'juridical' personalities).[61] However, Freud makes it clear that the superego derives its power from the *id* as the seat of the subject's enjoyment, which makes the superego cruel and aggressive.[62] Superego imposes senseless commands relentlessly tormenting the subject. The superego being linked to enjoyment (*jouissance*) is that which simultaneously inflicts pain and pleasure: it makes law powerful and at the same time vulnerable and contradictory:

> The connection between superego (the internalized compulsion to obey) and *jouissance* (excessive, destabilizing enjoyment) as constitutive of the law may seem contradictory, and yet, precisely as a contradiction, it captures the gist of the Freudian argument that the necessary implementation of the law (civilization) requires a sacrifice of enjoyment that is compensated by libidinally-charged superego pressure. To obey the law means, effectively, to renounce our desire to transgress it—a desire which the superego predates upon, thus making us feel guilty.[63]

This senselessness of command which has no particular content—it is a pure form—is, in fact, the repressed uncanny side of Kantian moral law, where an ethical act is ethical only insofar we act for the sake of morality itself; there cannot be any external motive to it, otherwise, it is not ethical, or to put it differently,

> in Kant we have the idea that what characterizes a truly ethical act is that it not only accords with the moral law but also is carried out exclusively because of the moral law . . . allowing *no other motive* but its unconditional, imperative command, devoid of all particular content.[64]

Guilt is inflicted on us by the empty form of the command because we can never truly execute the command addressed to us, since we never know what its content is.

61 Étienne Balibar, *Citoyen Sujet et Autres Essais d'anthropologie philosophique* (Presses Universitaires de France 2011) 409.

62 McGowan (n 28) 29.

63 Fabio Vighi, 'The Ambiguous Remainder: Contemporary Capitalism and the Becoming Law of the Symptom' in Laurent De Sutter (ed), *Žižek and Law* (Routledge 2015) 82.

64 Alenka Zupančič, *Let Them Rot: Antigone's Parallax* (Fordham University 2023) 55.

The effects of superego are twofold. First of all, it creates a mystical aura to the law, granting it an appearance of legitimacy. By proliferating the same empty command, law gets the illusion of depth. The guilt caused by the superegoic command is so palpable that it is tough to imagine it happens for no reason whatsoever. Surely, we can fabricate myriads of reasons why to obey the law: because it is rational, just, necessary, etc. But in the end, when we keep responding to the reasons of the law's legitimacy in a child-like manner 'why?', we are about to find nothing but emptiness; this is exactly the meaning of Derrida's *Mystical Foundation of Authority*, where Derrida famously quotes Blaise Pascal (quoting Montesquieu):

> . . . one man says that the essence of justice is the authority of the legislator, another that it is the convenience of the king, another that it is current custom; and the latter is closest to the truth: simple reason tells us that nothing is just in itself; everything crumbles with time. Custom is the sole basis for equity, for the simple reason that it is received; it is the mystical foundation of its authority. Whoever traces it to its source annihilates it.[65]

If the law is to remain effective, its violent origin, as well as its obscene underside cannot be disclosed; for this reason, we can say that one is taught not to trace the source of superegoic command. Public law in a sense of codes or institutions cannot provide us with reasons why to obey it, so the reasons have to be searched elsewhere. Hence, the superego is what helps to connect the dimension of the truth to the law.[66] But the truth of the Law is that there is no truth in it. Law does not stand on rock-hard pillars of justice; law cannot have any claim for truth. Its authority has no truth.[67] This confronts us with a radical openness of the legal and political field where anything is possible. So, the Real is this sense of open space where change can take root, which, of course, threatens the capitalist system.

Second of all, superego belongs to the Real because it produces an *impossible* command. And because the link between superego and enjoyment is an intimate one, the superego both strengthens and undermines the law. How exactly? Law, by stating the prohibition gives us an implicit message that if something is restricted, it may be the key to satisfy our desire, to get the *object a*, 'this is what the superego accesses in the law and activates, which is why Jacques Lacan states that nothing forces anyone to enjoy except the superego. The superego is the imperative of *jouissance*—Enjoy![68]

65 Jacques Derrida, 'Mystical Foundation of Authority' in Drucilla Cornell (ed), *Possibilities of Justice* (Routledge 1992) 12.
66 Žižek (n 15) 88.
67 ibid 36.
68 Todd McGowan, 'Superego and the Law' in Yannis Stavrakakis (ed), *Routledge Handbook in Psychoanalytic Political Theory* (Routledge 2019) 140.

It would be no exaggeration to say that the most magnificent triumph in the history of ideology was when capitalism recognized the gap in the subject as the motor of its own activity and connected it to the very principle of formal legal commandment which was changed from 'obey!' to 'enjoy!', or to be more precise, it changed the configuration of obedience, because to enjoy means to obey. The guilt of not enjoying ourselves enough—which, again, pertains to the insatiability both of superego and desire—is what drives us deeper into the superegoic abyss; when enjoyment 'becomes a responsibility, one becomes constantly aware of one's failure to enjoy oneself fully enough. The superego never enables the subject to do enough to satisfy it'.[69] That is what Lacan means by calling superego the law and its destruction; in a paradoxical way, it restricts and permits at the same time. Now, how to conceptualize legal form as a fantasy? As was mentioned a few times, fantasy is to be understood as:

> [A] schema that mediates between publically affirmed ideals on the one hand, and the darker side of those aspirations and aims on the other hand—a side that subjects would rather not consciously or officially affirm.[70]

In this definition we can see, in view of the previous interpretation, a clue to the connection between the form of law and fantasy. To summarize, I will demarcate two psychoanalytic accounts of the legal form.

First, Todd McGowan associates legal form with the superego and the aforementioned injunction 'enjoy!', although it would be more justified to translate McGowan's thesis into purely formal coordinates. That is to say, for McGowan, form of law coincides with form of an empty command 'do X!' without giving us any slightest idea to what this command aims or how to satisfy the commanding superego. Thus, the superego cannot be satisfied and it will never cease to command. We simply cannot win the game played against the superego, not because it is such a skilled gamer but because its annoyance is inconsolable. Superego derives its authority only from an empty command that is not justified in any way. Effectively, we are destined to find at the fundamental level of legal authority the law itself. In light of this, we can construct well-known tautology which bears witness to the law's stupidity: law is law. Or as Ludwig Wittgenstein poignantly remarked in his *Investigations*: How am I able to obey a rule?—if this is not a question about causes, then it is about the justification for my following the rule in the way I do. If I have exhausted the justification, I have reached bedrock, and my spade is turned. Then I am inclined to say: This is simply what I do.[71] Stupidity

69 ibid.
70 Jason, Glynos, 'Fantasy and Identity in Critical Political Theory' (2011) 32 *Filozofski Vestnik* 65.
71 Ludwig Wittgenstein, *Philosophical Investigations* (Basil Blackwell 1986) § 217.

represents the fact that contrary to the illusion of a sophisticated web of underlying justificatory mechanisms, law justifies itself, in the last instance, in the least savvy way imaginable, that is by a mere tautology. McGowan's idea aims at seeing through law's authority that is senseless and on the fundamental level unjustifiable. Ideological fantasy is then a smokescreen used to hide law's idiocy providing us with claims about justice, public good, freedom, etc. Crucial characteristics of McGowan's position is that he identifies legal form with the superego, wherein he also situates fantasy as a mechanism of concealment, which then belongs again to the superego.[72] Although, I overall agree with McGowan's analysis, if we want to get to the methodologically promising notion of fantasy *qua* legal form we need to focus on the fact of legal duality: public law/superego. If we connect legal form entirely to the superego it will not be wrong per se, but, nonetheless, such an approach is going to leave us with an epistemologically weak concept of fantasy which does not allow us to account for mutual transactions between two fantasmatic levels of public law and its obscene supplement, superego.

Second, Fabio Vighi proposes to conceive legal form as an overlap of explicit text and its disawoved-yet-fully-operative remainder, Vighi adds 'this overlap is by definition ambiguous since it captures both the coercive capacity of the law and its intrinsic, fundamental impotence'.[73] I claim Vighi's conceptualization of legal form is more methodologically sound since it enables us to count in the textual side of law, which is also a phenomenal side of law because our everyday contact with it is perceivable through its textuality and institutional base, while the superego remains hidden under the side of these juristic encounters. Vighi's concept of legal form is not elaborated further but Vighi, building on Žižek's insights, leaves us with an idea that I will try to mould into a methodological tool for critique of legal form. Vighi offers an indicia for such a project in connecting strategy of subversion with identification with law's lack, that is lack of fundamental justification and ambiguity stemming from a split between command and transgression:

> [I]f law and power are inherently inconsistent, 'lacking to themselves,' then, Žižek often argues, the strategy of subversion most likely to succeed involves not actively opposing the law but, as it were, endorsing its total grasp, fully identifying with it, so that the inconsistency might emerge as a destabilizing factor.[74]

In my opinion, Vighi goes a little bit further than McGowan and gives us more of a manoeuvring space for analysing legal form in terms of its critique.

72 McGowan (n 69) 144.
73 Vighi (n 64) 84.
74 ibid.

That is why I opt for Vighi's reading, not to mention McGowan's reading is already included in that of Vighi, so my further analysis is not to be understood as a dismissal of McGowan; rather, the opposite is true.

It is clear from the psychoanalytic views of legal form outlined above that McGowan neglects precisely what most common-sense non-Marxist alike legal dogmatists would consider to be legal form, that is law's textuality as a site of formal procedures, legislature, interpretative methods; in short, formalistic *lex artis*.[75] As fine as such view is from a psychoanalytic standpoint, which enduring agenda was to go against the grain of commonsensical thinking, we cannot neglect legal textuality as the level of libidinal investment, or the level of superegoic representation, or even as Peter Goodrich allegorically puts it:

> [L]aw enacts the symbolic form of human relationship and gives effect to those unconscious forces which would otherwise remain in the hands of the magician, the soothsayer, the diviner or the evil women who invoke the powers of Satan to perform impossible acts or to represent an invisible order of past or future causes.[76]

I do not intend to say that we should privilege textuality at the expense of criticizing the superego, because that would basically mean going back to the orthodoxy of symptomatic analysis and maybe, in effect, going back to ideology as false consciousness presuming the existence of the 'authentic reality' out there. Promoting this would send everything previously written down the drain. What I intend to do is to bring level of textuality (public law) and obscene underside (superego) together and to conceptualize this as legal form, which fantasmatic mechanism corresponds to that of fetishistic fantasy of commodity form, structuring our reality in a topsy-turvy way and concealing various manifestations of the Real within the Symbolic structure.[77] This way, we can arrive at a compact general notion of legal form, which is consistent with today's psychoanalysis-inspired critique of ideology and at the same time with Pashukanis' findings. With a dash of irony, we can look at it as a form of a contract: legal form provides fantasmatic critique with better understanding of its legal implications, and in return, phantasmatic critique provides legal form with explanation of its internal mechanism.[78]

75 Compare Brian Z Tamanaha, 'A Non-Essentialist Version of Legal Pluralism' (2000) 27 *J L and Soc* 296; Michael P Foran, 'The Rule of Good Law: Form, Substance, and Fundamental Rights' (2013) 78 *Cam LR* 570.

76 Peter Goodrich, *Law in Courts of Love: Literature and Other Minor Jurisprudences* (Routledge 2013) 169.

77 Pashukanis (n 3) 41.

78 Similar kind of contract was about to be concluded between Sigmund Freud and Hans Kelsen. Freud was supposed to provide Kelsen with psychoanalytic justification of pure

The starting point of connecting legal form and fantasy is that law is split between public law and superego. This necessarily requires the mechanism of covering tracks of splitting and mediating between the two halves. Initial need to understand the form of law in a dual configuration can be already read in Ronald Weitzer, stating:

> [capitalist legal apparatuses] operate independently to secure the common interests of capital by (1) juridically organizing and unifying the interests of isolated capitalist units, such as, for instance, disciplining wayward capitalists by commanding conformity to the dictates of a rationalized, predictable formal legal procedure and (2) organizing class struggle in such a way that general capitalists interests are protected from threatening antagonistic interests via mechanisms of legal repression, mystification, displacement, and exclusion, all of which restrict the scope of possible events within legal channels.[79]

At first glance, this split has nothing to do with the Lacanian notion of split law. But a closer look reveals that the administration of the class struggle would be nothing else than the administration of the social antagonism, that is, of the Real. Weitzer's division thus corresponds to a division in the sphere of public law, in a sense of describing tasks of capitalist legal apparatuses. But at the same time, this division refers to class struggle as something that traumatizes such administration; something that serves as a condition of the law and simultaneously, its threat.

Weitzer continues in assertion that what we call a subject is, in fact, an invention of the law itself. Now, we can recall Lacan and the law of signifier creating the subject, but to apply this to legal form means we need to be more precise, Weitzer, referring to Paul Hirst and Nicos Poulantzas says that:

> [I]t is in the law that men are constituted as subjects in the commodity form. Law interpellates individuals as possessive subjects. In this manner, law and juridical ideology originally contributed to the formal isolation or separation of social actors in order that they could be inserted into private property relations and capitalist labor practices. . . . The function of legitimacy shifts towards the impersonal and abstract instance of law at the very time that the agents 'loosen' and 'free' themselves from their personal-territorial bonds. It is exactly as if the abstract, formal and

theory of law, namely, showing that juridical order is autonomous from the collective will and subjective identification (law is situated in superego) and Kelsen, in return, would show that constitutional democracy will not do without psychoanalysis, see Balibar (n 62) 400.

79 Roland Weitzer, 'Law and Legal Ideology: Contributions to the Genesis and Reproduction of Capitalism' (1980) 25 *BJS* 137.

general character of law had rendered it the mechanism most suitable for fulfilling the key function of every ideology: namely cementing together the social formation.[80]

The 'as if' almost always marks some kind of uncertainty about how things appear to us, in a sense that if we make a shift in our point of view, things start to appear 'as if' they may be different. Superegoic imperative 'enjoy!' is what can make the 'as if' disappear, because it gives insight into what the capitalist operational mechanism essentially does: first, it creates an abstraction of a free subject; then, this subject is attached to the big Other by desire, and finally subject is through the object-cause of desire (*object a*) inaugurated into the realm of eternal enjoyment as a combination of pain and pleasure mixed in deferral of achieving the desired object. Phantasmatic frame structures our reality precisely as a stand-in for a void of the subject, placing into the void the mythical *object a*. Superego, as a remainder of signification and imaginary identification with fantasy creating the ego, is the whip that steers this mechanism, at the end of which stands the subject as an apparently free consumer and worker destined to enjoy for the desire is unsatisfiable and subject is unconsciously guilty for never enjoying enough. Put another way, what cements the social formation is the superegoic injunction to enjoy which, through the mechanism of legal form, pertains to the law's textuality as well as juridical principles.

So, not only does the emergence of law coincide with the emergence of free and rational agents, but more radically, what is created by legal form is the illusion that the legal subject is free and rational *thanks to the law*. Law creates a narrative of emancipatory force letting the subject breathe freely, and this subject supposedly becomes free even from the law itself, because desire and enjoyment seem to be strongly non-legal and non-ideological forces. Thus, the sophisticated trick played by law is that it creates a neutral framework, a sort of a playing field, where subjects are fully in charge of themselves and law as a coercive force is never present in their lives because the law is 'closed' in the textuality of codes; what remains is a space for indulging in private pleasures. Lacanian lesson here is that in:

> [T]he 'Discourse of Capitalism' we encounter rejection or better foreclosure of castration (symbolization), while this foreclosure happens when society more and more functions without limits and where there seems to be a constant push towards some kind of limitless *jouissance*. This push to *jouissance* at all costs is especially visible in all kind of forms of addiction—from excessive consumption of alcohol, drugs, shopping, workaholism and so on. Capitalism more and more transforms the

80 ibid 142–44.

proletarian slave into free consumer. However, limitless consumption paradoxically provokes the moment when the subject starts 'consuming himself'.[81]

The foreclosure of symbolization denotes law relinquishing its coercive function clearing the space for infinite pleasure. Law plays the role of a tool that can be used by endlessly creative subjects in various ways to actualize her freedom and quench her desires. But we can see that nowadays, we are far from being free from the law *qua* superego. As Pierre Legendre once remarked,

> the term enjoyment, if one gives it the meaning which psychoanalysis borrowed from Law, simply refers to the inscription of the human body in the mythological order of an unconscious fantasm . . . the fantasm has to capture and regulate the desires of the group.[82]

Conclusion

In this brief exposé are contained a few operational functions of the legal fantasy: 1) covering of constitutive split of law; 2) creation of 'free and equal subject' and 3) displacing law's force into the textual realm. But the 'microphysics of power', to use the words of Michel Foucault, is not reducible to codes or formal legal procedures. As we can see, the power of late capitalism lies in its ability to recognize the potential of superegoic force creating consuming subjects who are not able to see the political predicament in the lack of any true political choice. This lack is concealed by the possibility of choice between goods and services. And is not precisely what fetishism of commodity form means, in a sense that the subject's belief is displaced onto things, who believe instead of a subject? What Marx called 'social relations between things' is that originally human belief is incorporated into things which believe in the place of humans;[83] and from this traditionally Marxist assertion, we can infer that if commodities appear as free in terms of their movement and dissemination, and equal because they are commensurable through money; then we feel free and equal as well.

Another aspect is that, as we have seen, law is linked to its own transgression through enjoyment. It seems like the inherent contradiction between the form of command on the side of superego, that is unconditional command

81 Renata Salecl, 'Worries in a Limitless World' in Peter Goodrich, Lior Barshack, and Anton Schütz (eds), *Law, Text, Terror* (Glass House Press 2006) 138.

82 Peter Goodrich (ed), *Law and the Unconscious, A Legendre Reader* (Macmillan 1999) 129 cited in Adam Gearey, *Legal Aesthetics* (Hart Publishing 2001) 40.

83 Slavoj Žižek, *The Plague of Fantasie* (Verso 2008) 135.

'enjoy!', and the content of law in codes and legal documents, produces energy that drives the law. As Lacan commented:

> without a transgression there is no access to jouissance, and, to return to Saint Paul, that that is precisely the function of the Law. Transgression in the direction of jouissance only takes place if it is supported by the oppositional principle, by the forms of the Law.[84]

Lacan here clearly refers to the words of the apostle Paul in Romans (7:7): 'What then shall we say? That the law is sin? By no means! Yet if it had not been for the law, I would not have known sin.[85]

But law and transgression are not to be considered as some kind of 'ying and yang' or a binary opposition, however mutually connected; rather, to be precise, we ought to understand them as 'communicating vessels', where the word 'communicating' is to be taken literally. When thinking about law and transgression, we have something to do with the short circuit between the two: 'it is the Law itself that not only opens up and sustains the domain of sin, of sinful urges to transgress it, but also finds a perverse and morbid satisfaction in making us feel guilty about it'.[86]

In a similar manner, we can think about capitalism and its constitutive contradiction, allowing it to accommodate every obstacle into itself and generate power; to put it in a somewhat simplistic metaphor, capital's metabolism is able to turn virtually any trash into fuel. The connection of capitalist logic and legal form is more profound and does not rest on a mere similarity. A good example is illustrated by Laurent de Sutter showing, that the war on drugs conducted in the name of noble law (and the principle of restriction of pleasure) is what fuels the market and industry as well as the power of legal apparatuses:

> [T]he role played by the coke trade in the history of industrial development, as well as the model the substance represented in the turn to financialization, should have made us suspect that there was more going on with capitalism than simple amorality. Rather than a system accompanying (and even, largely, supported by) the powder that fascinated Freud, capitalism should be thought of as being completely innervated by it—in that it constitutes its energy, its substance, its goal and its model.[87]

84 Jacques Lacan, *The Ethics of Psychoanalysis* (Routledge 1992) 177.

85 Three most famous readings of St. Paul are provided by Giorgio Agamben (*The Time that Remains: A Commentary on the Letter to the Romans*), Slavoj Žižek (*On Belief; Ticklish Subject)*, Alain Badiou *(Saint Paul: The Foundation of Universalism*).

86 Žižek (n 42) 150.

87 Laurent De Sutter, *Narcocapitalism: Life in the Age of Anaesthesia* (Polity Press 2018) 43.

From such perspective, recalling Pashukanis' thesis that legal fetishism complements commodity fetishism,[88] we can finally say that it is only because capitalism and legal form share the very same logic, the logic of fantasy.[89]

This proves my initial claim that updating the work of Pashukanis and Marx with a psychoanalytic ideology critique is not only possible but also necessary. If the legal form is to be understood as a methodological tool to trace 'historical, economic, and political conditions where exchanges of legal positions take place',[90] then the radical critique of law consists in its ability to point to the essential characteristics of legal form and situate them in certain historical and material conditions.[91] This requires that we adopt a rigorous epistemic frame allowing for mapping the current logic of connection between capital and law. Further development of the phantasmatic logic can provide us with a lucid and schematic sense of how legal form operates in contemporary settings, thus giving us a potentially strong critical tool to engage with the ideological mechanism underlying legal structure.

88 Although Pierre Legendre never elaborated further on the intersection of law and fantasy, it is possible to see few allusions on potential benefit of broader theory of legal fantasy: 'Illustratively, I would say: any system explains itself out of its own dogmatic field, the equivalent of a fantasy scene where, if I dare say, the primordial truths take shape'. Pierre Legendre, *Le désir politique de Dieu: étude sur les montagnes, de l'état et du droit* (Fayard 1988) 59–60.

89 Pashukanis (n 3) 14; and Jason Glynos, 'There is no Other of the Other Symptoms of a Decline in Symbolic Faith, or, Žižek's Anti-capitalism' (2001) 24(2) Paragraph 78.

90 Gianfrancesco Zanetti, Mortimer Sellers, and Stephan Kirste (eds), *Handbook of the History of the Philosophy of Law and Social Philosophy, vol 3: From Ross to Dworkin and Beyond* (Springer 2023) 236.

91 Compare Brian Leiter, 'Radicalism of Legal Positivism' (2010) University of Chicago Law School, Public Law and Legal Theory Working Paper 303.

Chapter 5

On the 'relative' autonomy of the modern form of law

From Marx and Engels to Althusser*

Eduardo A. Chia

Introduction

The assertion of law's autonomy presents a conundrum. It suggests an ideal whereby law operates by itself, according to its own, yet its practical realisation emerges only within a network of interrelations and structures that determine it. One observes a tension between the aspiration for a self-sufficient law and its actual interrelatedness within society, which echoes the tension between agency and social dependence. Considering the law's ties to politics, morals and economic motions, the feasibility of autonomous law is questionable. However, negating its autonomy altogether compromises the law's claim to possess a unique self-standing status, potentially reducing it to an adjunct of morality or a mere device of political power. Therefore, the assertion of juridical autonomy proves ontologically, epistemically and politically significant. It underscores the law's reflexivity, enabling legal developments through its institutions and procedures. Likewise, it affirms the law's distinct methodologies and language as a separate discipline. Additionally, it reveals the law's political potential for emancipation. Simultaneously, however, the law is responsive as it reacts to, and processes, external social determinants.

The development of normative orders stems from dynamic historical interactions, leading to complex interrelations amongst myriad norms. Accordingly, entirely autonomous systems of norms developing in isolation are unrealistic because world phenomena are interwoven. Yet, recognising this interconnectedness cannot lead one to state the reductive view that everything in the world is relational. Thus, examining the

* The author thanks Javier Burdman, Daniel Dodds, José Duarte Daniel McLoughlin and Igor Shoikhedbrod for their insightful comments and reviews of early drafts of this work. The paper also benefited from the feedback received during the workshop on legal form organised by Nomos Centre at Jagiellonian University Kraków (April 14–15, 2023). Errors or inconsistencies that persist in the text are solely the author's responsibility. The study was funded by the National Agency for Research and Development of the Republic of Chile (ANID)/ DOCTORADO BECAS CHILE/2020-722104830.

DOI: 10.4324/9781032724713-6

specific nature of relationality and dependencies of law, which is simultaneously independent and influenced by other systems and phenomena, merits scholarly attention. This dilemma has prompted some legal scholars to suggest an aporetic combination: 'law's relative autonomy'. However, how could the law be autonomous and concurrently non-autonomous? For something being 'relative' suggests dependence and the presence of connections with other entities. Accordingly, the question arises: what exactly is 'relative' about the relative autonomy of law?

This chapter contributes to this debate by investigating the theoretical origins, intellectual development and articulation of the idea of the modern legal form's 'relative' autonomy. It argues that jurisprudential studies informed by Marx's and Engels' materialist-dialectical conception of history provide a theoretical basis for the 'relative autonomy of law'. These approaches suggested the conceptual compatibility between autonomy and determination, highlighting the law's self-determined reflexivity as concurrently responsive to and ineluctably dependent on the social whole's structures. Likewise, the chapter seeks to elucidate how selected scholarly interpretations build upon, diverge from and critically assess Marx's and Engels' original ideas while evaluating their strengths and limitations. Ultimately, the work will showcase discursive continuities and discontinuities within this paradigm. The chapter bridges historical and philosophical insights with jurisprudence, suggesting that scepticism towards law in materialist-dialectic law approaches targets not its concept but its modern form.

Study structure

Section one examines Marx and Engels' base and superstructure metaphor. It focuses on debates over the societal structure levels' self-standing movements *vis-à-vis* their determination by the material base. Engels' late clarifications are revisited to emphasise how he rejected determinism and economic reductionism. Section three revisits Karl Renner's and Franz Neumann's critical reworking of the base-superstructure model. From a legal-sociological perspective, they explored the interplay between legal order, economic conditions and social forces, challenging further deterministic approaches. Part four analyses the debate on law's 'relative' autonomy within Anglophone socio-legal scholarship, mainly through Isaac Balbus' perspective. This discussion reflects a transatlantic extension of the debates that Marx, Engels, Renner and Neumann initiated. Part five centres on Louis Althusser's contributions to comprehending law's relative autonomy. Althusser also critiqued deterministic views and introduced the concepts of structural causality and overdetermination to illustrate the dynamic interplay between economic substrate and superstructural instances. He re-signifies the base-superstructure model, introducing elements that amplify our understanding of how necessity, contingency and the tension between autonomy and determination operate within a complex social totality. Towards the end some concluding remarks are presented.

Tracing the source: base and superstructure

Marx's and Engels' thoughts offer conceptual precedents of contemporary discussions about 'relative' autonomy (of law). Namely, apropos of the dialectical interplay between material substructure (*Basis*) and superstructure (*Überbau*).[1] In the few texts where Marx and Engels resort to this scheme, they suggest that a social formation is composed of material bedrock upon which different ideas are mounted; these levels are both infrastructure-dependent but still identifiable as distinct self-sufficient edification parts. They contend that material relations of production are invisible, while what is noticeable are the structure's juridical-political façades. Hence, underlying conditions that make the entire edifice possible are not immediately discernible. Attention must be paid to the base supporting the building—the actual effectuation of relations of possession and property.

The figure of the optical inversion—the reflection—often employed by Marx and Engels, provides the same logic. The distorted reflected image shows the structure's upper levels as deceptively self-contained as if they were causes and not the bedrock's effects. The metaphor's argumentative merit is not necessarily explanatory or justificatory but might be a device of analogical reasoning or literary style whereby Marx and Engels illustrate their materialist-dialectic conception of history.[2] Despite this, considerable controversy and misunderstanding have stemmed from it. The place and function of law in this metaphor are also contentious, for the juridical forms were exemplarily presented as belonging to the ideological superstructure. This last suggestion opened debates and divergent interpretations.

On the one hand, certain theorists have dismissed the edifice model, arguing that legal relations and relations of production are equiprimordial. They

1 See Karl Marx and Friedrich Engels, *Die Deutsche Ideologie*, MEW vol 3 (first published 1846, Dietz 1969) 37–39; Karl Marx, *Vorwort zur Kritik der politischen Ökonomie*, MEW vol 13 (first published 1858, Dietz 1971) 8; Karl Marx, *Das Kapital*, vol III, MEW vol 25 (first published 1894, Dietz 1983) 799–800, ch XLVII, s 6. In different writings throughout their oeuvre, Marx and Engels also referred to the terms: *Konstruktion*, *Gestaltung*, *Gliederung*, *Unterbau*, *Superstruktur* and *Struktur*.

2 Ludóvico Silva, *El Estilo Literario de Marx* (Siglo XXI 1971) 57 ff. Cf. Siegbert Prawer, *Karl Marx and World Literature* (Verso 2011) 293–301; Raymond Williams, *Marxism and Literature* (OUP 1977) 75–82. In a different register, Stuart Hall, 'Rethinking the 'Base-and-Superstructure' Metaphor' in Jon Bloomfield (ed), *Papers on Class, Hegemony, Party* (Lawrence & Wishart 1977) 43–72, provides a clear explanation relying on Marx's and Engels' writings.

emerge concurrently, constituting the foundational elements of social structures. In this view, law would be integrated within the material infrastructure from inception.[3] On the other hand, further scholars, aligning more closely with Marx's and Engels' perspectives, situate law within the superstructure. The debate here centres on whether (i) law is mechanically determined solely by economic relations[4] or (ii) whether law displays *an extent of* reflexivity, manifesting as a capacity for self. At this stage, the idea of 'relative autonomy' was introduced to provide a qualification that helps discern the extent to which law has room for self-standing drives while remaining within a sphere of prior determination. Admittedly, according to this group of authors, it is a postulate that law is to be grasped as dialectically determined from antagonistic forces, simultaneously responsive and integral to a dynamically differentiated social *totality*.

By juridical self-determination, I refer to the process described by Hegel.[5] He suggested that the concept of law attains actuality as it manifests in positive existence autonomously. Consequently, it becomes a determinate particularity, embodying the formal universality of a specific sphere within the social whole.

Revisiting Engels' elucidation

Friedrich Engels raised some of the divergence's sources in understanding the interrelations between base and superstructure. In late works[6] and let-

3 EP Thomson, *Whigs and Hunters* (Allen Lane 1975) 261 supports this view: '[L]aw was deeply imbricated within the very basis of productive relations'. It implies that law is not merely a superstructural element shaped by the economic base but woven into the fabric of relations of production from the outset. See also, E.P. Thomson, *The Poverty of Theory* (Merlin Press 1978) 130 '[law] was imbricates within the mode of production and productive relations themselves'.

4 Pashukanis might be included in this hypothesis, especially considering his writings on the commodity form theory of law. Here, he suggests that legal forms are determined not by the relations of production but by commodity exchanges, equating legal relations to (social) exchange relations to some extent. See Evgeny Pashukanis, *The General Theory of Law and Marxism* (first published 1924, Barbara Einhorn tr, Transactions 2003). In later essays, a more sensitive Pashukanis towards the dialectical interplay between the base and superstructure and the prominence of relations of productions nuanced earlier assertions and hinted at a more decisive role of the juridical superstructure in law-determination process; thus, the author took distance from the idea of law as reflecting exchange relations. See esp. Evgeny Pashukanis, *Selected Writings on Marxism and Law* (Piers Beirne and Robert Sharlet eds, Peter Maggs tr, Academic Press 1980) 296–97. The article was entitled 'Marxist Theory of State and Law' (1932).

5 GWF Hegel, *Grundlinien der Philosophie des Rechts* (first published 1820, Felix Meiner 2013) § 207.

6 Friedrich Engels, *Ursprung der Familie, des Privateigenthums und des Staats,* MEW vol 21 (first published 1884, Dietz 1975); *Herrn Eugen Dühring's Umwälzung der Wissenschaft,*

ters on the meaning of the materialist conception of history,[7] he insisted on correcting their writings' mechanistic and reductionist readings. These misinterpretations presented a stationary rigidity of the social structure whereby the economy is *causa causans* as a single driver of epiphenomena. On the one hand, Engels acknowledges that the ultimate determining or decisive instance in history is the material production and reproduction of actual life ('*ökonomischen Bedingungen als das in letzter Instanz*').[8] On the other hand, this author hints that superstructural moments would have, to say, *own-account drives* for deploying concrete forms and even influence the mode of production through a dynamic dialectical interaction (*Wechselwirkung*) of uneven contradictory forces.[9] Engels' nuanced perspectives on non-determinism, complemented by Marx's writings,[10] triggered fruitful debates about the metaphor's meaning.[11] The dominant interpretation, particularly influential in the early 20th century, was shaped significantly by the pragmatic needs of Marxist-oriented political parties' agendas. Considerable readings during this period were not necessarily committed to a scientific analysis of Marx's and Engels' original texts.

Regarding the notion of 'relative autonomy', Marx and Engels did not explicitly refer to the *autonomy* of superstructural levels. Their approach to this term was cautious. Why intervene a term at the time significant for the Kantian moral philosophy, already complex and contentious, with an adjective? Nonetheless, Engels did employ the phrase '*relativen Selbständigkeit*', which translates to relative 'autonomy' or 'independence'. Although Engels elaborated on this subject in a series of letters, they have

MEW vol 20 (first published 1877, Dietz 1962); henceforth: *Anti-Dühring*; *Ludwig Feuerbach und der Ausgang der klassischen deutschen Philosophie*, MEW vol 21 (first published 1886, Dietz 1975) ch IV; henceforth: *Feuerbach*.

7 On law, amongst other things, see Friedrich Engels, *Brief an Joseph Bloch in Königsberg* (21 September 1890); *Brief an Conrad Schmidt in Berlin*, MEW vol 37 (first published 5 August 1890 and 27 October 1890, Dietz 1967) 462–65, 435–38, 488–95. *Brief an Franz Mehring in Berlin* (14 July 1893); *Brief an Walter Borgius in Breslau*, MEW vol 39 (first published 25 January 1894, Dietz 1968) 96–101, 205–8.

8 ibid. Engels to Walter Borgius, 206. Cf. Karl Marx, *Grundrisse der Kritik der politischen Ökonomie*, MEW, vol. 42 (first published 1858, Dietz 1983) 383 ff. esp. 403. Although these writings were preliminary drafts, here Marx suggests that the economy—producing and reproducing actual living conditions—is the ultimate determinant (*die letzte Instanz*) of superstructural developments.

9 ibid. Engels to Joseph Bloch, 463. Cf. Marx and Engels (n 1) 38.

10 Marx, *Vorwort* (n 1) 8. Cf. Karl Marx, *Einleitung zur Kritik der politischen Ökonomie*, MEW vol 13 (first published 1857, Dietz 1971) 640; see also Marx and Engels (n 1) 25 and Karl Marx, *Kritik des Gothaer Programms*, MEW vol 19 (first published 1891, Dietz 1973) 21.

11 On this debate, the literature is voluminous. An updated summary providing multiple references and sources can be found in the Legal Form blog: <>https://legalform.blog/archive/>.

been considered documents of significant scholarly value (*Engels Philosophische Altersbriefe*[12]). While explaining and systematising what he called 'materialist-dialectic', Engels emphasised that the superstructural developments acquired vitality of their own accord—independent existence—albeit primarily due to the motions of economic production. Nonetheless, superstructural moments are reacting continuously to the march of the economy and may modify it within certain limits. Engels' dialectical reasoning stressed that there is no room for crude determinism and that the societal totality is a matrix of complex dynamic forces' movements. There is compatibilism between autonomy and determination, contingency and necessity. Engels' elucidations are frequently misrepresented. They are prime scholarly sources of the law's 'relative' autonomy, later developed by subsequent authors. To illustrate the original idea, let us reproduce two cases discussed by Engels: politics and law.

Concerning the first one, Engels observed that politics pursues its own course by its inherent (*innewohnenden*) relative independence. This force for self-movement has, in turn, been transferred to it from the material relations of production and then gradually develops by itself. Overall, the economic movement prevails on a large scale, but it must also suffer a retroaction (*Rückwirkung*) from the political action that has instituted itself (*selbst eingesetzten*).[13] As for the second case, Engels illustrates the superstructure's relative autonomy regarding *Jus*. He says that legality unfolding corresponds to the economy in a modern state as it is its expression (*ihr Ausdruck sein*). However, law must have a certain coherence and internal logic, even to the extent that the ruling class cannot thoroughly instrumentalise it; otherwise, it would destroy the concept of law. He wrote: 'Und dies um so mehr, je seltner es vorkommt, daß ein Gesetzbuch der schroffe, ungemilderte, unverfälschte Ausdruck der Herrschaft einer Klasse ist: Das wäre ja selbst schon gegen den *Rechtsbegriff*'.[14] In other words, the law would be redundant if utterly instrumentalised, stripped of any autonomy.

Engels then discusses compulsory inheritance portions and the institution of mandatory heirs in continental Europe, contrasting these with the testamentary freedom in England. The inheritance of a patrimony has a materialist background. Nevertheless, it takes more than the economy's operation alone to determine the different concrete juridical forms that developed in the succession systems in Britain and the continent. Legal restrictions on testamentary liberty seek to protect the family's weaker parts while attempting

12 Consider that some of the ideas from the later Engels were more systematically articulated in his work Engels, *Feuerbach* (n 6). During that period, Engels endeavoured to explain and clarify Marx's works and his own, besides replying to misrepresentations and superficial readings of their writings. Cf. Gareth Stedman Jones 'Engels and the end of Classical German Philosophy' (1973) 79 *NLR* 17–36.

13 Engels to Conrad Schmidt, 490.

14 ibid 491. (Italics in the original). Cf. Marx, *Kapital III* (n 1) 801.

to distribute assets. In the latter case, the legal regulation of estate allocation may impact the performance of bourgeois material relations. The combination of freedom and solidarity of the Roman-based succession law systems is not usual in common law jurisdictions. It is a contextual feature of continental legal orders based on civil law tradition. If the economic imperatives of bourgeois society had been the primary determining factor, the codification of modern Western European inheritance systems would have adopted legal models boosting the free transmission of estates and the tendency to concentrate ownership. However, automatic conformity to purely bourgeois interests did not occur fully, indicating an extent of juridical autonomy.

Although no longer directly referring to the law, in other writings, Engels proposed the notion of 'certain independence' (*gewisse Selbständigkeit*) of the state[15] against its capture by the ruling classes. Exceptionally, Engels wrote, there have been concrete moments when the feuding social forces maintain such a close balance between them that the state power, as a mediator, momentarily acquires a 'certain independence' *vis-à-vis* both.[16] Notably, given historical contingencies, the state autonomously has balanced class antagonisms in a self-preserving function to safeguard the interests of those who have succeeded in imposing their rule. From this argument, one cannot infer the relative autonomy of law but of the state. Now, someone may think that since the modern state enacts laws, an alteration in lawmaking functions would also carry inevitable changes in the legal form. Nevertheless, this interpretation denies any law's autonomy because it reduces legality to the state's fate. Although the form of modern law is intimately related to the state, it is not reducible to the latter. Unifying the law's moves with that of the state presents practical and theoretical problems and does not seem like Marx's or Engels' suggestion.[17]

Marx's examination of the English Factory Acts[18] is another illustrative case of the juridical's 'relative' autonomy and law dialectical determination

15 Cf. Engels (n 6) 301. '... der Staat nicht ein selbständiges Gebiet mit selbständiger Entwicklung ist, sondern sein Bestand wie seine Entwicklung in *letzter Instanz* zu erklären ist aus den ökonomischen Lebensbedingungen der Gesellschaft'. (Emphasis added).

16 Engels (n 6) 167.

17 Marx and Engels criticised the modern notion of enacted positive laws (*Gesetze*) as expressing the people's general will, which the state operationalises by sanctioning them (actually, the ruling class will). In the *Deutsche Ideologie*, they indicated, for example, that those who govern must express the general will as the will of the state, as laws, expressions whose content is predominantly given by class relations, as private and criminal law proof. See Marx and Engels (n 1) 311. Similar thoughts Marx wrote in *Der achtzehnte Brumaire des Louis Bonaparte*, MEW vol 8 (first published 1852, Dietz 1960) 196, and in *Manifest der Kommunistischen Partei*, MEW vol 4 (first published 1848, Dietz 1972) 477. There is little evidence that they assimilated modern law into the bourgeois state.

18 Karl Marx, *Das Kapital*, vol I, MEW vol 23 (first published 1867, Dietz 1962) ch VIII, sec. 6–7, 294–319. I also considered Daniel McLoughlin and Talina Hürzeler, 'Marx on the Factory Acts: Law, Exploitation and Class Struggle' in Paul O'Connell and Umut Özsu (eds),

within the schema of base and superstructure. Originally legislated to ameliorate working conditions, these laws were the product of social struggles enacted on a political-economic terrain determined mainly by buoyant industrial capitalist production. Thus, while these statutes improved workers' quality of life, they paradoxically also served the capitalist system's long-term stability and efficiency in 19th-century England by *appearing* to be concessions to the working class. The enactment and application of the Factory Acts reveal concrete moments whereby bourgeois law operated 'relatively' autonomously. While influenced by the economic substrate and the dominant class's immediate interests, this legislative intervention opened new juridical avenues, though limited, for activism and reformist struggles (subsequently extended beyond Britain). Social and political pressures functioned as epiphenomena and contributed to the reconfiguration of modern law and the economy's run. This dialectical interaction exemplifies how the law is produced or determined by social forces and simultaneously produces or determines by itself material realities. It allowed historically marginalised groups to assert their claims through legal forms and contest established social hierarchies, concurrently affirming a strengthened economic performance. Accordingly, Marx's analysis of the Factory Acts illustrates, to a certain extent, in a concrete episode of the English industrialisation process, the law's reflexivity for adaptation and transformation and its ultimate responsiveness to the structure.

Marx's and Engels' discourse on the superstructure's 'relative' autonomy is fragmentary and unsystematic. Likewise, their limited exploration of law leads one to develop a reconstructive interpretation. Despite that, it is paramount to consider that they envisioned the potential for the autonomy of the legal form, mainly hinting at the consequences of the law concept's destruction. Indeed, by laying conceptual antecedents for addressing law's reflexivity and responsive integration within societal structures, Marx and Engels laid the groundwork for future theorists to elaborate further on law's 'relative' autonomy.

'Relative' autonomy of law early legal scholarship: Karl Renner and Franz Neumann

In the early 20th century, authors related to the social-democratic parties in Austria and Germany critically reinterpreted Marx and Engels based on continental legal sociology. Karl Renner, a member of the Austro-Marxist currents, and Franz Neumann, associated with the Frankfurt School, shed some light on the law's relative autonomy. They attempted to transcend orthodox base-superstructure interpretation, emphasising the complex dynamics

Research Handbook on Law and Marxism (Edward Elgar 2021) 21 ff. See also *infra* note N° 83.

between legal forms, social forces and economic motions. Their approach scrutinised the assumed rigidity of mechanical causalism and challenged the deterministic influence of the economic substrate on juridical and other superstructural forms.

Renner's questioning

Through an analysis of the writings of Marx and Engels, Renner[19] postulated the existence of interrelationships between various elements within a socio-economic whole.[20] He postulated that the emergence of the capitalist mode of production engendered a functional transformation in private law, diverging from its previous social functions. Renner argues that structural alterations in the legal form of private property were notably absent despite shifts in material development. Thus, while the economic base underwent substantial changes, the legal forms persisted, albeit with altered social functions. Thus his investigation aimed to demonstrate that 'der juristische Überbau vom ökonomischen Unterbau, seinem Substrat, völlig unabhängig ist, daß die Änderung des Rechtssystems aus anderen Quellen fließen müsse als aus der Wirtschaft'.[21]

Renner's analysis critically challenges the notion of legal forms as automatic extensions of the economic *substratum*, prompting some inquiries. If the relations of production are determinant for the functioning of a legal order, does this mean that legal forms are reducible to mere reflections of the economic order? Conversely, if certain legal forms are indispensable to the processes of production, exchange and circulation of commodities, does this suggest that the economy might be entirely subordinate to the legal order? Renner's empirically grounded, functional and socio-historical analysis negates both by introducing contingency. He argues that modifications in the social functions of law, particularly in private law norms, are not necessarily contingent upon shifts in the socio-economic base, especially when the latter remains unaltered. Likewise, transformations in the material base do not automatically precipitate changes in the law's social functions, which may remain static.[22] Consequently, technological advancements accompanying the development of productive forces while potentially catalysing social change do not inevitably lead to legal transformations. Similarly, changes in

19 Karl Renner, under the pseudonym Josef Karner, had published an essay called *Die soziale Funktion der Rechtsinstitute, besonders des Eigentums* in the Austromarxist journal *Marx-Studien, vol 1 (1904)*. The fundamental theses of the 1929 book are already stated in this work. The 1929 edition was a version intended for a broader audience.

20 Karl Renner, *Die Rechtsinstitute des Privatrechts und ihre soziale Funktion: ein Beitrag zur Kritik des bürgerlichen Rechts* (first published 1929, Gustav Fischer 1965) 58–63.

21 ibid 172.

22 ibid 60.

law do not uniformly exert a decisive influence on societal evolution. That is why he remarked that 'the relation between individuals and natural objects, the technical power of humans, the individual productive force, *develops under the eyes of the law, but not through the law itself*'.[23]

Renner implied that social and political forces might intervene and affect the interaction between the material substratum and legal forms. His observations on the historical development of law, recalling Engels' analysis of inheritance law and Napoleonic codification, emphasised the functional law variations independent of economic motions. This position made him question the prevailing deterministic interpretations about base and superstructure. Although he did not employ the same terminology, Renner's understanding involves postulating the case of a 'relatively' autonomous law. Upon these insights, Franz Neumann later expanded on the same topic.

Neumann's relative autonomy

Franz Neumann's work during the 1930s addressed law's 'relative' autonomy in a non-systematic fashion. Neumann's research programme sought to demonstrate the law's embeddedness in the socio-economic fabric, employing political and sociological arguments. Echoing Renner, Neumann reevaluated the social totality proposed by Marx and Engels, arguing against economic determinism. He posited that elements of the whole are dialectically interrelated, with no single dominant or determining factor. Incorporating a Hegelian[24] interpretation of Marx and revisiting Engels,[25] Neumann viewed the law as 'relatively autonomous' because 'legal forces' might evolve independently of the socio-economic base yet, under certain conditions, be influenced by it.

Neumann also contested the notion of the specific autonomous self-legality of law (*Eigengesetzlichkeit des Rechts*), challenging Hans Kelsen's *Pure Theor of Law*.[26] For Neumann, '[a] legal order for its own is unthinkable'.[27] His reservations emphasise constraints in Kelsen's epistemological approach, criticising a cognitively self-dependent law, which appears detached from

23 ibid 175. (Italics added). 'Das verhältnis Individuum-Naturding, die technisches Macht des Menschen, die individuelle Produktivkraft, entwickelt sich unter den Augen des Rechtes, aber nicht durch das Recht selbst'.

24 Franz Neumann, *The Rule of Law. Political Theory and the Legal System in Modern Society* (first published 1936, Berg 1986) 15–19. He references Hegel's *Grundlinien der Philosophie des Rechts*, particularly pointing to Hegel's commentary on Montesquieu in § 3. Hegel highlights Montesquieu's contention that legislation, both in its general and specific provisions, should not be viewed in isolation or abstractly. Instead, it should be regarded as a dependent component of a historical totality, interlinked with the myriad concrete determinations that define the character of a nation and an epoch.

25 References are to Engels' *Feuerbach* (n 6) ch IV.

26 Hans Kelsen, *Reine Rechtslehre* (first published 1934, Mohr Siebeck 2008).

27 Neumann (n 24) 17.

temporal and practical junctures in its pursuit of 'pureness'. This perspective suggests that while striving for theoretical aseity, Kelsen's account risks rendering law as a universal order, a timeless cognitive construct disassociated from societal life's actual relations that ultimately determine it. Yet Neumann objected not to the internal logical-conceptual soundness of the *Pure Theory* but to its little concern with concrete material reality, impracticality[28] and agnosticism concerning the question of law's ethical justification.[29] Neumann contends that Kelsen's notion of legal autonomy falls short of accounting for the complex ways law is embedded in societal structures. He argued, e.g., that legal transformations 'do not fall from the blue', *ex nihilo*, but result from social processes.[30] Opposing Kelsenian normativistic legal positivism, he emphasised the dialectical interplay between law, material forces and social relations in law determination.

In some passages, Franz Neumann presented a distinction between 'state law' and 'autonomous law',[31] as well as between 'legal norm' and 'general norm'.[32] This delineation reveals the ambivalent duality in modern law, embodying tensions akin to *lex* v. *ius* and *voluntas* v. *ratio*. Neumann characterises state law as a construct of posited legal norms articulated through lawmakers' decisions. In contrast, autonomous law aligns with the normative (rational) law concept, expressed through general norms. This differentiation reveals a conflict: state law, as a product of political decision-making, may not always align with the more comprehensive (rational) concept of law. When this lack of correspondence occurs, the autonomy of the law would be jeopardised (or, as Neumann wrote, 'destroy[ed]'). Neumann's dialectical interpretation of law suggests that juridical autonomy encompasses a dual dimension. In what might be termed a formal sense, law's autonomy is achieved not merely by insulating it from external influences in its self-determination but also through obtaining distinctiveness from other normative orders, thereby ensuring its specificity. Concurrently, the substantial dimension implies that for law to attain autonomy, its self-determination must be grounded in rational normative principles. Thus, Neumann's perspective underscores the ongoing tension

28 ibid 26. 'The pure science of law may indeed be self-contained and self-consistent, but it solves no political problem whatsoever'.

29 ibid. 12–13. Equivalent disapproval was formulated earlier by Pashukanis regarding Kelsen's Pure Theory of Law; see General Theory (n 4) 51–52, 75–76. Regardless, these criticisms hold no weight for the early Kelsen, as his neo-Kantian-based theory is indefeasible against objections derived from factual circumstances, which he would consider ideological 'impurities' that impede true legal knowledge. Neumann's further criticism of the 'Pure Science of Law' is found in Franz Neumann, *Behemoth* (first published 1942, Ivan Dee 2009) 46–47. For Neumann's criticisms of Kelsen, see Stanley Paulson, 'Neumanns Kelsen', in Mattias Iser and David Strecker (eds), *Kritische Theorie der Politik. Franz L. Neumann—eine Bilanz* (Nomos 2002) 107–124.

30 Neumann (n 24) 19.

31 ibid 15, 284.

32 ibid; Renner (n 18) ch I.

and ambivalent balance between law as an expression of sovereign power and its commitment to normative principles of justice and reason.

This interpretation is supported by Neumann's references to Hegel's *Rechtsbegriff*, which is broadly understood as a specific form of juridical normativity immanently reconstructed from the fundamentals of rational law. This conception is comprehensive and more substantive than the formal, positive idea of law. In that respect, Neumann observed the likelihood of law being shattered at its rational core by unbridled forces. His famous dictum encapsulates this idea: a non-autonomous law bereft of rationality is reduced to a mystic ruling device for concealing the exercise of authoritarian power: an *arcanum dominationis*.[33] Neumann's alignment with Hegel, Engels and Marx is not only based on this standpoint. As mentioned, he also considered law an integral component of a complex dynamic social totality, assuming that its internal oppositional elements unfold by themselves and engage in dialectical interplay.

It was thus that, synthesising Renner's, Engels' and Pashukanis' ideas (what he called 'Marxian sociology'), Neumann stated: 'law may develop relatively independently of social reality',[34] as well as 'autonomous legal forces may drive [law] development in another direction to that of the social substructure . . . as law is . . . a real social relationship'.[35] In that vein, '[t]he independence of the legal system from social forces is, however, as has been indicated by Engels with great firmness, only a relative one'.[36] What is crucial in these passages is that Neumann figured out that claiming 'law and the state are relatively autonomous' seems to be a truism, a 'meaningless statement'. The fundamental theoretical challenge lies in unravelling what is specifically 'relative' to relative autonomy. Therefore,

> [t]he central task of a sociological investigation into the legal system consists in indicating . . . *the conditions* under which law and the state can develop relatively independently and . . . *the forces* which go to destroy this relative autonomy and subject the law and the state with full force to the stream of social realities.[37]

In these excerpts, Neumann acknowledges the law's autonomy by referring to 'legal forces', suggesting that law has its own momentum to independently drive its self-determination, albeit dependent on the social totality. This perspective echoes Engels' abovementioned[38] suggestion that despite

33 Regarding the concrete case of the German Nationalist Socialist legal order see, Neumann (n 24) 285, 298; Franz Neumann, 'Der Funktionswandel des Gesetzes im Recht der bürgerlichen Gesellschaft' (1937) 6 Zeitschrift für Sozialforschung 587; Neumann (n 29) 448, 467.

34 Neumann (n 24) 16.

35 ibid. Footnote n 25 was incorporated.

36 ibid (quotations suppressed).

37 ibid. (emphasis added).

38 See section Revisiting Engels' Elucidation.

law's ultimate economic dependence, it possesses a unique reflexivity that allows it to reflect economic realities without being a direct automatic crude translation of economic forces. Similarly, aligned with Renner, Neumann posits that under certain conditions, the law may undergo an autonomous transformation in directions distinct from the underlying motion of the economic substructure. Nonetheless, Neumann emphasises that the occurrence of these movements is not severed from the interplay between law and social reality, characterising law's autonomy as 'relative'.

Commentaries

Following the thinking of Marx and Engels, Karl Renner and Franz Neumann contested economic determinism's misconceptions in sociological jurisprudence in early 20th-century Europe. Their account led them to elaborate, after Engels, on law's 'relative' autonomy. By attributing a more autonomous role to law, beyond viewing it as merely an ideological instrument, they recognised a liberating potential in bourgeois law. This shift likely reflected the era's political practices, as their involvement in social-democratic parties hinted at a pragmatic preference for gradual 'reformist' legal strategies. Historically situated, their stance critically contested the prevailing notion of economic determinism and the more formalistic and abstract jurisprudential conceptions of law divorced from the real material society.

Nevertheless, they did not fully articulate the relative specificity of the law's relative autonomy and the nature of the interrelationship of law with the economy and other social spheres.[39] Unlike Renner, Neumann attempted to deepen into the autonomy of law but left the conceptualisation of its relative independence unexplored. His own academic programme was not completed: [to] 'investigate the *conditions* under which law and the state can develop relatively independently'. Analytical challenges persist: What are the origins, the motor, of these independent legal movements, and what triggers them in historical development? How do the law's social functions autonomously unfold?

Thus far, we have examined jurisprudential discussions within continental legal theory regarding the 'relative' autonomy of law, following the initial postulates of Marx and Engels. The subsequent section will explore how this concept was received and debated in Anglophone legal theory across the Atlantic.

39 Further critiques of the limitations of Neumann's approach in this respect can be found, i.a., in Sonja Buckel, *Subjektivierung und Kohäsion. Zur Rekonstruktion einer materialistischen Theorie des Rechts* (Velbrück Wissenschaft 2007) 92–93; David Kettler and Thomas Wheatland, *Learning from Franz L. Neumann. Law, Theory and the Brute Facts of Political Life* (Anthem Press 2019) 126–28.

Reception in anglophone socio-legal studies

In the late 1970s and early 1980s, the discussion of law's 'relative' autonomy found resonance in Anglophone legal scholarship, albeit with adaptations.[40] A notable instance was the debate between David Trubek and Isaac Balbus in the United States. This dialogue, folkloric in North American socio-legal studies, revolved around Balbus' empirical analysis of 'legal power' based on Weberian and Marxist theories.[41] He investigated class and racial biases in the U.S. justice system during the 1964–1969 ghetto riots. Trubek, in a comprehensive review,[42] critiqued Balbus' methodology, questioning the compatibility between Marx and Weber. Likewise, he addressed aspects of Weber's sociology of law that supported a formal, unqualified autonomy of law.[43] This last perspective significantly influenced Anglophone liberal legal theories and socio-legal studies. It extended into discussions amongst empiricist-oriented legal realists and legal formalists and debates between instrumentalists and formalists. Within this context, Balbus, engaging in self-critique, addressed[44] Trubek's objections by proposing a resolution to what he perceived as a false dichotomy. Balbus responded to Trubek's criticisms by advocating for the 'relative' autonomy thesis, drawing upon materialist theories and the commodity exchange theory of law.

Isaac Balbus' relative autonomy

Balbus aimed to empirically demonstrate how law is deployed for domination, leading him to rework the notion of law's 'relative' autonomy based on commodity-form analysis. He proposed an argument to 'transcend' the tension between formalists and instrumentalists/reductivists in U.S. legal socio-legal scholarship. Balbus acknowledged the juridical domain's role

40 See amongst other things, in the United States, Robert Gordon, 'Critical Legal Histories' (1984) 36 SLR 101

> [R]elative autonomy means that (legal forms and practices) cannot be explained completely by reference to external political/social/economic factors. To some extent, they are independent variables in social experience, and therefore they require study elaborating their peculiar internal structures intending to find out how those structures feedback upon social life.

In the United Kingdom: Hugh Collins, *Marxism and Law* (OUP 1982) 63. 'The idea of relative autonomy refers to the institutional framework of the capitalist state and its freedom from direct control from the dominant class'.

41 Isaac Balbus, *The Dialectics of Legal Repression* (Russell Sage 1973). The theoretical foundations are mainly set out in ch. 1.

42 David Trubek, 'Complexity and Contradiction in the Legal Order: Balbus and the Challenge of Critical Social Thought about Law' (1977) 11 *L and Soc R* 529.

43 These explanations can be complemented by Christopher Tomlins' analysis, 'How Autonomous is Law' (2007) 3 *Annu R L and Soc* Sci 50–53.

44 Isaac Balbus, 'Commodity Form and Legal Form: An Essay on the 'Relative Autonomy' of the Law' (1977) 11 *L and Soc R* 572–87 (emphasis in original).

within a complex social whole, seeking to explain the intertwined nature of legal and capitalist commodity exchange forms. He paralleled legal and commodity exchange relations (recalling Marx and Pashukanis: 'the very cell[45] of capitalist society'), calling their resemblance 'homologous'. Drawing on Marx, Engels, and Lefebvre, Balbus suggested that modern legal forms abstract individuals, making them 'unequally equal'. Notably, he argued that bourgeois law, through its formal characteristics, masquerades relations of domination and naturalises practices that obstruct struggles for emancipation. Balbus, echoing Pashukanis' arguments, posited that the legal form transcends mere instrumentalism within capitalism, asserting a decisive role in facilitating exchange relations. Interestingly, he conceded that insights on the systemic parallels between commodity and legal forms were obtained independently from an in-depth examination of Pashukanis' work.[46] Balbus drew his conclusions from his own reading of Marx.

Law determination, social forces, capitalism

Balbus engaged in an exploration of the specific interplay between the legal form, capitalism and social forces. He presented a tripartite structure of society comprised of the system (capitalist mode of production), forms (commodity-legal) and agents (social forces, classes). He posited that law could be deemed autonomous if it remains non-responsive to influential social agents' interests. Nonetheless, he also argued that such autonomy concerning the will and preferences of social actors does not equate to independence from the capitalist economy as the basic structure of a societal organisation. Therefore, he argued that while the law may be autonomous from the direct influence of social forces, it is not from the capitalist mode of production. Accordingly, the imperatives of capitalism not only shape but may also 'articulate' legal forms with other spheres and even 'explain' the law. This interplay leads him to conclude that law possesses 'relative autonomy'. The following passages capture the main point:

> [T]he 'relative autonomy' of the legal form from the wills of social actors entails at the same time an essential identity or homology between the

45 Marx, *Kapital* (n 18) 12. 'Für die bürgerliche Gesellschaft ist aber die Warenform des Arbeitsprodukts oder die Wertform der Ware die ökonomische Zellenform'. Cf. Pashukanis *General Theory* (n 4) 85: 'The legal relation is the cell-form of the legal fabric: only there does law accomplish its real movement'. But the German edition reads: 'Das juristische Verhältnis ist die *Keimzelle* des Rechtsgewebes'. (73, emphasis added). These biological metaphors suggest that just as cells are elementary components enabling a living organism's growth, development and functionality, similarly, economic and juridical relations serve as the basic elements without which the structure and dynamism of a legal system in a capitalist formation could hardly be sustained.

46 Balbus (n 44) 577, note 5.

> legal form . . . and commodity form.[47] [The homology] guarantees both that the legal form, like the commodity form, functions and develops autonomously from the preferences of social actors *and* that it does *not* function and develop autonomously from the system in which these social actors participate.[48]

Balbus' account, presents certain challenges. Firstly, he distinguishes between the legal form and the concept of law, aiming to elucidate their roles within the capitalist economy. The former refers to the modern form of law—that is, the structural characteristics that law acquires in bourgeois society, marked by generality, completeness, systematicity and universality. Conversely, the concept of law captures normative structures and practices that govern social relations, going beyond the legal form's abstract formalism. Nevertheless, in several passages,[49] Balbus conflated one and the other, suggesting that both are relatively autonomous. This coalescence might obscure the elucidation of to what extent a genuine autonomous law that goes beyond bourgeois society might offer an emancipatory potential.

Secondly, the degree to which social forces alone effectively determine legal forms poses some queries. Does the logic of capitalism not already influence agents' decisions? To what extent does the economy shape social actors' consciousness and actions, considering their embeddedness in the material base? Balbus asserts that legal forms exhibit autonomy from the preferences of individual actors, suggesting that law may develop independently of social forces. Yet, such autonomy cannot be expected concerning the mode of production, as the economy determines legal forms. This delineation raises questions about the interaction between law, social agents and the material base. Balbus presents a tripartite structure: the system (capitalist mode of production), forms (commodity-legal) and agents (social forces, classes). The interplay and articulation of these elements, absent a dialectical approach, appear already preconfigured rather than dynamically interrelated.

Balbus's assertions highlight some distinctions: firstly, to what extent is law autonomous regarding the social forces? Secondly, to what extent is law autonomous from the economic order? Balbus seems to suggest that (i) capitalism determines law and legal forms, limiting their potential autonomy due to the 'essential identity' or 'homology' with the commodity form and precluding a 'last instance determination' or dialectical interplay; (ii) social agents are considered preconstituted entities, underestimating the role of ideology in shaping their consciousness and subjectivity. This perspective implies that the organisation of life's material aspects exerts a limited effect on shaping individuals' actions and preferences. Such an assumption takes little account of forming ideological, class-based social structures. Furthermore, it

47 ibid 573.
48 ibid 585. (Brackets added, italics in original).
49 ibid 573.

raises the question of whether the capitalist economy influences social actors' preferences and, consequently, legal determinations beforehand.

Commentaries

Balbus' view on the relative autonomy of law and legal forms aligns, in certain respects, with some concepts articulated by Neumann and Engels. His distinction between law and legal form echoes Neumann's differentiation between autonomous law and state law. Yet, as Neumann did, Balbus sometimes merged the two notions despite introducing the distinction. Similarly, Engels posited that legal forms, when enacted to serve only the interests of a specific ruling class at a given juncture, may destroy the law's autonomy and instrumentalise it in a manner that contradicts its concept (*Rechtsbegriff*).[50] Moreover, for Engels, legal forms (*Rechtsformen*)[51] are superstructural moments, subject to variation by dialectical movements. These legal forms, when determined, manifest contingently, reflecting societal forces' dynamic interplay in specific historical circumstances. This alignment suggests a continuity in materialist-dialectic law conceptions based on the conflicted interplay between normative principles of law and their actual posited legal articulations. Unlike Renner, Neumann and Engels, Balbus did not take a dialectical conception of the interaction between law, its forms and the economic base. Consequently, what precisely constitutes the operationalisation of the 'relative' of relative autonomy remains unclear.

Interesting parallels are identifiable, though, notably with Franz Neumann's scepticism towards conceiving law as autonomous without qualifications. One of Neumann's targets was Kelsen's *Pure Theory*, which claimed the law's dual unqualified autonomy as a self-referential normative order and independent scientific discipline. In turn, Balbus's critique primarily addresses the North American legal formalists' view of an autonomous law as posited legality endowed with intrinsic rationality that superseded individual will—a phenomenon Balbus termed, recalling Pashukanis, 'legal fetishism',[52] to denote the operations of a legal order that exists independently of, and detached from, actual social relations. This North American legal formalism, particularly influential in private law, carried a political motive to champion laissez-faire principles, thereby minimising state legal interference and regulation in personal business and contractual activities. Legal formalists[53] contend

50 See *supra* note n 14.

51 See *supra* note n 7.

52 Balbus (n 44) 583; cf. Pashukanis, *General Theory* (n 4) 87–88.

53 The literature on legal formalism developed in the tradition of American analytical jurisprudence is vast. Ernest J. Weinrib's The Idea of Private Law (OUP 2012) is seminal. Interestingly, in this book, in a footnote (139, n 32), this author indicates, quoting Pashukanis' *General Theory* (n 4), that the relationship of law to economics should be understood as the 'congruence of juridical and economic form' (emphasis added). It is unclear what this congruence, correspondence or harmony is meant to imply, as he references Pashukanis'

as a general claim that law possesses an 'immanent' ancient logic capable of self-regulation and autonomously generating unique cogent solutions. Hence, law is somehow always already determined by itself, without mediations, and adjudicators are presumed to access an autonomous 'legal reasoning'[54] that enables the law to unfold and apply according to its inherent rules.

These criticisms address the ideological narrative of law as 'fully' or unqualifiedly autonomous, divorced from social forces and obscuring the economy's ultimate determinant role. Legal formalists insist 'on treating law on its own terms, that is, unadulterated by history, politics and economics.'[55] For these authors, law autonomously would offer the right rational solutions, masquerading and naturalising capitalist productive relations and class domination through legally codified self-sufficient forms. This formulation implies that law is a self-standing impartial mediator detached from material influences and determinations. It then overshadows or distracts from the power relations that make certain legal forms' meanings prevail. In that vein, these objections align with Marx's commentary on the illusory 'fictive' function of supposedly autonomous legal forms, comparing the visible fetters of Roman enslaved people to the 'invisible strings' binding wage labourers. Thus, Marx posited that '[d]er Schein seiner Unabhängigkeit wird durch den beständigen Wechsel der individuellen Lohnherrn und die fictio juris des Kontrakts aufrechterhalten'.[56]

Likewise, despite his development regarding relative autonomy, Balbus faced accessory criticism because of essentialism[57] and the presupposition of the predetermined tripartite structure as 'first nature'.[58] Additionally, while innovative at the time, Balbus' focus on the 'homology' between the legal form and commodity exchange opens his arguments to similar critiques[59] faced by Pashukanis regarding the commodity-form law theory. Some years before Balbus elaborated his conception of the 'relative' autonomy of law, Louis Althusser in

book without indicating any specific page or phrase. An updated and expanded version of Weinrib's argument, grounded in a formalist approach with antecedents in Kant, is found in Ernest J. Weinrib's Reciprocal Freedom. Private Law and Public Right (OUP 2022). Similarly, see Arthur Ripstein, Private Wrongs (Harvard University Press 2016), who closely follows Weinrib's theses. For a critical appraisal of Weinrib's and Ripstein's legal formalism, drawing on the work of Pashukanis, see Igor Shoikhedbrod, 'Private Law's Estranged Bedfellows: Why Pashukanis Should Worry Contemporary Formalists' (2020) 33 *Can J L & Jurisprudence* 461–79.

54 On legal formalism's 'autonomy of legal reasoning', see Brian Bix, 'Law as an Autonomous Discipline' in Peter Cane and Mark Tushnet (eds), *The Oxford Handbook of Legal Studies* (OUP 2003) 975–87, who further clarifies and distinguishes jurisprudential discussions within the North American context.

55 Shoikhedbrod (n 52) 465.

56 Marx (n 18) 599.

57 Tomlins (n 43) 53–54.

58 Buckel (n 39) 136.

59 Amongst other things, Robert Fine, *Democracy and the Rule of Law. Marx's Critique of the Legal Form* (first published 1984, Blackburn Press 2002) 155–69; Igor Shoikhedbrod, *Revisiting Marx's Critique of Liberalism. Rethinking Justice, Legality and Rights* (Palgrave 2019) 97–110.

France provided insights into the specific nature of this notion. This perspective will be examined in the following section.

Louis Althusser's relative autonomy

In the context of Western Marxism,[60] Louis Althusser sought to develop a research programme with epistemological and political implications. His endeavour aimed to counter the evolutionist teleology of history, which prioritised productive forces over relations of production, and to challenge reductionist economism. This effort was set against the backdrop of policies endorsed by the USSR in left-wing politics and the fluctuations of international communism. Althusser aimed to renew Marxist theory by revisiting Marx's works, moving away from coeval interpretations that focused on Marx's early philosophical writings. These readings, often termed 'humanist' for emphasising the anthropological aspects of Marx's thought, sought alternatives to Stalinist dogmatism. Additionally, Althusser aimed to move beyond Marx's and Engels's empiricist orthodox interpretations that led to a mechanistic instrumentalism characterised by causal linearity ('historicism'), which overlooked the self-standing dynamics of culture, politics, law or art.[61]

Althusser's theoretical contributions eschewed determinism and economistic reductionism in orthodox Marxism whilst avoiding the situationist relativism prevalent in post Marxist tendencies. In Anglophone legal sociology and jurisprudence, Nicos Poulantzas is often cited as the primary advocate of the state and law's relative autonomy. Althusser's contributions to this subject, however, have received scant attention.[62] This oversight might first stem from Poulantzas's jurisprudential background, which informed his early writings on legal philosophy. Secondly, the posthumous 1995 publication of Althusser's manuscripts and essays in the volume *Sur la reproduction*,[63] edited by Jacques Bidet, introduced additional insights into his views on law.[64]

60 For context and explanations of Althusser's work, I am relying to a certain extent on William Lewis, 'Louis Althusser' in Edward Zalta and Uri Nodelman (eds), *The Stanford Encyclopedia of Philosophy* (2022) <>https://shorturl.at/EGNS7>.

61 The 'ideological' duality of humanism/economism is complementary. It is not an accidental link but an organic and consubstantial one. It is born spontaneously . . . of the bourgeois practices of production and exploitation, and at the same time, of the legal practices of bourgeois law and its ideology, which provide a sanction for the capitalist relations of production and exploitation and their reproduction. Louis Althusser, *Essays in Self-criticism* (first published 1973, Grahame Lock tr, NLB 1976) 85–86.

62 Exceptions in Anglophone sociology of law and legal theory are, amongst others, Alan Hunt and Maureen Cain (eds), *Marx and Engels on Law* (Academic Press 1979) and Roger Coterrell, *Law's Community. Legal Theory in Sociological Perspective* (OUP 1997).

63 Louis Althusser, *Sur la reproduction* (PUF 1995). On law, see especially chapters IV, V and XI. The condensation of these chapters was initially published in an abridged form in Louis Althusser, 'Idéologie et appareils idéologiques d'État' (1970) 151 *La Pensée* 3–38.

64 It was in 2013 that an insightful collection of articles on Althusser's thinking and law theory was published in the English language; see Laurent de Sutter (ed), *Althusser and Law* (Routledge 2013).

Regarding juridical autonomy, Althusser, by revisiting Engels' elucidations of their collective work with Marx, wondered about the precise interplay amongst relations of production, productive forces and the resulting political, juridical and ideological superstructural elements. He sought to develop a conceptual paradigm that articulates and mediates the determination by the economy *in the last instance* and the 'relative' self-standing specific efficacy of the superstructures within a total social structure.

While maintaining a critical stance towards Engels' interpretations of Marx, Althusser adapted and reinterpreted fundamental materialist-dialectic tenets stressed by the late Engels. These included the notion of 'relative autonomy', the principle of retroactive interaction and the ultimate determination by the economy. Nonetheless, Althusser's interpretation advances beyond Engels by presenting arguments for redefining the interrelations between base and superstructure.

Central concepts

The concept of *coupure épistémologique* in Marx's thought, particularly concerning Hegelianism, marks one of Althusser's significant intellectual contributions. This thesis suggests a transformation in Marx's oeuvre, moving away from philosophical categories derived from Hegel's idealism and Feuerbach's materialism to concentrate on social structures. This shift prompted Althusser to make a contentious distinction between the early 'ideological' pre-scientific Marx and the later 'scientific' non-ideological Marx, starting from his critiques of political economy (1845 onwards). In a series of articles from the early 1960s, Althusser laid the groundwork for arguing Marx's epistemic rupture with Hegel, moving away from Hegelian philosophy. This departure led to some outcomes: Marx's dialectics would have been sublimated, thus transitioning from a system of 'simple' contradictions to 'overdetermined' contradictions. Moreover, the social unity invoked by Marx would not be a mere spiritual *Totalität*, as Hegel indicated, but a unity of a complex and differentiated material *tout*. Althusser also moved away from the Hegelian-inspired dialectical progression of history towards a concept of 'structural causality', drawing from Spinoza's philosophy. For Althusser, given Hegelian idealism's teleological and subject-centric nature, it would be categorised under the 'humanist' ideological approach.

Althusser's invocation of *surdétermination*—a term appropriated from Freud's psychoanalytic concept of *Überdeterminierung* and de Saussure's linguistic theories—played a central role in his *reading* of Marx's dialectics. Despite Althusser's own stated ambivalence towards the term, he employs it, in his words, 'faute de mieux', as both an *indicator* and a *problem* because it aptly illustrates why he is dealing with something fundamentally different from Hegelian contradiction.[65] For Althusser, *surdétermination* signifies an

65 Louis Althusser, *Pour Marx* (first published 1965, La Découverte 2005) 100. In another article in the same collection, he adds that it was not a capricious decision as the concept '. . . possède une "connotation" objective dialectique, et —particulièrement en

essential quality within a contradiction: the reflection (*la réflexion*), within the contradiction itself, of its conditions of existence, its position within the structure in dominance (*structure à dominante*[66]) of a complex *tout*.[67] He underscores that, in historical development, the economic base is not a monolithic determinant but is dynamically interwoven with and influenced by multiple elements within a social formation that simultaneously affect and are affected by it (via *action en retour* or Marx's and Engel's *Rückwirkung*). This perspective maintains that while the economy may *ultimately* drive historical conjunctures, it does so through a network of interactions and reactions rather than by itself alone.

This argument aligns with Engels' concepts and prior interpretations, but Althusser went beyond Engels. He systematically articulated and conceptually clarified the rationale behind the superstructure's elements, achieving autonomy within dependency. Althusser posited *overdetermination* as a creative nexus where concrete actions, movements and events intertwine with the material base, being 'determining but also determined in one and the same movement'.[68] Althusser argued against the primacy of a single contradiction (e.g., capital v. labour), suggesting instead a network of primary and secondary contradictions[69] that shape and are shaped by each other within a societal formation.[70] Echoing Engels, for Althusser, the mode of material production, embodying both productive forces and relations, in the last instance (*en dernière instance*), determines the concrete society's dominant structure at a given historical juncture.[71]

Althusser's *lecture symptomale* reevaluated the dialectical interaction between the economic base and the ideological superstructure. Within this context, Althusser presents an argument concerning the relative autonomy of superstructural elements, including the legal apparatus. This re-elaboration carries implications for the present study. Firstly, Althusser's interpretation of Marx and Hegel's philosophies provokes controversy, yielding diverse

psychanalyse— formellement assez apparentée au contenu qu'il désigne ici' (212, note N° 48).

66 On Althusser's '*structure à dominante*', consider Marx's assertion that in all social formations, a particular production assigns *rank* and *influence* (*Rang und Einfluß anweist*), thereby determining all the rest of relations. Marx, *Einleitung* (n 1) 637.

67 Althusser (n 65) 215. About 'réflexion', see 212.

68 ibid 99–100.

69 'es contradictions secondaires sont essentielles à l'existence même de la contradiction principale . . . tout comme la contradiction principale constitue leur condition d'existence' Althusser (n 65) 211.

70 Cf. Engels, *Brief an Conrad Schmidt in Berlin* (n 7) 436 '[D]ie materielle Daseinsweise das *primum agens* ist, das nicht ausschließt, daß die ideellen Gebiete eine reagierende, aber sekundäre Einwirkung auf sie hinwiederum ausüben'.

71 In a similar fashion Étienne Balibar, 'Sur les concepts fondamentaux du materialisme historique' in Louis Althusser and others (eds), *Lire Le Capital* (first published 1965, PUF 1996) 452.

conclusions from those who critique his postulates.[72] While this chapter recognises the contentious nature of Althusser's ideas, it will accept his premises as a basis for further analysis. Secondly, Althusser's reformulation of the interrelations between substrate and superstructure has implications for the relative autonomy of law. This chapter contends that Althusser's viewpoint of the period under analysis signified an insightful theoretical attempt to comprehend the distinct character of juridical autonomy in its interdependence with the social whole. Althusser's analysis foregrounds how the juridical superstructure maintains its autonomy while being embedded in and responsive to the material base.

Reconciling autonomy and determination?

Althusser's invocation of relative autonomy marks a departure from orthodox economic determinism, suggesting superstructural instances, such as law, are not automatically determined by economic forces.[73] Althusser pointed out that more complex dialectical interactions operate within societal formations by reworking Marx's dialectics and moving beyond the Hegelian philosophical system. For Althusser, interrelations within the social totality are not only linear and binary, as he believes could be inferred from a Hegelian dialectic. On the contrary, because of overdetermination and structural causality, all movements comprise various forces and elements simultaneously interacting in an intricate constellation of contradictions, effectuating the whole concurrently. Therefore, a social structure emerges historically from specific modes of production as decentralised networks of self-organised 'structures of structures'. These possess distinct specificities, engaging in a dynamic of overdetermined contradictions beyond 'linear' (Descartes) or 'expressive' (Leibniz/Hegel) causality.

While the economy is the ultimate determinant of changes in a mode of production, it does not invariably assume the role of the dominant instance. As a result, superstructural elements might become predominant at specific historical junctures. One example could be the prevalence of the Catholic religion during Western European feudalism (as 'structure à dominate'). Nonetheless, this predominance is dynamic rather than static, as each component within the social totality possesses its own *efficacité spécifique*, enabling an extent of independence amongst the structures. Despite their

72 Amongst the scholars who suggest the ongoing influence of Hegel's postulates on Marx's writings are Friedrich Engels, György Lukács, members of the Frankfurt School, Shlomo Avineri, and, more recently, Igor Shoikhedbrod.

73 Peter Dews, 'Althusser, Structuralism, and the French Epistemological Tradition' in Gregory Elliott (ed), *Althusser: A Critical Reader* (Blackwell 1994) 114.

autonomy, these diverse structures can only be fully understood within this complex *tout*, marking the critical point at which the idea of 'relative autonomy'[74] becomes significant.

Althusser further elucidates the idea of 'structural' relative autonomy. He emphasises that Marx provides 'deux bouts de la chaîne', exhorting one to explore between them: on the one hand, the ultimate determination by the mode of (economic) production; on the other, the relative autonomy of superstructures and their specific effectiveness.[75] This metaphor of 'the ends of the chain' signifies a shift from dialectical movement to a relation of structural causality, described as 'the simultaneous unity of distinct and unequal modes of determination'.[76] Althusser additionally notes that Marx suggested the economic determination of the whole and the relative autonomy of superstructural elements by highlighting their irreducible singularity.[77] Althusser draws attention to historical instances where superstructural elements have demonstrated their own articulations, thus possessing their unique historicity. He also observes that immediate political superstructural outcomes should not necessarily be expected from contradictions between productive relations and forces within the material base.

Subsequent works between 1968 and 1970 delve further into the superstructure's relative autonomy. These texts highlight how every structural level, operating autonomously influencing each other through mutual interactions within the *tout*, effectuates specific determinations (*indice d'efficacité*). Althusser also emphasises the importance of addressing the theoretical challenge of 'derived' efficacy within the superstructure. This idea, expressed by Althusser's phrase 'penser ce que la tradition marxiste désigne sous les termes conjoints d'autonomie relative de la superstructure, et *d'action en retour* de la superstructure sur la base',[78] underscores the key of relative autonomy: the reciprocal interactive influence (*reaction back on* or *Rückwirkung*) between superstructure and base, alongside the index of determination. The autonomy of superstructural levels is underpinned by their unique capacity for self-movement, imbuing them with a distinctive agency that ultimately depends on the material base.

74 [L]a spécificité de chacun de ces temps, de chacune de ces histoires, autrement dit leur autonomie et indépendance relatives, sont fondées sur un certain type d'articulation dans le tout, donc sur un certain type de dépendance à l'égard du tout.

Althusser and others (n 71) 284

75 Althusser (n 65) 117 (emphasis in original).

76 Robert Resch, *Althusser and the Renewal of Marxist Social Theory* (University of California Press 1992) 38–39.

77 See *supra* note N° 1.

78 Althusser (n 63) 276.

Juridical superstructure

The above interpretation presents two scenarios for the juridical superstructure: at the emergency moment, the law is shaped by societal and economic conditions rather than existing apriori as a pre-social or pre-political order; it is an effect of the structure itself. Subsequently, socio-economic relations facilitate autonomous legal developments aligned with concrete material human practices during the reproduction moment of a legal order. The structural dynamic assigns the law a specific *location* and *function* within the social formation, guided by the principle of structural causality, which orchestrates the diverse interactions within the societal *tout*. Poulantzas elucidates this point: '[T]he specificity and efficacy of a structure's particular level—let us say the law—does not depend on its nature but on its location and function in a type of relations of the levels within a complex unity'.[79]

The idea might be more comprehensible when illustrated with a specific example, like the forms of the feudal order of Western Europe during the early medieval age. These feudal societies were characterised by the plurality of normative orders and regional divergences, each with its own form of 'relative' self-contained or 'semi-autonomous' organisation. It consisted of agricultural and craft production based on a non-free immediate labour force exploiting manors or fiefdoms/feuds. These landed estates were owned or effectively possessed by non-labouring landlords.[80] In most regional variations (e.g., Manorialism, *Grundherrschaft*, *Señorío*), land ownership was concentrated amongst magnates (secular and religious), and the peasantry's immediate labour produced economic value. Unlike capitalism, where the surplus produced by the labour force is effected via market transactions, under feudalism, the surplus was obtained and transferred through direct political, legal and military coercion. The productive social relations stemming from landholdings in exchange for labour at the material base gave form to the entire hierarchical structure of feudal society. The core of these

79 Nicos Poulantzas, 'A propos de le théorie marxiste du droit' (1967) 12 *Arch philo droit* 145, *passim*. In this essay, while maintaining his original viewpoint, Poulantzas provides detailed expositions and interpretations of Althusser's structuralism applied to philosophy of law. Elements of this article were later integrated into the introduction to Nicos Poulantzas, *Pouvoir politique et classes sociales de l'État capitaliste* (first published 1968, Maspero 1982) 10 ff.

80 On feudal mode of production, amongst others, see Marx, *Kapital III* (n 1) ch XX, s 4, 335 ff., ch XXXVI, 607 ff., ch XLVII, 790 ff. According to John Pryor, 'The Historical Foundations of a Feudal Mode of Production' (1985) 2 Feudalism: Comparative Studies 70, the above is the broad sense in which Marx and Engels would have understood 'the medieval mode of production' according to his archaeological and historical sources. John Pryor, 'Karl Marx and the Medieval Economy' (1996) 18 *Arts: The Journal of the Sydney University Arts Association* 68–86. Cf. Paul Hirst and Barry Hindess, *Pre-Capitalist Modes of Production* (Routledge 1975) 222 ff.

relations was the feudal oath of fealty between the vassal and the lord. This agreement was juridically expressed in a contractual form and was fundamental for medieval productive relations.

Religion was the ideological structure in dominance (*structure à dominante*), as the power of religious orders and ecclesiastical institutions extended beyond their landowner roles. They exerted substantial normative, political and cultural influence, shaping norms, values, legal institutions and principles to the extent that canon law rules sometimes prevailed over local customary norms. In that sense, Engels remarked that theology had annexed all other forms of ideology during the medieval age: philosophy, politics and jurisprudence, turning them into subdivisions and forcing every societal and political movement to adopt a theological form.[81] Concurrently, the juridical structure[82] manifested prominently through public law rules infused with ecclesiastical doctrines and canon law. Meanwhile, private law was based mainly on the remnants of Roman concepts and Germanic customary law yet was also influenced by regional social practices and the *ius commune*, such as those norms codified in the Lombardian *Libri feudorum*.[83] Over time, these systems underwent gradual transformations, influenced by local customs, mercantile disputes and shifting power dynamics amongst feudal lords, monarchies and the Church. These interrelationships illustrate, to some extent, the superstructural interplay, leading to overdetermination and the material base determination as the last instance.

This concrete historical example underscores law's 'relative' autonomy, demonstrating its reflexivity and responsivity to interact, adapt and react, keeping its specificity yet still overdetermined by societal, economic, and ideological religious elements. Law contours were blurred but still identifiable; their preponderant role in the efficient performance of productive relations was not yet fully settled. Nonetheless, law's 'relative' autonomy during this era is noticeable in its dual function: adjusting and reinforcing feudal hierarchies and obligations associated with status and maintaining a 'relative' *location* within the fragmented and conflicting structure of medieval political and productive relations.

81 Engels, *Feuerbach* (n 6) 304. These observations must be complemented by the fact that, during the Western European Middle Ages, the Catholic Church was not merely a dominant religious and spiritual structure but also exercised significant political power, which led, for example, to persistent conflicts with the princes' secular authority.

82 On 'feudal law' I am relying on Joseph Canning, 'Feudal Law' in Henrik Lagerlund (ed), *Encyclopedia of Medieval Philosophy* (Springer 2011) 354–56; Dirk Heirbaut, 'Feudal Law' in Heikki Pihlajamäki and others (eds), *The Oxford Handbook of European Legal History* (OUP 2019) 547. Indeed, this general description only covers the surface of the complicated multifarious processes that define feudalism.

83 Attilio Stella (ed and tr) *Libri Feudorum* (Brill 2023).

How is the modern form of law 'relatively' autonomous?

On the juridical level, productive social relations, though not juridical, *generate* content abstracted by law. Legal forms and relations are ultimately determined by material production. Yet they also influence the motions of the economy. The early Poulantzas highlighted that the superstructure's component levels are, in their own specificity, the actual existential conditions[84] of the economy and vice versa.[85] Legal relations formalise the bridge between relations of production and productive forces while actualising social relations of production (e.g. property relations) through juridical expressions (e.g. *ius in re*) after a series of dislocations.[86] The employment contract is another example. It is a quintessential illustration of formal labour relations, a fundamental component of capitalist productive relations. It legally encapsulates the agreement whereby an employee exchanges labour power for wages. While the material base determines the contract's content, its form hinges upon the juridical instance, highlighting an interdependent interplay. Without labour contracts, capitalist production relations falter. Simultaneously, the contract form and content are moulded by prevailing justice ideologies, customs or the influence of another temporarily dominant structure. Thus, as Marx suggested, legal forms are expressions of conflicting existing productive realities—the dialectic between productive forces and relations of production.[87]

One can observe that the juridical moment is not decisive within the *tout* because it is subject to the overdetermination of various other structures. Regardless, the overarching structural whole determines the *location* of each superstructural element. Law is continuously affected and crossed by ideological, cultural and economic structures that delineate its *function* within the mode of production. Thus, the juridical level is *overdetermined*, reacting to diverse influences from distinct instances and simultaneously impacting them. This structural overdetermination of law requires detailed consideration. Juridical determination involves 'external' socio-economic law-determination

84 Cf. Marx (n 1) 621.

85 Poulantzas (n 79) 150. There would be a dual occurrence: the legal form is both an effect and an existential condition. This observation finds support in Marx's writings. He suggested that law might dialectically influence the material base while discussing the inevitability of the universalisation of Factory Acts. 'Mit den materiellen Bedingungen und der gesellschaftlichen Kombination des Produktionsprozesses [the legislation] reift sie die Widersprüche und Antagonismen seiner kapitalistischen Form, daher gleichzeitig die Bildungselemente einer neuen und die Umwälzungsmomente der alten Gesellschaft.' Marx (n 18) 525–26. In the same chapter, Marx also noted the ambivalent effects entailed by the dialectic of modern law.

86 Étienne Balibar in Althusser and others (n 71) 462.

87 Marx already identified this dialectic as problematic: 'Dialektik der Begriffe Produktivkraft (Produktionsmittel) und Produktionsverhältnis, eine Dialektik, deren Grenzen zu bestimmen und die realen Unterschiede nicht aufhebt.' Marx (n 1) 640.

and 'internal' juridical self-determination and self-reproduction.[88] Law, embedded in complex material processes, faces structural conditions that might lead to contingent imbalances with the economy. These decouplings, triggered by instances' self-drives, reveal the uneven performances of law in specific historical conjunctures. For example, hypothetically, a concrete legal order may achieve high degrees of autonomy, even being the dominant structure (as it was the Catholic religion in the European medieval age) yet remains part of the determinations of the whole. It is dependent in its very independence: '*relativement autonome, donc relativement indépendant dans sa dépendance même*'.[89]

The idea of juridification[90] (*Verrechtlichung*) is a more contemporary example that may illustrate law's 'relative autonomy', overdetermination and contingent structural dominance. Juridification describes processes of modern legality's expansion into previously unlegalised areas that have taken place mainly in complex Western capitalist societies; likewise, it denotes the increasing technical detail of existing legislation, emphasising the intensification of the uses of modern legal forms. Juridification also entails raising administrative regulations, including, e.g., environmental and natural resource laws at national and international levels, besides the increasing clout of constitutional and international human rights laws. Here, the law appears as a *structure à dominante* consolidated via extensive legislative reforms, judicial decisions and legal doctrines indispensable for the operation of specific capitalist markets. Concurrently, these legal forms maintain their unique juridical logics, gaining momentum and direction autonomously, yet are ultimately determined by economic and political forces at concrete moments (e.g., the social law in the context of Western European welfare state). Nonetheless, simultaneously, the juridical structure is still overdetermined by normative ideological constraints, the power of social forces and the demands of the capitalist economy. Whilst potentially dominant in given historical circumstances, these constellations of laws, regulations and legal norms may be ultimately innocuous against the power of economic forces' actions in global capitalism.

88 Cf. Nicos Poulantzas, *Nature des choses et droit* (L.G.D.J. 1965) 255. Law displays inner self-determination through an internal dialectic, with its relativity manifesting via mediation by an external dialectic that engages with other societal spheres. This conceptual approach was hinted at in the doctoral dissertation of the young Poulantzas.

89 Althusser and others (n 71) 284.

90 Hugo Sinzheimer, 'Die Zukunft der Arbeiterräte' in Otto Kahn-Freund and Thilo Ramm (Hrsg), *Hugo Sinzheimer. Arbeitsrecht und Rechtssoziologie. Gesammelte Aufsätze und Reden*, vol 1 (first published 1919, Europäische Verlagsanstalt 1976) 351–55; Otto Kirchheimer, 'Zur Staatslehre des Sozialismus und Bolschewismus' in Hubertus Buchstein (Hg), *Otto Kirchheimer. Gesammelte Schriften*, vol 1 (first published 1928, Nomos 2017) 132–51. Cf. Jürgen Habermas, *Theorie des kommunikativen Handelns*, vol 2 (Suhrkamp 1981).

Commentaries

In contrast to other theorists discussed here, Louis Althusser's account departs from figures like Engels and Neumann regarding Hegel's influence on their analyses. He advanced his thesis on Marx's rupture with Hegel, simultaneously reassessing Hegelian dialectics. In this regard, Althusser's approach to Hegel, at least considering his writings from 1960–1973, differs from previous versions of Marxist-Hegelianism by authors such as Engels or Neumann.

Althusser's relative autonomy thesis builds on Marx's and Engels' preliminary conceptual insights into the base and superstructure scheme. His re-elaboration provided a sounder philosophical ground to counter Marx and Engels' economic reductionist and deterministic teleological readings. Althusser's redefinitions furnish a conceptual foundation for justifying historical-political realities' contingency, instances' specificity and their unforeseen development. This approach dispels oversimplified claims that negate the possibility of any agency's actualisation. Indeed, Althusser admitted the existence of an ultimate social determinant driven by material life's production and reproduction processes. Nevertheless, concurrently, he noted the complex, dynamic interplay of multiple elements and temporal sequences, each moving according to its own and overdetermining each other.

Althusser's reworking of 'independence in dependency' marked a theoretical advancement within the materialist-dialectic tradition. This affirmation is so because 'relative autonomy' embodies the tension between autonomy and determination, which Althusser endeavours to overcome. He posited that this elaboration refers to self-standing movements of diverse instances, each possessing different temporalities and effectuations yet maintaining a structural correspondence within the complex social whole. The introduction of Althusser's concepts of 'overdetermination' and 'structural causality' prevents the monocausal and monodirectional simplification of the interplay of the structural instances' movements. In other words, structural causality implies that the totality of the structure underpins levels' self-standing movements, manifesting as the structure's effectuation. Through a model of causation different from the 'linear' and the 'expressive' one, he aimed to reconcile agency and conditioning, contingency and necessity.

Althusser's account of the relative autonomy of law indicates that law is ineluctably related to a complex social structure. As part of the superstructure, the law is never an inert epiphenomenon of economic relations but has its own particularity, internal logic and self-sufficiency that can likewise influence societal structures and relations via overdetermination. Legal norms, institutions and practices are determined by—but also determine—the material base and other superstructural elements. Hence, a given mode of production ultimately determines the law's specific effectiveness, granting it 'relative autonomy'. Nevertheless, as structural interactions are not perpetually static, a concrete structural instance might 'overdetermine' this interplay at some historical juncture, for an extended period, even to the point of being dominant. For Althusser, the economy's determination in the 'last instance' characterises the overall constitution of a social formation, the specific hierarchical structuring of the juridical superstructure and its articulation with other ideological forms.

Despite Althusser's enhanced theoretical development during the period under analysis, one persistent problem remains not fully resolved. In the absence of pre-given, pre-constituted 'first nature' elements, in which ways is the interrelation between the economic base and the superstructure's autonomous movements concretely operationalised? What exact type of procedures mediate the realisation of this interplay? Furthermore, how might one precisely define the nature of this mediation in terms of linking the determinant or conditional instance with the determinate or conditioned element, thereby activating self-standing movements? In other words, what precise mechanisms make it possible for the base-superstructure dialectic to function without reverting to raw determinism?[91] Indeed, Althusser identified the puzzle, reflected on it and illuminated it philosophically, sought to take up the baton left by Engels, and offered conceptual solutions like structural causality and overdetermination. However, it seems that Althusser's suggestion still needs to exhaust the exact causal mechanism that enables the 'relative' effectuation of the superstructures' autonomy and thus unravels what is specifically 'relative' about relative autonomy. Engels could not completely solve this enigma, nor was it overcome by the theoretical programmes of Renner, Neumann, Balbus or Poulantzas.

Concluding remarks

The notion of 'relative autonomy' of the modern legal form, as developed within materialist-dialectic jurisprudence, draws from the philosophical foundations laid by Marx and Engels. This idea posits the law as ontologically autonomous regarding its self-determination and reproduction. Simultaneously, it recognises the law's integration within a differentiated societal totality. Such interweaving requires reciprocal interaction and continuous dependence on law in various social realms, like morality, politics and the economy. Grasping the interplay amongst the various elements and moments within the structure is obtained by examining them through the materialist-dialectic method developed by Marx and Engels.

This perspective also carries epistemic implications as it contests knowing the law as an absolute, unqualified order, entirely autonomous and isolated from societal determinations. By categorising autonomy as 'relative',

91 In different variations, these doubts have also been formulated, amongst other things, by Michael Kelly, 'Louis Althusser and the Problems of a Marxist Theory of Structure' (1978) 78 PRIA 199–212; Gillian Rose, *Hegel Contra Sociology* (first published 1981, Verso 2009) 39–42; Sheelagh Strawbridge, 'From 'Overdetermination' to 'Structural Causality': Some Unresolved Problems in Althusser's Treatment of Causality' (1984) 38 *Radic Philos* 9–16.

the materialist-dialectic tradition stresses the law's ineluctable connections to, and dependencies on, particular social structures. This approach fosters a relational understanding of the law's nature, whereby autonomy allows the law's constant interrelation with non-juridical elements. Yet, all this is attained by maintaining the law's unique identity as a relational normative order, keeping its juridical distinctiveness within the tapestry of social interactions. The law is neither co-original nor equiprimordial with the economy nor is entirely subsumed by it; it neither precedes the entirety of social structures nor can it determine in *the last instance* the unfolding of other structures.

Regarding the history of legal ideas, the explicit articulation of law's 'relative' autonomy arguably originated from Engels' critiques of reductive economism amidst broader debates on the interrelations between the material base and superstructures. The qualification of law's autonomy proved epistemically tenable when acknowledging its concomitant inescapable relationality to other societal elements. Concerning law's existential status, the 'relative autonomy' thesis fosters more responsive juridical self-determination, avoiding reduction to a mere instrumentality of dominant social forces. In this sense, the juridical 'relative' autonomy claim is situated between the poles of formalism and instrumentalism in jurisprudential theories.

The political significance of 'relative' juridical self-determination involves questioning to what extent the modern form of law enables emancipatory potential. The latter status might be achieved by synthesising law's responsiveness and reflexivity for social freedom: law, through self-reflection, looks at itself to guide the determination of legal forms, which are inevitably linked to socio-political interconnectedness. Thus, the implications of conceiving law in this sense are as follows. The less self-reliant law is, the more its legal forms become static and instrumental. Conversely, the fewer external interferences in law's self-determination, the broader the scope for autonomous movements. The stronger the self-sufficiency, the more likely modern legality will have an emancipatory outcome. With little autonomy, law may remain a mere motionless reflection of the naked forces that determine it, wrecking its potential for emancipatory purposes.

Chapter 6

Struggle to see the law

Legal form beyond the object totality

Hedvig Lärka

Introduction: *the legal form* and the limits of *form* in contemporary Marxian scholarship

The formal equality of legal subjects, as an ideal, if not as a reality, is generally considered to be the specificity of the legal form. This is true in mainstream legal theory as well as in popular legal consciousness, where law is often presented as a neutral and more or less autonomous social totality under which everyone is, or should be, equal.[1] But it is also true of some Marxist readings, which present formal, general equality as a necessary moment arising within capitalist exchange.[2] In this chapter, I argue for a

1 Equality as a central tenet of classic theories of law: Ronald Dworkin, *Taking Rights Seriously* (Harvard UP 1977); Ronald Dworkin, *Sovereign Virtue: The Theory and Practice of Equality* (Harvard UP 2000); John Locke, *Two Treatises of Government and a Letter Concerning Toleration* (Yale UP 2003); HLA Hart, *The Concept of Law* (3rd edn, OUP 2012); John Rawls, *A Theory of Justice* (Harvard UP 2005); Hans Kelsen, *Pure Theory of Law* (Lawbook Exchange 1967); Hans Kelsen, *General Theory of Law and State* (Harvard UP 1945). Moreover, it is the ideal present in critique of law, for example in critical legal studies or even deconstructive critique, over the failure of law to live up to its promises. At the same time, it is present in contemporary, law-affirming streams of law and economy, where the meaning of equality and neutrality is one of efficiency, transparency, and wealth maximation, see on both points Corinne Blalock, 'Neoliberalism and the Crisis of Legal Theory' (2014) 77 *Law and Contemporary Problems* 71. On the more general question of 'what specifies law as a distinct social field'?

2 For example, see: China Miéville, *Between Equal Rights: A marxist Theory of International Law* (Brill 2005); Carl Wilén, 'Why Pashukanis was Right: Abstraction and Form in The General Theory of Law and Marxism' (2023) *Capital & Class*, https://doi.org/10.1177/03098168231215417 (online first); Isaac D Balbus, 'Commodity Form and Legal Form: An Essay on the "Relative Autonomy" of the Law' (1977) 11 *Law and Society Review* 571; Matthew Dimick, Paul O'Connell and Umut Özsu, *Research Handbook on Law and Marxism*', *Chapter 8: Pashukanis' Commodity-Form Theory of Law* (Edward Elgar Publishing 2021). These works all leave the equality of legal form more or less intact—leading to for example Balbus declaring, in the midst of monopoly and state-regulated capitalism, a crisis of legal form itself, and the general equality that Balbus believes specifies the form (see p 586 ff).

DOI: 10.4324/9781032724713-7

Marxist critique of law that presents the specificity of law not as general equality, but *as equality before the value-form*. In other words, the legal subjects are not equal amongst each other, but equally and universally transparent and measurable from the standpoint of value-form itself, as a world-making abstraction.

Thinking of the legal form as equality before the value form means three things. *First*, that the concrete form of the legal subject, the form of its abstract and concrete *will* or *interest*, and its formal competence to accumulate value through rights and claims, appear itself as a manifestation of the historically specific form of class struggle that constitutes and is constituted by the value form. Thus, a general equality of legal subjects cannot be assumed, nor can it be seen as constituting the form of legal subjectivity itself. This point highlights the inherent tendency of the legal form to stratify legal subjects alongside abstractions such as state and citizenship or race and gender, etc.[3] *Second*, that the legal subject, sprung from the legal form, exists only if and to the extent that it represents capitalist value, as well as the capacity to accumulate this value. This means that the *abstract will*, an a priori undergirding much of jurisprudence, can be grounded in the larger totality of capitalist accumulation, its form and movement rendered more visible in critique. Third—and finally—it means that Marxist critique of law, building on Pashukanis insights, offers nothing less than the seed of a new ontology of law for jurisprudence as a discipline and, in general, social understanding. This seed provides the methodological starting point for a praxis of critique of concrete appearances of the legal form, uncovering the real movements of these more concrete forms of appearances *and* of their abstract essence and notion.

I present this reading of the legal form in three steps. *First*, I reiterate the Marxian concept of totality in a presentation of the ontological and epistemological roots of the dialectical method and the wager of class struggle as the motor of history. *Second,* I embark on a critique of how the Marxian concept of form has been developed in contemporary Marxian critique, particularly with regard to i) how the Marxist sense of *totality* has been truncated and ii) how *class struggle* as a historically specific, pervasive relation

For alternatives see for example Brenna Bhandar and Alberto Toscano, 'Race, Real Estate and Real Abstraction' (2015) *Radical Philosophy*, https://www.radicalphilosophy.com/article/race-real-estate-and-real-abstraction; Brenna Bhandar, 'Status as Property: Identity, Land and the Dispossession of First Nations Women in Canada' (2016) 14 *Darkmatter Journal* 1.

3 See for example, on this tendency of legal form Rob Knox, 'International Law, Race, and Capitalism: A Marxist Perspective' (2023) *AJIL* Unbound 55D; Donatella Alessandrini, J del Pilar Cortes-Nieto, L Eslava, A Yilmaz Vastardis, 'The Dream of Formality: Racialisation Otherwise and International Economic Law' (2022) 25 *Journal of International Economic Law* 207.

has been simultaneously deformed and eclipsed. Here, I use a critique of systematic dialectics and social form theory as a case study, focusing on the epistemological notion that grounds the dialectic of this movement: the so-called *object totality*. *Third*, I present my critique of the legal form as grounded in the classical Marxist sensitivity to the real, unbridled totality of *'Being with a capital B'*.[4]

While my reading does provide a clear methodological starting point of the legal form, I stress the need precisely to withhold the use of the legal form as a conceptual a priori. In encountering the fetishized appearances of the legal form as they intuitively appear in the objective, critique should strive to reveal the inner movements of these forms rather than impose a finished definition or 'content' upon them. Only in this way, through the constant derivation of abstract class struggle from the more concrete legal form, can the *real* form, shape, and inner relations of law be laid bare in social understanding. Only in this way can the plasticity of objective totality be made justice.

Planting the wager of the capital relation in social understanding

Central to Marxist understanding, such as I will present in this chapter, is the notion that there is such a thing as an objective reality.[5] But this is not the timeless, that is, *dead* objectivity of the bourgeoisie horizon, held forcefully in stasis through dogma, a priori and brute violence. It is instead the living, thinking and acting objectivity of social understanding, *the absolute*, *the concrete*, of *the idea* or *ideal*, of the *common good*, to name a few iterations.[6] In this section, I shortly introduce the two great *wagers* of historical materialism, the wager of the absolute—with the self-moving, self-grounding Idea as the real movement of history and as the measure of truth—and the wager of *class struggle* as the real albeit hidden and still under-realized content of this

4 Vanessa Wills, 'What Could It Mean to Say, "Capitalism Causes Sexism and Racism?"' (2018) 46 *Philosophical Topics* 229.

5 ibid, Vladimir Lenin, *Philosophical Notebooks*, vol 38 (Collected Works, Progress Publishers 1976); Karel Kosík, *Dialectics of the Concrete: A Study on Problems of Man and World* (Springer 2012); Evald Vasilyevich Ilyenkov, *The Dialectics of the Abstract and the Concrete in Marx's Capital* (Aakar Books 2008); Raya Dunayevskaya, *The Power of Negativity: Selected Writings on the Dialectic in Hegel and Marx* (Lexington Books 2002); Agnes Heller, *A Theory of History* (Routledge and Kegan Paul 1982); Katie Terezakis, 'Telling the Truth: Heller as Philosopher of History and Personality' (2014) 125 Thesis Eleven.

6 ibid, Georg Wilhelm Friedrich Hegel, *Georg Wilhelm Friedrich Hegel: The Science of Logic* (Cambridge Hegel Translations, CUP 2015). Keti Chukrov, *Practicing the Good: Desire and Boredom in Soviet Socialism* (University of Minnesota Press 2020). Georg Lukacs, *History and Class Consciousness: Studies in Marxist Dialectics* (MIT Press 1971).

Idea.[7] This wager or *notion* of class struggle has the potential to unravel the true and inner relations of the objective and to do so in a way that must necessarily change it, or rather; to allow history and all of its attendant abstractions, to change itself.[8] The purpose of this section is to introduce the critique of object-oriented ontologies of capitalism, using systematic dialectics as a case, as well as the critique of law.

The great wager of the idea: absolute immanence and unity in difference

In Marxist thought, the dialectic is the real movement of history, as well as the key to grasp this movement and the abstractions, forms and relations that structure social reality.[9] The wager of absolute totality entails that every abstraction and every concrete instance forms a whole and that this *whole* of reality and history must be critiqued, its inner relations laid bare, according to its own logic, as it unfolds. However, due to the reifying force of capitalist abstractions, the objective, such as it really is, remains largely hidden to us, subjects under capitalism, even as we are sprung from and given form through these very abstractions and their inner movements. In order to become conscious of ourselves—of our acts and thoughts, tastes, desires, and entire worldviews—as well as to gain true freedom through this consciousness, it becomes necessary to *critique* the forms and abstractions that rule and govern all life. Abstractions such as value, labor, will, subject, law, and state, forming the bourgeoisie horizon, must be critiqued in way of sublation, forced by way of their own inner logic to offer up the hidden contents and relations by which they move, their inner *notions*.[10]

7 The idea of the historical wager is closely connected to the social nature of both knowledge and society and the social unity between them. If history alone explains history, and history as a material process and as a form of knowledge is socially produced, then the history embedded in our acts and thoughts is always partial, historizised by our informed guesses or wagers on the nature of the forces that propel history forward. On this idea of the *wagers* of history see Heller (n 5). Terezakis (n 5). When a wager has been made, for example, that history provides its own grounding, or that the motor of history and of the legal form is class struggle, then this wager will pay off—or not pay off—through the concrete appearances that it engenders, and the other way around. For example, if there ever is a truly successful socialist revolution, we will see if the law withers away, proving its transhistorical nature, bound to capitalist totality; and, as a second example, at the end of this chapter, you will see if you find my argument on the convincing.

8 Lukacs (n 6).

9 Karl Marx, *Capital*, vol I (Penguin Classics 2004). Karl Marx, *Grundrisse, Foundations of the Critique of Political Economy (Rough Draft)* (Penguin Books in Association with New Left Review 1973). Karl Marx, 'The Value-Form, Appendix to the 1st German Edition of Capital, vol 1, 1867' (1978) 4 Capital and Class.

10 This notion of the bourgeoisie horizon is a metaphor for the way that the concepts and acts through which one approaches the world decides, in a very real way, how the world appears

The great wager of absolute totality entails that the objective such as it really is, the truth of the world, unravels in understanding as if from the middle. Among other ways, dialectics can be described as a bidirectional movement from the abstract to the concrete, from the concrete to the abstract, striving toward unity in difference of the different levels; moving toward a greater social understanding of totality through attention to the blank spots of this social or objective understanding, sublating and deepening this understanding. In this way, the abstract is *grounded* by the way it necessarily relates in or to the concrete, and vice versa, and truth is unraveled as the proper logic of the object of study itself. Through this *kneading* of concrete and abstract in dialectic unity, understanding can *first* be made aware of the abstractions and forms that *already* structure its concrete worldview, and *second* through suspending and sublating these abstractions and this worldview, lay bare the real movement behind their empty, one-sided shells. Through dialectic critique, one is made aware of how the fetishized forms, which are not only of the mind but of action, of labor, how these forms not only hide but actively *withhold* from life the ontology of socialism, of the idea of true freedom and beauty.

Given that the dialectic is 'living, many-sided knowledge (with the number of sides eternally increasing), with an infinite number of shades of every approach and approximation to reality (with a philosophical system growing into a whole out of each shade)' it is 'immeasurably rich'.[11] The *truth* of this immeasurable movement, and of the absolute itself, cannot be presented as some final proof. Instead, it is a process of *praxis*, through which the objective reality is reformed, kneaded, made clear, always anew in light of its own, inner notions: the final validity of the absolute is always postponed. Lenin, scribbling down his thoughts on Hegels *Science of Logic* in his philosophical notebooks, commented on this aspect of the dialectic and the postponement of truth that it entails: 'Hegel actually *proved* that logical forms and laws are not an empty shell, but the reflection of the objective world. More correctly, he did not prove, but *made a brilliant guess* [italics added]'.[12]

Through dialectic critique, the 'reflection' of the objective world can be made to iteratively offer its inner depth as totality. The idea of the absolute is not a theory, but an inescapable way to meet, act, and live in the world,

and the ways that the world may appear, they decide the horizons of imagination as well as of action. See for example Marx, *Capital* (n 9) 96

> In so far as political economy is bourgeois, i.e. in so far as it views the capitalist order as the absolute and ultimate form of social production, instead of as a historically transient stage of development, it can only remain a science while the class struggle remains latent or manifests itself only in isolated and sporadic phenomena.

11 Lenin (n 5) 360.

12 ibid 180. On these notions of guesses and wagers see footnote 7.

ultimately a becoming of the world in such a way that action and thought are extensions of the same movement, of the same idea. In this way, the separation between knowledge and action is undone. Practice or praxis is the inextricable unity of action and thought. Again, in the words of Lenin: '[M] an's practice, repeating itself a thousand million times, becomes consolidated in man's consciousness by figures of logic. Precisely (and only) on account of this thousand-million-fold repetition, these figures have the stability of a prejudice, an axiomatic character'.[13]

Through or *as* the idea of the world, praxis or labor stretches out in a movement that is history. So, what is the *idea* of history, the *will* of the world? It is not yet socialism, and it is *class struggle* only as a notion, a secret longing, and a great bet of historical materialism.[14] Identity of this notion with the objective can only be established through the praxis of ruthless critique of all that exists so that the hidden kernel of reality is finally laid bare. In time and praxis, another worldview will spring from the dry shell of the old, one-sided, inadequate forms and notions of unreflected capitalist modernity.

The great wager of the capital relation: historically specific class struggle

When the wager of unity in difference of the abstract and the concrete has been placed, it is made clear that no intuitive understanding of the concrete can exist in isolation from abstract thought forms. The objective abstractions and worldviews which give form and shape to all capitalist life are ever-present and fully constitutive. For all disciplines, as well as for the general objective consciousness, this means that there is always some silent and most basic assumption sitting heavily at the floor of understanding. And that, as one gets to know and move in the world, it is through this assumption that knowing is made, and the world unravels along the gravity of this most basic Word. Through the wager of historical materialism, it is the task of Marxist or socialist thought to place *class struggle* firmly at the center of social understanding. For jurisprudence and other social sciences, this means to develop systems and methods by which the legal form can iteratively be critiqued, its real movements discovered.

Emancipatory, socialist theory is often named Marxism, because Karl Marx showed with great clarity, in the right place and at the right time, not only that the key to social emancipation rests within the contradictions immanent to the mode of production of a society, that is, *class struggle*, but what particular form such struggle assumes in capitalist society. With this

13 ibid 216.
14 Lukacs (n 6).

singular finding and its expert presentation, Marx unleashed a whole new continent of thought, knowledge, and history.[15] It has been named a new continent since every moment of capitalist reality can be made through the wager of historical materialism to offer their inner secret and fully transform so that this wager offers another world of thought, hidden within the forms of old. For the legal form, I will argue, this continent of thought offers nothing less than a proper ontology for the discipline of jurisprudence, grounded in the abstract notion of class struggle. In a capitalist society, Marx shows, class struggle takes the form of the law of value or of the *capital relation*: The drive of capital—that is, of self-valorizing value—to accumulate surplus value, against the drive of everything that is not capital, to resist the value form.[16]

The value form must indeed be resisted because, at its core, it is wholly empty. It is pure, abstract relation—it exists either as a form of the capital relation, or it does not exist at all. As an abstraction, the value form can produce mountains of materials, massive enough to block the flows of oceans, melt the Arctic, and blot out the sky—but it cannot produce *more* of itself, because not only is it simply a social relation, but a totalizing one. The only way for capital to produce surplus value, and for the value-form to endure, is for capital to find a way to de*value* other iterations of *itself*; such as the cost of labor power, or the purchasing power of an entire nation, or the consumer of monopolized goods. Thus, the value form, as a pure relation, can only produce a surplus value *in relation to itself*. Most abstractly vampiric or cannibalistic, the value form will only endure as long as it reproduces itself in this way. Value, as a form of the capital relation, is voracious, yet insatiable, and must never cease to reproduce a world in its image. This is the *notion* of the capital relation. The capital relation creates a productive, real abstraction—the value form—from which sprouts, historically and logically, the continuous reorganization of all social relations—from which sprouts a world. As forms of the totality of the capital relation, value, money, price, race, the commodity, law, and state, etc., co-emerge dialectically, iteratively reworking all of social relations in their wake.

Up until now, I have laid down the theoretical groundwork of historical materialism in the dual wagers of dialectical materialism and class struggle as the motor of history. In the following I will contrast these wagers with the truncated dialectics of object-oriented models of capitalism, using systematic dialectics as a case. In conceptually banning capitalism to the object realm, this dialectic simultaneously loses grasp of the objective world as an

15 Dunayevskaya (n 5). Raya Dunayevskaya and others, *Marx's Philosophy of Revolution in Permanence for Our Day: Selected Writings* (Bibliography, Brill 2018) 263 and Louis Althusser, 'Philosophy as a Revolutionary Weapon' (1970) 64 *NLR* 3.

16 John Holloway and Sol Picciotto, 'Capital, Crisis and the State' (1977) 1 *Capital & Class* 76.

absolute totality of shifting social relations *and* of the worldmaking relation of class struggle. Because of this loss, as I will show in the next section, object-oriented ontologies of capitalism—such as social form theory and systematic dialectics—are unable to critique the legal form, as to make visible that inner relation which fundamentally transforms its many forms and appearances: the capital relation.

Critiquing Marxian 'object models' of capitalism

In order to underscore the importance of totality and class struggle, I will, in this section, critique *the systematic dialectic* of contemporary, so-called social form theory.[17] The systematic dialectic aims at recreating the method applied by Marx in the writing of *Capital* and, in so doing, it beautifully clarifies the different abstract forms that, throughout Marx's presentation, found their genesis in the capital relation. However, in being ultimately unable to *let go* of the systematically constructed object totality as an epistemological, totalizing notion, and in so doing escape the confines of a world of *things* and *facts* for one of *relations* or *notions*, social form theory cannot account for the notion of the capital relation in and for itself. Consequently, and like other leading Marxian accounts that share this tendency, it deradicalizes social theory, being able only to account for the causality of 'capital' or the 'capitalist system' as an *object totality*, while tending to present class struggle simply as a moment within this object totality (that is, to the extent it can at all account for such struggle). In this subsection, I will show how the gravity of *object totality* as an epistemological assumption, forecloses the vital praxis of grounding of the capital relation in social understanding in general and of the legal form.

Introducing systematic dialectics and its reliance on the object totality

One of several things to appreciate with the systematic dialecticians is that they are indeed very systematic, and transparent, in their presentations.

17 Patrik Murray, *The Mismeasure of Wealth* (Brill 2016); Patrik Murray, *Methods* (The SAGE Handbook of Marxism SAGE 2021); Chris Arthur, *The Spectre of Capital: Idea and Reality* (Brill 2022); Tony Smith, *The Logic of Marx's Capital Replies to Hegelian Criticisms* (State University of New York Press 1990); Geert Reuten, *The Unity of the Capitalist Economy and State: A Systematic-Dialectical Exposition of the Capitalist System*, vol 186 (Brill 2019); Geert Reuten, 'An Outline of the Systematic-Dialectical Method: Scientific and Political Significance' in Tony Smith and Fred Moseley (eds), *Marx's Capital and Hegel's Logic* (Brill 2014) 241–268.

Patrick Murray, one of the foremost social form theorists, presents the systematic dialectic presentation as follows:

> i) a systematic dialectical presentation will have identifiable premises or presuppositions given by nature and history; ii) it will represent the moments of the object under study in their inseparability as uncovered by phenomenological inquiry into that object, and in so doing it will disclose the essence of what is under study; iii) in introducing those moments, the presentation will proceed from the conceptually simpler to the conceptually more complex; and iv) though the conceptual development proceeds from the conceptually simpler to the conceptually more complex, the former will be presented, at least implicitly, as presupposing the latter: there is a structure of mutual presupposition among the simpler and more complex categories.[18]

For Murray, it is very important that the systematic dialectic relies in its presentation on certain phenomenological presuppositions.[19] In his own words, Murray understands the concept of '"phenomenology" in a broad sense, not specifically Hegelian or Husserlian, to mean experience-based inquiry into when the distinguishable is separable'.[20] Consequently, Murray's account of systematic dialectics rests on a split notion of validity. First, the systematic dialectic is valid because it follows from certain premises about the human condition, nature, and history. Second, the systematic dialectic is valid because of the internal coherence of the presentation, in which all the necessary conditions are posited and mutually presupposed as to make up an object totality.

Finally, in starring facts as being phenomenological, Murray means to say that social forms can act as facts and that facts coemerge with social forms. With this move, Murray claims to transcend what he calls a 'purist split' between the 'empirical' and 'the conceptual' spheres of thought.[21] In other words, social forms interact with phenomenological truths by i) depending on these truths as premises and ii) having causal power among phenomenological facts posing as premises in the finding of these facts.[22] The two epistemological notions coalesce in Murray's account, but they never fully collapse

18 Murray, *The Mismeasure of Wealth* (n 17) 106.

19 ibid 97 and especially p 486 with Murray's account of the "general, phenomenological truth of historical materialism as follows: 'human beings are needy, self-conscious, symbolising, social, sexually reproducing animals who are in (and of) non-human nature, which they purposively transform according to their perceived wants'.".

20 Murray, *The Mismeasure of Wealth* (n 17) 168.

21 ibid 69 ff. Murray coins the concept 'formal causality', see p 70.

22 Murray, *The Mismeasure of Wealth* (n 17) 70.

into each other. While social forms can be posed as phenomenological facts, all phenomenological facts cannot be posed as social forms and have 'formal causality'. For a social form to be a social form, it must be presentable as an object totality.

Murray's account can be contrasted with that of Geert Reuten, which is very similar except on some core points. Reuten is very intricate and transparent indeed, in explaining the grounds for validity of the systematic dialectic presentation.[23] At its base, his systematic dialectic is about unity in difference and, through unity, the *eradication of all presupposition*. For Reuten, the systematic dialectic is about i) finding and explicating an object totality ii) through one unifying concept (he often calls this concept 'the starting point') iii) which is grounded in presentation through a series of mutually presupposing presuppositions.[24] According to Reuten, 'the key to the reliability of [systematic dialectics] lies in the interconnection of all relevant knowledge about some object totality'.[25] Consequently, a condition of possibility for systematic dialectics, is that 'its object realm, in our case capitalism, is inherently systemic, that is, it consists of interacting constituent parts forming an integrated whole'.[26] For Reuten this is an ontological matter, that is, Reuten presupposes that the world consists of distinguishable and separable systemic wholes—object totalities. This presupposition is 'grounded' for Reuten, by

23 Reuten, *The Unity of the Capitalist Economy and State* (n 17) 602 ff.
24 ibid 614.
25 ibid 15.
26 ibid 606. For more on Reuten's dialectics, see Reuten, *The Unity of the Capitalist Economy and State* (n 17):

> The pre-systematic research (A§3) leads up to the starting point of an SD exposition. This starting point is an all-encompassing conceptualisation of the object totality. It is abstract in the sense of it being an as yet non-grounded conceptualisation. At the starting point we merely have the appropriation of analysis as an abstract determination (α in Figure 14.4). Or, we have 'merely' posited a unity-in-difference.

continued:

> At the beginning it is unclear how the starting point can have existence. At the beginning it is, as yet, unproven that the starting moment (α) indeed is the unifying concept of the object totality. This has to be shown in the process of setting out its conditions of existence, along which the starting point appears progressively less abstract. Thus we have a process of progressive concretization and differentiation (β). As Hegel says, at the beginning "difference is still sunk in the unity, not yet set forth as different". Only on completion of the exposition, he continues, will we know that "[t]he truth of the differentiated is its being in unity. And only through this movement is the unity truly concrete". 14 Once the exposition is complete—and thus when the initial unifying concept is shown to be inherent in the object totality, in its full concreteness (γ)—we will have come full circle, confirming the truth of the abstract starting point. Thus the ultimate test of a starting point is the success of the exposition itself.
>
> Reuten, *The Unity of the Capitalist Economy and State* (n 17), 614

the way that epistemologically, object totalities can be presented as such through the systematic dialectic. Thus, the validity of the systematic dialectic presentation depends on the presentation of social forms, and the other way around, in a perfectly circular logic that is reflected in the presentation itself.

For both Murray and Reuten, the object totality that is presented is proven by the way it logically presupposes and is presupposed by the starting point, or the most abstract moment—the lowest form of abstraction—of the presentation. The validity of the method, in turn, is proven by the possibility of this result. The relation of validity springs thus, in Hegelian terms, from a circle of circles. Murray breaks this circular logic somewhat, by insisting on the importance of certain silent presuppositions about history and the human condition that predate the systematic dialectic. Murray insists that *this*, namely the posing of premises before the systemic dialectic, is what for Marx, separated his (Marx's) account from that of Hegel. In the words of Murray,

> These premises, which are given by nature and are not themselves subject to incorporation as "results" of some more cosmic systematic dialectic, reappear in *Capital* and testify to Marx's explicit and frequently reaffirmed divergence from strictly Hegelian systematic dialectics (at least as he, questionably, understood Hegel).

In the end, however, Murray's systematic dialectics lend their validity from these premises only indirectly. It is the systematic dialectic presentation, and the premises with them, that is proven as valid by the way that the object totality as a systemic whole, appears.[27] According to the social form, and many value form theorists, social forms are what they are precisely because they can be presented in the form of object totalities, through the systematic dialectics of presentation.[28] The object totality is deemed to exist as an object, because of the systematic dialectic presentation, and the other way around.

The circle outside of circles: the frozen circle of object totality

To summarize, systematic dialectics serve to first find and later present an *object totality*, through positing 'its' mutually presupposing forms, at different levels of abstraction, thereby simultaneously grounding the lowest level of abstraction of the presentation as a whole. Later in this section, I will question the *necessity* of the object totality, which systematic dialectics deem

27 Murray, *Methods* (n 17) 49 ff.

28 Murray, *The Mismeasure of Wealth* (n 17) 95 ff; Arthur (n 17) 27 ff; Reuten, 'An Outline of the Systematic-Dialectical Method' (n 17) 241–68.

constitutive. But before I go into this, I would like to discuss what's at stake: what the object totality *does* with the presentation and with the Marxian dialectic as a whole.

First, and this is the most important critique, according to the logic of object totality, capitalism can only be presented in the abstract. The abstract object of capitalism and its attendant forms can then have causal effects in 'the real world'. This central, constitutive moment of systematic dialectics introduces an arbitrary cut or separation between the abstract and the concrete, that *completely truncates the historically specific relation of class struggle*. At the same time, it clouds the view of the concrete *and* of abstract forms. The abstract and the concrete, distinguishable but *inseparable* moments, cannot be made within the dialectic to reveal their own, inner relations when the object totality as epistemological and ontological form is forced upon them this way. The forms of capitalist totality, including the forms of wage labor and class struggle are, with systematic dialectics, presented with the goal of creating a mutually presupposing abstract whole. The goal is *not* to understand, unravel, and regard for differences in concrete and abstract phenomena. Because of this, the forms of systematic dialectics and any other object-oriented presentation of capitalist totality and capitalist forms, *lack movement*. Because of this lack of movement, there is a clear limit to the conceptual force of the systematic dialectic in unravelling class struggle into social understanding, transforming the *worldview* of this understanding. This way, the systematic dialectic fences in the absolute and explosive power of historically specific class struggle.[29]

More specifically, the way it is presented by systematic dialectics, capitalism as an object totality withholds understanding of the capitalist forms of law, state, racism, imperialism, and other, more concrete phenomena.[30] It

29 Compare Hegel on the *release* of the concept from the object totality posed by the dialectics of being and essence, in footnote 46 and in Georg Wilhelm Fredrich Hegel, *The Science of Logic* (CUP 2010) 521–22: 'When this manifestation of essence is set free, then we have the concept. . . . The present position to which this development has led is that the form of the *absolute* which is higher than being and essence is *the concept*. Viewed from this side, the concept has *subjugated* the spheres of being and essence to which, from other starting points, feeling, intuition, and representation, which appeared to be its antecedent conditions, also belong; it has demonstrated itself to be *their unconditional foundation*. But this is one side alone. There is a *second side* left to which this third book of the Logic is devoted, namely the demonstration of how the concept forms within and from itself the reality that has vanished in it. It is conceded, in other words, that the cognition that does not go past the concept, purely as concept, is still incomplete, that it has only arrived at *abstract truth*. But its incompleteness does not lie in its lack of that alleged reality as would be given in feeling and intuition, but in the fact that the concept has yet to give to itself its *own* reality, one that it generates out of itself'.

30 Reuten, in his presentation of capitalism, abstracts from colonialism, racism, etc, because 'capitalism can exist without these'. Reuten, 'An Outline of the Systematic-Dialectical Method' (n 17) 529. This is the sort of claim made necessary when the course of history

can only either i) incorporate the legal form as a necessary moment of itself, ii) regard the law, the state, and concrete phenomena as forms of distinct object totalities, or iii) view these forms and appearances either as functions to, mediated by, or as distorting itself.[31] This, too, follows from the lack of movement, the muting force of the object totality. When class struggle has been reduced to a set and introverted moment of object totality—for example, the extraction of surplus value from specifically wage-labor—then the legal form can only be regarded by the way it is *necessary* to enable surplus value extraction from wage-labor. For example, this can be done by positing the general equality of legal subjects as a necessary moment of capitalism as an object totality, keeping this supposed equality of liberal jurisprudence relatively intact.[32] This functional and purely abstract view of law renders invisible i) how legal form and indeed the struggle between wage-labor and capitalists are forms of appearances of class struggle at the most abstract level and ii) how law, as a form of appearance of abstract class struggle, has laws of motion of its own, which can be rendered visible by critique.[33]

Importantly, through the obfuscating figure of the object totality, the notion of class struggle in and for itself is made unseen, defused, or heavily

is truncated by the abstract agency of the object totality as epistemological and ontological notion. This account may be compared with for example Ramón Grosfoguel, 'The Global Contributions of Black Decolonial Marxism—A Foreword' in Sabelo J Ndlovu-Gatsheni and Morgan Ndlovu (eds), *Marxism and Decolonialization in the 21st Century Living Theory and True Ideas* (Routledge 2022) xviii. 'Black Radical thinkers . . . have emphasized the fact that racism and the idea of race are not simply part of the ideological "superstructure" of capitalism but an organizing/articulation/structuring principle inherent to capitalist exploitation and the accumulation of capital at a world scale'. And with Hegel (n 29) 519 'Abstractive thought (. . .) is not to be regarded as the mere discarding of a sensuous material which does not suffer in the process any impairment of reality; it is rather the sublation and reduction of that material as mere *appearance* to the *essential*, which is manifested only in *the concept*.' In a full Hegelian view, the notion inherent in the concept of *object totality*, that abstraction *must* entail the ontological separation of a certain sphere of reality (i.e. capitalism as object totality), is foreign the idea of absolute truth, which entails a grasp of universal and self-moving ground. Simply put—if our concept of capitalism (or rather class struggle) cannot and indeed must not be able to account for, that is, the manifold appearances of actually imposed racial difference, then our concept of class struggle is inadequate.

31 Among social formalists, racism is often seen as 'distorting' the concrete appearance of 'capitalism as object totality', see, for example, Murray, *The Mismeasure of Wealth* (n 17) 175: 'Houses may be commodities, but racist real estate practices do not play by the rule that one person's money is as good as another's'.

32 See for example Wilén (n 2).

33 For example, when Patrick Murray asserts that racist pricing of American real estate *distorts* the commodity form (and we might add, the legal form), he places a severe cut between capitalist and *other* social relations (see footnote 30). If he did not uphold this cut between the abstract and the concrete, he could see that the legal form moves precisely by stratifying formal legal subjectivity *differently*, that the struggle to become equal or render unequal is a manner of class struggle over the form of legal subjectivity.

reconstructed. This defusal of class struggle lies at the missing heart of the stasis of capitalism as object totality. Murray, Reuten, Smith, Arthur, among other social form theorists, all end up producing their own, slightly different object totalities. Even if the differences among these object totalities are minute, the debates that flower around them are grand bordering on imposing.[34] Never are the debates more considerable than around the question of how surplus value is produced, which is precisely where, in Marx's *Capital*, the capital relation is found.[35] Like Marx, social form theorist seeks the answer within *abstract, value-producing labor* as social form. However, where Marx turned to *labor* in order to *critique it* as a fetishized appearance within classical economics, an unquestioned a priori, social form theorists turn to labor as a Marxian concept in order to either reify wage labor as the singular source of surplus-value or nullify any notion of how value is created. Because of this, they lose track of the capital relation in and for itself, and so they blind critique to the work that this relation does in or *as* the world.[36]

For example, Murray lists his description of the conditions under which abstract labor is value producing, in Murray's terms called 'practically abstract labor'.[37] He does this in answer to Reuten, who believes that the labor theory of value has no place within a true systematic dialectic, seeming

34 For example, see Moseley, another social form theorist, in a heated book-long debate with Michael Heinrich's particular interpretation of Marx's value-form theory, in Fred Moseley, *Marx's Theory of Value in Chapter 1 of Capital: A Critique of Heinrich's Value-Form Interpretation* (Palgrave Macmillan 2023).

35 As explained above, the capital relation, as a purely social relation, is the seed from which the totality of capitalist social forms and relations spring. This relation is, simply stated, the way that value form and capitalist social totality are reproduced. The secret of the value form is that it can only be produced in relation to itself, by devaluing itself, in its many concrete forms, such as labor power, see page five ff. Consequently, the capital relation—the historically specific form of class struggle—is the drive of value form to reproduce itself through devaluing itself, against everything and everyone that resists this existential drive.

36 Also, they take up a lot of academic and intellectual space, that could be filled with the task of positioning class struggle at the heart of social understanding, through critique of concrete phenomena, and theory production informed by such critique.

37 Murray, *The Mismeasure of Wealth* (n 17) 264–65:

> for an hour's labour to count as an hour's worth of value, it must meet several conditions: 1. It must be an hour of 'simple average labour'; hours of complex labour count for more. And what counts as simple average labour is historically variable, not naturally determined. 2. To be 'socially necessary', the hour of labour must produce the number of commodities equal to the number produced in an hour averaged across all producers of that commodity. An hour's labour that produces more commodities than the average counts as more value, and conversely. An hour of labour that is socially necessary in sense (2) is socially necessary in a further sense—one that builds demand into the very concept of value—only if the demand for that type of commodity matches the supply. If the supply of a commodity exceeds demand, an hour's labour on that commodity that is socially necessary in sense (2) produces less than an hour's value, and conversely.

as it does, according to Reuten, to assume 'value' as 'physical substance'.[38] For Arthur, a social formalist that I have yet to present, labor is something which capital-as-subject posits to be its own precondition, in order to subsume it in the form of value.[39] The critique that Marx presented of how surplus value reproduces never truly fits, it seems the moment in constant need of reordering or the mistake to be overlooked. It sits uncomfortably squeezed amidst the folds of the object totality.

In contrast, through a full Hegelian view of dialectics, the spirit, not the object, lends movement to history. What Marx saw, and what many have since then seen, is that the idea of history is *class struggle*. He also saw that this idea is still but a notion, hiding behind or being withheld by the false totality of interlocking idealist abstractions; this interlocking totality is never better presented than throughout Hegel's logic, albeit uncritically so.[40] Marx showed that is exactly through the praxis of *uncovering* the notion of class struggle, that its movement as a motor of history is *unleashed* from fetishized thought forms—frozen in stasis around their secret kernels, their secret longing—in such a way that *it*, the notion of class-struggle, may make itself true upon the world.

Truncated Hegelian dialectic: the epistemological roots of object totality

The Hegelian logic is of central importance for the whole structure of Marx's *Capital* and of the systematic dialectic, including their notion of the object totality. However, social form theorists only draw from the *Logic of Essence* of Hegel's *Science of Logic*, foregoing the *Subjective Logic* partly or fully.[41] This way, I argue, the systematic dialecticians truncate the revolutionary dialectic of historical materialism in such a way as to make it inert. Without the subjective logic, the movement of history is frozen in abstract stasis. However, if systematic dialectic were to affirm the subjective logic, in other words, to reincorporate itself into the Marxian sense of not object totality but absolute totality of being, social form theory still has considerable merit. As such, may help illuminate and make clear and true the rule of abstractions generally, and the rule of abstract the legal form specifically.

In his own rendering of Hegelian terms, Reuten makes use of the logic of Essence of capitalism, without minding the logic of Idea of capitalism.[42] He

38 Reuten, *The Unity of the Capitalist Economy and State* (n 17).
39 Arthur (n 17).
40 See Rosie Woodhouse in this volume.
41 Reuten explicitly states that he foregoes the Subjective logic, see Reuten (n 30) 615. See also Smith (n 17). See also Murray, *The Mismeasure of Wealth* (n 17) 67, 274, 345, 389, 393.
42 Reuten (n 30) 615.

does this for reasons similar to those of Tony Smith—who is appalled by the subjective logic, proclaiming that

> [w]hereas in reality *thoughts are properties of real human subjects*, here it seems that "Thought" or Spirit is hypostasised into a supersubject, *while real humans are made into its predicates*. Obviously such a topsy-turvey metaphysics is incompatible with a materialist ontology [italics added].[43]

Reuten and Smith alike are not able to let go of the sovereignty of human, transhistorical agency. Because of this, they are driven to affirm the very mystical, cosmic dialectic that Hegel himself presented, through which man and his thoughts and his reason are their own beginning, and the source of the real movement of history. In refusing the Hegelian subjective logic—ironically—Reuten and Smith seal this very logic in social understanding. Their stance is therefore foreign to historical materialism and the dialectic that would instead seek to affirm *and abolish* these forms, by looking at history and its abstractions, its many fold forms and appearances, from the standpoint of class struggle.

Murray and especially Chris Arthur are more inclined towards the Hegelian subjective logic.[44] In his latest work, *The Spectre of Capital*, Arthur casts *Capital* itself as a subject which recognizes itself in the world and returns to itself transformed, imprinting its terrible twisted shape upon the world.[45] Still, I will argue, wedged beneath the towering object totality of capital, the notion of class struggle remains hidden. Arthur insists that value is accumulated by being posited by capital in the form of wage labor, and then in a second step extracted by capital. This is how capital accumulates—by reflecting itself upon life only to gorge upon its own image; vampire-like, it poses its own presuppositions and taps the life out of being. Arthur paints a vivid and properly eldritch frame, from which *Capital with a capital C* burst, spirals out to feed. However, the notion of capital cannot quite be regarded in and for itself. The notion appears the great maw of *a particular object*; it is the gaping gob of an object totality rather than the utmost seedling of absolute totality.[46] And so it is that the abstract concept of class struggle is truncated,

43 Smith (n 17). Compare this with the contrasting account of Hegelian Angelica Nuzzo: 'Philosophy is, more precisely, an immanent dimension of that very world and time, namely, the dimension of rational (self-) comprehension of the world itself'. In Angelica Nuzzo, 'Changing the World of Spirit in Hegel's Philosophy of Right' (2021) 8 *Crisis and Critique*.

44 Murray, *The Mismeasure of Wealth* (n 17) 67, 274, 345, 389, 393 and Arthur (n 17).

45 Arthur (n 17).

46 On the Hegelian notion of Notion (in German *Begriff*, and in the cited work translated into *concept* rather than *notion*, see Translators note in the *Science of Logic*, p XVII), see p 526:

> The concept, as considered so far, has demonstrated itself to be the unity of *being* and essence. Essence is the *first negation* of being, which has thereby become *reflective shine*;

and critique is made to encounter social forms and concrete phenomena from the standpoint of capital as an automatic subject rather than from the standpoint of the abstract relation of class struggle.

From the one-sided standpoint of *Capital* as subject, the real movement of forms and appearances remains hidden. There is no way of knowing what social forms under capitalism *must do*, other than reproducing the wage labor form. This form, moreover, is fetishized, being seen as the sole 'source' of surplus value.[47]

Also, and eldritch appearances aside, capital doesn't seem all that bad. If value stems from the act of capital of positing labor as the wage labor form—in order to then extract this labor in the form of surplus value—surely it could just, with the right politics, be forced to posit more wages? And if I am a relatively well-off wage laborer—and there are many—why would I complain? What tools am I given to notice my own complicity? The diehard idea that the great beast of capital could be domesticated, its divine milk distributed through socially controlled forms, maintains its irreducible presence.

Things fall apart: class struggle and the abolishment the object totality

In this chapter, I argue that a proper critique of law must rest on the dual wagers of *absolute totality* and of *class struggle* as the real motor of history. One central thesis of this argument is that capitalist social relations shouldn't be seen as a mere object totality, but a shifting, moving, ever-present social and absolute totality, springing in the abstract from the capital relation and the spirit of class struggle. The capital relation, which has many names, is the historically specific notion of class struggle. Marx found this relation by way of critiquing the appearance of the commodity in classical economics in such a way that the secret of value was laid bare. This secret is *not* that it only comes from wage labor, but that as a totalizing relation, it can only

the concept is the *second negation*, or the negation of this negation, and is therefore being which has been restored once more, but as in itself the infinite mediation and negation of being. . . . The concept is the truth of the substantial relation in which being and essence attain their perfect self-subsistence and determination each through the other. The truth of substantiality proved to be the *substantial identity*, an identity that equally is, and only is, *positedness*. Positedness is *determinate existence* and *differentiation*; in the concept, therefore, being-in-and-for-itself has attained a true existence adequate to it, for that positedness is itself being-in-and-for-itself. This positedness constitutes the difference of the concept in the concept itself; and because the concept is immediately being-in-and-for-itself, its *differences* are themselves *the whole concept—universal in their determinateness and identical in their negation.*

47 Arthur (n 17) 242, 239.

accumulate in relation to itself.[48] It is the task of critique not to reiterate eternally the finding that Marx already accomplished, but to get to work in *grounding this most abstract and worldmaking abstraction*—the capital relation—in the concrete, rendering greater clarity to both these levels of abstraction and the possibility of revolutionary action alike.[49]

The object totality rests on a notion of validity, which states that something is true when it can be shown as an object totality, defined by the way its distinguishable but inseparable moments are logically necessary for each other, grounds each other. But under the wager of absolute totality, the world in its thousandfold appearance is identical in difference, and not a single moment is ontologically separable from any other. This wager of the absolute entails approaching a world of difference that can be unentangled in its unity. Historical materialism, in turn, provides the methodological starting point for such work: it provides the wager that class struggle in the abstract structures of world history, such as it appears to us, beings of history.

And indeed, immanent to systematic dialectics lies the key to releasing both the epistemological notion of the absolute and its historical motor, the notion of class struggle. Social form theory can be shown as true, but insufficient, in that it beautifully clarifies social forms, but has failed to release the notion of class struggle in and for itself. The compelling aspect of systematic dialectics, according to Murray, is its ability to demystify seemingly standalone, fetishized forms by integrating them into a larger totality. This approach allows for a more relational and comprehensive understanding of the world, and the dialectic presentation is deemed valid through the way it succeeds in presenting an object totality in the most compelling way. But, and this is the simple yet central point: *it is not compelling to hold fast to object totality when it sits in the way of concrete critique*. If object totality as the utmost notion of validity is abolished and reinscribed in social understanding, in the absolute,

48 See footnote 31 and page five ff.

49 Compare Hegel (n 29) 522, on the dialectics of 'derivation' of the concept and the real: 'The derivation of the real from the concept, if

> "derivation" is what we want to call it, consists at first essentially in this, that the concept in its formal abstraction reveals itself to be incomplete and through a dialectic immanently grounded in it passes over into reality: it passes over into it, however, as into something which it generates out of itself, not as if it were falling back again onto a ready-made reality which it finds opposite it, or as if it were taking refuge, because it sought for something better but found none, into something that has already been proven to be the unessential element of appearance.

The concept of class struggle in its formal abstraction is true but incomplete. It exists, also, as its manifold appearances, in the unity of itself as totality. See also p 508:

> the concept is at first to be regarded simply as the third to being and essence, to the immediate and to reflection. Being and essence are therefore the moments of its becoming; but the concept is their foundation and truth as the identity into which they have sunk and in which they are contained.

then the dialectic presentation is free to engage concrete difference. When the idea of capitalism as static object is abolished for an understanding of class struggle as critique, when the notion of class struggle is *released* from the systematic dialectic presentation of capitalism, a true dialectic of the abstract and concrete can continue. In such a dialectic, every new presentation is not some *final proof*, indeed such proofs are suddenly impossible, but more of a wager or *a brilliant guess*, or a *wager*, and a *kneading* of social understanding toward social consciousness and revolutionary praxis.

The failure to comprehend the notion, the seed, the utmost law that is the historical form of class struggle under capitalism—in this chapter named the capital relation—leads to endless debates centered on the nuances of object totality which, while seemingly endless, overlook the already established concept of the capital relation, the law of value, class struggle, whatever its name. In fact, the debates are endless precisely because of the way they truncate the dialectical materialist method, relegating the absolute to the realm of myth, the way they refuse to release the notion of class struggle in social understanding; keeping it instead well-hidden between the folds of their respective and looming object totalities. They are endless because their epistemological and ontological ground is the object totality, which is a fickle castle built on the rolling dunes of absolute totality. The outer walls of their respective object totalities, constructed against the rush of history, can never be truly fixed and have no final logical ground.

Importantly, these endless debates have at the moment of writing put a pause to the singular and pivotal task of Marxist theory, which is to ground the capital relation in the manifold forms and appearances of infinitely rich concrete social understanding. The task now is *not* to rediscover but to ground this relation in the analysis of concrete phenomena, recognizing the capital relation and its various forms of appearance as inherent aspects of the absolute. This means developing methods across disciplines, by which the silent dogmas of knowledge creation can be made visible and abolished under the abstract force of class struggle as a concept and as a worldmaking abstraction. In the next subsection, I exemplify the failure of social form theory in approaching the concrete, by presenting the legal form such as it appears or can be made to appear within systematic dialectic presentations of capitalism as an object totality. Later, and in contrast, I will present my thoughts on a Marxian or historical materialist *critique* of the legal form from the dual standpoints of absolute totality and historically specific class struggle.

Two peas of a bourgeoisie pod: capitalism and law as object totalities

As a basis for legal critique, Arthur's and Murray's accounts of capital as an automatic subject are interesting but one-sided. They cannot ground the revolutionary praxis of abolishing liberal legal thought forms by grounding the legal form in abstract class struggle. This is because neither of them truly manages to *let go* of the object totality, a move that would make visible class struggle in and for itself as a worldmaking abstraction. This failure entails that the abstract appearance of the legal form will be incorporated and sealed into the necessary moments of object totality, where it *should* instead be sublated through critique. In fact, where a legal theory to be derived from their theoretical projects, that theory would look much like mainstream classical and modern legal theory. As does such legal theory, Arthur and Murray assume the formally free and equal subject. In this subsection, I shortly note the limits of systematic dialectic in critiquing the legal form.

Both Murray and Arthur *assume* the doubly free worker.[50] On this assumption, they build their object totality models of capitalism. For the commodity to exist, they say, it requires the abstractly equal subject, who is equally free to own and sell his labor power. This assumption finds its mirror in jurisprudence, which implicitly or explicitly builds on the abstraction or form of the *formally equal legal subject*. One could assert here, that as the Soviet jurist Evgeni Pashukanis writes that 'when the product of labour becomes a commodity and a bearer of value, man acquires the capacity to be a legal subject and a bearer of rights',[51] he draws attention to the fact that the enforced general equality of the law is a necessary moment of capitalist totality. In the language of systematic dialectics and the quest to erase or minimize the use of presuppositions through the creation of a fully systemic object totality, the legal subject appears as a historically specific form, necessary to the object totality of capitalism.

In this way, one can incorporate the legal form into the schema of systematic dialectic. But when this is done, and we translate the theory into a Marxist approach or method to the movements of jurisprudence and to law in social understanding, a certain lack of direction arises. We have given a definition of law, but we cannot really say what the legal form actually *does*, except to submerge the exploitation of the wage worker in a mystifying fog. We see now that the legal form is *not* transhistorical—that it is indeed specific to capitalist social relations—but *not much else*. Also, and this is a pivotal failure; we have uncritically accepted and eternalized the fetish of universal, general equality. For, under the cryogenic seal of object totality, we have frozen the legal form into a ready definition by which to order social understanding. We have reified that which we set out to *critique*.

If the systematic dialectic had in a final step abolished the object totality to release the notion of class struggle in and for itself, the methodological approach to critique the legal form would have been different. In a first

50 Arthur (n 17) 242, 239.
51 Evgeny Pashukanis, *The General Theory of Law and Marxism* (Routledge 2002).

step, legal critique would study concrete and abstract appearances of law, in order to find, detangle and present the abstractions that already structure social understanding. Depending on the shape of the concrete appearance of law, this would include perhaps the diehard thought form of abstract general equality. In a second step, legal critique would have these forms of understanding abolished by their own real movement and inner relations. For example, the thought-form of abstract general equality of legal subjects would be *unmade* into abstract equality before the value form. With this *critique* of law, legal form and its forms of appearances follow a clearer understanding of the real inner relations and movements of law, as well as a novel horizon of legal and social praxis. It is this clarity of understanding, this disentanglement of the absolute, that *grounds* the legal form and its true movements, rather than some fantasy of object totality, turned *a priori* in its relegation to the abstract realm.

Conclusion

At its core, systematic dialectics seeks to describe capitalism in terms of a static object, in order to use this totality in object form, with its sub-forms, to then explain relations in the concrete. This means that the theoretical constructions will subsume difference, rather than account for difference, in the simplest, clearest, and most explicit way possible. When the concrete is thus bent inward toward, and to be explained by theory, Marxist critique will lack direction. The central relation of the class struggle is to a large extent sealed in advance and therefore cannot be discerned and presented anew in each new instance. One could say that class struggle in this case remains bound to grand narratives when it could also be an intuitive way to meet the world, an optics, or a methodology of moving in and approaching the social.

The systematic dialectic, as it is understood by Murray, Reuten, and Arthur, etc., presupposes and reproduces the 'object totality' as an epistemological notion. However, through a tracing of the inner connections of the object totality, and of that which grounds the object totality as an epistemological notion, I find it to be inseparable from the absolute. When the 'object totality' of systematic dialectics has thus produced a notion, the notion of the absolute, it has achieved its goal, and the object totality falls away. Or rather, the object totality as an ontological notion presents itself unbound, as so many forms, as social formalism, enlivened by the force of a new such notion—the notion of the absolute, of the objective such as it truly is or of the idea. To paraphrase Hegel: through critique of the systematic dialectic, *these dead bones can be quickened by spirit.*[52]

52 Hegel (n 6) 53.

The center cannot hold: the legal form as social critique

Marx famously asserted that the role of theory is not just to describe history but to change it.[53] In the realm of legal critique, this statement has a very acute meaning. Law is an abstraction that lives on through forced immediacy. To be a legal practitioner is to describe law in its immediate appearances, in order to pronounce law *just right*. Legal practitioners are trained well in this skill, trained differently depending on their particular contexts, and there is no strict need for the practitioners to understand *why* something is *just right* rather than something else, and *how* the larger totality of law moves beyond their own bounded acts. In this way, the legal practitioner is much like the store clerk, happily pricing his wares, unaware of the mind-bendingly vast social totality through which any one commodity measures its value. The task of *legal critique*, in contrast, is to unravel precisely this larger and unseen totality, and through this presentation force law to display its own truth, its own moment of undoing.

In his work on the legal form, *General Theory of Law and Marxism*, the Soviet jurist Evgeni Pashukanis describes how every discipline is defined by the unity of its methods and particular notions, in other words by the standpoint and manner by which the discipline moves through knowledge.[54] In this section, I start by describing the methods and notions of legal practice and conventional jurisprudence. I then continue by presenting Marxist the legal form as precisely a *critique* of the legal form, grounded in the notion of class struggle. As a *critique* of the immediacy of law's appearances, Marxist legal theory could bear the task of *reforming* law in social understanding, laying bare the inner depth of its immediate appearances.

The suspension of history: the legal form as unreflected praxis

Law or the legal form, whatever it may be, moves through the world as an abstraction and appears as people, institutions, and the acts of states as a *method* or a *praxis*. Most of all, law is a doing, and part and parcel of this doing are certain forms of thoughts, that come *from outside* and cloud this doing in mystery whilst extending it uncritically onto history.

The role of legal practice is to *know the law*, to pronounce the law, and to do this from a particular standpoint. It is seldom if ever clear—for the jurist and in general understanding—*what* this standpoint is, in a sense it is perhaps *any standpoint* that *makes law work*. In another sense, and according to some

53 Karl Marx, 'Theses On Feuerbach' in *Marx/Engels Selected Works*, vol 1 (Progress Publishers 1969) 11th thesis.

54 Pashukanis (n 51).

legal theory, it is the standpoint of *the audience*—but who, or *what* is the audience?[55] Looming, shadowy, glistening limbs aloof, the audience holds its breath: ready to Act on the Word of the Law. It is presently fashionable to say that law does not truly exist, that it is simply a shared *thought construct*, as if we—the lawyers, the practicians, the motley crew of law—could simply *think together differently or* mobilize the audience differently. However, the materiality of the law is demonstrated when the jurist deviates (too much), and the spectral *Audience* suddenly slashes at the jurist's throat; when the jurist ceases to be a prophet, the voice of the law, and might as well be speaking gibberish.

In short, to be a lawyer is to be versed in *the legal method*. It is to get to know and feel the eerie winds blowing through that extra-dimensional space where only law lives and which only law truly knows. To stick your finger in the air and just *know* what law will be, how the law will work—in so many words *to become law*, to incorporate the doing of law itself.

And so, the task of legal practice is precisely to describe law, to *pronounce law* just right but *never* to change it. Under no circumstances is the task to *change it*. To change law, would be to destroy law, and this is either impossible or can only be done at great personal risk: because whilst the jurist is mortal, exchangeable and insignificant, the legal form is *as eternal* as the social relations of capitalist totality (i.e. not all that eternal). And let's be clear—some jurists *love this*. They know that they are insignificant; that they speak for some unspeakable force and never for themselves. Their idea of the common good is identical to that of law, even though most of them have no clear or true idea of what law really wants (this knowledge is the task of critique). Conventional, uncritical jurists grovel before the majesty of the law. They want to be *filled* to the brink with law. Law makes giants out of mice. These jurists are some of the most despicable folks on this forsaken planet and, in fact, all of us trained jurists, no matter our toil to differ, share this eldritch bond, the irreducible *pest* of pure, unreflective law.

However, behind the immediacy of law's forms and appearances passes shadows, barely visible. The immediacy of law is not a construct of reason but of the social relations of capitalist totality. Through *critique*, the immediacy of the legal forms can be forced to offer up their inner, secret notions, the relations that truly make law move. This way, law is indeed made to change, if only in its developed self-knowledge. While the practicing jurist, critical or not, *is law, is legal immediacy*, critical jurisprudence can from some healthy distance journal the relations and notions through which the foul, foamy breath of law passes.

55 On this notion of the audience, a common trope among certain scholars of legal realism and legal positivism, who seek to explain where the meaning of law is ultimately derived from, see for example Martti Koskenniemi, *To the Uttermost Parts of the Earth: Legal Imagination and International Power, 1300–1870* (CUP 2021).

The legal form as a praxis of critique: towards a new ontology of law

Law meets the gaze of critique in a myriad of ways. This is not a testament to its radical relativity, to its radical indeterminacy, but to its objectivity as a social form.[56] In the words of Lenin: 'Philosophical idealism is only nonsense from the standpoint of crude, simple, metaphysical materialism. From the standpoint of dialectical materialism, on the other hand, philosophical idealism is *one-sided* [italics added]'.[57] It is the task of legal critique to force law's immediate appearances, in the abstract and the concrete, to offer up their inner dialectical unity, their depth as forms of capitalist totality. Lenin continues:

> Human knowledge is not (or does not follow) a straight line, but a curve, which endlessly approximates a series of circles, a spiral. Any fragment, segment, section of this curve can be transformed (transformed one-sidedly) into an independent, complete, straight line, which then (if one does not see the wood for the trees) leads into the quagmire, into clerical obscurantism (where it is anchored by the class interests of the ruling classes). Rectilinearity and one-sidedness, woodenness and petrification, subjectivism and subjective blindness—voilà the epistemological roots of idealism. And clerical obscurantism (= philosophical idealism), of course, has epistemological roots, it is not groundless; it is a sterile flower undoubtedly, but a sterile flower that grows on the living tree of living, fertile, genuine, powerful, omnipotent, objective, absolute human knowledge.[58]

Today, much legal practice and understanding is made through the prism of *a priori* assumptions. But through the wager, notion or methodological standpoint of class struggle, the objective the legal form can be made to offer its secret longing for a sociality that has yet to come, its inner longing toward abolishment.[59] In light of this, Pashukanis worked toward formulating the proper method for Marxist jurisprudence, and also to offer a preliminary general theory of law and Marxism. At least this is true if one reads Pashukanis as being grounded in a materialist dialectic of knowing in the absolute.

Marxist legal form *as* critique could develop the inner movements of law from any one-sided appearance of law in the abstract or the concrete. However, in his *magnum opus General Theory of Law and Marxism*, Pashukanis chose to critique the forms specifically of bourgeoisie natural law. Natural law is a theory that certain rights are natural and universal and that they are

56 Lenin (n 5) 110.
57 ibid 361.
58 ibid 361.
59 Lukacs (n 6).

linked to a certain transhistorical human nature. Pashukanis turned to criticizing natural law for two interlocking reasons. First, because it flourished at a time when the bourgeoisie was formulating its demands and carrying out revolutions (Pashukanis 2002 p 76). Second, because it most poignantly and explicitly articulated what Pashukanis saw as the core notion of the legal form: the sovereign, free, and equal legal subject.

In Pashukanis' time, the natural law abstractions of equality and freedom had become accepted as truths since the victory of capitalism over feudalism: they had become reified and were seen as a natural part of society. For this very reason, because of the central role of bourgeois natural law in society, it expresses, according to Pashukanis, a great truth about law, but a one-sided one, which must be developed in dialectical criticism. For Pashukanis, who considered every idealist legal theory to be a theory of natural law, including Kelsen's theory, natural law where most acutely attuned to the manifold forms and appearances of the legal form.[60] Consequently, Pashukanis drew on natural law's understanding of the legal subject, of the social contract, and of the state as a nodal point of 'free'; in Pashukanis' view, value representing legal subjects, and showed how these abstractions were valid only under capitalism, and how their respective movements were completely tied to the accumulation of the value form. In the words of Pashukanis:

> [L]aw in its general definitions, law as a form, does not exist in the heads and the theories of learned jurists. It has a parallel, real history which unfolds not as a set of ideas, but as a specific set of relations which men enter into not by conscious choice, but because the relations of production compel them to do so. Man becomes a legal subject by virtue of the same necessity which transforms the product of nature into a commodity complete with the enigmatic property of value. To the kind of thinking which does not transcend the framework of the bourgeois conditions of existence, this necessity must appear as none other than natural necessity. That is why all bourgeois theories of law are based, consciously or unconsciously, on the doctrine of natural law [emphasis added]. The school of natural law was not only the most marked expression of bourgeois ideology at a time when the bourgeoisie acted as a revolutionary class, formulating its demands openly and consistently; it also provided the model for the deepest and clearest understanding of legal form. It is not by chance that the period when the doctrine of natural law flourished coincides approximately with the appearance of the great classical bourgeois political economists. Both schools set themselves the task of formulating in the most general and consequently the most abstract manner, the fundamental

60 Pashukanis (n 51) 68.

conditions of existence of bourgeois society, which they regarded as the natural conditions of existence for absolutely any society.[61]

In short, Pashukanis' aim and method were to return to the categories of bourgeois law (especially as they appear in bourgeois natural law), which he sublated in critique as true but *insufficient*, one-sided, from the historical materialist standpoint. From the standpoint of class struggle, and focusing on the categories of natural law, Pashukanis abolished the liberal legal subject, the state, and the social contract as eternal and transhistorical and reinscribed them as necessary manifestations of the self-perpetuation of the value form. Pashukanis could have chosen another theory to critique, but he wanted his object of critique to already approximate the real movements of law, as far as possible: he found that natural law best did so.

However, it would have been easy for Pashukanis to critique, for example, Kelsen's pure theory of law. Rather than centering on the legal subject, Kelsen's theory centers on the legal norm, and the way that systems of norms interlock perfectly, as to create object totalities of the *pure ought*. These systems, subsuming reality, ensure coherence of law in hierarchical systems, rising all the way up to the *Grundnorm*. The *Grundnorm* is the *notion* of Kelsen's object totality, the concept that ties the system together, and it is a hypothetical ground that must simply be *assumed*, lest the validity and practical functioning of the whole project falls together. This is an open goal for Marxist critique, premised as it is on uncovering the inner depth of one-sided a-priories. The hypothetical assumption of the *Grundnorm* easily finds its historical ground in the immanent imperative of capitalist social forms to accumulate value. Kelsen's *pure theory of law* explains not a contract of free men, but a structure that perpetuates and is structured by the drive toward self-accumulation of the value form through its many forms, especially through those of the legal subject and the state. Sonja Buckel has presented a reading of law somewhat to this effect, although she, as is Kelsen, is not grounded in an epistemological standpoint of absolute totality.[62]

In this return to the most basic concept of bourgeois jurisprudence, which he finds to be *the legal subject,* Pashukanis finds that it expresses the very cell of the legal form. However, in his critique, Pashukanis finds that equality is not to be confused with equivalence and that the liberal legal subject is equal *not* in relation to a natural law of human nature, nor to one another, but before the value of the commodity and the imperative that seals the existence of the commodity—the imperative of value to self-valorize in class struggle. The freedom, abstract will, or interest of the subject of law was sublated in

61 ibid.

62 Sonja Buckel, *Subjectivation and Cohesion: Towards the Reconstruction of a Materialist Theory of Law* (Brill 2021).

Pashukanis' critique as a *paradoxical* freedom or will. The subject of law, which exists only insofar as it represents value, *must* accumulate value in order to survive, or perhaps more accurately, to survive, to reproduce itself as form. Just as Marx showed how the commodity ultimately depends on the self-perpetuating relation of value the historically specific expression of the class struggle—Pashukanis shows that the general equality and free will of law is nothing other than the equality and will before the value form and its inner notion of class struggle.

Thus, Pashukanis unveils the contradiction within the legal subject's freedom under capitalism. The legal subject, seemingly free and equal, is compelled to pursue surplus value generation, and is only as a matter of class struggle formally equal to this task. Concrete forms of appearances of legal subjects are not specified by general equality, rather their very form and the form of their will are subject to class struggle. This, he argues, is the essence of the natural law social contract, where the abstractions of states and legal subjects dialectically reproduce a world stratified by not only real inequality, but also formal inequality within the frameworks notably of racialized difference and of global imperialism.

With Pashukanis, I argue that the legal subject as a real abstraction—a form not merely of capitalist domination, but of *class struggle*—must, in order to exist, strive to accumulate value—the corporation forming the most obvious example of this imperative, the waged or unwaged laborer forming another. Through or as law, legal subjects and their abstract wills are made alike before the eldritch senses of the value form, and the formal inequality of legal subjects forms a *rule* rather than an exception.[63] More to the point, the legal subject appears as a form of appearance of class struggle in the concrete as well as abstract, and central for the social reproduction of surplus value on a global scale, stratified as it is in global color lines by imperialism as racism.[64] Through critique, the specificity of the legal form can be found in the equality of legal subjects *not* in general, but specifically *before the value form*.

63 Lindsay M Orchowski and others, 'Integrating Sexual Assault Resistance, Bystander, and Men's Social Norms Strategies to Prevent Sexual Violence on College Campuses: A Call to Action' (2020) 21 *Trauma, Violence, & Abuse* 811; Bhandar (n 2); Bhandar and Toscano (n 2).

64 Katrina Quisumbing King, 'The Global Color Line and White Supremacy: WEB Du Bois as a Grand Theorist of Race' in Aldon Morris and others (eds), *The Oxford Handbook of WEB Du Bois* (Oxford Academic 2022); WEB Du Bois, *The Souls of Black Folk* (The Project Gutenberg eBook 1996); Vladimir Lenin, *Imperialism, the Highest Stage of Capitalism*, vol 1 (Collected Works, Progress Publishers 1963); Ramón Grosfoguel, 'The Global Contributions of Black Decolonial Marxism—a Foreword' in Sabelo J Ndlovu-Gatsheni and Morgan Ndlovu (eds), *Marxism and Decolonialization in the 21st century living theory and true ideas* (Routledge 2022); Rob Knox, 'Law' in Sara R Farris and others (eds), *Sage Handbook on Marxism* (Sage 2021). Knox (n 3).

Conclusions

In this chapter, I have argued that the Marxist critique of law must proceed from the dual wager of absolute totality and of class struggle as the seed and appearance of totality. This dual wager can be formulated in many ways. Key is the notion that knowledge always knows itself and that Being with a capital B unravels according to its own, absolute logic and totality, a logic that can be unraveled in social understanding through critique.

Regarding the legal form, I have alongside Pashukanis presented a new ontology of law in social understanding and jurisprudence. I have argued that Marxist jurisprudence should primarily be a method of critique, eschewing formal definitions in favor of a dialectical approach to law's immediate appearances in the abstract and the concrete, but still I have presented the specificity of the legal form by way of a methodological standpoint: equality of the legal subject before the value form. By continually presenting this new legal ontology, grounded in the necessity of class struggle, legal critique can re-*form* legal abstraction in social understanding. The irreducible rest of an abstraction, that law is somehow created and managed by *human beings* (whatever those are), can be made to offer its inner truth in critique. With time, this approach, this new ontology of critique, can replace liberal legal formalism with an understanding of law as a social form rooted in class struggle, thereby transforming the general, legal consciousness.

Place your bets: the legal form and the great wager of historical materialism

The wealth of society presents itself as an immense accumulation of horrors. One knows that the value form is there, because when one speaks its name, these nameless, senseless horrors appear as forms of its ascension, and are almost rational. The purpose of this chapter has been to present one of these horrors, namely the legal form, as a form of the capital relation.

In the first part of this chapter, I introduced the dual wagers of totality and class struggle that I argue must undergird Marxist legal critique. Following this, I showed in a second part how contemporary Marxian critique of social form tends to perpetuate liberal, fetishized thought forms by separating the abstract from the concrete, thereby denying absolute totality, and displacing the foundational class struggle relation to too advanced a level of concreteness. I argue that a Marxist critique of law, and indeed a broader critique of form, must begin and end with the historical materialist wager that it isn't some abstract man, will or reason, but *the abstract, historically specific form of class struggle* that structures and manifests as the social, its essential abstractions and myriad appearance. Most importantly this *grand wager*, in order to be won, must sustain a materialist dialectic, through which the bifurcation of the logical and the historical are united in their difference. In other words, the ontological separation of the abstract from the concrete, or perhaps the 'conceptual' from the 'empirical', must be *undone* in order for the living dialectic to reveal *class struggle* as the real movement of history.

Consequently, in my critique of the Marxian concept of *form,* I focused on the core epistemological and ontological notion that simultaneously founds, grounds, and defangs mainstream Marxian theory: *the object totality.* The object totality truncates true totality while leaving open a space for *universal man*, or the fetish of irreducible sovereignty, or whatever diehard abstraction, that secretly inundates intuitive thought forms under capitalism.[65] This subject, *enslaved* as it were by the domination of capitalist abstractions, obscures in social understanding the constitutive complicity of what passes as 'humans' under capitalism. At its heart, the ontology of object totality serves to sever the abstract from the concrete, not in order to ground both modes in their unity in difference, but in order to reduce the concrete to one-sided forms grounded solely in the abstract. In this way, capitalism as an *object totality* and the legal form is presented in a frozen state, unmoving in the abstract, delivering a static and thus weak understanding of class struggle, and of law.

I argue that the very motor and objective measure of immanent critique is the dialectical unity in the difference of the abstract and the concrete. It is only through a critique that aims at and is capable of unravelling such a unity, such an unbridled sensitivity to the inner yet hidden connections of the objective, that social understanding and the inept thought forms that *already* structure such understanding can be suspended and transformed. This is true for critique in general—and it is particularly true for the critique of law.

Only when the *object totality* as epistemological and ontological notion has fallen away, can sensitivity be reinscribed in social, Marxist critique for the shifting, historically specific forms of appearance of class struggle, in the abstract as in the concrete. The notion of class struggle unleashed in the writings of Karl Marx, structures social reality and understanding through fetishized forms. Today, abstractions rule our lives and yet their real inner connections and roots remain hidden. These abstractions come *from outside* and give shape and form to thoughts, relationships, and actions: like eldritch monsters, they burst forth from a world history structured by class struggle, and speak through our mouths, move our limbs, distort our faces, and make us horrid and inhuman. Importantly, they turn us into *legal subjects.*

As legal subjects, we are represented by the value we accumulate as well as our formal *capability* to accumulate this value (citizenship, social rights, et cetera) and we embody the singular will to do and believe *anything* to keep our value and our status.

65 Przemysław Tacik, *New Philosophy of Modernity and Sovereignty, A: Towards Radical Historicisation* (Bloomsbury 2021); Heller (n 5).

I say *we* in the sense of shared, universal, legal subjectivity, *our* shared and automatic, existential complicity in the objectively murderous totality of capitalist social relations *as* legal subjects, *to the extent* we are legal subjects actively representing and accumulating capitalist value.

The only hope of reversal in this inverted hellish dialectic of global inhumanity, the only real hope of absolution, rests in the abolition of the legal form of capitalism. Jurisprudence specifically, and the more general critique of law, has a small role here. This role or method of critique lies in the presentation, through thought and action, of class struggle at law's heart. This presentation cannot be a formal systematic presentation of the solely abstract and inert: it must be a living, social critique capable of imploding fetishized forms, time and again, to reveal their secret, inner center of struggle, and of promised yet unfulfilled *humanity*.

Chapter 7

From critique of abstraction to speculative legal form

Hugo Lundberg

Introduction

In the plan for what was to become *Dialectic of Nihilism*, social theorist Gillian Rose had hoped to include a chapter on Evgeny Pashukanis, Karl Renner and the Frankfurt school.[1] Rather than speculating as to what that chapter may have contained, this text turns to the speculative[2] in a broader sense to address the critique of abstraction that has long haunted the legal form theory of Pashukanis. By retrieving Gillian Rose's speculative reading of law, I show how the work of Pashukanis displaces some aspects of this critique of legal form theory.[3] Drawing on Rose, I explore a possible response to the critique of Pashukanian abstraction by reading the concept of legal form through the Hegelian categories of the *abstract, dialectical and speculative* as Rose interprets them.[4] Building on abstraction and the dialectic, the speculative is, in essence, a way of handling contradictions, trying to grasp how seemingly opposed concepts are actually dependent on each other and united. What if Pashukanis is not too abstract, but rather not speculative enough? This question invites us to rummage through the trash of discarded Pashukanis readings to salvage the speculative in the garbage, negating the negation.[5]

1 Andrew Brower-Latz, 'The Social Philosophy of Gillian Rose: Speculative Diremptions, Absolute Ethical Life' (doctoral thesis, Durham University 2015) 132.

2 Recently, there has been an uptick in what is called speculative legal thinking. There is for instance a network that researches speculative legal theory springing from a diverse background of new materialism, actor-network theory and accelerationism. For the purpose of the present work, such theorizing is seen as speculative in its Kantian sense, rather than the Hegelian variation I am relying on here. See Gillian Rose, *Hegel Contra Sociology* (Athlone 1995) 48.

3 I use legal form theory to mean Pashukanian theory which emerged specifically from the General Theory of Law and Marxism, and later works building on this both in law and beyond.

4 This piece is not an exegesis of Hegel. It relies on Rose's reading which manages to be heterodox and orthodox simultaneously, indebted to a lot of other theorists. See Tony Gorman, 'Gillian Rose and the Project of a Critical Marxism' (2001) 105 *Radical Philos* 25.

5 See for instance, the grounds on which Ntina Tzouvala objects to legal form and its abstractions. I take this critique to be indebted to Critical Legal Studies. See Ntina Tzouvala, 'International Law and (the Critique of) Political Economy' (2022) 121(2) *S Atl Q* 297, 297.

DOI: 10.4324/9781032724713-8

To retrieve this however, we must first consider the Marxian link between Rose and Pashukanis. Interpretations of legal form theory, just as any other Marx-adjacent concept have been conditioned by the broader epistemic trends in Marxist theory at their given point in time. This conditioning, though inevitable, has not always been acknowledged. In reassessing Pashukanis' work, much can be gained by an awareness of the various strands of Marxist thinking influencing a certain interpretation. In attempting to read Pashukanis speculatively through the work of Gillian Rose, I rely on contemporary value-form theory as a bridge to develop legal form speculatively.[6] Rose adds an important question to jurisprudence here: what can a theory about the rupturing of the social relations of law offer when that rupture remains unclear? Law is not an optional extra for understanding the so-called diremptions of modernity, but central to understanding them and how their mending remains unclear.[7]

After introducing Rose, I begin by summarizing the widespread critique of abstraction in the reception of Pashukanis' work and then move on to explain how Rose's Hegelian concept of the abstract and dialectic can be used to defend legal form against such critique. I then question the influence of negative dialectics and why that would be problematic for Pashukanis, building on Rose's critique of Adorno. If, as Pashukanis argues, the legal form will wither away, there must be a budding of social relations to come after.[8] I conclude with an outline of what a positive, speculative legal form may entail and why it could be useful as the opposite of the critique of abstraction. The *raison d'être* of this chapter is therefore to suggest that by means of the speculative, we can move away from schematic understandings of law and acknowledge legal form not simply as 'homological'[9] with the commodity form but see how it can be understood as a system, and a workable tool in that system instead of a re-totalizing method. This essay does not claim to sustain any form of final speculative experience for legal form theory but rather culminates in the suggestion of a few propositions that could serve as tentative invitations to seeing legal form as speculative, or in other words: attempting to think the jurisprudential absolute.

6 For important work in making Rose's speculative ambitions relevant for contemporary value-form theory see Michael Lazarus, 'The Legacy of Reification: Gillian Rose and the Value-Form Theory Challenge to Georg Lukács' (2020) 157(1) Thesis Eleven 80.

7 Diremption is part of the Hegelian system of logic and part of the speculative system of handling contradictions. See Gillian Rose, *The Broken Middle: Out of our Ancient Society* (Blackwell 1992).

8 Fernando Quintana, 'On the Withering Away of Law: Radical Politics Beyond Legal Fetishism' (*Legal Form*, 25 January 2024) <https://legalform.blog/2024/01/25/on-the-withering-away-of-law-radical-politics-beyond-legal-fetishism-fernando-quintana/> accessed 11 March 2024.

9 Isaac D Balbus, 'Commodity Form and Legal Form: An Essay on the Relative Autonomy of the Law' (1976) 11 *Law and Soc'y Rev* 571, 573.

Legal form and the critique of abstraction

Abstraction is often portrayed in negative terms. The paradigmatic and general example of this is Alfred North Whitehead and his calling the 'intolerant use' of abstractions the 'major vice of the intellect'.[10] Whitehead famously argued that this results in 'misplaced concreteness': that which happens when an abstraction is treated as something endowed with physical properties.[11]

It is against this backdrop of general mistrust of abstraction, not surprising that the movement around Critical Legal Studies (CLS), in part due to legal realist influences, is suspicious of the *doctrinaire* connotations implicit in Marxist concepts such as real abstraction.[12] Abstraction can for these fields of inquiry become equated with bourgeois (or just doctrinal) theorizing that presupposes a transhistorical and thus eternally valid legal subject. Such rigidity is an obstacle to progressive interpretations of juridical concepts.

The critique of abstraction can also be understood with reference to the hermeneutic of suspicion and its hegemonic position in much of the work of the CLS tradition.[13] Even though the hermeneutic of suspicion in CLS supposedly takes aim at ideology in a somewhat Marxist-influenced tradition, it has at the same time often come close to a broader aversion toward theoretical abstraction in general.[14] Such critique aims to unmask the hidden subjectivities presupposed in a given approach. The 'politics all the way down' approach of Anne Orford is another contemporary representation of this CLS critique.[15] If (international) law is indeed politics all the way down, why do we need abstraction? Such an epistemology would rather just shed all ideology.

I suggest we must see this as CLS taking part in a reaction against juridical orthodoxy, expressed by opposition to disembodied doctrinal concepts and jurisprudence as removed from social reality. In this perspective, it becomes natural to see theoretical abstractions as (wrongfully) naturalizing legal phenomena that are socially constituted. For *the crits*, critique consisted in part of showing how reified and abstract juridical concepts such as the legal subject could be de-naturalized, in contrast to how they appear in traditional legal scholarship.[16]

10 Alfred North Whitehead, *Science and the Modern World* (Free Press 1997) 19.

11 ibid 54–56.

12 Alfred Sohn-Rethel, *Intellectual and Manual Labour: A Critique of Epistemology* (Macmillan 1978); Mark Tushnet, 'Post-Realist Legal Scholarship' (1980) *Wis L Rev* 1383.

13 For an overview see Duncan Kennedy, 'The Hermeneutic of Suspicion in Contemporary American Legal Thought' (2014) 25(2) *L and Crit* 91.

14 Alan Hunt, 'The Critique of Law: What is 'Critical' About Critical Legal Theory?' (1987) 14(1) *J L and Soc* 5.

15 Anne Orford, *International Law and the Politics of History* (CUP 2021) 315.

16 For an intra-CLS discussion on this see Peter Gabel and Duncan Kennedy, 'Roll Over Beethoven' (1984) 36 *Stan L Rev* 1.

However, the critique of abstraction of Pashukanis' legal form begins much earlier than CLS. As the commodity form theory was beginning to lose its hegemony in early soviet jurisprudence, P.I. Stutchka—fellow Marxist but somewhat theoretically competing—contributed to the mounting critique by urging his fellow scholars to confine themselves in 'the abstract world of simple commodity producers for no longer than is necessary to reveal the secrets of the abstractions of bourgeois law. Once this is done, back to reality, to class society'.[17] This is the important split between Pashukanian and non-Pashukanian Marxist legal theory.

Another version of Stutchkan's critique is levied more recently by Ntina Tzouvala. In *Capitalism as Civilization*, she argues for the dismissal of Pashukanis and the legal form on the following grounds:

> Pashukanian approaches to law largely assume that the commodity-owner is a natural figure and not one that emerges through bureaucratic and legal techniques of individualisation and, crucially, the separation of individuals from the means of production and their traditional (legal) links to family, land and community.[18]

This critique of Pashukanis especially and of abstraction more broadly has had several iterations between Stutchka and Tzouvala.[19] Tzouvala and others, such as Paul Hirst and B.S. Chimni have also advanced similar critiques on more immanently traditional Marxist grounds: the circulationist charge that Pashukanis made the mistake of deriving law from exchange rather than production and that he is overly focused on form at the expense of content.[20]

Igor Shoikhedbrod puts forward a version of this critique which is even more specific in critiquing abstraction. He claims that Pashukanis 'at no point . . . conclude[s] from his critique that the abstract categories of liberal jurisprudence are somehow illusory constructs that exist only in the minds of legal formalists and their pedestrian adherents'.[21] According to Shoikhedbrod, this makes Pashukanis strangely appealing to the formalists he

17 Peteris Stuchka, 'State and Law in the Period of Socialist Construction' (1927) 2 *The Revolution of the Law*.

18 Ntina Tzouvala, *Capitalism as Civilisation: A History of International Law* (CUP 2020) 25.

19 Ronnie Warrington, 'Standing Pashukanis on His Head' (1980) 4(3) *Capital & Class* 102.

20 Tzouvala (n 5); Paul Hirst, 'The Law of Property and Marxism' in *On Law and Ideology* (Springer 1979); Bhupinder Singh Chimni, *International Law and World Order: A Critique of Contemporary Approaches* (Sage 1993).

21 Igor Shoikhedbrod, 'Private Law's Estranged Bedfellows: Why Pashukanis Should Worry Contemporary Formalists' (2020) 33(2) *Can J L & Jur* 461, 467.

critiques, with Lon Fuller being the most notorious example.[22] Shoikhedbrod again, raises the Korschian point of Pashukanis' supposed exclusive focus on exchange at the expense of production.[23]

Before defending the Pashukanian notion of abstraction, we need to examine the framework Rose and, in extension, Hegel offer us for thinking about the abstract.

Rose's Hegel and the abstract, dialectical and speculative

In 1812, Hegel wrote Friedrich Immanuel Niethammer attempting to explain how philosophical content can assume three forms: abstract, dialectical and speculative.[24] In her work, Rose attempts to retrieve the latter, what she calls the speculative experience for modern social theory, understood in relation to the other two categories.[25] These distinctions between forms are invitations to think about how the legal form theory of Pashukanis can be read beyond the traditional critique of abstraction above. Conceptualizing a speculative legal form is thus a way of radicalizing it. In the letter, Hegel claims that abstraction comes before the dialectical and the (truly) speculative. The abstract signifies something which is isolated and known in its 'fixed distinction'.[26] This means that all the particularities are dissolved away. What is lacking in *the abstract* is the dialectical understanding of abstraction as movement and relationality in the world. Instead, abstraction as a fixed distinction may align with what is critiqued above, an abstraction only in thought, something that is removed from its concrete circumstances.

If those circumstances are included, we move into the dialectical form, which according to Hegel is:

> more difficult [than the first]. . . . The antinomies contain deep fundamentals of the antinomical [content] of reason. Yet these antinomies lie concealed and are recognised in the antinomies so to speak unthinkingly and insufficiently in their truth.[27]

22 Lon L Fuller, 'Pashukanis and Vyshinsky: A Study in the Development of Marxian Legal Theory' (1948) 47 *Mich L Rev* 1157.

23 See Korsch's afterword in Pashukanis; see also Shoikhedbrod (n 21) 469; Sonja Buckel, *Subjectivation and Cohesion: Towards the Reconstruction of a Materialist Theory of Law* (Brill 2020).

24 Georg Wilhelm Fredrich Hegel, *The Letters* (Indiana UP 1984); Gillian Rose, *Judaism and Modernity: Philosophical Essays* (Blackwell 1993).

25 To a large extent, she outlines how thinkers contemporary to her time moved between the speculative and dialectical with Lukács being the notable example. See 'From Speculative to Dialectical Thinking' in Rose (n 24) 53–63.

26 Hegel (n 24).

27 ibid; Rose (n 24).

The dialectic is a negative stage of reason.[28] It is no longer fixed or static, but relational. Behind the dialectical form we may glimpse the world that makes a concept contradictory and complex, but only to pick it apart, to dismantle and work toward a point of no return. But Rose teaches us that this point of no return is a Sisyphean horizon that can never be fully reached. What the speculative form offers is a striving toward reaching it—even if risking failure. Moving from negative reason to a positive moment, the speculative proceeds out of the dialectic.[29] This procedure involves recognizing the limits of legal form as what Rose calls relative ethical life in contrast to absolute ethical life.

This does not mean that Rose offers a ready-made roadmap of getting out of legal form/relative ethical life. Rose firmly rejects such methodologism and instead favors the absolute system. She goes as far as to say that 'Hegel's philosophy has no social import if the absolute cannot be thought'.[30] System and method then, cannot be meaningfully separated without losing the speculative character and thinking the absolute means comprehensive thought that works with diremptions, which for Rose means certain splits, such as law and ethics or finite and infinite.[31]

Breaking the link between system and method by adopting the method to help draw out social contradictions subdues the most radical aspects of Hegel. It does this by not acknowledging the fact that Hegel's (and Marx's) critiques largely take aim at the method as such. By not recognizing this grounding, the critique becomes transcendental and Neo-Kantian.[32] It is Neo-Kantian in the sense that it puts forward a general logic of *a priori* forms, becoming a justification for thought that is prior to itself. Furthermore, if this prior form is unknowable, it is because of inherent limitations in the Kantian schema where the 'unconditioned' or infinite is unknowable.[33] This is precisely why Rose argues that we must think the absolute because thought without a system which can cognize infinite knowledge renders us 'powerless', and unable to change the social, economic and legal *forms* which determine much of human social relations.[34]

In place of the transcendental method with pre-judged forms of thought, Rose puts forward, via Hegel, the idea of phenomenology—specifically concerning the '*quaestio quid juris*', the question of right.[35] This phenomenology forms a trinity with the ideas of absolute ethical life and logic.[36]

28 Rose (n 24) 53–63.
29 Hegel (n 24).
30 ibid 42.
31 Kate Schick, *Gillian Rose: A Good Enough Justice* (Edinburgh UP 2012) 31.
32 Rose (n 2) 32.
33 ibid 44.
34 ibid 45.
35 ibid.
36 ibid.

Taken seriously and applied to legal form, this trinity makes it a form of knowledge that cannot be pre-judged or reduced to crude economism, but rather needs to affirm such knowledge according to the methodological standards present in law and its consciousness as phenomenologically defining appearance. But in this, it must also be shown that the out-defining of the absolute or the infinite from consciousness is also, in fact, a product of consciousness itself.[37]

The thought of Rose thus serves as a link between Pashukanis and Hegel. Although first and foremost a social theorist or philosopher, Rose treats law and jurisprudence as central to that endeavor. The limits set by of legal form are implicit in her work. Read into the work of Pashukanis, a cannon of reason cannot legitimate itself without the infinite, just as legal form cannot legitimate itself without reference beyond the narrow confines of bourgeois right. In the words of Pashukanis: 'the legal form only encompasses us within its narrow horizon for the time being. It exists for the sole purpose of being utterly spent'.[38] Rose complements this by urging us to neither cast aside abstractions nor treat them as beyond reach.

Pashukanian abstraction and jurisprudence

What does the triune structure of abstract-dialectic-speculative entail for the critique of abstraction? Why bring it up at all? First, what those skeptical of the merits of legal form call abstraction may not be abstract according to the Hegelian schema. Second, accepting this, why should legal theorists unconvinced by Pashukanis care about some Hegelian schema? In what follows below I try to answer these questions in drawing out what is specific to Pashukanis' use of abstraction.

A possible genesis of Pashukanian abstraction is to be found in Marx's claim that '[i]n the analysis of economic forms neither microscopes nor chemical reagents are of assistance. The power of abstraction must replace both'.[39] This Marxian origin is important to bear in mind when considering possible Pashukanian responses to the critique of abstraction. At the beginning of the *General Theory of Law and Marxism* Pashukanis claims, in opposition to approaches oriented toward concrete class relations, that:

> to think that the juridical concepts which express the sense of the legal form have been quite arbitrarily dreamt up is to fall into the error which

37 ibid 46.

38 Evgeny Pashukanis, *The General Theory of Law and Marxism* (Transaction Publishers 2002) 133.

39 Karl Marx, *Capital: Critique of Political Economy*, vol 1 (Penguin Classics 1990) 90; See also Michael Heinrich, *An Introduction to the Three Volumes of Karl Marx's Capital* (NYU Press 2012) 40, for whom '(t)his remark shows that Marx intends to do more than simply describe the immediately visible phenomena of capitalism'.

> Marx pointed to in the work of the Enlightenment scholars of the eighteenth century. According to Marx, these scholars were still unable to account for the origin and development of the enigmatic forms assumed by human relations, so they tried to render these forms less incomprehensible by declaring them to be in fact human inventions rather than something which appeared out of the blue.[40]

The critique of instrumentalism in Pashukanis' work is thus inextricably bound up with form-analysis. Pashukanis offers a systematic critique that does not accept class rule as a conclusion but justifies its approach through engaging with the forms themselves. As I pointed out previously Stutchka argued against this, for a class-centric approach. Should we grapple with abstractions and then return to the realities of class society, as Stutchka argues? Or is it the case that the abstractions of bourgeois law make up the reality of class society?

Rather than viewing Pashukanis' legal form theory as reductive, we can better understand it as what Moishe Postone defined as a 'category of singularity and totality at once', from which the whole of capitalist modernity unfolds in *Capital*.[41] Legal form as both categories would entail an inversion of the idea that Pashukanian abstraction equals 'fixed distinction'. Instead, abstraction is shown to be dialectical because it springs both from the single commodity and the commensurability of all commodities. This need not be understood as some pre-judged and presumed totality at the outset of investigating the relation between law and capitalism, but by virtue of the commodity as a specific social form. In this mode of presentation, capital is the subsequent justification for the commodity as the starting point. But Rose's insistence on the centrality of the system can radicalize such a version of legal form even further.

Giving priority to totality rather than reduction recalls Lukács' understanding of the commodity in *History and Class Consciousness*.[42] Rose develops a condensed version of her speculative approach from working with Lukács' notion of Marxism as a method, where 'the whole is the true'.[43] It opens for the speculative by avoiding a return to Kantian dualism. According to Rose,

> Lukacs shows that exposition of the universalizing of commodity relations and of legitimate domination complement each other; they are not metaphysically or sociologically incompatible. The ineluctable confrontation

40 Pashukanis (n 38) 61.
41 ibid 139.
42 Rose (n 24) 57.
43 Georg Lukács, *History and Class Consciousness: Studies in Marxist Dialectics* (MIT Press 1972); For the importance of Lukács for Rose see Rose (n 24) 53; Brower-Latz (n 1) 155.

with legal forms is at the heart of this speculative exposition: the commodity has and is the form of legal-rational domination.[44]

Even if Rose relies on Weberian terms such as legal-rational to make it, this argument echoes the Pashukanian legal form since it attempts to preserve the commodity form without reduction to reification.[45] The commodity comes to mirror the form that law necessarily assumes in capitalist modernity. But this is an argument that is predicated on the universalizing of generalized commodity exchange specifically, and thus, as Pashukanis readily points out, it is a form of right and of law that is not only historically specific but also illustrates that it is not the result of specific theorizing, but rather a claim that these abstractions result from processes necessarily structuring capitalism. This means it cannot arise from a single commodity as it is a real abstraction, co-constitutive with the processes of bureaucratic and legal individualization, as these processes cannot make sense without it. As Lukács illustrates, the personification of commodities and the commodification of persons is this process of individuation.[46]

What is critiqued by sceptics of abstraction in jurisprudence then, is not a reading of Pashukanis such as this one, but rather the 'fixed distinction' of Hegel's first category. Pashukanis on the other hand, theorizes this abstraction as something that arises with the dialectic. Thus, the conceptualization of legal form is not one of law existing in the heads of learned jurists but rather unfolding with a 'real history'. Just as a specific set of social relations compel nature into the form of the commodity, legal subjecthood is afforded by the same totalizing effects of the commodity form—both with the 'enigmatic property of value'.[47]

There is, therefore, a tendency in CLS, and its adjacent theorists, to misconstrue the power and responsibility of abstracting processes as if legal scholars and Marxists rather than in the forms of value and commodity

44 Rose (n 24) 58.

45 Rose's legal form must avoid reification as she argued it had been adopted to bear an enormous weight—even 'abused' in social theory. While Rose's critique takes aim at reification, she is not opposed to deriving concepts from commodity-exchange in abstraction, but rather argues reification is reductive to a single feature of Marx's theory of the value-form. See Gillian Rose, *The Melancholy Science: An Introduction to the Thought of Theodor W. Adorno* (Verso 2014) 36. It is furthermore the awareness of the commodity-form as a basic, mediating social unit that is lost in Habermasian critical theory, where state and law become *sui generis* forces rather than derived from capital relation. See also the state and world-market-debates on how the tendency to create the concept (*Begriff*) of the state and world-market is inherent in Capital itself. Christel Neusüss, *Imperialismen og det kapitalistiske verdensmarked* (Kurasje 1976).

46 Rose (n 24) 58; Lukács (n 43); for an opposing view see Tzouvala (n 5) 25.

47 Pashukanis (n 38) 68.

were responsible. The figure of the commodity owner is social, not natural, and assumed precisely because it emerges through the forms described by Pashukanis.[48]

Furthermore, Stutchka's emphasis on simple commodity production reveals a position on the structure of Marx's capital that has been subject to intense scrutiny in later years. In the philological work of the *Marx-Engels Gesamtausgabe* (MEGA^2), this viewpoint of simple commodity production in the beginning of *Capital* as a phase already superseded by Capitalism has been shown to rest on assumptions that do not find much support in Marx's manuscripts before Engels edited them.[49] This entails that Pashukanis is much closer to Marx than Stuchka was. In other words, class society contains aspects that are necessarily abstract from a juridical point of view. The critique of perspectives that preside certain notions of class over the unfolding of form can be seen as a microcosm of wider developments in Marxism, represented by Pashukanis turning Soviet legal theory toward form-analysis.

One tool for understanding abstraction as a dialectical form is reading Pashukanis as compatible with value-form theory.[50] Value-form theory can be contrasted with substantialist accounts of *Capital*, which view labor as something embodied in the commodity, value-form theory (broadly) views the act of exchange as central to obtaining objective forms of value.[51] In other words, the way we perceive Marx's argument on the forms of value to unfold becomes central to the limits and possibilities legal form.[52]

What then, may be the criterion to ascertain when an abstraction expresses something real and when it becomes an ideological mask for a contingent

48 This is not unlike Delezue and Guattari's critique of Chomsky, wherein the fact that Chomsky's generative grammar is hierarchical throws doubt on his system of thought as an Anarchist. See Gilles Deleuze and Felix Guattari, *A Thousand Plateaus: Capitalism and Schizophrenia* (Bloomsbury Publishing 1988).

49 See Engels' preface in Karl Marx, *Capital: Critique of Political Economy* (Penguin Classics 1990); For critique of this see Heinrich (n 39) 81–85.

50 As Dimick rightly points out, value-form theory of law may have been a more suitable name for Pashukanis theory than the conventional 'commodity-form theory of law'. Matthew Dimick, 'Pashukanis' Commodity-Form Theory of Law' in *Research Handbook on Law and Marxism* (Edward Elgar Publishing 2021) 4.

51 Heinrich (n 39) 55.

52 For a thorough engagement with the latter, that is, the unfolding manner of presentation of argument see Heinrich (n 39). It should also be noted that to a certain extent, China Miéville's reconstruction of Pashukanis already responded to some of these critiques, in that Pashukanis does use abstraction but in a distinctively different manner compared to the Neo-Kantians. Miéville builds on the movement from the abstract to the concrete and views legal categories as determinate forms expressing a certain abstract notion necessary for analysis of the concrete. Although Miéville seems to have a grasp of how Pashukanis use of abstraction corresponds to that of Marx, his engagement with the question is somewhat cursory as he favors a reading based on what he calls historical materialism. China Miéville, *Between Equal Rights: A Marxist Theory of International Law* (Brill 2005) 79.

order? It would be absurd to claim all abstractions are relevant only by merit of being classifiable in a Hegelian system. On the contrary, ideology critique has been essential in illustrating the contingency and naturalization of human rights, civilization and other similar terms.[53] Analytically, the difference can be understood along the lines of formal and determinate abstraction. By making this distinction, legal form theory can distance itself from the bourgeois conceptualization of terms as autonomous and pre-given. Simon Clarke describes formal abstraction in political economy as:

> not gratuitous inventions, but express real abstractions in a mystified form. Thus the "abstract individual" really exists in a capitalist society. However the individual is a "formal" abstraction when it is considered in abstraction from its historical foundation, ... In abstracting its fundamental concepts from the social forms of capitalist production and reproduction, political economy abstracts from the social relations which alone determine the qualities which it calls on to give its concepts their explanatory powers.[54]

Contrary to this, determinate abstractions for Marx correspond to determinate social processes, which is why the abstract and the concrete describe generality and particularity, or totality and singularity.[55] Pashukanis traces the abstraction not as a pre-given method, but as a system in which the relational nature of the legal subject is the only way in which legal form can express something meaningful. By drawing out these different forms of abstraction, it is possible to see how one is abstract (formal) while the other becomes dialectical (determinate). The formal abstractions of traditional political economy, such as Smith's *Wealth of Nations*, were an attempt at describing but not explaining.[56] Thus, what Marxian critique of political economy attempts to do is peer beyond this bourgeois horizon and not only describe but explicate.[57] When Pashukanis proclaims that legal fetishism

53 Susan Marks, *The Riddle of All Constitutions: International Law, Democracy, and the Critique of Ideology* (OUP 2003).

54 Clarke 108.

55 ibid. Clarke is here drawing on Marx's *Grundrisse* in which he writes that only in a society with a very developed totality can labor be abstract. Homogeneity in the abstraction of labor is then not simply a fictions figure in the mind of the theorist but develops from a real social form in which labor is transferable and homogeneous. See Karl Marx, *Grundrisse: Foundations of the Critique of Political Economy* (Penguin Classics 1993) 140. Totality and singularity are Postone's terms.

56 Ana Cecilia Dinerstein, 'Denaturalising Society: Concrete Utopia and the Prefigurative Critique of Political Economy' in *Social Sciences for an Other Politics* (Springer 2016).

57 Patrick Murray, *The Mismeasure of Wealth: Essays on Marx and Social Form* (Brill 2016) 5.

complements commodity fetishism, he emphasizes the way in which the legal subject is simultaneously dreamt up and structuring social reality.[58]

Understood in this way, the theory of legal form cannot be reduced to the concrete commodities being sold in generalized market exchange. But must be read as the commodity, through value, becoming a category that encompasses the totality of capitalist modernity on which a historically specific legal form is predicated. As Marx writes in volume III of *Capital*, 'we are only out to present the internal organization of the capitalist mode of production, its ideal average, as it were'.[59] Abstraction in Marxist theorizing of law not only means something the theorist wishes into being but must account for something that emerges through the fetishism resulting from how human social relations come to relate to each other through commodity exchange.

Thus, Pashukanis departs from what may be seen as traditionally Marxist in significant ways, here exploitation takes place by way of the full value of labor being withheld by the owners of the means of production.[60] By putting more emphasis on how production cannot exist without circulation and legal form, Pashukanis knowingly or unknowingly questioned the epistemic framework of his contemporary Marxism. If one attempts to read Pashukanis back into this tradition, disappointment awaits. In the turn to political economy, Pashukanis appears to be sidelined precisely because he attempts to *critique* political economy in its complete form and not only its workings or effects.[61]

One task of critical social theory for law should be to dissolve the dogmatic appearance of society as a manifestation of economic nature, to paraphrase Werner Bonefeld.[62] But unlike CLS, such dissolving is not opposed to the idea of abstraction *per se,* but by illustrating the historically specific nature of forms of being in capitalism.[63] These forms are abstractions that are not eternally valid as thought, but only exist in the dialectical logic of capital.[64] By generalized commodity exchange, the exchange abstraction

58 Pashukanis (n 38) 14.

59 Marx (n 39) 970.

60 Murray (n 57) 5.

61 An example of this is the law and political economy (LPE) movement at large. 'Political economic critique', 'critical political economy' and critique of political economy often seem to blend together in legal theory, See Tzouvala (n 5); For critical social theory see Werner Bonefeld, *Critical Theory and the Critique of Political Economy: On Subversion and Negative Reason* (Bloomsbury 2014).

62 Werner Bonefeld and Chris O'Kane, *Adorno and Marx: Negative Dialectics and the Critique of Political Economy* (Bloomsbury 2022).

63 Kirstin Munro and Chris O'Kane, 'Marxian Economics and the Critique of Political Economy' in Werner Bonefeld and Chris O'Kane (eds), *Adorno and Marx: Negative Dialectics and the Critique of Political Economy* (Bloomsbury 2022) 78–79.

64 Moishe Postone, *Time, Labor, and Social Domination: A Reinterpretation of Marx's Critical Theory* (CUP 1995) 5.

subsumes social relations which at the same time makes the regulation of these same social relations assume legal character and form.[65] This unfolding logic of the commodity form cannot take place in abstraction from the category of capital as self-valorizing value, as capital becomes its subsequent justification by retrospective illumination of the determinations being valid only in looking back.[66] The owl of Minerva begins its flight only with the onset of dusk, and the legal form can only be understood as capital comes to dominate social relations.

Dialectic considerations

In the sections above I have attempted to show, against the critique from CLS and others, that legal form can be understood beyond the fixed distinction that the Hegelian category of abstraction entails. In the hegelian schema of forms, philosophical content may assume, legal form is dialectical, not abstract. I came to this conclusion through an underlying reliance on value-form theory, broadly construed. But how do these abstractions operate in the world?[67] What difference would a dialectical understanding of abstraction entail? The dialectic is only the second stage, so while the critique against abstraction has been critiqued, this is not enough. Rose sees several issues pertaining to the nature of critique of political economy as critical social theory in its Adornian variation which this section makes use of to level similar critique at Pashukanis.

In the glossary section of her doctoral dissertation, Rose explicates the nature of concepts for Adorno as 'not only the universal, that is, what we possess when we grasp the sense of a word. . . . Concepts are thus real, substantively conceived, and not mere ideas or ideal-types'.[68] For Rose's Adorno too, we see that abstract concepts are not just abstractions. But, in *Negative Dialectics*, Adorno points out that his dialectic is no longer compatible with Hegel as it does not tend to the difference in identity of object and concept but is suspicious of all identity. He calls this a logic of disintegration.[69] How does such a view of dialectics affect modern value-form interpretations? While contemporary value-form theory is indebted to Pashukanis and what appears as his anachronistically early understanding form analysis, it also relies heavily on the critical theory lineage from Adorno to his students Hans-Georg Backhaus and Helmut Reichelt.[70] The relevance of Adorno in

65 ibid 189.
66 ibid 269.
67 This question comes from Buckel (n 23) 232.
68 Rose (n 45) 196–97.
69 Theodor Adorno, *Negative Dialectics* (Continuum 1983) 143.
70 A recent volume has shown that the connection to Adornian thought is still present though often unacknowledged in value-form theory. See Bonefeld and O'Kane (n 62).

value-form theory is symbolically present in a shorthand lecture transcript taken by Backhaus wherein Adorno claims that:

> Exchange itself is a process of abstraction. Whether human beings [die Menschen] know it or not, by entering into a relationship of exchange and reducing different use-values to labour-value they actualise a real conceptual operation socially. This is the objectivity of the concept in practice. It shows that conceptuality lies not only in the minds of the philosophers but also in the reality of the object itself.[71]

While one cannot disregard the influence of Sohn Rethel, Adorno claims that this idea is the *differentia specifica* for Frankfurt School sociology, which may be true, it is *not* true for jurisprudence, as Pashukanis had pointed out some 40 years earlier:

> In reality, of course, the category of the legal subject is abstracted from the act of exchange taking place in the market. It is precisely in the act of exchange that man puts into practice the formal freedom of self-determination.[72]

In other words, the way abstraction entangles with reality is a central insight into both the work of Adorno and Pashukanis. But justifying Pashukanis' use of abstraction in the legal form in this way opens it to the same critique that can be leveled at Adorno's dialectic and its negativity. We have already seen that the commodity can be read as both singularity and totality and that there is nothing in Pashukanis that *prima facie* hinders such a reading.[73] Regardless of whether Pashukanis himself makes this supposed break from traditional Marxism toward form analysis, the Marxian commodity cannot be understood as just any type of trans-historical commodity, it has to be grounded in the unfolding categories of its dominant social form. The commodity exists in tandem with capital and other social categories even if it is presented in abstraction from them. When Marx and, subsequently,

71 Theodor Adorno, 'Theodor W. Adorno on "Marx and the Basic Concepts of Sociological Theory": From a Seminar Transcript in the Summer Semester of 1962' (2018) 26(1) *Historical Materialism* 154, 2–3.

72 Pashukanis (n 38) 117.

73 It should be noted that China Miéville had already read as well as corresponded with Chris Arthur and does bring up social form or 'capital-logic' several times in *Between Equal Rights*. However, although mentioning how Pashukanis could be reconciled with these ideas, it is not his focus, so he does not bring it into full fruition. See Miéville (n 52); Chris Arthur, *The New Dialectic and Marx's Capital* (Brill 2003) 33; Murray (n 57).

Pashukanis make use of the commodity, it is of its dual character as use- and exchange-value in capitalist society.[74]

An important insight made by both value-form theorists and Pashukanis in the transition away from traditional—or indeed Ricardian—political economy was presenting capital not as a map for an alternative political economy but to stress its critical aspects.[75] But this reaction against a perceived orthodoxy has turned toward the overly negative at times. According to Werner Bonefeld, for instance, 'as critical theory of society, the critique of political economy is devoid of affirmative traits'.[76] What would a legal form without affirmative traits look like? What would it mean for it to be only negative? Just as the form of value cannot be filled with new non-capitalist content, the legal form cannot encompass content beyond that of 'bourgeois law' for Pashukanis.[77] But for Rose, form is glossed as not to be contrasted with content but rather 'process or essence'—form, thus means form of appearance of certain social relations.[78] We have gathered that the *form itself* arises dialectically through social relations, and thus becomes an operative abstraction beyond forms of thought. But for Rose, several issues remain with this type of theorizing.

One of these issues is the engagement with economic forms, which Rose finds lacking in the work of Adorno. Even though Rose supposedly reads as an *intriguer* it seems difficult to accept this contention considering the value-form critique reiterated above. Given that exchange is always an act of abstraction, economic forms must exist as real abstractions for Adorno, although sometimes in the background.[79] In my view, the most devastating critique levied by Rose against Adorno—and by extension, large parts of the value-form paradigm and Pashukanis—occurs in *Hegel Contra Sociology* rather than in her dissertation. She argues that by favoring Nietzsche over Hegel, Adorno's so-called *Melancholy Science* inherits Kantian aporia, that is, insoluble issues which are relegated beyond comprehension. Rather than struggling with such aporia in Hegelian fashion as Rose would have it, Adorno is left with a methodological moralism of infinite and abstract striving rather than one that can develop through the social forms that underlie its relations.[80]

This is expressed through the renunciation of social form as totality (which in our case includes legal form), when Adorno rejects the Lukácsian

74 Postone (n 64) 128–30.
75 Heinrich (n 39).
76 Bonefeld (n 61) 221.
77 Pashukanis (n 38) 61.
78 Rose (n 45) 198.
79 ibid 37. See also Schick (n 31) 23.
80 Rose (n 2) 33–34.

proposition that the whole is the true, inverting it to become the whole is the false.[81] In *Minima Moralia* for instance, Adorno employs a form of negative reason which never gives itself up to the real movement of the dialectic. By refusing this, Rose explains that Adorno is left standing on the sideline, 'merely judging' with a harsh irony that never fully cognizes juridical aporia since irony cannot reconstruct them through their constitutive social forms.[82] So, both the negative nature of Adorno's mode of inquiry and the fact that 'dialectical thinking is not speculative thinking' are the issues at stake.[83]

What does this have to do with the legal form, then? First, in our reading of Pashukanis, the equivalent issue arises when the method accepts the aporetic conclusion of the value-form paradigm as given not through its constitutive social forms, but as abstract methodologism which we can freely apply to the object of inquiry. We have on the one hand, the law, which we study—and on the other a proposition that legal form is either a constitutive part of the commodity form, structurally mirrored by the commodity form or another variation. Such a reading risks succumbing to an instrumentalist paranoia which can only ever confirm the capitalist origin of certain legal phenomena. Wielding the hammer of legal form in such a manner, every juridical inquiry may present itself as a nail reduced to formalist economist tendencies.[84] It is thus an interpretation of Pashukanian legal form that manages to be both formalist and instrumentalist, reproducing the very spectrum that Pashukanis sought to critique.[85] Part of the skepticism against abstraction we saw in the previous section, I think comes from seeing Pashukanis as methodologically rigid in this sense.

The second issue pertaining to reading legal form as a dialect through the value-form scholarship is that it runs the risk of an overly negative reading, one that, as Rose would say, 'revels without repose'.[86] In Rose's reading of Hegel, one must at a certain point arrest the dance of the dialect and locate the totality as a result of one's movement. But there is a certain allure in avoiding this—issuing such judgement carries an inherent risk, especially regarding the reified forms of thought under capitalism. This risk, however, must be taken in any kind of legal theorizing because, as the speculative is tied to Rose's concept of the broken middle, it is impossible for the owl of Minerva to see before it spreads her wings at all—but it is only in this flight, in dusk

81 Theodor Adorno, *Minima Moralia Reflections on a Damaged Life* (Verso 2006) 50.
82 Rose (n 24) 60.
83 ibid 59.
84 See Przemysław Tacik, 'Subjectification Through Normativity: Legal Form as a Modern Device' in this volume.
85 On this last point see Carl Wilén, 'Why Pashukanis was Right: Abstraction and Form in The General Theory of Law and Marxism' (2023) *Capital & Class*, https://journals.sagepub.com/doi/epub/10.1177/03098168231215417 (online first)
86 Rose (n 24) 62.

that it can 'herald the return of Athena, freedom without domination'.[87] The concept of jurisprudence is for Rose also tied to the speculative, Here Pashukanis is not his radicalized reading of form allows him to see that private and public law are indeed interdependent and not merely aporetic antitheses:

> Yet it is precisely this contradiction which is the most typical attribute of the legal form as such. The division of law into public and private law characterises this form from the historical as well as from the logical aspect. Thus the very concept of "public law" can only be developed through its workings, in which it is continually repulsed by private law; so much so that it attempts to define itself as the antithesis of private law, to which it returns, however, as to its centre of gravity.[88]

Value-form theory, in turn, often lacks engagement with law beyond reference to form and occasional homage to (without engaging with) Pashukanis. At first, this may seem natural, but when accepting the argument above, legal form always plays a role in facilitating exchange, without which there could be no form of value. In a closing world where the narrow horizon of bourgeois right is crumbling for the wrong reasons, it is not difficult to see why thinking beyond that very horizon seems far-fetched. Nevertheless, the legal form cannot wither away without new social relations to replace it, and these are in dialectical tension with social regulation. Rose suggests that the way to overcome these reified forms of thought is the movement from so-called relative to absolute ethical life.

Toward a speculative jurisprudence of legal form

The speculative is the opposite of dogmatism, in that it is 'knowledge of what is opposed in its very oneness, more precisely, the knowledge that opposites are in truth one'.[89] Things are defined by not being another and so cannot be thought of in isolation. To this end, this section provides a first sketch of Rose's trinity of ideas from *Hegel Contra Sociology:* absolute ethical life, phenomenology and logic, as an attempt at expanding legal form in a systematic way.

Hegel Contra Sociology is structured along the dialectic of relative and absolute ethical life [*Sittlichkeit*] as standpoints in an unfolding phenomenology.

87 Rose (n 2) 91. Tony Gorman has an interesting reading of this which understands Rose's later work such as *Mourning Becomes the Law*, through her work that is part of her project on 'Critical Marxism'. This speculative understanding is suitably aporetic in a Rosean way, see Gorman (n 4) 35.

88 Nevertheless, this is not a purely speculative approach, but it shows how Pashukanis is open to such theorizing. See Pashukanis (n 38) 106–7.

89 Rose (n 2) 88.

For our present purposes, these standpoints can be read as the legal form (relative ethical life) and its withering away in communism (absolute ethical life). Rose writes that the sphere of abstract right comes to be represented as civil society (capitalism).[90] Contrary to the idea that civil society and spheres such as the family are emanations of the state, Hegel is here seen to argue that such categories 'presuppose an overall economic and political organization which may not be immediately intelligible'.[91] This organization is what results from generalized commodity exchange in Pashukanis' account. Law becomes dependent on this specific *form* of social regulation. As Pashukanis illustrates, mutual recognition of subjectivity is integral. But the purported universality of this form is an illusion in which the particular individual mistakes for a totality, which is rational.[92] This mistake is inevitable because:

> civil society as a whole considers individuals as universal, as "man", without reference to class, religion or nationality. But the designation "man" in a society based on private property relations is only the form of universality, not the content or actuality.[93]

Viewing posited law as universal for Rose, then, is dependent on relative ethical life, or legal form. It amounts to form because bourgeois property relations can never be 'rational in content'.[94] And so while it may appear as a very Eden for rights, the way the form of value dominates means that class, race and gender are not dissolved away in content or actuality, because this very right presupposes inequitable property relations, otherwise it would be meaningless.[95] To paraphrase Pashukanis, the right to property merely affords 'equal opportunity to attain inequality'.[96] The alternative to this is changing standpoint from relative ethical life to one of absolute ethical life, wherein law would become subsumed in the totality of social institutions, that is, the withering away of law, familiar from the work of Pashukanis, but restated from within Rose's thought.[97] But before returning to purported ends of law, we need to consider other ways of deriving legal form from Rose's work as well as the specificity of a speculative legal form.

The other explicit conceptualization of legal form in Rose's work can be found in *From Speculative to Dialectical Thinking*.[98] Legal form is there

90 ibid 88.
91 ibid 55.
92 ibid 88.
93 ibid 89.
94 ibid 88.
95 ibid 109.
96 Pashukanis (n 38) 123.
97 Rose (n 2) 89.
98 Rose (n 24) 53–63.

derived from combining Lukács' speculative reading *(in spe)* of the commodity form with Weber's theory of legal-rational domination. This form also bears similarities to the legal form Pashukanis presents.[99] Legal form can be, and is for Lukács, at the heart of speculative exposition. This means that the legal form for Rose, building on the commodity form, both lead to *commodification* and *personification*. Because the invention of the modern legal subject cannot be adequately understood without reference to how labor-power assumes the form of commodity and thereby necessarily results in a breaking down of the subject-object dichotomy represented by this speculative moment. The (in)famous spectral objectivity Marx ascribes to the commodity is very difficult, if not impossible, to fully grasp without the legal form mediating social relations.[100] The commensurability that affords the commodity with its form is saturated by law. This can be contrasted with the now classical Marxist theory of international law presented by Miéville, where he consistently turns toward an idea of historical materialism and finds the rejection of 'capital logic' and 'derivation' to be key to understanding Pashukanis. In this move, Miéville does not allow the legal form to assume shape through the speculative unfolding of social mediations, opting instead to build on the assumptions implicit in historical materialism.[101] But to allow the legal form to take form speculatively can mean very different things depending on what type of speculation is put forward. Rose contrasts the use of the speculative in Hegel and Kant, whereas for the latter it means incorrect use of correct principles, while Hegel relies on speculation to illustrate the impossibility of 'Kantian justification'.[102] This means that Rose has a concept of the speculative which is far removed from contemporary speculative legal theory which speculates as to possible post-human, post-capitalist future from Kantian premises.

For Rose, speculative propositions revolve specifically around the non-identity of subject and predicate. To read propositions speculatively means to equally affirm both identity and non-identity between subject and predicate. This is what Rose refers to as severe style.[103] The meaning of a proposition can only be speculatively affirmed by identity and non-identity clashing in a series of relations to each other—'only when the lack of identity

99 On Rose reading Pashukanis see Brower Latz (n 1).
100 Marx (n 39) 128.
101 This does of course not take away from the fact that few people have done as much for Marxist currents in international law as Miéville, essential in paving the way for contemporary debates and opening the field. But he does so in a way that builds on conclusions that are implicit in historical materialism. See Miéville (n 52) 129.
102 Rose (n 2) 89.
103 'The severe style is concerned to give a true representation of its object and makes little concession to the spectator. It is designed solely to do justice to the integrity of the object' ibid 51.

between subject and predicate has been experienced, can their identity be grasped'[104] Speculative legal form must therefore be retrieved as *experience* rather than theorized spontaneously or without reference to the dialectic nature of law's relation to the value form. For example, when Rose re-reads Hegel's Philosophy of Right considering speculative propositions, it transforms into a critique of liberal natural law. Parts of the supposedly conservative Hegelian system which before appeared as natural and immediate, such as the family, work and civil society, are through this dialectical movement revealed only to assume form under a very specific set of social relations. Far from naturalized, they rely on presuppositions that are violent and repressive.[105] The use of Pashukanian thought is that it allows us to ascertain that such relations translate into law by being mediated by the value-form. Marx saw the commodity as abounding with 'theological niceties', Pashukanis saw how legal abstractions come to dominate, and Rose allows us to see how this happens through a specific set of social relations in each case: not being pre-judged but allowed to assume form through the unfolding of relations.

Rose and Pashukanis thus both take aim at a perceived lack in Marx's theory: for Pashukanis it is the development of law, for Rose *stasis*. Because Marx separated the speculative system from its dialectic method, his account of subjectivity is seen by Rose to be overly rigid.[106] But Marx's project is salvageable, especially the concept of commodity fetishism from which Pashukanis derives legal fetishism. According to Rose, this is the most speculative moment in Marx because substance becomes misrepresented as the subject, which leads to the illusion of legal equality.[107] This does not mean that any specific subject necessarily knows itself as a substance, but regardless of consciousness, it is still a determination of that substance. According to Rose, this transformation can only be unveiled by a philosophy of history, but Pashukanis arguably provides a functionalist legal history of the same metamorphosis.[108] While this fills a gap in Marx, it is also the crux of so-called relative ethical life, because while it looks like the legal form encompasses the universal, it is only able to re-cognize its interests in disputes and clashes which by necessity become dominated by formal property law.[109]

The tension between subject/substance or freedom/domination may lead to the type of legal nihilism which is sometimes ascribed to the work of Pashukanis and those inspired by it. To a certain extent this must be true, the telos of Pashukanian thought entails the sublation (a term which in this case also needs to take the form of the speculative) of law. But this sublation

104 ibid 49.
105 ibid 50.
106 ibid 216.
107 ibid 217.
108 ibid 105.
109 ibid 176.

is never expounded on by Pashukanis, instead the project of understanding the intricacies of legal form itself largely relies on Roman law. Pashukanis' few own suggestions of what may come after, including a type of technical regulation where 'singleness of purpose' reigns as opposed to contestation, are unsatisfactory and underdeveloped.[110] Legal form theory is then a theory from the standpoint of relative ethical life, a change of which requires formal law and custom need to merge. Rose is here referring to custom as *Sittlichkeit* and not the type of customary law one would find in international law and *jus gentium*. Such customary law is also just another form of relative ethical life which is illustrated by Pashukanis in his text on international law.[111]

Just as legal form remains internal to law necessarily must view law both from the inside and outside—as really existing but historically specific—Rose suggests that there is an implicit and hidden ought, *Sollen* in Hegel's work, even if it strives to be presuppositionless. This ought exists to the extent that the real relations which underpin his philosophy are concretely incompatible with it. To fall back into the language of reification: the type of thinking that becomes reified in a society can never fully contain absolute ethical life. Despite this hindrance, Rose suggests we must attempt to think the absolute, even if we then, like Hegel, need to begin to develop it as an abstract imperative 'because it arises in a society where real recognition has not been achieved'.[112] What is the social import of thinking the absolute? Rose cites Hegel as saying that the idea man has of God corresponds to himself, or that our concept of God is the concept of ourselves. Without thinking of the absolute then, we are powerless to change our underlying social relations.[113] The Kantian unknowable thing-in-itself—or God, then, means that we have no way of knowing ourselves, much less our political and social relations. Rose writes:

> "Subjectivity" is the correlate of the legal definition of persons as bearers of private property rights. Misrepresentation of the absolute is the correlate of subjectivity.[114]

Suppressing thinking of the absolute leads to a misrecognition of the very circumstances and reality of legal abstraction, taking the form of the critique against Pashukanis' tendency toward abstraction with which I opened this text. But more than that, legal subjectivity is then by itself necessarily

110 See C.J. Arthur's introduction in Pashukanis (n 38) 16.
111 Pashukanis argues international law is one of the first and purest forms of appearance of social regulation mediated by value. Evgeny Pashukanis, 'International Law' in *Pashukanis, Selected Writings on Marxism and Law* (Academic Press 1980); See also Rose (n 2) 114.
112 Rose (n 2) 78.
113 ibid 92.
114 ibid 93.

a misrecognition. But this misrecognition needs to be recognized as part of retrieving the speculative experience. Pashukanis' beginning with the 'atom of the legal relation'—the subject—can thus be understood as the beginning of a speculative proposition. Compare this with Hegel's treatment in the *Philosophy of Right* which contains two speculative propositions, one being that religion and state are identical. Read speculatively, however, this means that they are *not* pre-judged to be identical but rather opposition that must be experienced to gain knowledge. This experience implies the misrecognition of both state and religion, that is, of bad state and bad religion. Contrary to these abstractions which can only misrepresent, the absolute must be thought from real social relations. But thinking only of real relations without the absolute also entails misrepresentation.[115] The absolute can, instead, be thought of by the 'philosophical completion' of religion and its corresponding social relations.[116] The philosophical completion of the speculative reading of the law is further expounded on by Rose when she takes Hegel's *Logic* as the final part of his trinity of ideas.[117] Rose reads Hegel as coming to grips with the issue of how formal law dominates absolute ethical life, which is the mirror image of legal form hindering communism. Both appear unattainable considering the misrepresentation above. The logic can contribute to a speculative understanding of legal form insofar as it describes the identity and non-identity of law.[118] This means remaining aware of the limits posed by the value-form and in extension capital by understanding it not as a split between the economy and the political, but as a totality that comes into being from a series of form determinations. I am not arguing that logic cannot achieve freedom from domination. Rather, by speculatively exposing how abstraction dominates contemporary life, jurisprudence will not necessarily be limited to reforming its concepts but rather critique the way in which they are determined.[119]

In this, the critique of abstraction made in the name of legal form as theory is correct insofar as it identifies a form of relative ethical life attempting to present itself as a naturalized order of things or truth, using abstraction. But critique must importantly illustrate how the violence of abstraction comes into being, through its various determinations. It must be aware of both identity and lack of identity.[120] This last step is where critical legal theory outside of Pashukanis often is lacking. As an example, Miéville theorizes this violent nature of legal form and its abstraction but his reliance on Schmitt and

115 ibid 93.
116 Rose (n 24) 94.
117 Georg Wilhelm Fredrich Hegel, *The Science of Logic* (1st edn, CUP 2010).
118 Rose (n 2) 187.
119 ibid 187.
120 ibid 57.

Koskenniemi obscures the nature of this violence. It takes the route through Schmitt, rather than the contradictory experience of the value-form as both equality and inequality, that law must be the bloody world around us.[121] There is nothing wrong with this conclusion *per se* but rather in the way it is reached. The merits of a speculative exposition would be that it could outline how legal form bears the seeds of its own destruction. While the technical regulation presented by Pashukanis appears as a failure to salvage something from the legal form, forms of judgement and social relations that are not subsumed by the value form need to be thought about. Drawing on Rose, legal theory should do so from the standpoint of absolute ethical life. Speculative philosophy must always sit between tragedy and utopia, which in legal form means acknowledging its brokenness while attempting to find ways out of it.[122]

Mending brokenness requires striving toward 'real re-cognition'. Even in contemporary forms of mis-cognition, real cognition is implied but can again not be pre-judged, instead taking form through a series of systematic movements. Law and value as forms cannot just be done away with, however much one agrees with the fact that they are the bloody world around us. They remain, and in critically theorizing their afterlives, it may be productive to think of them speculatively, transforming beyond what is. Rose calls this 'looking back' without denying or subsuming the difference.[123] Such a process will inevitably require some form of abstraction while at the same time differentiating Rose from the negative dialectics of Adorno and value-form theory. Rose offers so-called repose in the bacchanalian revel[124] as a positive moment from which something else can be born. Applying real recognition, this is far from a transcendental or trans-historical absolute, but instead, something that is implied by contemporary intuition and the dialectic movement of value becoming capital.[125] Rose shows us the impossibility of overcoming legal form by way of an abstract *Sollen* as well as the hidden *Sollen* of striving for something beyond, even in the most presuppositionless of doctrines. She offers us a way out: thinking the absolute, that is through the

121 Miéville (n 52) 319.
122 Schick (n 31) 37.
123 Rose (n 2) 65.
124

> The True is thus a Bacchanalian revel, with not a member sober; yet because each member collapses as soon as he drops out, the revel is just as much transparent and simple repose. In the whole of the movement, seen as a state of repose, what distinguishes itself therein, and gives itself particular existence, is preserved as something that recollects itself, whose existence is self-knowledge, and whose self-knowledge is just as immediately existence.
>
> See introduction in Georg Wilhelm Friedrich Hegel, Phenomenology of Spirit (OUP 1977)

125 Gorman (n 4) 30; See also Rose (n 24); Postone (n 64) 142–43.

dirempted forms as truth in their wholeness. But that would be law divorced from the legal form. In the words of Rose herself:

> In an ethical community law would not be set apart from the totality of social institutions. It would not be private property law. In a simple, just, ethical community real recognition would be enshrined in custom, Sitte. Hence ethical life, Sittlichkeit, would be natural, the concept and intuition equal, and the life of the community would be "a natural history of spirit". This life would consist of mutual recognition in all social institutions.[126]

Conclusion

This chapter opened with the now familiar critique of abstraction and its use in legal form theory, it has argued that through engaging with form as it is conceptualized in Marxist theory rather than approaches internal to law—as for instance, CLS—the critique appears to be misplaced. The ways in which Pashukanis relies on abstraction do not correspond to those of traditional bourgeois jurisprudence. Viewing jurisprudence through the Hegelian schematic of the forms which philosophical content may assume suggests that what is generally understood to be an abstraction in the work of Pashukanis is instead a form of dialectical derivation taking place through acts, not thought. If the theory indeed describes something real, such phenomena cannot be overcome by simply favoring a theory that is supposedly less abstract.

But such a reading in turn becomes susceptible to Rose's critique of Adorno and negative dialectics. Accepting the conclusions of value-form theory without subjecting it to a systematic critique of the contradictory experience of those very forms leaves them undissolved and rigid in a similar vein to how critiques of abstraction take aim at Pashukanis. It is also, for Rose, a critique that never gives itself up to the dialectic, becoming ruthless in form but never in content as it never risks issuing a judgement.

To this end, Rose's speculative project could expand legal form theory beyond such impasses. A speculative reading of legal form attempts to think of the absolute because it is the only thought which can go beyond not only the abstractions of bourgeois law but the very determinations of their forms. This requires shifting standpoint from relative ethical life, that is, legal form, to absolute ethical life, which for Pashukanis would be communism. Doing that has been beyond the scope of this present work, but to that end, I offer the following tentative proposition for retrieving speculative experience for legal form: *the subject and property are one and the same.*

126 Rose (n 2) 89.

Chapter 8

Legal form and the anarchist critique of the law

Christos Marneros

Introduction

In this chapter, I examine and discuss the potential way(s) that the understanding of legal form, as this is articulated and developed by the Marxist jurist Evgeny Pashukanis,[1] could be utilised by anarchists and legal theorists who engage with an anarchist and/or anarchic critique of the law and who aim to seriously think about the possibility of living a life which is dictated by legal norms—in short, of a life *beyond the yoke of the law*.

While, as I argue, Pashukanis' examination of the legal form and its overall 'legal scepticism'[2] is a significant step towards a call for the abolition of the law, it does not go all the way. My central argument tries to shed light on how the notion of legal form might be a useful tool in the effort to better grasp how the law becomes, perhaps, the most useful tool in the state's ability to justify and enjoy a monopoly of violence. In doing so, I aim to demonstrate that the Marxist notion of the legal form and its reduction to mere 'economism'—at least, the critique of the law and its form advanced by Pashukanis[3]—suffers from a significant shortcoming. This is its inability to account for and take seriously the powerful ability of the law and juridical mentality to produce a special category of reactionary (legal) subjectivity, what I call here, the 'perfect citizen.' This 'perfect citizen' as a pacified, decadent and alienated form of subjectivity, consciously (or not) acts as the most faithful 'agent' of the law and the state by justifying the state's monopoly of

1 Evgeny Bronislavovich Pashukanis, *The General Theory of Law and Marxism* (first published 1924, Barbara Eihorn tr and Dragan Milovanovic intro, Transaction Publishers 2003).

2 For a brief overview of how Pashukanis' account of the legal form relates to a broader sceptical approach towards the law, see Cosmin Cercel, 'Through a Glass Darkly': Law, History and the Frontispiece of the Exception' in Cosmin Cercel, Gian-Giacomo Fusco, and Simon Lavis (eds), *States of Exception: Law, History, Theory* (Routledge 2021) 42.

3 Nancy E Anderson and David F Greenberg, 'From Substance to Form: The Legal Theory of Pashukanis and Elderman' (1983) 7 *Social Text* 69, 69–70.

DOI: 10.4324/9781032724713-9

violence.[4] Thus, it is paramount that we rethink in terms of a potential anarchistic legal form or think beyond it.

The chapter starts with a brief examination of Pashukanis' understanding of the legal form (Section I). It proceeds with a reading of the anarchist critique of the law and its ability to justify the state's monopoly of violence, by focusing on the writings of two important thinkers of the anarchist tradition, albeit in a very different sense from one another, Peter Kropotkin and Max Stirner (Section II). Finally, the chapter concludes with an evaluation of how the legal form could be utilised—or become redundant—by an anarchist critique of the law (Section III).

From an instrumentalism to a Marxist critique of the law and its form: Pashukanis on legal form

The multifarious ways of thinking about the nature of the law and the state, their relationship and coexistence during the 20th century have rendered necessary the close engagement of theory with this particular subject matter. The 20th century witnessed the co-existence, utilisation of and even opposition between legal systems and forms with different ideological positions and political systems. The capitalist market's flexibility and the different legal form(s) were used accordingly by Western liberal democracies, both in their social democratic and more conservative forms, fascist and other forms of totalitarian regimes, such as the military juntas in Greece, Portugal and Spain.[5] These changes rendered the (re)examination of the role, function and ultimate place of the law in a future communist society which would have succeeded the 'withering away' of the bourgeois state and the provisional stage of the dictatorship of the proletariat.

A first step towards this renewed interest in the science of jurisprudence in Marxist juridical and philosophical circles was to recognise that the

4 These distinct approaches on who or what is the central enemy of any radical, emancipatory effort, lies at the very core of the schism between Marx and his followers on the one hand and anarchists on the other, with Bakunin being a central figure of this feud. See Friedrich Engels, 'Versus the Anarchists' in Robert C Tucker (ed), *The Marx-Engels Reader* (W.W. Norton 1978) 728. Engels writes:

> Bakunin has a peculiar theory of his own, a medley of Proudhonism and communism, the chief point of which is, in the first place, that he does not regard capital and therefore the class antagonism between capitalists and wage-workers which has arisen through social development but the state as the main evil to be abolished.

5 For a discussion on the formation and characteristics of these kind of dictatorships as opposed to the Fascist regime of Italy and the Nazi regime of Germany, as well as the different operation of the law and legal form(s), see Nicos Poulantzas, *Fascism and Dictatorship* (Judith White tr, Verso 1979) 299–333; *The Crisis of Dictatorships: Portugal, Greece, Spain* (David Fernbach tr, New Left Books 1976).

instrumentalist understanding of the law, as this is mainly found in young Karl Marx's writings, was not particularly well-equipped to respond to the realities of the 20th-century states. In particular, the central position of an instrumentalist, Marxist perspective on the place of law in capitalism started to seem ineffective in appreciating the unique role of the law and the science of jurisprudence more broadly in justifying, creating, sustaining and, more importantly, *abstracting* the oppressive social relations of the capitalist state of affairs and apparatuses—'committee for managing the common affairs of the whole bourgeoisie.'[6]

For example, Marx's understanding of the law and the state, in his 'On the Jewish Question', limits their role in a process of political alienation. In the passage, Marx, correctly identifies that the emancipation of politics, the state and the individual from religious dogmas is nothing more than a sham that successfully hides the true face of oppression which stems from the social and economic alienation and exploitation of the working class in capitalist states. As he explains, 'to be politically emancipated from religion is not to be finally and completely emancipated from religion, because political emancipation is not the final and absolute form of human emancipation.'[7] To that extent, a clear distinction must be drawn between human emancipation and state emancipation. Whereas the state can emancipate itself from religious superstitions, it creates at the same time—by utilising the law and its promises of equality and rights—an even more powerful form of oppression for the working class, enchanting it with these false and abstract promises[8] of equality and representation, when the material conditions and the abstraction of their labour are sustained, if not deteriorating.

For the purposes of this examination, we can draw the following conclusions. First, the law is not objective but rather reflects the prevailing power relations in society. Laws are made by the ruling class to favour their interests and protect their property rights. The legal system also helps to maintain the status quo by criminalising the dissenting voices and legitimising state violence against the working class. Secondly, the state functions to maintain social order by enforcing the laws and regulations that are in the interest of the ruling class. In this sense, the state is a repressive apparatus that uses force to control the working class, maintain the status quo and protect the property interests of the ruling class. Thus, both the state and the law function as instruments of the bourgeoisie to sustain the status quo and their hegemonic position.

6 Karl Marx and Friedrich Engels, 'Manifesto of the Communist Party' in Robert C Tucker (ed), *The Marx-Engels Reader* (W.W. Norton 1978) 475.

7 Karl Marx, 'On the Jewish Question' in Robert C Tucker (ed), *The Marx-Engels Reader* (W.W. Norton 1978) 32.

8 With perhaps the first and foremost the so-called 'right to liberty' which in capitalism is only translated in practice as 'the right to private property'. (ibid 42).

Despite the merits of Marx's analysis, this approach towards the law downplays its unique position and the role it played in the emergence and subsequent triumph of capitalism not only as an economic system but as a mode and process of *individuation*. In the preface to the German edition of his *General Theory of Law*, Pashukanis begins by emphasising this position: 'In bourgeois society, jurisprudence has always held a special, privileged place. Not only is it first among the other social sciences, but is also leaves its mark on them.'[9] As such, his quest is to offer an analysis that pays the necessary attention to the law's ability to (re)produce a legal subject which serves in its totality the function of the capitalist system.

Pashukanis explains that it is paramount to pay closer attention to the abstract categories of juridical notions and concepts that are taken for granted, such as 'legal subject,' 'norms,' 'legal relations' and so forth.[10] This is because these abstract notions and the general ideology of juridical science hold the key to an effective understanding of the machinations of the law and its form. It is through this critical examination that we should be able to 'demonstrate [the] true significance and lay bare the historically limited nature of the legal form.'[11] In particular, this reference to a 'true significance' of the law and its abstract categories already shows that juridical science enjoys a certain element of independence from the wishes of the bourgeoisie. The law—or in better terms—its form is thus not only an instrument of the ruling class or a mere force of coercion but something beyond that. *It is a protagonist itself within the capitalist system, as it dictates social relations in a similar fashion that Marx argued for the role of political economy.*[12]

To that extent, Pashukanis aims to develop 'a commodity theory of law.'[13] In order to achieve that, he proceeds by demonstrating how an analogy or homology exists, as Dragan Milovanovic describes it,[14] between the 'commodity fetishism,' that characterises the social relations as these are formed by political economy and legal form. As he states, 'the critique of bourgeois

9 Pashukanis (n 1) 33.
10 ibid 47.
11 ibid 64.
12 See, Dragan Milovanovic, *Introduction to the Sociology of Law* (3rd edn, Lynne Rienner Publishers 2003) 89. In his chapter on Marx, law and political economy, Milovanovic argues that Pashukanis' starting point for his analysis of the legal form is Marx's first volume of *Capital*. Just like Marx developed there his notion of 'commodity fetishism' and commodity form, Pashukanis follows 'a similar logical development: that is, there exists a *homology*'.
13 Pashukanis himself did not use this term to describe his study but it is rather a term which was coined by Andrey Vishinsky and Pashukanis approved this. This information is mentioned in Tormod Otter Johansen, 'Minor Law: Notes Towards a Revolutionary Jurisprudence' in Cosmin Cercel, Gian-Giacomo Fusco, and Simon Lavis (eds), *States of Exception: Law, History, Theory* (Routledge 2021) 78.
14 Milovanovic (n 12) 89.

jurisprudence from the standpoint of scientific socialism must follow the example of Marx's critique of bourgeois political economy.'[15] Just like the way the political economy of the capitalist system produces abstractions such as 'the independence of the market' which is based on so-called natural phenomena and not the volition of the capital owners, buyers and sellers of commodities (for example, the price or value of commodities), the law and its form behaves in a similar manner. The law presents abstract notions such as rights, norms and legal subjectivity, as naturally given and universally applicable. The legal form, then, effectively separates the legal subject from its social, political and economic relations. The legal subject via the medium of the bourgeois legal form is reduced to the abstract bearer of rights, irrespective of its material conditions and societal position, in a fashion that is similar to the way Marx understands the fictitious equality which is promised by the law, political or constitutional rights and the rights of man.[16] To that extent, this commodity form veils the way that the law operates in a concrete situation, where the very reality of the position of a person, for example in terms of class, is at stake. Pashukanis wants us to become aware of this sham and understand the very reality of the operation and machination of the law and its form:

> Hence [the] law in its general definitions, law as a form, does not exist in the heads and the theories of learned jurists. It has a parallel, real history, which unfolds not as a set of ideas, but as specific set of relations which men enter into not by conscious choice, but because the relations of production compel them to do so. Man becomes a legal subject by virtue of the same necessity which transforms the product of nature into a commodity complete with the enigmatic property value.[17]

What is important to notice here, is that while the legal form operates by normalising or even naturalising abstract, legal concepts, it is not void of any content or history. Nonetheless, this content of the legal form is something which has been produced by the capitalist relations based on commodity value and exchange.[18] Thus, the way that the human being becomes the legal subject under bourgeois jurisprudence suggests that this subject will always act—or in better terms, be acted upon—in a mode of abstraction, by being the bearer of so-called universal rights that profess to be uninterested in its

15 Pashukanis (n 1) 64.

16 ibid 115: 'The legal subject acquires a double in the shape of a representative, and himself attains the significance of a mathematical point, a centre in which a certain number of rights is concentrated.'

17 ibid 68.

18 Ruth Fletcher, 'Legal Forms and Reproductive Norms' (2003) 12(2) *Soc of LS* 217, 219.

material condition (or as the usual narrative of pseudo-equality goes: 'the law is equal for everyone and applies equally to everyone').[19]

From the above examination, we can deduce two further closely interconnected points which relate to the way that the legal form operates under capitalism. The first point is that with this abstract category of the legal subject, we also witness the formalisation of the legal norms that apply in every aspect of legal process and decisions. This means that the laws are supposedly applied universally by supposedly disregarding the material context and uniqueness of a situation, that is, the unique characteristics and particularities of a legal case. The second point, and the more important one, relates to the way that the legal form in capitalism understands the notions of liberty, rationality, autonomy and equality. The legal subject is considered to be an entity that finds its origins in the Enlightenment and Kantian notions of rationality and autonomy. Yet, as John Locke has taught us, these notions of autonomy, rationality and liberty are interwoven with the possession of private property.[20] Pashukanis' account takes this last point and demonstrates that the critique of the legal form must focus on a critique of the sphere of private law. This is the legal sphere where the legal subjects are recognised as merely the bearers of 'equal' property rights.

Indeed, Pashukanis maintains that private law is the primary level of any juridical practice while all the rest disciplinary forms of law, be that constitutional,[21] criminal and so forth, are simply dictated by private law and the socio-economic relationships based on commodity exchange. He explains that in a system which is based on commodity exchange, the basis is an 'atomised economy.'[22] In its turn, this atomised economy presupposes that there is a link or relation between 'isolated private economic units.'[23] This link is maintained through business transactions. In the sphere of political economy, these isolated private economic units are the products of labour

19 A similar observation can be made for the way that the modern common law, in particular when it comes to private areas of law, such as tort and contract, has based much of its tests on the equally abstract and generally uncontested notion of the so-called 'reasonable person'. On how this abstraction came to become naturalised see, Joanne Conaghan, 'Reassessing the Feminist Theoretical Project in Law' (2000) 27(3) *JL & Soc* 351; John Gardner, 'The Reasonable Person Standard' (2019) International Encyclopedia of Ethics 1.

20 See for example, how Locke's recognition of a 'right to revolution' is subjected to someone's recognition as a property owner. In order for someone to have the 'right to rebel' they must suffer a violation of their right to private property. See, John Locke, *Second Treatise of Government* (CB Macpherson ed, Hackett Publishing 1980) 111.

21 Pashukanis (n 1) 103–4: Constitutional law is only able to exist as a reflection of the private-law form in the sphere of political organisation, otherwise it ceases to be law entirely. In other words, the public realm of the law and the constitutional rules are simply an outcome of the relations that are cemented in the sphere of private law.

22 ibid 85.

23 ibid.

that turn into commodities. In the juridical sphere, they are the legal subjects who are supposedly free to enter into legal relations. To that extent, for Pashukanis, 'the legal relation is the cell-form of the legal fabric; only there does law accomplish its real movement.'[24] On the contrary, the general view of law as purely a matter of norms and regulations (here Pashukanis names Kelsen as the central figure of this understanding of the law), is false because fails to take into consideration the fact that these norms or regulations are either 'derived directly from relations already in existence'[25] or they will be the originator of the emergence of future relations. For example, a state decree which prevents theft is a regulation which, according to Pashukanis, is based on existing social relations, in that case, perhaps, the fact that the law of contract suggests that a form of exchange should be given for acquiring any goods or services. Furthermore, this anti-theft decree will lead to the emergence of novel social relations, for example, the fact that the exchange of commodities can only take place if the monetary value of the good or service which is asked by the one party to the relationship, is met by the other party. Subsequently, if the very core of legal relations is the commodity exchange, then the legal form comes to its peak with the emergence and domination of the capitalist system.[26] In its turn, every legal relation presupposed that the legal subject is at the heart of it—'the subject is the very atom of legal theory, its simplest, irreducible element.'[27] Ultimately, the legal form then produces the narrative of the legal subjects as the supposedly free consumers who have the liberty to enter into commercial relations—'a liberty' that they have to take if they want to enjoy the societal recognition as property owners and the abstract protections that their rights offer them.

The next question then becomes, what will the future of the legal form be when the capitalist system dies out? Or how will the law look in a future classless or communist society when private property is abolished and thus, the legal relations that shape the legal form cease to exist? Following in Marx's footsteps, Pashukanis is not very clear about the image of the law under communism. He seems to acknowledge that a certain element of legal relations might exist during the transitional period from the fall of the bourgeois regimes and the dictatorship of the proletariat, in order to facilitate necessary actions such as the redistribution of private property or the distribution of

24 ibid.
25 ibid 87.
26 This is perhaps another issue of Pashukanis' account of legal form and its understanding as a homology with political economy. While he may be right that the legal form comes to its peak with the emergence of capitalism, the existence of the legal form is rather a matter of any hierarchical system or any legal system. Hence, as I argue, the anarchist critique of the law might offer a better understanding of the problem with the law, while also utilising some of Pashukanis' powerful insights.
27 Pashukanis (n 1) 109.

necessary goods.[28] Yet, he is very clear that with the arrival of the endpoint of communism and the complete triumph of the revolution, the law just like the state, private property and all the remnants of bourgeois society and system will 'wither away.'[29] As he explains (in a fragment worth quoting extensively):

> The withering away of certain categories of bourgeois law (the categories as such, not this or that precept) in no way implies their replacement by new categories of proletarian law, just as the withering away of the categories of value, capital, profit and so forth in the transition to fully-developed socialism will not mean the emergence of new proletarian categories of value, capital and so on.
>
> The withering away of the categories of bourgeois law will, under these conditions, mean the withering away of law altogether, that is to say the disappearance of the juridical factor from social relations.[30]

This position is consistent with the way in which Pashukanis understands the notion of the legal from. Since the legal form achieves its highest level of dictating the formation of the legal subject as an abstract bearer of rights and owner of private property, with the abolition of private property and the demystification from the pseudo-equality and liberty of the bourgeois state, the law and any element of legal relations will cease to exist because, to put it simply, they will be worthless.

Pashukanis' account of the legal form is without a doubt, a valuable contribution not only to Marxist examination and serious engagement with

28 ibid 62.

29 In later writings and due to the direct threat that this position had for his life during the Stalinist purges, Pashukanis amended it. For example, we read in his short piece, 'State and Law Under Socialism' in Piers Beirne and Robert Sharlet (eds), Peter B Maggs (tr), *Pashukanis: Selected Writings on Marxism and Law* (Academic Press 1980) 354, 356:

> It is just as opportunistic to assert that law will wither away under socialism as it is to affirm that state authority should wither away the day after the bourgeoisie was overthrown. In this context it is appropriate to offer once again deserved criticism of those erroneous positions put forward by the author of *The General Theory of Law and Marxism*. This is essential if the old mistakes and confusion are not to be repeated in other forms and other ways.

In few pages later:

> The real and concrete history of Soviet law as a weapon of proletarian policy-which the proletariat used at various stages to defend the conquests of the revolution and the reconstruction towards socialism-was replaced by abstract and mistaken conclusions about the withering away of law, about the "disappearance" of the legal superstructure etc.

Of course, this change in his position was not enough to save him.

30 ibid.

the question of jurisprudence and the law[31] but more generally to a radical demand for the abolition of the law and the rethinking of our social relations and the ways that we are constantly coming to be into (legal) subjects. Despite this, his account has been criticised—and correctly so—for being too narrow and too focused on private law, something that has as an outcome the underestimation of how the law, in other spheres, also plays an important role in maintaining and extending the status quo.[32] In addition, the Marxist theoretician of fascism, dictatorship and the state, Nicos Poulantzas, criticised Pashukanis' purely materialist approach to the law as something that reduces the notions of the law and the state to the base. This is—according to Poulantzas—due to a misconception of the superstructure as a form of an ideal, a Kantian transcendent, that goes beyond the real or material social relations.[33] Nonetheless, Poulantzas correctly identifies that the ideological aspect of the law and the way that it (re)produces its legal subjects is something that does not necessarily belong to an ideal and otherworldly transcendent. Ideology is also *real*, 'it too is genetically integrated into the—Marxist—totality, in praxis starting out from the base.'[34] Furthermore, further critiques correctly identify that Pashukanis' representation of the legal subject is oversimplistic because it fails to take into account the complex processes of individuation and legal techniques that lead to the shaping of a (legal) subject. By illustrating the legal subject as 'a natural figure,'[35] he fails to take into consideration how subjectivity is racialised or gendered.[36]

All the aforementioned critiques of Pashukanis' account of the legal form seem to speak in one way or another about the narrowness of his encapsulation of the law and its function in society. By reducing the operation of the law to a mere homology with the way that political economy functions and shapes our social relations, Pashukanis, ironically, fails to recognise the

31 Within the Anglo-American, Marxist legal circles and especially so in international law, Pashukanis' account of legal form has gained significant prominence after the publication of China Miéville, *Between Equal Rights: A Marxist Theory of International Law* (Brill 2005). More recently, the work of Robert Knox has drawn extensively on Pashukanis' theory of law. See, for example, Robert Knox, 'Marxism, International Law, and Political Strategy' (2009) 22(3) LJIL 413.

32 Johansen (n 13) 80–81.

33 Nicos Poulantzas, 'Marxist Examination of the Contemporary State and Law and the Question of the "Alternative"' in James Martin (ed), *The Poulantzas Reader: Marxism, Law and the State* (Verso 2008) 26–28.

34 ibid 30. I should note here, however, that Poulantzas' rather positive view on the law, which suggests that the law can function as a sphere that certain gains of the working class (e.g. certain rights) are to be preserved, is something that I find problematic. As I will explain in the next section, the law must be extinguished but this should not be a matter of a gradual 'withering away' but rather a matter of direct 'attack.'

35 Ntina Tzouvala, *Capitalism as Civilisation: A History of International Law* (CUP 2018) 25.

36 Fletcher (n 18) 223.

special position that the law enjoys in societies which are based on dogmatic and hierarchical relations of oppression and domination. This is done despite the fact that he claims that his study has as one of its main purposes to acknowledge the special position that the law holds. In doing so, he expected the law to 'wither away' just like the state and this inability to recognise that the gradual demise of the law and the state will not happen, but it will probably lead to a new hierarchy, which paid with his life. My argument in the next section is that the anarchist critique of the law succeeds where he fails, by recognising the law (and the state) as a fundamental enemy that must be directly attacked and vanquished.

The 'perfect citizen' as a pathology: the law's 'favourite'

Mikhail Bakunin, commenting on the need to abolish juridical law, states something very important not only about the anarchist position on the matter of law but also something which defines ontologically what it means *to be* an anarchist:

> In a word, we reject all legislation—privileged, licensed, official and legal—and all authority, and influence, even though they may emanate from universal suffrage, for we are convinced that it can turn only to the advantage of a dominant minority of exploiters against the interests and the vast majority in the subjection to them. *It is in this sense that we are really Anarchists.*[37]

This passage from Bakunin manifests the ferocious animosity of anarchists against all facets of legalism, juridical thinking and the law in general. If being an anarchist means automatically to refuse every aspect of legalism, then the law is automatically elevated to the position of the main target for anarchist politics of emancipation. At the same time, it is perhaps this animosity that held back anarchist thinkers, groups, activists and scholars from delving into an analysis of the relationship between law and anarchism, because they may have considered any 'serious analysis' to be unattainable or a matter which is already resolved. Critics, on the other hand, find the above position as something that demonstrates the utopian—in an 'immature,' or 'unscientific' sense—of the anarchist position. For example, Friedrich Engels ferociously attacks Bakunin for holding, according to him, a rather absurd position.

37 Mikhail Bakunin, 'Law, Natural and Invented' in GP Maximoff (ed and tr), *The Political Philosophy of Bakunin: Scientific Anarchism* (The Free Press of Glencoe 1964) 241 [emphasis added]. Similarly, for Kropotkin, anarchy is the refusal of 'submission to law.' See, Peter Kropotkin, 'Anarchism' in Emile Capouya and Keitha Tompkins (eds), *Essential Kropotkin* (Palgrave Macmillan 1975) 108.

Engels considers Bakunin to be naïve for believing that the state and the law are the main 'evils' that have to be attacked and not capital.[38] Similarly, in his rather controversial book on Stalin, the Italian philosopher and political theorist, Domenico Losurdo, often talks about the 'anarchoid messianism' that is characterised by a rather imbecile 'demand of absolute freedom.'[39]

The central mistake of these critics is that they reduce a very conscious and carefully developed position of the anarchists as a 'hot-headed' attitude which lacks the 'scientific' analysis and critical position to understand the process of class antagonism and the ultimate 'end of history' with the dissolution of class and the coming of communism. The reason why anarchists are very clear and direct when it comes to the need of getting rid of the state and the law from the beginning is because they realise the way that the law operates and that the survival of the law (even during a transitional period, as Pashukanis suggested) means outright the end of any emancipatory, non-hierarchical political project. The reason is simply because the law's main function is to produce a form of (legal) subjectivity which is completely pacified, dependent and resentful. By doing that, the law achieves to create 'the perfect citizen' who is not only ready to accept the state's monopoly of violence but to also justify it as necessary or even just.[40] Just like the Marxian concept of the lumpenproletariat, the 'perfect citizen' is

> [t]he "dangerous class," the social scum, that passively rotting mass thrown off by the lowest layers of old society, may, here and there, be swept into the movement by a proletarian revolution; its conditions of life, however, prepare it far more for the part of a bribed tool of reactionary intrigue.[41]

Yet, unlike the lumpenproletariat, the 'perfect citizen' does not belong to the old, but it is part of every fabric of our society, with each one of us being capable of turning into one at any point. Furthermore, what renders the 'perfect citizen' more dangerous is that it does not belong to a specific class—thus, Pashukanis' reduction of the legal form to a matter of private

38 Engels (n 4) 728.

39 Domenico Losurdo, *Stalin: The History and Critique of a Black Legend* (Salvatore Engel-Di Mauro and Henry Hakamäki trs and intro, Iskra Books 2023) 111.

40 In another instance, I demonstrated how deeply this pathology of the 'good citizens' runs in society and how rotten it is. I discussed the example of Greek society, where the 'common people' were ready to justify the execution of the teenager Alexis Grigoropoulos in December 2008 by a cop, simply because he was in the anarchist neighbourhood of Exarcheia in Athens—which is apparently a good reason, according to them, for the cops to murder someone. See, Christos Marneros, 'Μ.Γ.Δ.: The Figure of the Cop in the Anarchic Lyrics of Greek Punk' in Jim Donaghey, Will Boisseau and Caroline Kaltefleiter (eds), *Smash The System!: Punk Anarchism as a Culture of Resistance* (Active Distribution 2022) 250.

41 Marx and Engels (n 6) 482.

law, a mere 'economism,' fails to properly encapsulate the figure of the 'perfect citizen'—but it can subdue and shape anyone.

The radical collective of French philosophers and activists, Tiqqun, defines the citizens as

> those who, at the very heart of the general conflagration of the social sphere, persist in *proclaiming* their abstract participation in a society that now only exists negatively, through the terror it exercises over everything that threatens to abandon it and, in so doing, to *survive it*.[42]

In that sense, there is a persistence to continue participating in an already 'dead and buried' social, political environment due to a lack of thinking an alternative, a certain 'pacification' and 'numbness' of any of its capacities to resist this condition due to a nihilistic disinterest on behalf of this 'perfect citizen' to explore different ways of living. At the same time, the 'perfect citizen' participates and offers its services consciously (or not) to this dying society by recognising the legitimacy of its laws and its monopoly of violence. This figure of the 'perfect citizen,' while not explicitly portrayed, was, as I argue below, present in the anarchist critique of the law and this is what makes such a critique a powerful tool against the law.

'No more Laws!': Kropotkin's attack on the pacified legal subject

In his 'Law and Authority,'[43] Kropotkin argues that the law, against the common (mis)understanding, is a modern invention; he situates its origins back to the 18th century. As he explains, after the conclusion of the French Revolution, the law and the newly formed republics developed a very successful narrative of their willingness to serve and promote equality for everyone, through a call for societal cohesion.[44] The law was thus presented as a system which honours, respects and incorporates pre-existing social and moral values, and which at the same time effectively managed to present itself as a necessity. A necessity whose absence would have led to total chaos and the collapse of any civilisation.

This process has as a result the production of a specific category of a human being, one which is completely dependent on the law and its commands. Kropotkin portrays this decadence and the ultimate dependency of

42 Tiqqun, *This is Not a Programme* (Joshua David Jordan tr, Semiotext(e) 2011) 102.
43 Peter Kropotkin, 'Law and Authority' in Emile Capouya and Keitha Tompkins (eds), *Essential Kropotkin* (Palgrave Macmillan 1975).
44 ibid 29.

human beings on the commands of the law by describing the following fictitious situations where:

> If the road between two villages is impassable, the peasant says, "There should be a law about parish roads." If a park-keeper takes advantage of the want of spirit in those who follow him with servile observance and insults one of them, the insulted man says, "There should be a law to enjoin more politeness upon park-keepers." If there is stagnation in agriculture or commerce, the husbandman, cattle-breeder, or com speculator argues, "It is protective legislation that we require." Down to the old clothesman there is not one who does not demand a law to protect his own little trade. If the employer lowers wages or increases the hours of labour, the politician in embryo exclaims, "We must have a law to put all that to rights." In short, a law everywhere and for everything![45]

The law takes the form of 'a cult'[46] that indoctrinates the human being, turning it into the subject of the law, or what I named here the 'perfect citizen.' This indoctrination is something that happens since our age of infancy, through our everyday social relations and in particular, the education that we receive from institutions such as the family and the school. As a result, any inclination to question, critique and our 'spirit to revolt'[47] against the state of affairs, no matter how oppressive they are, dies out. Being completely submissive, pacified and dependent on the law, the law manages to make its yoke tighter through a powerful blackmail.[48] It is not only impossible to demand a life beyond the boundaries of the law, but it is impossible to think that such a possibility exists. 'Our society seems no longer able to understand that it is possible to exist otherwise than under the reign of law, by a representative government and administered by a handful of rulers. And even when it has gone so far as to emancipate itself from the thraldom, its first care has been to reconstitute it immediately.'[49] For Kropotkin, the law then is not only useless because in reality it does not offer something new, but it rather 'codifies' certain behaviours and beliefs which were already there long before the law acquired the official position that it currently enjoys in contemporary states.

More importantly, though, Kropotkin considers the law to be also harmful. This is because the law is presented as something natural and thus, a

45 ibid 27.

46 Errico Malatesta, 'The Duty of Resistance: Anarchists and The Law' in Davide Turcato (ed), Paul Sharkey (tr), *The Method of Freedom: An Errico Malatesta Reader* (AK Press 2014).

47 ibid 27.

48 Christos Marneros, "It is a Nomos Very Different From the Law': On Anarchy and The Law' (2021) 96 *Folia Iuridica* 125, 127–28.

49 ibid 27–28.

society in the absence of it is rather unnatural, at best problematic and at worst uninhabitable, if not a living hell. To that extent and in order to avoid the civilisation's collapse, the 'perfect citizen's' servitude and respect for the law is not only considered as a matter of option or 'taste' but rather an indication of 'virtue.' Ultimately, the 'perfect citizen' lives a life of total alienation,[50] in the sense that every aspect of its life is or *should* be dictated by the law's commands.

The 'perfect citizen' as a (un)willing 'agent' of the law: Max Stirner's spooks

Max Stirner's *Unique and Its Property*[51] can be read as a direct and ferocious assault on the emancipatory promise of the Enlightenment, an era which is, often, defined as the point of departure for the centrality that humanity enjoys in the universe. The 'era of reason' is usually thought of as the historical period when the human was liberated by the bondages and the commands of the Divine, the era when all forms of authority became the subject of strong doubt and criticism. The words of the Scriptures or any other Holy Book are subjected to strong criticism and the Divine becomes even something which is subjected to 'mockery.' Yet, this revolution of humanity remained rather incomplete, because, according to Stirner, even the most radical of the revolutionaries remained entrapped and in need of a highest essence to believe in.[52] Similarly to Kropotkin, he identifies the law as one of the fundamental tools that sustain this belief to higher principles—what he calls *phantasms* or *spooks*. Moving beyond the superstitions of religion, now 'a person should bend to the human calling, should be obedient, become humble, should give

50 Here, I use the term in a much broader sense from the Marxian one and his understanding of alienation as 'the turn' of the human being into a commodity. With 'alienation,' I want to describe a condition that expands on much broader categories or even the whole of the human experience, which can be described as a totality of a *disinterested passivity* towards the human milieu and themselves, a form of a nihilistic stalemate. This understanding of alienation is influenced by the work of Tiqqun. In their *Theory of Bloom* (Robert Hurley tr, Little Black Cart 2012) 124, they explain that the human being of today's Western society is completely alienated from its environment and itself, because all its relations are mediated by the dominant language and the *spectacular* images and signs of today's world order (Empire, as they call it). Hence, for Tiqqun, 'this is how Bloom [this is the concept they use to define the condition of today's Western human being] would like to understand himself: as foreign, as external to himself.'

51 Max Stirner, *The Unique and Its Property* (Wolfi Landstreicher tr, Underworld Amusements 2017).

52 See, also, Friedrich Nietzsche, *The Gay Science, With a Prelude of Rhymes and An Appendix of Songs* (Walter Kaufmann tr and commentary, Vintage Books 1974) Aphorism 108, 167.

up his will to an alien one which is set up as rule and law; he should abase himself before something higher: self-abasement.'[53]

Stirner identifies that the law is deeply entrenched in the psyche of the contemporary subject that even in the situation where this subject revolts against an oppressive regime, it does so *in the name* of the law, that is, in order to reinstate the law which is supposedly violated by a regime which becomes illegitimate, or in order to create a new form of law, which is supposedly more progressive and emancipatory:

> People felt few reservations about revolting against the existing state or overturning existing laws, once they had decided to no longer let what exists and is tangible impose itself on them; but to sin against the concept of the state, to not submit to the concept of law, who would have dared that? So one remained a 'state citizen'; a 'law-abiding'; loyal person; indeed, one seemed to himself only to be so much more law-abiding, the more rationalistically he did away with the former defective law in order to honour the "spirit of the law."[54]

In the passage, we see that Stirner acknowledges the law's powerful ability to turn the human being into the law-abiding subject; ready to sacrifice itself in order to secure that this 'spirit of the law' survives no matter the cost. Its freedom is seen as a freedom which is determined by the boundaries of the state and its laws. Thus, anything or anyone who questions the need of the law is automatically classified as an enemy. This loyalty of the 'perfect citizen' is tested by its ability to contribute to the permanence of the legal status quo. To that extent, the 'perfect citizen' recognised the violence used by the state as legitimate, while any insurrectionary violence against oppression is condemned as criminal or immoral. Ironically so, the readiness of the perfect citizen to condemn anything that questions the law, makes it the most successful agent of the violence of the state and the oppressive institutions that utilise this monopoly of violence. Stirner correctly notes that '[t]he people go utterly nuts, sending the police against everything that seems immoral, or even only unseemly, to it; and this popular rage for the moral protects the police institution more than the mere government could possibly protect it.'[55] The reactionary and alienated (legal) subjectivity of the 'perfect citizen' is now complete by turning this subject into the perfect 'cop,' a resentful snitch that not only is unable to revolt and resist but is, perhaps, the biggest threat to any promise of an emancipatory project.

53 Stirner (n 51) 98.
54 ibid 103–4.
55 ibid 253.

This particular form of the subject as the perfect 'cop' is a fundamental feature of the modern subject that Pashukanis' account of the legal form fails to fully grasp. This is due to his insistence to attach the legal form to the sphere of political economy and to that extent, to reduce it to a matter of mere 'economism.' On the other hand, the anarchist critiques of the law in general—and the critiques of Kropotkin and Stirner, in particular—demonstrate that the examination of the legal form and the opposition to the law, in general, must try to understand this multifaceted (legal) subjectivity beyond the realm of political economy. Indeed, a serious engagement with the formation of this form of subjectivity and its relation to the law and its form seems to be necessary if we are to seriously engage in a struggle for the total abolition of the law and the dissolution of its form.

Beyond legal form and towards the total abolition of the law?

In this chapter, I argued that Pashukanis' account of legal form makes an important contribution to our understanding of how the law alienates and abstracts our social relations by producing and recognising the human being as a legal subject only by virtue of being a property owner and the holder of abstract rights. In addition, Pashukanis' call for the need to abolish the law and the legal system, or in better terms, the call for 'withering away' of the law is also useful in, partially, pointing towards the idea that it is impossible to think of any emancipatory political project that remains within the boundaries of the law, and which tries to think of an account of the law which is progressive and emancipatory.

Nonetheless, as I further argued, Pashukanis homology between the way that the law operates and the way that political economy operates has as a result a fundamental flaw in his theory. This is the reduction of the juridical science and the relations that it creates to mere economism which gives primacy to the area of private law, but it neglects the broader ways and technologies of individuation that the law uses in order to (re)produce a form of (legal) subjective which is pacified, reactionary and resentful. This has a result in the expectation that the law and the state will 'wither away' with the decline of the social relationship that emerged through the capitalist market.

As the anarchists rightly observed, this cannot be achieved if we do not pay closer attention to the insidious ways that the law operates and the need to directly attack the law as one of the fundamental and primary tactics of any emancipatory political project worthy of its name. As I further argued, the subject of the law becomes the 'perfect citizen.' A totally alienated, reactionary subject that acts in order to sustain the status quo and ensure the failure of any potentiality of the coming of the new. The question then becomes: *how is this to be done?*

Kropotkin argues that a way out of the yoke of the law is by paying attention to our 'natural' inclinations for cooperation and mutual aid and try to reclaim them. While this reference to natural qualities is rather outdated and problematic for many reasons,[56] we may read this as a call of trying to reshape our habits and priorities and to a certain extent, to change our politics and strategies. Perhaps, we do not yet have the words or the thought to articulate this or as Giorgio Agamben suggests what we need is 'a thought capable of thinking the end of the state and the end of history *at one and the same time*, and of mobilising one against the other.'[57] Only then perhaps, we may be able to also think the end of the law and an anarchist vision *beyond the law*.

56 Elena Loizidou, *Anarchism: An Art of Living Without Law* (Routledge 2022) 33–34. Loizidou makes a similar remark regarding the problem of referring to natural instincts or inclinations.

57 Giorgio Agamben, *Means Without End: Notes on Politics* (Vincenzo Binetti and Cesare Casarino trs, University of Minnesota Press 2000) 109.

Chapter 9

Law beyond the legal form

Tormod Johansen

In this chapter, I will place Evgeny Pashukanis' concept of the legal form, as well as its inherent theoretical view of progression toward and beyond the highest development of legal form, in a broader conceptual perspective. The aim is to show the tensions between the concepts of legal form, law in general, and social ordering—and through this analysis argue that the end of the legal form (as Pashukanis and others have envisioned it) does not mean the end of rules, and not even the end of law. I argue that the lack of clear distinction between legal form and law which is prevalent in the Marxist legal discussion needs to give way to more fine-grained distinctions and categories, which could also allow for a clearer understanding that beyond the end of legal form, we find law.

The chapter starts off with a first section that discusses the notion of legal form in Pashukanis' work and the notion of development that it is based in. In the second section, I broaden the notion of law with the help of Thanos Zartaloudis' study of the Greek *nomos* and Lorraine Daston's schema of three types of rules. In the third section, an even deeper perspective is built out with the help of legal anthropology and the concept of social ordering in the work of Simon Roberts. The fourth section builds on the previous sections in understanding law as going beyond legal orders and legislation, in that it can and often does contain notions of ideals toward which we can strive. In the final section, these threads are brought back to the issue of legal form, and I put forward the argument that the potential end of legal form cannot mean the end of law.

Legal form

For Evgeny Pashukanis, the atomic component of law is the legal subject, which like the commodity is stripped of all specific properties and shows itself to us in an abstract way. While the commodity is only defined by its value on the market, the legal subject is only defined by her subjective will. The capacity to exchange transactions, which is just a specific ability that actual

DOI: 10.4324/9781032724713-10

physical humans possess, is thereby raised to become the primary function of the subject. With the support of the whole edifice of the state, with its police, courts, and other agencies this abstraction becomes functional and through successive historical development is purified. There is therefore an intimate connection between the development from primitive exchange into markets, parallel and connected to the centralisation of violence from its origin in the individual or smaller group into the state with its legally organised and legitimised sanction, including threat of and exercise of violence:

> Just as chance acts of exchange and primitive forms of exchange, . . . preceded the exchange transactions of developed commodity production, so too the armed individual . . . is the morphological precursor of the legal subject with his sphere of legal power extending around him. This close morphological link establishes a clear connection between the lawcourt and the duel, between the parties to a lawsuit and the combatants in an armed conflict. But as socially regulative forces become more powerful, so the subject loses material tangibility. His personal energy is supplanted by the power of social, that is, of class organisation, whose highest form of expression is the state.[1]

This whole development in Pashukanis' theory is tending toward an ever-purer form of legal abstraction based on the creation of markets with their necessary adjuncts, individual property, money, etc. While the original primitive forms were direct and based on the exchange between concrete physical persons, in the case of proto-markets through goods and in parallel through the use of physical coercion or threat. This clear developmental and progressing path is then fundamentally the same in its rise as in its endpoints: the combination of capitalist markets and bourgeois society with its legal arrangements.

In the development of bourgeois society, we witnessed a transition from the feudal structure where rights were privileges and which 'lacked any notion of a formal legal status common to all citizens, to all men'.[2] There simply was no concept of a universal man or subjectivity. There was neither any distinction between 'objective law and subjective rights or legal powers'.[3] So, while many of our present legal concepts and institutions have their precursors in the medieval era, they are transformed or replaced by the ultimate incarnations of legal arrangements in bourgeois society. For Pashukanis this

1 Evgeny Pashukanis, *The General Theory of Law and Marxism* (Transaction Publishers 2002) 118.

2 ibid 119.

3 ibid 120.

is clearly a teleological development, pointing towards the fullest expression of the legal form, as well as towards reaching a state which is logical and fulfils the final potential of his concept of law. As he writes,

> Only when bourgeois relations are fully developed does law become abstract in character. Every person becomes man in the abstract, all labour becomes socially useful labour in the abstract every subject becomes an abstract legal subject. At the same time, the norm takes on the logically perfected form of abstract universal law.[4]

Law has finally reached its 'logically perfected form' when 'bourgeois relations are fully developed' as abstract law. The peak of the development of law is the legal form, which also takes as its central concept the *contract* or agreement. While the contract now is only one of a multitude of legal transactions, Pashukanis argues that the historical development is opposite—the contract is what gave rise to the universal category of legal transactions as such.

One fruitful aspect of Pashukanis' argument is that it critically intervenes in more fundamental questions of the existence and possible cessation of law as such. This continues to be the case, even if we disregard the question of whether one agrees with his peculiar transposition of the theory, the commodity form to the legal form, and his speculative and utopian proclamations of the perfection of bourgeois law and its disappearance in communism. Considering the question of the cessation of the legal form, and the question of what the relation is between legal form specifically and law in general, requires us to place ourselves in a broader conceptual and philosophical frame of reference.

Nómos, rules, ideals

In his study of the term *nómos* and its related concepts in Ancient Greek, Thanos Zartaloudis suggests that its earliest uses are 'perhaps, in a modern sense, an "objective" rule or ordering, but it is not separable from the life to which it applies'.[5] Law, to use an imprecise word in translation, is here not 'distinguished from the living that it "commands"'.[6] I would argue that the suggestion that law could be inseparable from human life is simultaneously a fascinating and threatening notion. Law is in modernity precisely that which is separable or separate from human life, a force that acts upon it from the outside. Life, both for individuals and for society as such, is structured by a

4 ibid 120 f.

5 Thanos Zartaloudis, *Birth of Nomos* (Edinburgh UP 2018) xxxviii.

6 ibid xxxviii.

multitude of normative structures which never reach a harmony or a total control of life.

This is not to say that laws and legal orders are a wholly external force acting upon humans and society. Of course, they originate and are mediated through, as well as aimed upon, human life and actions. But the legal sphere is a sphere of specific institutions and normative structures that are not identical with the other spheres and activities of human society that they act upon.[7] The factory is not identical with the legal regulation structuring the activities in the factory, and the same with schools, offices, families, voluntary associations, et cetera. The legal system is not unconnected to other spheres—it might require certain permits, order the vacation of a property, or prosecute and ultimately imprison a person. But all of these actions are based on the autonomy and distinction between the legal order and the legal system *vis à vis* the spheres of society it acts upon.

This does not mean that legal rules are the only ones ordering and affecting human lives and these different spheres of society. Normativity and rules are not the exclusive domain of the legal order. In all human conduct, there arises certain rules, of different kinds, that structure the interactions between the people involved. Lorraine Daston in her wide-reaching study of rules argues that there are three semantic clusters of meaning that map out the meaning of rules: 'tools of measurement and calculation; models or paradigms; and laws'.[8] These three paradigms all have ancient roots and are with us today although in differing fashion and configured in different ways than in other periods.

Among these three paradigms, the first and third are most recognisable as rules for us moderns, who understand both the rules concerning physical measurement as well as abstract mathematics as being structured as or just the effect of the application of rules. The very word rule attests to that, in English and other languages, connecting concepts such as ruler (as in a prince or sovereign) and ruler (as in a device for measuring), as well as the ancient and absolutely modern concept of algorithm—steps by which a calculation or other activity is performed, a recipe for how to produce a result.[9] So we are well acquainted with the first type of rules as scientific or practical tools. We are also steeped in the third, since laws are not only important but in many ways a sort of hegemonic type of rule in our era.[10] All important rules

7 See, e.g. Hans Kelsen, *Introduction to the Problems of Legal Theory* (first published 1934, Bonnie Litschewski Paulson and Stanley Paulson trs, OUP 1992) 58–60.

8 Lorraine Daston, *Rules: A Short History of What We Live by* (Princeton UP 2022) 2.

9 Emile Benveniste, *Dictionary of Indo-European Concepts and Society* (HAU 2016) 312. Daston (n 8) 23.

10 This is not least visible in the continous expansion of the number of legal regimes and laws that are produced. Already in 1953, the Italian jurist Francesco Carnelutti pointed to the

of society (and quite a few of minor importance) are created, codified or promoted to the status of legislation. In this sense law understood as legislation seems to us as the most natural form of rule—we take it for granted that the most important and proper rules are those backed up by the state and ultimately by the tools of coercion invested in the state.

But where does this take us in relation to law? Is law simply the term we should use for legislation and legal structures originating in, controlled by or assented to by the state?[11] While Daston uses the term 'rule' as her overarching concept under which she categorises law as distinct from her other two categories, the word law and its synonyms or translated terms have quite often been understood in a sense broader than how it is now usually understood. This is true concerning her first semantic cluster of measurement and calculation rules, which seldom have been called 'laws'. But more importantly, here the mostly forgotten type of rule, or type of law, is the second in Daston's schema: the *model* or paradigm. She points out that from a deeper historical perspective, this is quite surprising, considering that this meaning was synonymous with the word rule from ancient Greece to the Enlightenment.[12] The *kanon*, *paradeigma* and *regula* referred to the primary type of rule—the ideal towards which actions or ways of life were defined and regulated. We will return to this point.

Social ordering

Considering the discussion in the previous sections on the diverse meanings of the term law and its cognates and synonyms, we can take a further conceptual step up from the problem of law. We can consider even broader concepts than the different semantic clusters of rules, that already encompass a wide range of normative structuring of human life. In the anthropological work of Simon Roberts, we find an important critique of the outlook of legal anthropology which also serves as a further decentering of the legal hegemonic perspective of today.

Roberts' critical account, both part of and intensely critical of the general outlook of the field of legal anthropology, is based on two main arguments: 1) that legal anthropology has made itself a disservice by identifying diverse social phenomena in the societies it has studied as 'law' based on Western-centric conceptions of what organs and functions are required in human society (such as magistracies, legislatures, courts, police, etc.), 2)

'hyperthrophy' of law. Francesco Carnelutti, 'La morte del diritto' in *La crisi del diritto* (Ceram 1953) 177–90.

11 Consider that many legal rules originate in private rulemaking (through contracts or other means) but that these are accepted and supported (as well as restricted) by the legal order and its public law functions in the courts, bailiffs, et cetera.

12 Daston (n 8) 11.

that anthropology studying these phenomena should be focused on 'broader questions of order in society' rather than just law in this narrow and historically contingent sense.[13]

He illustrates these points with several interesting examples, among them referring to Clifford Geertz's study of the Balinese kingship.[14] While a Western conception of kingship focuses on the political aspects such as the Weberian 'explicit exercise of a steering role, the business of telling other people what to do', Roberts argues forcefully that this 'can only ever be part of the picture'.[15] The Balinese king which Geertz described in his seminal study was not 'only, or even primarily, an office of command', but rather the king together with his court provided 'a model, a paragon, a faultless image of civilized existence' in which the life of the court was 'paradigmatic . . . of social order' and on which men should 'seek to pattern their lives'.[16] It does not make sense to say that there is no normativity in this scenario, rather it is a normativity of the highest order since the performance of the king and his court reflects the world of the gods, which is the ultimate source and paradigm for human action.

This shows how the model/paradigm/ideal form of normativity can be as important a law as the legal or legislative form of normativity. Roberts argues through several different examples against the identification of normative orders in general with Western legal institutions. But Roberts' other central anthropological claim is that the underlying issue here is social ordering rather than a narrow understanding of law, meaning that social ordering here is understood as a broader concept in which legal institutions are only a subset:

> First, it is taken for granted here that a degree of order and regularity must be maintained in any human group if the basic processes of life are to be sustained. Secondly, it is recognized that quarrels will inevitably arise, and that these may disrupt that order if they are not resolved or at least contained. So the questions are no longer: "Have they got law?" "How closely do their legal institutions match our own?" Instead they become: "How is order maintained?" "By what means are quarrels dealt with?"[17]

For Roberts' purposes, this argument is mainly used in his attempt to provide an anthropological description of small-scale societies that he calls 'acephalous', in other words, those which do not contain legislative and

13 Simon Roberts, *Order and Dispute: An Introduction to Legal Anthropology* (Quid Pro Books 2013) unnumbered preface.
14 Clifford Geertz, *Negara: The Theatre State in Nineteenth-Century Bali* (Princeton UP 1980).
15 ibid.
16 Geertz (n 14) 13.
17 Roberts (n 13) 3.

adjudicative organs and centrally organised sanctions.[18] Here he polemicises against H.L.A. Hart's suggestion that '[f]ew societies have existed in which legislative and adjudicative organs and centrally organized sanctions were all entirely lacking'.[19] Instead, Roberts suggests that 'many societies *have* existed without them' and 'how order is secured in such societies' is the theme of his study.[20] We do not here need to adjudicate the empirical question which divides Hart and Roberts, on the issue of the prevalence of such societies, but, instead, we can take seriously what they both suggest: that order in a society does not crucially depend on the existence of those legal organs and such a recognisable modern legal order that Hart is concerned with in his theory. Societies can both exist and function, and this in a normatively structured fashion, without what we would necessarily recognise as a legal order and most certainly without legislation.

Law and nomos to regulation and ideal

Roberts chooses the term *ordering* to describe a wide array of functions of society that could alternatively be referred to as *law* in a broad sense.[21] Considering the discussion above, law and its synonyms have often referred to ordering in this wider sense. And here we can connect this back to the second semantic cluster of Daston's systematic treatment of rules. The existence of

18 There of course exists critiques of this view, for example, from Hans Kelsen in his polemic against Engels' idea about a state and lawless society in the *Ursprung der Familie*:

> There can be not the slightest doubt that the societies to which Engels refers have lived under a strict coercive order characterised by legal institutions, such as blood revenge and expulsion from the community, collective property in land and more or less individual property in movable things. That there was no state organisation is true in so far as the coercive, and that means the legal, order of these societies did not institute special organs for the creation and application of the law, that there were no legislative and judicial organs and, in particular, no special organs for the execution of the sanctions provided for by the legal order. The principle of self-help prevailed, but this principle was a legal principle.
>
> Hans Kelsen, *The Communist Theory of Law* (Library of World Affairs 1955) 39

19 HLA Hart, *The Concept of Law* (2nd edn, Clarendon Press; OUP 1994) 293.

20 Roberts (n 13) 13.

21 Roberts prefers not to:

> Given this lack of "fit" between our own legal arrangements and the control mechanisms in the societies we shall be considering, and the consequent inapplicability of much of our legal theory, it seems best to avoid centering the discussion upon law altogether. Were we to insist upon doing so, the term "law" ' would either have to be used excessively loosely, or else we would need to exclude from consideration control mechanisms which in many societies hold central importance.
>
> Roberts (n 13)

normativity and the maintenance of order in societies does not exclusively, and historically not even mainly, rely on legal institutions, but rather on normativity—or law for short—that functions as paradigms or models of action and performance.

Zartaloudis, in his book on the concept nomos (or rather the two words *nómos* and *nomós*, and their respective families of concepts), argues in line with Giorgio Agamben against a distinction between law and pre-law or the legal and pre-legal.[22] Agamben criticises the idea put forward by Louis Gernet[23] that we can make a distinction between pre-law, where there is not yet a distinction between the action and its effects, but rather functions through an effective performativity, where religion-magic and law are indiscernible. While there might be a certain truth to these aspects of pre-'archaic law', the problem Zartaloudis sees with this approach is that these practices are understood in terms of what they supposedly aimed at developing into, namely the 'proper' legal structures that followed. Zartaloudis refers to Bronislaw Malinowski's *Crime and Custom in Savage Society* in which the latter is explicit in his description of Melanese practices and institutions that

> "law" and "legal phenomena". . . do not consist in any independent institutions. . . . Law represents rather an aspect of their tribal life, one side of their structure, than any independent, self-contained social arrangements. Law dwells not in a special system of decrees, which foresee and define possible forms of non-fulfilment and provide appropriate barriers and remedies. Law is the specific result of the configuration of obligations, which makes it impossible for the native to shirk his responsibility without suffering for it in the future.[24]

This is exactly the kind of historical development argument that permeates Pashukanis' theory.

For his part, Agamben argues that the split between law and religion is not preceded by 'more ancient law' or 'more primitive religion' but rather preceded by an 'unknown X' that does not presuppose the character of this preceding phenomena with the latter known phenomena.[25] Zartaloudis therefore states that it would be

> misplaced to suppose that the Greeks at some point lifted the veil of "religious" rites and found underneath it the autonomous and liberating

22 This is connected also to the common distinction between primitive law and law in the modern sense, as, for example, in Hart (n 19) 3.

23 Louise Gernet, *The Anthropology of Ancient Greece* (Johns Hopkins UP 1981) 143.

24 Bronislaw Malinowski, *Crime and Custom in Savage Society* (K. Paul, Trench, Trubner & Co., Ltd. Harcourt, Brace & Company, Inc. 1926) 58–59.

25 Giorgio Agamben, *The Signature of All Things: On Method* (Zone Books 2009) 90.

"secular" law-giving of the polis or, lastly, to presume the "developmental" transposition of cognition from the obscurity of (oral) poems to the lucidity of (written) law and prose (including that of Plato's "philosopher-king").[26]

This is an important point about the history, or prehistory and genesis of what we now talk about as law. But it also shines the light on an important aspect of the idea of the legal form. What we must question is whether the legal form is as closely tied to a broader understanding of law as we might at first presuppose. We can also use the insight that phenomena that are nowadays mostly split into different domains or spheres are not so by necessity. What is now distinguished as custom, law, religion, politics, does not necessarily need to be so distinguished.

To draw a distinction between law in a broader sense and legislation as part of modern legal order is not only prudent for a contemporary analysis, but it is an important issue both in legal anthropology and conceptual analysis. That order or regulation of conduct both predates and is conceptually prior to legislation and juridical regulation seems clear. From a fundamentally different ideological perspective, Friedrich Hayek formulated this argument succinctly: 'Law in the sense of enforced rules of conduct is undoubtedly coeval with society; only the observance of common rules makes the peaceful existence of individuals in society possible'.[27] So law, according to Hayek, was never actually invented, in contrast to legislation, insofar as 'the deliberate making of law, [which] has justly been described as among all inventions of man the one fraught with the gravest consequences, more far-reaching in its effects even than fire and gun-powder'.[28] Even Pashukanis argues that a type of ordering or rule-following precedes a normative behaviour which has acquired what he calls the 'legal character' of social regulation:

> The same applies to the second apparent tautology, according to which law regulates social relations. If one strips this formula of a certain anthropomorphism attached to it, it reduces itself to the following: under certain conditions the *regulation* of social relations assumes a *legal character*.[29]

Here regulation in general is put in contrast to one of its sub-categories: legality. This is one way of formulating the distinction but it has a drawback. It confuses what has been called the 'legal form' with law in general. What Pashukanis assumes here is that regulation of social relations or social

26 Zartaloudis (n 5) xx.

27 Friedrich A Hayek, *Law, Legislation and Liberty: A New Statement of the Liberal Principles of Justice and Political Economy* (Routledge Classics 2013) 69 f.

28 ibid 69.

29 Pashukanis (n 1) 79.

ordering (as Roberts puts it) or 'enforced rules of conduct' (as Hayek puts it) is fundamentally different than law. And there is of course something to this from the perspective of modern law, as it is difficult to disentangle from the view that law is the product of legislation, and furthermore something that is fought over and decided on in courts.

Karl Marx and Friedrich Engels saw the need for both ordering in the form of administration and regulation in different forms. They were clear that some forms of authority were necessary in order to organise social life.[30] Their vision of communist society was not a formless existence, but rather a society in which social life had developed both rationally and humanistically beyond the anarchy of capitalist society, which relied on and produced subjugation of workers as well as destruction of both resources and life worlds for no other purpose than the profit of capital.

In one sense it is a question of terminology, and following Roberts we could confine the use of the term law for phenomena that we identify with modern Western societies, and then talk about other forms of *social ordering* when discussing other societies. This could then be transposed to the speculation of a future communist society (which would however grow out of these societies with what everybody recognizes and refers to as societies with law) and we could restrict our usage of the terms so that such a society does not contain law.

But we might question what is won by this approach. It is different with *legal form* as distinct from *law*. Legal form might fruitfully be used to describe a specific configuration of law (and social ordering, as well) that arises in modernity and finds its fullest development in the private law relations that are the main focus of Pashukanis' theory. But then it becomes even more urgent to acknowledge that *legal form is not equal to law*. Legal form is a type of legal phenomena or a subcategory of law in general. For Pashukanis in his developmental and teleological theory, it is both the basis (in concepts such as the subject, the contract, the dispute) and the endpoint of historical legal development in that law finds its highest expression in the legal form. Pashukanis actually identifies two epochs where law found its 'highest point of development': in ancient Rome with its system of private law, and in the emergence of bourgeois society, in 'the seventeenth and eighteenth centuries in Europe, during which time philosophical thought discovered the universal significance of the legal form as a possibility which bourgeois society was destined to embody'.[31] For Pashukanis this represents its 'full flowering'

30 Friedrich Engels, "On Authority" in Marx-Engels reader (W.W. Norton & Co. 1978) 730–33. Consider also the famous formulation from Engels' Anti-Dühring: 'the government of persons is replaced by the administration of things', Karl Marx and Friedrich Engels, *Collected Works, vol 25: Anti-Dühring Dialectics of Nature* (Lawrence & Wishart, Progress Publishers 1987) 268.

31 Pashukanis (n 1) 71.

while, before, the legal form was only 'in an embryonic state, with minimal internal differentiation, and with no clear demarcation from neighbouring spheres (mores, religion)'.[32]

End of legal form

Let us draw some tentative conclusions from the preceding. Without minimising the significance of the shift that an end of the legal form (or at least its shift into a minor position relative to other hegemonic normative structure[33]) would entail, I want to insist on the important distinction between the three categories of 1) social ordering, 2) law, and 3) legal form. *The end of the legal form is not the end of rules, and not even of law in general.* Social ordering will, according to the argument brought forward here, always exist in human society (bar an actual messianic event). This social ordering takes many different forms and is often normative in its structure, in which case it is also common to use legal language to describe the duties put on persons or groups and legitimations for sanctions against those who are in breach of the norms.

Roberts in his anthropology of small acephalous (non-state) societies argues that in many cases there does not exist what we would recognise as separate legal institutions, nor that there exists any real distinction between legal rules and other forms of normativity. What we call sanctions often do not take the form of coercive force (like violence, imprisonment, fines or forfeiture).[34] This leads him to argue that we should not use terms such as law or legality to describe these forms of social ordering. That argument has some merit, but it also becomes somewhat blind to how the term 'law' has been used in the deep historical context of Western societies. The lack of separation between political, religious, and judicial organs has often been a feature of these societies from antiquity to the present. It is of course clear that the invention of a distinction between these functions has also arisen in the Western tradition. But let us take just one illustrative example of a situation without this distinction. The judicial function has often been vested in the monarch, arguably this being the oldest construction.[35] In mediaeval law

32 ibid.

33 Tormod Johansen, 'Minor Law: Notes Towards a Revolutionary Jurisprudence' in C Cercel, GG Fusco, and S Lavis (eds), *States of Exception: Law, History, Theory* (1st edn, Routledge 2021).

34

> In many acephalous communities the most dreaded and effective sanction in the face of sustained anti-social behaviour is withdrawal by other members of the society from social contact and the withholding of essential forms of economic cooperation: quite the reverse of what we commonly understand as coercive force.
>
> (Roberts n 13)

35 Luca Mannori and Bernardo Sordi, 'Science of Administration and Administrative Law' in Damiano Canale, Paolo Grossi and Hasso Hofman (eds), *A Treatise of Legal Philosophy*

there was no clear distinction between what we now recognise as legislation, jurisdiction, and administration, they were all collected under the heading of *iurisdictio* which in essence refers to a broad conception of justice. As Mannori and Sordi pointed out,

> At the basis of this choice lay the idea, quite well rooted in medieval culture, that the true *raison d'être* of power consisted in making everyone observe a law of natural origin, immanent to things themselves and prior to every creative act by man. Sovereigns and magistrates were not intended by God to rule over men by their own will, but to guarantee respect of the rules which He had already inscribed in the natural order of the world. Every act of power, therefore, was aimed at revealing, declaring and imposing *an already given law*; and only towards this end were rulers invested with certain rights of supremacy over their subjects.[36]

Law is here not only a tool to be used for ordering society but a fundamental structure at the basis of both natural and social order. It is also pointed toward a telos in the form of the order that all these measures and decisions were aimed at realising:

> The prince's law, the judge's sentence and the magistrate's order were not truly different from one another. Though on a different level, each of them contained the authentic statement of a legal rule, and was therefore the expression of a unitary function, which the medieval legal vocabulary indicated everywhere with the same expression: "*iurisdictio*".[37]

This indistinction points towards central aspects of our problem. It concerns both the appropriate use of the word 'law' and its cognates and related terms, as well as the problem of finding a useful system of definition and systematicity in the use of these terms. It makes little sense to restrict the use of the word 'law', due to a number of reasons. To specific contemporary uses in present societies, as if to refer only to legislation or those types of normativity that arise from the system of the distinct institutions of legislature—executive (including administration)—courts. Neither is it useful to limit it to only being related in the end to a sort of ideal form of legal regulation as

and General Jurisprudence. Volume 9: A History of the Philosophy of Law in the Civil Law World, 1600–1900 (Springer 2009), 225–61. See also Kantorowicz' discussion of the 'law-centered kingship' (Ernst Kantorowicz, *The King's Two Bodies: A Study in Mediaeval Political Theology* (Princeton UP 1957) 141, 191), and the king as the 'Fountain of Justice' (ibid 4). See also Harding 2002, 19 on the 'royal function of arbitrating' and Weiler 2009 on 'the king as judge'.

36 Mannori and Sordi (n 35) 226.

37 ibid.

Pashukanis does in his theory of the legal form, where all legal regulation in class societies develop towards the pure form of legal relation in contracts between legal subjects. It must, however, also be pointed out that it makes little sense to have an all-too-encompassing concept of law, where every form of normativity or even spatial and physical opportunities and restrictions in space and time becomes 'law'.[38]

What can be argued, however, is that there is a more or less precise relation between different forms of normativity, where the rough categories *coercive normativity* and *non-coercive normativity* relate to each other so that the deflation of one, in general, might lead to an inflation of the other.[39] It is of course possible that the inflation of non-coercive normativity in a society goes together with the inflation of simultaneous or parallel inflation of coercive measures, although it is probably unclear in that case whether they are just correlated and not causally linked. It is at least a plausible hypothesis that a functioning normativity without coercion alleviates the need for coercive normativity.

Law in the wider sense is then a category that both contains legislation and positive law, as well as, for example, natural law or divine law. This does not mean that all social ordering is law; both because some social ordering is the result of norms that no one would call law (such as common courtesy or other social rules), but also because law is a concept that is broader than just social ordering. Furthermore, what has often been called divine law can contain injunctions or norms directed at us which goes much further than simple social (or civil) ordering.[40]

Law in the sense of a normative structure that functions as a paradigm of action seems not only possible but perhaps even more necessary, in a future situation without the existence of legal institutions and the practices of the legal form (legal subjects agreeing to contracts under the supervision of a state). One basis of social ordering could be through the normativity of the ideal (paradigm or kanon). While not investigated here, a hypothesis might be that this is what is actually partially developed and suggested in the Marxist and communist tradition in the speculation of a future classless society. The reliance on both fundamental morality (natural law) and technical rules as form of soft normativity structuring the social ordering and practical activities of society and social action. 'From each according to his ability, to each according to his needs' could be the basis for a coercive normative order, but also a principle of a non-coercive order, a law of a society that has chosen

38 Cf. the idea of 'lawscape', which I find all too inclusive to actually function as a concept of law or legality. Andreas Philippopoulos-Mihalopoulos, *Spatial Justice: Body, Lawscape, Atmosphere* (Routledge 2015).

39 I have called this position 'minor law', see (n 33).

40 Consider Matthew 5:21–48. Ágnes Heller discusses these issues in her book *Beyond Justice* (Basil Blackwell 1987) 53.

to produce and distribute goods without coercion and without the mediation of the legal form.

In conclusion, if we accept this broader concept of law, it is clear that *after the end of the legal form we will find law*. The question of what law can and should be beyond the legal form is a task for the future. But we should make sure not to let it be restricted by our contemporary narrow presuppositions about law.

Chapter 10

The withering away of the legal form

Revisiting past debates for future movements

Dimitrios Kivotidis

Introduction

The debate on the role and place of law in society has returned with extreme urgency over the last decades. During the capitalist crisis of 2008, several countries were treated like 'guinea pigs' through the introduction of far-reaching legal measures that aimed to 'treat' the causes of the crisis, based on heavily contested diagnoses and with very controversial results. The legal implementation of structural adjustment programmes to save national economies about to default raised serious concerns about the role of law in contemporary society where 'even the most solid constitutional norms can melt into air when confronted with capital interests'.[1] This legal implementation relied heavily on the use of the doctrine of judicial deference, as well as on notions such as 'public interest', 'emergency situation', 'law of necessity', etc.[2]

The same legal notions were applied to accommodate an unprecedented restriction of individual freedoms in the name of dealing with an unforeseen public health (and subsequent economic) crisis, during the COVID-19 pandemic. Yet, notably no Western state adopted measures that would threaten private property, particularly the property of multinational corporations, even though such measures would have been much more suitable and proportionate to deal with the public health crisis.[3] It seemed like the majority of rights (especially social rights) were treated like not being worth the value of

1 Ioannis Katsaroumpas, 'De-Constitutionalising Collective Labour Rights: The Case of Greece' (2018) 47 *Ind L J* 465, 465.

2 Dimitrios Kivotidis, 'The Form and Content of the Greek Crisis Legislation' (2018) 29 *L and Crit* 59.

3 Such measures could include the requisition of private clinics, the commandeering of productive units to redirect their production to health material and equipment, as well as the contravention of the patent protection afforded by the Agreement on Trade-Related Aspects Intellectual Property Rights (TRIPS) through the use of compulsory licences and the parallel imports of medicines. See Dimitrios Kivotidis, 'Public Interest of Social Need? Reflections of the Pandemic, Technology and the Law' in Carl Stychin (ed), *Law, Humanities and the Covid Crisis* (University of London Press 2023) 13–30.

DOI: 10.4324/9781032724713-11

the paper they were written on, while others (especially the right to property) were granted an almost sacred status. The recent new round of capitalist crises (the so-called 'cost-of-living crisis') see further devaluation of social and economic rights, as well as further enhancement of authoritarian structures and institutions.[4]

These developments have also given rise to a notable rise in Marxist legal studies.[5] This is the case mainly because Marxist theory is an analytical paradigm that can help explain the ways in which law interacts with the economy from a critical perspective that questions the foundational elements of liberal thought, especially the free market and private property. However, for all the growth of the Marxist literature on law and the state, there is a disproportionate lack of engagement with the idea of the withering away of law and the state.

The withering away thesis was put forward by Marx, Engels, and Lenin. The classics of revolutionary socialist thought shared the view that the state will wither away as a result of a long and arduous historical process of social transformation. They focused explicitly on the withering away of the state, which was, after all, the main issue of revolutionary praxis.[6] In Lenin's *The State and Revolution*, the 'theoretical exegesis' to the October Revolution, the idea of withering away of the state features centrally, occupying several sections.[7] In the aftermath to the October Revolution, the focus shifted more explicitly to the question of the withering away of the other institutional apparatus essential to modern societies, that is the legal system.[8] There we find the most prominent of all contributions, Pashukanis' critique of the legal form. This critique is discussed in more detail in section two of the chapter.

In this chapter, I will show that the withering away of the law is an important topic for discussion which might inspire the exploration of alternative constitutional arrangements and judicial structures in a society that has transcended the contradictions of capitalism. Thinking about a historical phase

4 Dimitrios Kivotidis, 'The UK Economic Constitution: Between Authoritarianism and Democracy (2023) 4 *Pub L* 650.

5 See Paul O'Connell and Umut Özsu (eds), *Research Handbook on Law and Marxism* (Edward Elgar, 2021); Rob Hunter, Rafael Khachaturian, and Eva Nanopoulos (eds), *Marxism and the Capitalist State: Towards a New Debate* (Palgrave Macmillan 2023); as well as the Legal Form website (https://legalform.blog/).

6 See Friedrich Engels, 'Anti-Duhring' in Karl Marx and Friedrich Engels (eds), *Collected Works*, vol 25 (Lawrence and Wishart 2010) 129–276, 5–312; Friedrich Engels, 'Origin of the Family, Private Property and State' in Karl Marx and Friedrich Engels (eds), *Collected Works*, vol 26 (Lawrence and Wishart 2010); and Karl Marx, 'Critique of the Gotha Programme' in Karl Marx and Friedrich Engels (eds), *Collected Works*, vol 24 (Lawrence and Wishart 2010) 75–99.

7 Vladimir I Lenin, 'The State and Revolution' in Vladimir I Lenin (ed), *Collected Works*, vol 25 (Progress Publishers 1976) 385–498.

8 Evgeny Pashukanis, *The General Theory of Law and Marxism* (Transaction Publishers 2003).

that will occur—if it occurs at all—a very long time from now might seem like a distraction, as well as leave Marxist analysis vulnerable to accusations of utopianism. It is still a task I consider worth pursuing for two main reasons. First, capitalist society has reached such levels of sepsis and decay that engagement with a new vision of post-capitalist society is essential to inspire the social movements necessary to supersede the contradictions of capitalist society. A second reason for engaging with the institutional forms of a future communist society is the mistreatment of the idea of communism by non-Marxist currents.[9] There is now a growing literature engaging with the place and role of politics and the political form in communist society.[10] This includes some serious and well-thought contributions that demand our attention. They signify a renewed attempt at approaching communism from a Marxist perspective and respond in a scientific manner to the idealistic representation of this idea by various exponents of post-Marxism.

My hypothesis is that the legal form, that is, the predominant form of viewing and understanding capitalist society, may be replaced by new forms of social consciousness based on the notion of 'ethical community' and the principle of the 'free and full development of the individual' in a post-capitalist society. In other words, I will explore the thesis that the legal form may wither away. To do so, the first section of this paper assesses the analytical value of the notion of the legal form based on the work of Evgeny Pashukanis. The next section discusses the withering away thesis as developed by the classics of Marxism and received by Soviet theorists, while section three examines the more recent contributions to this debate, with emphasis on Shoikhedbrod's compelling argument for a notion of communist legality. The final section explores the main tenets of our hypothesis based on Hegel's idea of the 'ethical community' and Tony Smith's work on socialist constitutionalism.

Legal Form

We wish to start our discussion of the legal form by emphasising the analytical value of this notion. This is key to answering the question 'why is law so crucial for the reproduction of capitalism'. It allows us to escape the hurdles of both a content analysis and an interest-based analysis of legislation and

9 See Costas Douzinas and Slavoj Žižek, *The Idea of Communism* (Verso 2010); Alain Badiou, *The Communist Hypothesis* (Verso 2009); Jodi Dean, *The Communist Horizon* (Verso 2012).

10 Bruno Leipold, *Citizen Marx: The Relationship between Karl Marx and Republicanism* (2017) <https://ethos.bl.uk/OrderDetails.do?uin=uk.bl.ethos.740967>; Alexandros Chrysis, *O Marx tou Kommounismou [Marx of Communism]* (Kapsimi 2020); Igor Shoikhedbrod, *Revisiting Marx's Critique of Liberalism: Rethinking Justice, Legality and Rights* (Palgrave Macmillan 2019).

legal principles, which can only be ad hoc, and instead opt for a general theory of law from a Marxist perspective.

Furthermore, the notion of the legal form enables us to understand law and right, not only as normative standards regulating social behaviour but also as forms of social consciousness. Indeed, the legal form is here approached as a form of social consciousness.[11] Social consciousness refers to 'collectively-organised', 'harmonised' modes of conceiving reality, which are shared by individuals in a society, and which reflect and counter-act upon social processes, practices, relations, and institutions. According to Soviet philosopher Evald Ilyenkov, social consciousness 'from the very beginning precedes individual consciousness as something already given, and existing before, outside, and independent of individual consciousness'.[12] In its 'individualised form, in the form of the consciousness of one's closest teachers, and after that, of the entire circle of people who appear in the field of vision of a person', social consciousness determines individual consciousness to a much greater degree than the 'material world'.[13]

Law is commonly perceived as an objective and ineradicable form of the external world, based on which we understand and analyse the totality of socio-political processes. Yet, it is only the 'fetishised' or 'reified' forms of collectively organised experience.[14] Legal and political forms have crystallised in social consciousness and are reinforced by force of habit and tradition.[15] However, forms of social consciousness are historical. This means that new forms may develop on the basis of different social relations. It follows from the above that the withering away of the state and law refers not only to the 'dying out' of political and legal institutions but also to the abolition of the predominant forms of social consciousness in capitalist society and their replacement by other new forms of social consciousness, particular to the social relations that transcend capitalism. Additionally, it follows that

11 See Karl Marx, 'A Contribution to the Critique of Political Economy' in Karl Marx and Friedrich Engels (eds), *Collected Works*, vol 29 (Lawrence and Wishart 2010) 257–420, 263:

> In the social production of their existence, men inevitably enter into definite relations, which are independent of their will, namely relations of production appropriate to a given stage in the development of their material forces of production. The totality of these relations of production constitutes the economic structure of society, the real foundation, on which arises a legal and political superstructure and to which correspond definite forms of social consciousness.

12 Evald Ilyenkov, *Leninist Dialectics and the Metaphysics of Positivism* (New Park Publications, 1982).

13 ibid.

14 ibid.

15 ibid.

the process of developing new form(s) of social consciousness is equally, if not more, long, and arduous as the process of developing new institutional forms.

The historicity of the legal form was argued by the most prominent thinker to ever engage with the concept, namely Evgeny Pashukanis. He defined the legal form as a 'specific set of relations which [human beings] enter into not by conscious choice, but because the relations of production compel them to do so'.[16] According to Pahuskanis, one 'becomes a legal subject by virtue of the same necessity which transforms the product of nature into a commodity complete with the enigmatic property of value'.[17] In this definition, the legal form appears as a form of social consciousness which consists of both institutional and ideational elements.

For Pashukanis, 'the conflict of private interests' is a basic prerequisite for legal regulation and, consequently, it is the origin of the legal form.[18] The legal form is the inevitable reflex of the commodity relation.[19] According to Pashukanis, the legal form emerges with the beginning of commodity exchange, which reaches its full development with the onset of the capitalist mode of production, for only then does it acquire 'universal significance'.[20] The legal form's existence is contingent upon 'the integration of the different products of labour according to the principle of equivalent exchange' and not according to 'needs and abilities'.[21] It follows that if the distribution of the social product is carried out in accordance with different principles (namely 'according to needs') from those of equivalent exchange, the legal form will be made redundant.

The following points follow from Pashukanis' analysis regarding the historicity of the legal form: i) the legal form has pre-existed capitalist society; and ii) the legal form becomes the dominant form of social consciousness in capitalist society. However, the reasons Pashukanis gives to substantiate these claims are not fully convincing. His argument is that *the possibility of a dispute* between sovereign, formally equal individuals, which is inherent in commodity exchange, requires a specific form of social regulation: the legal form formalises the method of dispute resolution without weakening the sovereignty and equality of the guardians of commodities.[22] However,

16 Pashukanis (n 8) 68.
17 ibid.
18 ibid 80–81.
19 ibid 82.
20 Sonja Buckel, *Subjectivation and Cohesion: Towards the Reconstruction of a Materialist Theory of Law* (Brill 2021) 90; see also Pashukanis (n 8) 114, 45.
21 ibid 63.
22 China Mieville, *Between Equal Rights: A Marxist Theory of International Law* (Brill 2005) 7.

the possibility of a dispute between sovereign and formally equal individuals pre-exists capitalist society and cannot adequately explain why the legal form became the dominant form of social consciousness at this historical period.

I argue that it is not the possibility of the dispute but the *actuality of exploitation* which renders the legal form the dominant form of social consciousness and social regulation in capitalism.[23] It is not the general relation of exchange between formally equal individuals, but the special exchange relation where labour power is sold as a commodity that necessitates the role and place of the legal form is capitalist society. The legal form is an essential precondition for the non-coercive extraction of surplus value, on which the reproduction of the capitalist relations of production rest. As Marx showed in 'Capital', the profit of capitalist enterprises consists of the surplus value extracted through surplus labour.[24] Profit, the substance which oils the engine of capitalist production, relies on the exploitation of labour, which in capitalism relies, on the one hand, on the private ownership of the means of production by a social minority, and, on the other, on the exchange relationship between the owners of these means of production and the immediate producers who contract with the former as owners of their labour power.[25] The legal form ensures the formal freedom and equality of the subjects entering into the contract of a wage-employment relationship.[26]

This point allows us to more firmly grasp the historicity of the legal form, as well as the argument for the withering away of the legal form. Let us elaborate by focusing on the main characteristics of the legal form in general before comparing these to the characteristics of the legal form specific to capitalist society. Possible differences between the two might give an answer as to why the legal form assumes a dominant role in capitalist society.

To begin with, the legal form is characterised by *formalism* (which obscures social and economic divisions and contradictions), *individualism* (which presents social processes from the standpoint of self-interested

23 This argument to a large extent echoes the classic Marxist critique of Pashukanis for ignoring the sphere of production and reducing the law's significance to the sphere of circulation. According to this argument, the bourgeois law is based not upon the general fact that all owners of commodities have to consider each other as equal in their economic transactions, but on the underlying special exchange relation between wage labourers and capitalists. See Oskar Negt, '10 Thesen zur marxistischen Rechtstheorie' in Hubert Rottleuthner (ed), *Probleme der marxistischen Rechtstheorie* (Suhrkamp 1975) 48. Additionally, see Karl Korsch, 'Einleitung' in Eugen Paschukanis (ed), *Allgemeine Rechtslehre und Marxismus* (Neue Kritik 1970) XI; Burkhard Tuschling, *Rechtsform und Produktionsverhältnisse: Zur materialistischen Theorie des Rechtstaates* (Europäische Verlagsanstalt 1976) 12–13. For an overview of this critique see Mieville (n 22) 91ff.

24 Karl Marx, *Capital*, vol 1 (Penguin 1976) 320–39.

25 ibid 874.

26 ibid 270–71.

individuals), and *conflict* (which involves an adversarial setting for dispute resolution in the social sphere).[27] These characteristics derive from Pashukanis' commodity-form analysis of the legal form. Furthermore, the legal form as a form of understanding and regulating social processes is premised on a system of organised violence that ensures rules are adhered to. This is precisely what distinguishes law from other systems of rule, such as custom. Coercion is essential to the legal form not because it belongs to a transhistorical idea of the legal form, but because the law has historically been a medium of regulating social relations and facilitating social processes in class-divided societies, where different social groups with conflicting interests would often resist rules that adversely affected their conditions.

It follows that these characteristics are incompatible with a classless society. At the same time, these characteristics the bourgeois legal form arguably shares with the legal form of pre-capitalist social formations. Indeed, the notions of personhood, freedom, and equality, as well as the institutions of private property and contract existed in legal systems corresponding to pre-capitalist social formations—they are encountered in Roman law, for instance.[28] I argue that the characteristic which gives the bourgeois legal form its distinct identity is the *universality* of the above principles.

Earlier social formations could reproduce their conditions of existence on a limited and sporadic application of the principles of freedom and equality. This is not true of the capitalist social formation. Capitalist production relies on the law of value, which presupposes the expropriation of surplus labour through economic means, that is, without violence (at least immediately). The structure of capitalist economy and the market is predominantly consensual and does not rely on extra-economic coercion, which appears in feudal societies and economies. The free and consensual contract of employment between employer and employee, as well as the freedom of contract and right to property, which is rid of old feudal burdens, are essential conditions for the operation of capitalist relations. Therefore, consensus becomes a fundamental organisational principle on an economic, as well as a political, level.

This resulted in the universalisation of the principles of freedom and equality, which are to be found in foundational constitutional documents of bourgeois revolutions, like the *Declaration of the Rights of Man and of the Citizen*. Karl Marx was the first to advance a comprehensive critique of the function and formal nature of these principles in capitalist society. His

27 Louis Althusser, *On the Reproduction of Capitalism* (Verso 2014) 57–69.

28 Michael E Tigar and Madeleine R Levy, *Law and the Rise of Capitalism* (Monthly Review Press 1977).

critique of the bourgeois rights-form 'On the Jewish Question'[29] is furthered in 'Capital' where he effectively shows that the principles of freedom, equality, and property—which the bourgeois legal form presents as universal – are essential to the process of capital's valorisation. He argues that the universal validity of equality and property is essential 'in order that the owner of money may find labour-power on the market as a commodity'.[30] Freedom ensures that workers are liberated from other relations of dependence and are free to appear on the market. Property is essential so that workers appear on the market as free proprietors of their labour-power which they then offer for sale as commodity.[31] Last but not least, equality is essential so that the worker and the owner of money 'meet in the market and enter into relations with each other on a footing of equality as owners of commodities'.[32] The legal form consists in the universal application of the formal and individualist principles of freedom and equality, as a result of the capitalist mode of production resting on economic means of surplus value extraction. These principles are essential to the process of capital's valorisation because they sustain a false consciousness of social production and mask the reality of exploitation.

We may thus conclude that the legal form emerges in pre-capitalist social formations but reaches its full development in capitalist society. Formalism, individualism, adversarial mode, as well as the universal validity of freedom, equality, and property, constitute the essential traits of the bourgeois legal form. These essential traits of the legal form are necessary for a class-divided society premised on commodity exchange and labour exploitation. However, the existence of the legal form in pre-capitalist social formations leave open the possibility of post-capitalist social formations where the legal form exists but is not the predominant form of social consciousness and regulation of social conduct. It also leaves open the possibility for a social formation where the legal form has been replaced (partly or wholly) by other forms of social consciousness and social regulation.

This brings us to the following questions: are all the characteristics of the bourgeois legal form incompatible with a society that has transcended these obstacles to human emancipation? Is the legal form historical, as Pashukanis, argued or are there any transhistorical elements to it? Can it be replaced by other forms of social consciousness in a future post-capitalist society? What are the conditions for the legal form to wither away? What meaning can this

29 Karl Marx, 'On the Jewish Question' in Karl Marx and Friedrich Engels (eds), *Collected Works*, vol 3 (Lawrence and Wishart 2010) 146–74, 162.

30 Marx (n 24) 270.

31 ibid 271.

32 ibid.

proposition have in contemporary context? The next section will turn to the withering away thesis.

The withering away of the legal form

This section will engage with the withering away thesis. The withering away of the state and law is a hypothesis that, albeit not proposed by Marx himself, arguably flows from the general tenets of Marxist analysis of the capitalist mode of production and its juridico-political forms of social consciousness. Friedrich Engels, in *Anti-Dühring*, describes a stage in the development of communist society where the state really represents all of society and is rendered superfluous. At this moment state interference in social relations withers away and 'the government of persons is replaced by the administration of things, and by the conduct of processes of production'.[33] Furthermore, in his *Origin of the Family, Private Property and State*, Engels claims that

> society, which will reorganise production on the basis of a free and equal association of the producers, will put the whole machinery of state where it will then belong: into the museum of antiquities, by the side of the spinning-wheel and the bronze axe.[34]

As mentioned previously, it was Lenin who put this idea into political practice. His *State and Revolution*, the theoretical guide to the October Revolution, addresses the question of how the transition from capitalist to communist society is possible.[35] Both Engels and Lenin echo Marx's view that the withering away of the state (and law) can only be the result of a long and arduous historical process—indeed a process of class struggle—which would involve the development of the proper material conditions.[36] Marx mentions three historical milestones that need to be achieved before the 'narrow horizon of bourgeois right' is crossed in its entirety and a new principle of production; distribution is inscribed on society's 'banners': i) elimination of the subordination of the individual to the division of labour; ii) the transformation of labour, as well as the conception of labour, from a means of life to life's prime want; and iii) the expansion of productive forces so that 'all the springs of common wealth flow more abundantly'.[37]

Among these conditions, we find the development of social consciousness necessary for a paradigmatic change in the government of social affairs and

33 Engels, 'Anti-Duhring' (n 6) 268.
34 Engels, 'Origin of the Family, Private Property and State' (n 6) 272.
35 Buckel (n 20) 104.
36 Marx, 'Critique of the Gotha Programme' (n 6) 87.
37 ibid.

regulation of social behaviour. This was a point further developed by Lenin. For Lenin, the question of the withering away of the state is a question of the development of the necessary consciousness and ethics (which Lenin refers to as 'habit') and the creation of the necessary economic conditions for such consciousness and ethics to develop. Lenin observes 'millions of occasions' where people readily become 'accustomed to observing the necessary rules of social intercourse when there is no exploitation, when there is nothing that arouses indignation, evokes protest and revolt, and creates the need for suppression'.[38] The economic basis for this ethical stance to take over involves such a high development of communist production that the distribution of products will not call for a system of norms to regulate how many products are to be received by each; each will take freely 'according to their needs'.[39] Additionally, individuals will have become 'so accustomed to observing the fundamental rules of social intercourse', when their labour is so productive, 'that they will voluntarily work "according to their ability" '.[40]

The fulfilment of these conditions would eventually lead to the transition from a government of persons to an administration of things. Engels's idea is echoed in Pashukanis' distinction between legal regulation and technical regulation. As we saw above, for Pashukanis the opposition of private interests is the logical (and historical) precondition of the legal form and legal regulation.[41] It follows that the abolition of social conflict and the achievement of a unity of purpose for society as a whole that would eliminate the material basis of the legal form. Unity of purpose is the premise of technical regulation. Pashukanis uses the example of railroads: 'the legal norms concerning the liability of railroads presume private claims, private individualiszed interests; the technical norms of railroad movement suppose a single purpose, e.g. the achievement of maximum freight capacity'.[42] He accepts that coercion is not eliminated from technical regulation,[43] but its role changes in the context of a single purpose: 'considered from the perspective of the same single purpose (both for the rulers and the ruled), it remains solely a technically expedient act'.[44]

It should not be forgotten that Pashukanis and Soviet theorists expressed their views on the withering away thesis in the context of revolutionary change and intense class struggle. The first revolutionary period in Russia was characterised by a strong condemnation of the legal form in the process

38 Vladimir Lenin, *The State and Revolution* (Penguin 2009) 80.
39 ibid 87.
40 ibid 86.
41 Pashukanis (n 8) 81.
42 ibid.
43 See also Andreas Harms, *Warenform und Rechtsform. Zur Rechtstheorie von Eugen Paschukanis* (Nomos 2000) 147.
44 Pashukanis (n 8) 81.

of class struggle. Emphasis was placed on the distinction between formal legal rights and the material conditions for their exercise. According to Nikolai Bukharin, a leading Bolshevik, 'paper laws are of no use to the working class unless the possibility of their realization exists'.[45] Law's formalism and its contribution to the reproduction of exploitation were criticised. The idea that law was essential to the subjugation of the working class led many Soviet lawyers to view law itself as a purely bourgeois phenomenon.[46] According to Alexandr Goikhbarg, a Soviet jurist, 'the temple of bourgeois authority is legislation and its fetish is the law'; this makes law 'the sanctuary of the exploiting classes'.[47] On the contrary, 'the temple of the socialist world system is administration and its divine service is work'.[48]

During the first revolutionary period, Soviet legal theorists questioned the need for law and stressed instead the need to perfect society, arguing that this would render law unnecessary.[49] According to Pashukanis, there could be no such thing as a socialist or proletarian law. Law had emerged in the process of commodity exchange and would disappear with the revolutionary overthrow of the bourgeoisie.[50] Pashukanis was not the only one to argue that the 'administration of things' would replace the rule of 'man by man': 'law, the role of which is to sanction the existing social relationships, will not be needed as long as [social] relationships are observed voluntarily'.[51] True justice, it was argued, 'rested less on procedures and courts than on a just ethical and social order in society'.[52]

This particular view of Pashukanis seems to contradict both the preceding section's analysis on the historicity of the legal form and the classics' view of the withering away of the state (and law) as the result of a long and arduous historical process. Of course, the argument could be made that the legal form operating during the process of socialist construction is still bourgeois law (insofar as the 'narrow horizon of bourgeois right' is not crossed yet). The verification of this claim would necessitate an investigation into whether we can speak of a socialist legal form as a legal form with distinct characteristics

45 Nikolai Bukharin and Evgenii Preobrazhensky, *The ABC of Communism: A Popular Explanation of the Program of the Communist Party of Russia* (University of Michigan 1966) 175–76.
46 John B Quigley, *Soviet Legal Innovation and the Law of the Western World* (CUP 2007) 55.
47 Alexandr G Goikhbarg, 'Justice, the Ideology of Law, and Revolution' in Michael Jaworskyj (ed), *Soviet Political Thought: An Anthology* (Johns Hopkins UP 1967) 121.
48 ibid.
49 Vladimir A Tumanov, 'O pravovom nigilizme' [On Legal Nihilism] (1989) 10 *Sovetskoye gosudarstvo i pravono* 20, 22–23.
50 Quigley (n 46) 55.
51 I Podvolotskii, 'The Withering Away of Law' in Michael Jaworskyj (ed), *Soviet Political Thought: An Anthology* (Johns Hopkins UP 1967) 114–17.
52 Tumanov (n 49) 21.

that differ from those of the bourgeois legal form. This task—albeit closely related to it—unfortunately lies outside the scope of this chapter.

In reality, the second revolutionary period saw a change in the Soviet jurists' views on the role of law in socialist society. During the 1930s, in conditions of intense class struggle between the different social elements, as well as deep antagonism between socialist relations of production and market elements, law was not withering away but increasing. Socialist society was a society where commodity production co-existed with socialist relations of production and distribution and, therefore, arguably the legal form still had a role to play. In that context, Soviet jurists argued that the need was not to eliminate all law but 'to eliminate the bourgeois features of law'.[53] Additionally, socialist law was not considered as merely a further development of bourgeois law but a new type of law that was the expression of the will of the entire Soviet people, following the elimination of the exploiting classes.[54]

It seems then that objective reality had forced the recognition of the dialectical movement between law and social change. Where does this leave us with regard to the doctrine of the withering away of law and the state? It has been argued that this doctrine was unable 'to prevent or even inhibit repressive developments in Soviet legal history'.[55] On the contrary, it was sometimes used to 'justify authoritarian brands of socialism'.[56] According to Christine Sypnowich, 'Marxism should be concerned with the inadequacy of an ideal of socialist society as offering both liberty and democracy with neither the legal nor political mechanisms which, in bourgeois societies, have been their guarantee'.[57] In other words, the historical experience of 'actually existing socialism' casts doubt on the possibility of the withering away of the state and law, since legal and political institutions are essential preconditions for human emancipation as guarantors of liberty and democracy.

More questions arise from such statements—which of course cannot be adequately answered unless in a future process of building a post-capitalist, communist society, and corresponding social relations. Are political and legal forms essential to human emancipation? Are these the political and legal forms of capitalist society, or can we speak of a different kind of juridico-political institutional form (e.g. socialist or proletarian)? There have

53 I Naumov, 'A Critique of Legal Nihilism' in Michael Jaworskyj (ed), *Soviet Political Thought: An Anthology* (Johns Hopkins UP 1967) 250.

54 Mikhail S Strogovich, 'Sovetskoe sotsialisticheskoe pravo—vyschii tip prava' [Soviet Socialist Law—The Highest Form of Law] in Mariia P Kareva (ed), *Teoriia gosudarstva i prava [Theory of State and Law]* (State Publishing House of Legal Literature 1949) 348.

55 Christine Sypnowich, 'Withering Away of Law' (1987) 33(4) *Studies in Soviet Thought* 327–28.

56 ibid.

57 ibid.

been a few recent and important contributions to the 'withering away' debate which address these questions. The following section will turn to these.

Communist legality

The recent contributions to the debate on the withering away thesis approach it in an innovative way, arguing that legal and political institutions might have a role to play in a communist society.[58] These arguments are based on the need for structures that will enable interpersonal deliberation, negotiation, and authoritative decision-making in communist society. Based on this, Alexandros Chrysis argues that even if the state withers away in communist society, the political (especially the democratic) form will not necessarily do so. Chrysis's argument relies on a wide definition of the political form, which is not reducible to the state form and the repressive superstructures of class-divided societies.

Narrowly defined, the political can be understood as a form of social consciousness with institutional manifestations which pertain to class societies and contribute to the reproduction of class division and exploitation. This conception of the political is associated with social antagonism and is reflected, for instance, in the definition of the concept provided by one of the major contemporary thinkers of bourgeois political theory who famously claimed that 'the specific political distinction . . . is that between friend and enemy'.[59] In this sense, the political withers away with a transition to a classless society. On the other hand, the political can also be defined in broader terms as something pertaining to human nature – in the Aristotelian conception of human as *zoon politikon*.[60] In this broader sense, the political form cannot be reduced to the political forms of class societies. If interpersonal deliberation, negotiation, and authoritative decision-making are understood as political matters (in the broad sense of the term), then the argument could be made that a classless society might also have a political form, in the broad sense of the term.

Chrysis claims that

> the communist formation, a classless and stateless society, is projected on the historical horizon as a post-capitalist society with persons and politics; it is constituted as demos, within which autonomous personalities, free from the burden of class exploitation and the state as political power, deliberate and co-decide coexisting as members of a communist polity.[61]

58 Alexandros Chrysis, *Marx of Communism* (in Greek) (Kapsimi 2020); Igor Shoikhedbrod, *Revisiting Marx's Critique of Liberalism: Rethinking Justice, Legality and Rights* (Palgrave Macmillan 2019).

59 Carl Schmitt, *The Concept of the Political* (University of Chicago Press 2007) 26.

60 Aristotle, *Politics* (University of Chicago Press 2013) book 1, ch 2.

61 Chrysis (n 58) 216.

His argument is based on an analysis of the main characteristics of this social formation, to the extent that these have been described by the classics. The development of productive forces in communism is set out, regulated, and controlled by fully developed, conscious humans. The rational operation of the 'realm of necessity' presupposes weighting processes, plans, and decisions of conscious and autonomous personalities.[62] The members of communist society have 'the ethical-political responsibility to evaluate, decide and discern the criteria and limits, the measure of production and needs satisfaction'.[63] This necessitates the existence of forms of association and collective decision-making and planning. On this basis, Chrysis articulates the following hypothesis: communist society, as the organised collective of fully developed personalities, is constituted as a communist polity, whose members weigh and decide not narrowly technocratically, but politically.[64] Politics in communism tends to assume the characteristics of praxis as a process of free and creative life.[65]

This is quite a compelling argument on the need and role of institutional forms in communist society. A similar argument is developed by Igor Shoikhedbrod, who focuses more explicitly on the legal form. Shoikhedbrod argues that Marx's critique of liberal rights did not result in the withering away of the law thesis.[66] Instead, Marx's 'new materialist outlook' allows for an alternative conclusion, 'one in which the revolutionary transformation of capitalism leads to the development of a communist conception of right and a structure of rights that would be appropriate to the needs of socialised individuals under a communist mode of production'.[67] His strongest and arguably most significant claim is that communist legality is born out of the need for forms that would mediate among the diverse and potentially conflicting projects pursued by socialised individuals.[68] This argument for communist legality is based on a similar premise as Chrysis's argument for the existence of a sublated version of the democratic form in communism.

In several instances, Shoikhedbrod makes the point that 'every mode of production creates its own legal relations, including a corresponding structure of rights and duties'.[69] This point is arguably based on Marx's view of the relationship between social relations and the legal and political superstructure, as outlined in the 'Preface' to *A Contribution to the Critique of Political Economy*.[70] In rejecting the withering away of the law thesis,

62 ibid 221.
63 ibid 220.
64 ibid 225–26.
65 ibid 234.
66 Shoikhedbrod (n 9) 7.
67 ibid.
68 ibid 7.
69 ibid 82, 85, 86.
70 See Marx (n 11) 263.

Shoikhedbrod expresses the view that only 'positive law changes' as a 'consequence of transformed material circumstances, which means that even a developed communist society would require a system of legal justice'.[71] This view seems to accept the transhistorical nature of the legal form, recognising only the content of law as historically contingent.

Additionally, Shoikhedbrod argues that Marx did not view legal rights 'as an insurmountable barrier to the development of communism', but instead as 'a technical and cultural precondition for the free development of individuals'.[72] Therefore, he claims that the undoing of legal rights conferred on individuals in capitalist society 'would mean reverting to pre-juridical relations in which human beings are not even formally recognised as persons'.[73] This argument seems to reproduce Sypnowich's aforementioned point on legal and political institutions (as developed in capitalist society) being guarantors of liberty and democracy and, therefore, essential preconditions for human emancipation.

In the spirit of furthering this debate, we wish to express some concerns regarding Shoikhedbrod's compelling analysis of communist legality. Particularly, the point that different modes of production give rise to different legal relations should be approached with caution. Legal relations are social relations mediated by law as a form of social consciousness, as well as by legal institutions. The fact that in capitalism (as well as in pre-capitalist, class-divided social formations) law as the predominant form of social consciousness gives to such social relations the form of legal relations, does not mean that social relations in communism, especially in terms of decision-making or dispute-resolving processes, cannot be mediated by other forms of social consciousness.

Furthermore, the argument that rights are a precondition of communism and cannot, therefore, be undone runs the risk of absolutising the value of the rights-form, ascribing a transhistorical value to it. Marx certainly considered liberal rights as a historical advance, yet with this he meant a relative advance compared to precapitalist forms of mutual recognition. It is not necessary that the abolition of the rights-form in communism will revert historical movement backwards instead of advancing it forward. In the same way that the law of value is abolished in communism, while socialised production and concrete labour remain, the abstract legal form can be sublated and replaced by other forms of social consciousness.

We saw above that the debate on the future of the legal and political forms in post-capitalist society depends to a certain extent on how these terms are

71 Shoikhedbrod (n 9) 109.
72 ibid 119.
73 ibid 120.

defined. A wide definition of the political might allow us to argue for the existence of political forms in communism. Similarly, the definition of the legal form is important for the debate. In that respect, it is crucial to take into account that the legal form includes not only the institutional manifestations of legality but also the ideational elements of law. The rights form consists of both the legal institution of rights and the predominant conception of rights and justice in a social formation. In that sense, one might argue that even in a communist society a type of communist legality would operate, if by that we mean a set of institutional forms for the interpersonal deliberation and resolution of dispute combined with and determined by the corresponding conception of justice (and ethics, we might add).

Regardless of the above concerns, Shoikhedbrod makes a valid and compelling point regarding the need for institutional forms of mediation in communist society. This point compels us to explore what form these mediations would take if. Before we move to our hypothesis, let us look closer at Engels's brief exposition on this issue, which Shoikhedbrod also quotes. According to Engels, in communist society the contradiction between individual man and all others is eliminated, social peace takes the place of social war, and the axe is put to the root of crime.[74] These developments will render 'the greatest . . . part of the present activity of the administrative and judicial bodies superfluous'.[75] Conflicts in communist society can, thus, only be rare exceptions 'and will be easily settled by arbitrators'.[76]

Shoikhedbrod argues that Engels's statement seems to support a system of technical, rather than judicial, arbitration in communism. Yet, he claims that the 'rigid distinction between legal and technical rules is dubious'.[77] According to him, the process of arbitration 'would still require an impartial system of justice for adjudicating between opposing claims, however rarely these might occur', as arbitration by bureaucratic decrees or unconstrained officials, would not suffice.[78] At this point, Shoikhedbrod seems to distinguish between legal regulation, which is predominantly democratic, and technical regulation which presupposes relations of expertise, technocracy, and delegation impermissible from the standpoint of a society of associated producers. Indeed, earlier in his critique of Pashukanis, Shoikhedbrod opposes Marx's emphasis on collective self-determination, for a 'democratically managed production and legislation by the associated producers' in communism, to Pashukanis' 'technical regulation' which involves delegating 'the task of

74 Fredrick Engels, 'Speeches at Elberfeld' in Karl Marx and Friedrich Engels (eds), *Collected Works*, vol 4 (Lawrence and Wishart 2010) 243–64, 248.

75 ibid.

76 ibid 248–49.

77 Shoikhedbrod (n 9) 122.

78 ibid.

determining the most efficient means for realizing collective ends to specialist agencies and bureaucrats'.[79]

But what if technical regulation does not mean bureaucratic regulation? It need not necessarily mean so. If everyone has the potential as well as the material conditions enabling them to become experts, then a technical decision can also be a collective decision. With the abolition of the division of labour in communist society, technical issues need not be restricted to particular social classes or social groups. Judicial and political expertise is eliminated with the abolition of this division of labour since communist society provides all individuals with the opportunity of acting as arbitrators as well as decision-makers. Thus understood, Engels's concept of arbitrators does not refer to a group of bureaucrats but rather potentially to the people at large, whereas Pashukanis' technical regulation does not refer to rules arbitrarily developed by a group of experts but rather to a system of rules collectively produced by the people.

On this basis, we could claim that communism warrants a system of rules collectively produced and consensually adhered to, rather than a system of legality. I believe this claim describes more accurately the difference between the bourgeois legal form and communist right (or ethics). Related to this, we could also advance the hypothesis that the separation of powers is abolished, too, in communism, as a result of the abolition of the division of labour. Forms of evaluation, planning and decision-making may simultaneously operate as forms of dispute resolution in communist society. The abolition of the division of labour enables the resolution of disputes by the community as a whole—since everyone is a judge of their peers.

All the above points must be understood under the lens of the dialectical notion of sublation (*Aufhebung*). Institutional forms for collective planning, decision-making and dispute resolution may continue to exist, but on the basis of different social relations, they assume different functions and different formal characteristics. In this sense, we may speak of a sublated version of right or democracy. The abolition of both the division of labour and technical barriers in education and consciousness enables collective rule-making and collective rule enforcement since everyone can be a decision-maker or an arbitrator for his peers. This is arguably a pragmatic and realistic, rather than utopian, approach to the question of the role of institutional forms of decision-making in communist society.

The communist ethical community

Let us now turn to a tentative exploration of what replaces the legal form as the predominant form of social consciousness in communism. The discussion

79 ibid 106.

will proceed with extreme care and caution, recognising that the answers to these questions—as well as the questions themselves—will be modified as a result of the historical process of superseding capitalist contradictions and building a socialist society. As Marx himself put it, we do not purport to 'write recipes for the cook-shops of the future',[80] but rather aim to make a contribution to the writing of the 'poetry of the future'.[81] We have already put forth the hypothesis that the legal form is replaced in communism by a form of institutionalised ethics. This hypothesis can only be tested in revolutionary praxis and the historical process of class struggle. Yet, it might be possible to outline some initial characteristics of this form of social consciousness if we draw inspiration from Hegel's notion of ethical community (*Sittlichkeit*) which we shall approach as a form of institutionalised ethics.

It has been argued that Hegel developed the notion of ethical community in his *Philosophy of Right*[82] to critique the two central forms of bourgeois consciousness, that is, the legal person and the moral subject.[83] In developing this concept Hegel addressed the main shortcomings of the first two levels of his outline of a philosophy of right. The first level, (namely abstract right) is dominated by the figure of the legal person, while the second level, (namely morality) is dominated by the figure of the moral individual. Yet, both levels and their main figures are characterised by one-sidedness and lack of reference to the totality of social relations. According to this argument, the analysis of law and morality must move beyond the abstraction of individualism and individual responsibility and put emphasis on the concreteness of social totality.[84]

On this basis, the ethical community (*Sittlichkeit*) appears as 'the set of institutions and objective norms, sanctioned by custom, through which the members of a living and rational social order fulfil the demands of the social whole to which they belong'.[85] The above serves as a basis for a materialist conception of the ethical community. Marx endorsed Hegel's critique of the 'abstractness' and 'formalism' of bourgeois morality and extended this critique to the notion of private, individual rights.[86] According to Marx, objective moral (and juridical) norms reflect the relations of the existing social

80 Marx (n 24) 99.

81 Karl Marx, 'The Eighteenth Brumaire of Louis Bonaparte' in Karl Marx and Frederick Engels (eds), *Collected Works*, vol 11 (Lawrence and Wishart 2010) 99–209, 106.

82 GWF Hegel, *Outlines of the Philosophy of Right* (OUP 2008).

83 Georgios Kolias, 'Hegels Materialismus in der Rechtsphilosophie' 1 (2014) *Hegel-Jahrbuch* 248–53.

84 ibid.

85 Allen W Wood, 'Marx's Immoralism' in Bernard Chavance (ed), *Marx en Perspective* (Editions de l' Ecole des Haute Etudes en Sciences Sociales 1985) 686. See also Hegel (n 82) 154.

86 Michael Rosen, 'The Marxist Critique of Morality and the Theory of Ideology' in Edward Harcourt (ed), *Morality, Reflection and Ideology* (OUP 2000) 5.

formation, thereby representing the fundamental needs of the prevailing mode of production. As a result, the 'Sittlichkeit of bourgeois society will indeed be . . . merely bourgeois prejudices masking bourgeois interests'.[87] Thus, the bourgeois ethical community reflects and is determined by capital's "radical" need for profit. Hegel's goal of superseding the abstract individualism of the legal person and the moral individual cannot be achieved in bourgeois society and the modern state. But his analysis of the objectivity of moral norms opens the way towards conceiving an alternative form of social consciousness in a society where the material conditions for transcending this abstract individualism will have been created.

The ethical community (*Sittlichkeit*) is present in any social formation. In communist society, this form of institutionalised ethics might replace the legal form as the predominant form of social consciousness. According to Philip Kain, Marx's conception of mature communism would involve this higher form of community (*Sittlichkeit*) where 'individuals do not perceive moral laws as constraints, as obligations, or as duties to be fulfilled', but rather 'their behaviour is rooted in ethical custom which permeates their interests and inclinations'.[88] In the ethical community of communism, social behaviour is sanctioned by custom. Individual morality and the principles of right and justice have been transcended. Custom and tradition, which are indispensable to any mode of production will remain, but the communal relations 'which give rise to custom and tradition will be subordinate to conscious and rational control'.[89]

The emphasis on custom and tradition as forms of social consciousness and social regulation is strongly reminiscent of Lenin's remarks on the role of habit in the process of the withering away of the state and law.[90] The legal form is transcended, having shaped custom and tradition in the process of socialist construction, and replaced by the form of institutionalised ethics. In this analysis, democracy and rights are not rejected or abolished from the outset. The legal and political forms are rather sublated (*Aufgehoben* in Hegelian terms). They are realised first and then transcended, meaning that the rights which were realised in the first immature phase of communism will have shaped custom and tradition and thus no longer appear as formal constraining principles in mature communism but would instead be embedded in the customs and traditions of the ethical community.[91]

Communist social consciousness thus takes the form of institutionalised ethics, conceived as the objectified form of the totality of subjective acts of the associated producers shaped by custom and tradition. In terms of its form,

87 Wood (n 85) 687.
88 Philip J Kain, *Marx and Ethics* (OUP 1988) 186.
89 ibid.
90 VI Lenin, 'The State and Revolution' *Collected Works*, vol 25 (Progress Publishers 1976) 431, 467.
91 Kain (n 88) 202.

communist ethics supersede the legal form. We saw above that the characteristic of coercion, essential to the legal form, is transcended by custom, habit, and institutionalised ethics. Furthermore, the formalism of the legal form is transcended through the communist ethic's focus on many-sidedness and the adoption of the standpoint of the social totality. As a result, the legal form's individualism is also transcended. Communist ethics goes beyond the individualism of bourgeois morality and rights. Justice as 'suum cuique', as well as individualist rightsism are transcended in a society that prioritises the concept of social needs in its ethical standpoint.

This brings us to the more concrete principles and notions that provide this form of communist social consciousness with content. Communist ethics cannot be conceived as an exhaustive list of principles, as this would run the risk of reducing what will be the result of a long historical process and reflection of a totality of social relations, which are born in capitalist society but cannot be anticipated in their entirety, to an idealist exercise. Nevertheless, we wish to cautiously suggest a way of approaching the principles that might substantiate a communist ethics. This involves focusing on the primary goal of communist society, that is, the free and full development of the individual. This ruling principle of the communist system of needs will arguably be equally central in the communist form of social consciousness, as profit is in capitalist society and its legal and political forms. Furthermore, it will translate into several other principles, such as the need for creative labour and leisure time, the need for collective decision-making forms and processes, as well as the principles of solidarity and emulation.

The role of the needs principle in communist ethics has already been discussed, albeit in a limited and non-systematic manner, in Marxist literature. It has been argued in this respect that the concept of human need is fundamentally an ethical category which features centrally in the principle of justice reflected in communist society.[92] The need for freedom, self-determination, and self-realisation constitutes the highest need of human beings and can only be satisfied within an ethical community.[93] Yet, the system of needs in capitalism contradicts human needs. Indeed, the moral ideals of capitalist society require 'the reduction of physical and spiritual needs to a minimum in order to maximise profits and capital accumulation'.[94]

Human needs can only be met and flourish in a

> society which has understood that needs call forth production and that production transforms needs—a society that thus would begin to experience *a need to control production consciously so as to produce in*

92 George E McCarthy, *Marx and Social Justice: Ethics and Natural Law in the Critique of Political Economy* (Brill 2018) 248, 268.

93 ibid 248.

94 ibid.

> *individuals higher needs, needs which would be ends in themselves, needs for a totality of human manifestations of life*, or *for the full development of the powers and capacities of the individual.*[95]

Accordingly, the goal of communist society, its ideals and principles, 'would arise from and come to be felt as needs'.[96] Furthermore, this also means that the need for free and full development of the individual's capacities assumes extreme significance for the social consciousness of communist society.

Notably, there is a scarcity of systematic elaborations on this principle, despite its importance for the Marxist conception of social emancipation. Indeed, it is only in Tony Smith's recent work on the principles of a socialist constitution that we find a detailed discussion of this concept and its implications.[97] Tony Smith discusses the principle of 'free and full development of every individual' as the foundational principle for a socialist constitution. This principle appears in the *Communist Manifesto* where Marx and Engels call for a society where 'the free development of each is the condition for the free development of all',[98] as well as in *Capital*, where Marx refers to the highest form of society where 'the full and free development of every individual forms the ruling principle'.[99]

This principle is, according to Smith, 'a dimension of material social life that reflects and is reflected by institutional frameworks and systems of social practices'.[100] It is, we would add, a principle understood in a materialist and not idealist way, as the ruling principle of both communist production and all sorts of institutional frameworks and systems of social practice, including decision-making and dispute-resolving processes. It is thus a ruling principle in the sense of a 'radical' need, that is, the fundamental principle lying at the roots of a social formation.

In his work, Smith proceeds with a concrete analysis of the central aspects of this principle. He begins with the aspect of 'free development' and notes that the notion of 'freedom' does not merely refer to the 'formal freedom to act without external interference so strongly emphasised in the republican constitutions of modern capitalism'.[101] It rather conveys that 'socialism does not aim at a state of well-being paternalistically bestowed on passive

95 Kain (n 88) 195 [emphasis added].

96 ibid.

97 Tony Smith, *The Full and Free Development of the Individual: A Socialism for the Twenty-First Century* (Forthcoming, 2024).

98 Karl Marx and Friedrich Engels, 'Manifesto of the Communist Party' in Karl Marx and Friedrich Engels (eds), *Collected Works*, vol 6 (Lawrence and Wishart 2010) 477–519, 506.

99 Marx (n 24) 738.

100 ibid.

101 ibid.

recipients'.[102] Instead 'every individual must have a freedom to develop on the basis of their own actions'.[103] This freedom presupposes the existence of institutional forms for collective evaluation, planning and decision-making, which are 'created, continually renewed, and periodically modified through the collective actions of the members of the socialist society'.[104]

We can see, thus, how the ruling principle of 'free development of the individual' is concretised into principles that relate to institutional forms of decision-making in communist society. The principles of electivity, revocability, democratic centralism, and immanent (or non-political) representation based on the abolition of the division of labour, are relevant in this respect, to ensure that communist society is regulated by a system of rules not only consensually adhered to by habit, but also collectively produced. Of crucial significance is the principle of workplace democracy, at least in the form in which it will appear in communist society, according to which the workplace is the primary locus and nucleus of collective decision-making. According to Smith, all sites where collective decision-making takes place (e.g. workers collectives, community associations, public forums) are part of an extended commons.[105] Furthermore, the notion of 'free development' necessarily affects and reflects developments in the sphere of production, since the production and allocation of social wealth in general, and the social surplus in particular, is the issue of collective decision-making par excellence.

This brings us to the aspect of full development. Smith begins by noting the impossibility of fully developing 'every potential latent in the human species in a single lifetime'.[106] Nevertheless, he moves on to concretise the principle of 'full development of the individual' into two sets of needs: universal and particular needs. Universal needs are needs that 'all members of the community have qua members of a geographical or virtual community', while particular needs refer to the 'particular goods individuals require for their particular life plans', and which are provided 'to the greatest feasible extent compatible with the principle of solidarity'. Both sets of needs are met with a view to expanding the realm of freedom.

As far as universal needs are concerned, these include a collective universal need for the resources required to establish and maintain the essential institutions and organisations of self-governance; a collective universal need for a built social environment conducive to the full development of social individuals; a collective universal need for an effective innovation system furthering human flourishing; as well as a collective universal need for a natural

102 ibid.
103 ibid.
104 ibid.
105 ibid.
106 ibid.

environment within which human beings can flourish.[107] Particular needs refer to essential capabilities, which are met according to the principle of solidarity. These include the need to live healthy lives of normal length; the need to exercise agency in creative ways; the need to develop the capacity for sensation, imagination, theoretical and practical thought; the need to have appropriate emotional connections with other beings; the need to experience ourselves as part of the natural world in relationship with other parts; the need to engage in play; the need to cooperate with others in households, workplaces and other organisations and associations; and the need to participate as an equal in the institutions and social practices of self-governance without domination.[108]

Conclusion

This chapter defended the withering away thesis by focusing on the notion of the legal form. This is an important topic for those interested in and struggling for a different kind of society. Abolishing market relations and profit as the main regulator of social relations can only be the result of a long historical process of struggle. This process involves the development of the consciousness necessary for the struggle and the creation of this different society. In this context, the 'free and full development' can be approached as a radical principle for a different kind of society—a principle that unites institutions of justice and relations of production.

If we accept the historicity of the legal form and the possibility of its historical transcendence, we can envisage a new form of social consciousness, a form of communist ethical community that might eventually supersede it. This would enable a novel understanding of the world, that is, natural and social relations, not through the lens of law, coercion, and the false consciousness of capitalist democracy, but through institutional forms radically different and conducive to the free and full development of the individual. This analysis of the 'free and full development of the individual' as the ruling principle of communist society provides us with the content of communist ethics or communist rights. In other words, it gives us a few pointers on what principles and institutions a new form of social consciousness in a communist society would accommodate.

However, it needs to be stressed that examining this principle is not just an idealistic exercise. Neglecting or abandoning this principle during the course of socialist construction has resulted in dire historical developments. The historical outcome of the process of socialist construction in the Soviet Union, for instance, proves, among other things, that the 'full and free development

107 ibid.
108 ibid.

of the individual' and the expansion of 'the realm of freedom' should constitute constant concerns and demands in the process of socialist construction. They should act as ruling principles guarding against the reintroduction of profit as the main regulator of production. It is, thus, important to firmly establish how antagonistic these principles are to market relations and the capitalist need for profit not only in an abstract theoretical manner but also by examining the historical process of socialist construction during the twentieth century, in order to draw inspiration for the urgent struggles that lie ahead, while avoiding the pitfalls and setbacks of the past, in this long and arduous process of social emancipation.

Index